AF768987

Studies in Legal History

Published in association with the
American Society for Legal History

Editor: Stanley N. Katz

Editorial Advisory Board
John D. Cushing
John P. Dawson
Lawrence M. Friedman
Charles M. Gray
Oscar Handlin
George L. Haskins
J. Willard Hurst
S. F. C. Milsom
A. Arthur Schiller
Joseph H. Smith
L. Kinvin Wroth

Earlier volumes

Frederic William Maitland: A Life
C. H. S. Fifoot

Impeachment: The Constitutional Problems
Raoul Berger

The Autobiographical Notes of Charles Evans Hughes

Edited by David J. Danelski and Joseph S. Tulchin

Harvard University Press Cambridge, Massachusetts 1973

© Copyright 1973 by the President and Fellows of Harvard College
All rights reserved
Library of Congress Catalog Card Number 72–88130
SBN 674–05325–7
Printed in the United States of America
Book Design by David Ford

Acknowledgments and a Note on Editing

We wish to thank Mr. and Mrs. William T. Gossett, son-in-law and daughter of Charles Evans Hughes, for permission to edit and publish this volume and for their encouragement and help in carrying out the project. We also wish to thank Alan Hubbard, Otto E. Koegel, and Judge Edmund L. Palmieri for their willingness to discuss various aspects of Hughes's career; A. J. P. Taylor of the Beaverbrook Library in London who, in behalf of the Beaverbrook Newspapers, Ltd., gave permission to quote from the Lloyd George Papers; Paul T. Heffron, Kate Stewart, and the staff of the Manuscript Division of the Library of Congress for their assistance; Max Hall, Dorothy Whitney, and Denise Thompson of the Harvard University Press for their support and suggestions about editing; and Yale University, the R. J. Meigs Fund at Cornell University, and the Center for Advanced Study in the Behavioral Sciences for financial and other assistance. Charles Evans Hughes deserves credit for the Notes. We accept full responsibility for their editing and preparation for publication.

A microfilm of the original Notes is in the Manuscript Division of the Library of Congress and has been available to scholars with the permission of Mrs. Gossett. Because of the importance of the Notes as a primary source concerning Charles Evans Hughes and significant events with which he was associated, they deserve the widest possible dissemination, and that is the reason for their publication at this time. In preparing them for publication, our objective has been to maximize their utility — to historians, those interested in the legal profession, and the general public — without altering their character. We have provided the reader with footnotes identifying persons and events to which Hughes refers. Wherever possible, we have incorporated material from the Beerits Memoranda which Hughes consulted as he dictated these Notes. In every case, our additions are marked by brackets. There are two major editorial interventions. The opening chapter, as dictated by Hughes, contained a long genealogical parenthesis which now appears at the end of the Notes as Appendix I. The series of memoranda on Hughes's years as secretary of state have been reordered and combined into three chapters (14–16). The titles for these chapters, as well as Chapter 1, are added by the editors. Both interventions, like the explanatory notes and minor changes in punctuation, were made with a view to enhancing readability. We sought to edit the Notes as objectively and unobtrusively as we could. What opinions we have concerning Hughes are stated briefly in our introduction. But the Notes are his, and we have done our best to present them so that he speaks for himself.

Contents

Illustrations

Charles Evans Hughes

April 11, 1862	Born at Glens Falls, New York
1876–1878	Student at Madison (now Colgate) University
1881	A.B., Brown University
1881–1882	Instructor, Delaware Academy, Delhi, New York
1884	LL.B., Columbia University
	A.M., Brown University
1884–1891	Practiced law in New York City
December 5, 1888	Married Antoinette Carter
November 30, 1889	Son, Charles Evans, Jr., born
1891–1893	Professor of law, Cornell University
January 11, 1892	Daughter, Helen, born
1893–1906	Practiced law in New York City
1893–1895	Special lecturer at Cornell University
1893–1900	Special lecturer at New York Law School
August 11, 1898	Daughter, Catherine, born
1905	Counsel in New York gas investigation
1905–1906	Counsel in New York insurance investigation
1905	Nominated by Republican Party for mayor of New York City (declined)
1907–1910	Governor of New York
August 19, 1907	Daughter, Elizabeth, born
1910–1916	Associate Justice of the Supreme Court of the United States
1916	Republican Presidential Candidate
1917–1921	Practiced law in New York City
1917–1918	Chairman, Draft Appeals Board, New York City
1921–1925	Secretary of State in Cabinets of Presidents
	Harding and Coolidge
1924–1925	President of the American Bar Association
1925–1930	Practiced law in New York City
1928–1930	Judge of Permanent Court of International Justice
1930–1941	Chief Justice of the United States
August 27, 1948	Died at Cape Cod, Massachusetts

Editors' Introduction

On June 2, 1941, Charles Evans Hughes presided over the Supreme Court for the last time. At the conclusion of the Court's business that day, he announced his retirement, thus ending some thirty-six years of public service. He was in his eightieth year and still in good health, but he could no longer keep up the pace he had set for himself as chief justice and hence knew the time had come for him to step down. Retirement would be a time for reflection and summing up. Eight years earlier he had engaged Henry C. Beerits, a young Princeton graduate, to arrange his papers and write memoranda on various aspects of his life. Between November 1941 and the end of 1945, Hughes, with Beerits' memoranda and other materials concerning his life before him, leisurely dictated his "Autobiographical Notes."[1] He thought the memoir might be interesting to his children and grandchildren and useful to others who wished accurate information about his life. It was first used by Merlo J. Pusey, whose prize-winning biography of Hughes was published in 1951.

The Notes directly and indirectly reveal the man. They provide an initial basis for understanding his personality and its relation to his public image. They suggest that certain of his characteristics — unusual intelligence, strong sense of duty, and self-sufficiency — were directly related to his rise in public life, and they provide insight into his political style. The Notes are also an important primary source concerning the times in which Hughes lived, portraying perceptively, for example, college life in the 1870s, law practice in New York City in the 1880s and 1890s, and the Supreme Court in 1910. In a prefatory note, Hughes states that he has no intention of writing an apologia, but he is, of course, aware that he is before "the bar of history" presenting his final case.[2]

[1]The original title of Hughes's manuscript was "Biographical Notes."

[2]Alpheus Thomas Mason, "Charles Evans Hughes: An Appeal to the Bar of History," *Vanderbilt Law Review*, VI (1952), 1–19.

I

Hughes's description of his parents' contrasting temperaments is a clue to his personality. His father, he said, "was emotional, impulsive — with the Celtic warmth — generous, sociable, and with a flair for adventure"; his mother was "delicate, reserved, reflective, and cautious, but of strong will." [3] In varying degrees, and at different times, Hughes exhibited many of his father's traits and all of his mother's. Those close to him saw two sides to the man — a serious side when he was at work, and a genial, sometimes humorous, side when he was relaxing or in a social situation. Justice Roberts said that Hughes was "an intense man," and when he "had serious business to transact, he allowed no considerations to interfere with his operations. He was so engrossed in the vital issue that he had not time for lightness or pleasantry. But he realized as well as the next man that there is a time for work and a time for play, and when he played, he played with zest. The personal relations between him and his brethren were genial and cordial. He was considerate, sympathetic, and responsive; and in his social contacts in Washington he not only had the fullest enjoyment, but everyone who came into contact with him was charmed by his personality." [4] Hughes's work, recalled Justice Frankfurter, "took possession of him — whether in masterly examination of witnesses in the insurance investigation, or in his devastating campaign against Hearst, or in carrying to the people his policies as Governor, or in his various official appearances as Secretary of State, or in the Supreme Court, alike when arguing before it or presiding over it." At such times Hughes appeared intense and aloof, but that, said Frankfurter, was only the man's public face. Referring to Hughes's other side, which Frankfurter thought was his true face, he said the chief justice was "genial though not promiscuous, full of fun and whimsy, a delightful tease and sparkling story-teller, a responsive listener, and stimulating talker." [5]

The Notes themselves show the two sides of Hughes's personality. When he writes of his nonofficial life — especially his boyhood, college days, and early years at the bar — he is a raconteur telling his story with a certain amount of humor, and when he writes of his relationship with Justice Holmes, he does so warmly. But his discussion of his official life is matter of fact and formal.

[3] Notes, p. 3.

[4] U.S. Supreme Court Bar, *Proceedings of the Bar and Officers of the Supreme Court of the United States in Memory of Charles Evans Hughes* (Washington, privately printed, 1950), p. 127.

[5] Felix Frankfurter, "The Impact of Charles Evans Hughes," in Philip Elman, ed., *Of Law and Men: Papers and Addresses of Felix Frankfurter, 1939–1956* (New York, Harcourt, Brace & Co., 1956), pp. 147–148.

Hughes's public image was spectacularly established in the gas and insurance investigations in 1905–06.[6] His serious side was then exposed and distorted by the press. "Hughes," wrote Mark Sullivan almost a quarter of a century later in *Our Times*, "emerged upon the American scene as a Hercules about to clean the insurance stables, in cartoons that overemphasized virile whiskers and big white teeth, and in newspaper sketches which overemphasized Puritan austerity, and emphasized, but did not overemphasize — because it would be difficult to exaggerate this quality of Hughes — intellectual sinew." Sullivan's image of Hughes was that of an unemotional investigator who was "as undramatic . . . as an adding machine."[7] The distorted image of Hughes — as cold, austere, overly cerebral, humorless — persisted despite occasional public glimpses of his warmer side. When Hughes became secretary of state, Gus Karger, the newspaperman, wrote to his friend, William Howard Taft: "Mr. Hughes has been a revelation to us. He is not the same man we knew formerly. His manner is gracious and affable."[8] In 1924, Hughes sailed to Europe accompanied by several leaders of the American bar. Charles Cheney Hyde, then State Department solicitor, wrote that they expected "a cold, detached, self-centered individual, living and thinking on a plane aloof from his fellow citizens, and not particularly interested in their concerns," but they were pleasantly surprised to find him "a friendly and genial person, quite unconscious that any change had overtaken him and the last to suppose that he was different from what he had always been."[9]

II

A necessary condition for Hughes's rise in public life was his extraordinary intelligence. He was able to read at the age of three and a half; before he was six, he was reading and reciting verses from the New Testament, doing mental addition, and studying French and German; at seven, he began to learn Greek; and before he was nine, he had read Bunyan, Moore, Byron, and Shakespeare. When he was admitted to church membership at the age of nine, the deacons were amazed by his mastery of denominational doctrine. For young Hughes, books were not only a source

[6]Years later Felix Frankfurter remembered Hughes in the gas investigation. "When first you touched my young imagination as counsel in the Gas Inquiry," he wrote Hughes on April 10, 1942, "I felt a free and courageous, as well as a powerful, force in our public life." Felix Frankfurter Papers, Library of Congress.

[7]Mark Sullivan, *Our Times: The United States, 1900–1925*, 6 vols. (New York, Charles Scribner's Sons, 1926–1935), II, 52–55.

[8]Karger to Taft, Apr. 6, 1921, William Howard Taft Papers, Library of Congress.

[9]Charles Cheney Hyde, "Charles Evans Hughes," in Samuel Flagg Bemis, ed., *The American Secretaries of State and Their Diplomacy*, 10 vols. (New York, Alfred A. Knopf, 1929), X, 327–328.

of knowledge; they were also a stimulus for his active imagination, and sometimes he pretended to live in the world of his books. With Thomson's *Land and the Book* before him, he would gallop across Palestine on his hobby horse.

Hughes began school at the age of six, but when he protested that it was a waste of time, his parents allowed him to pursue his studies at home. At the age of eight, he tried school once more; again the "experiment" was a failure. The next year he entered a public school a year below the graduating class, and when he graduated two years later, his grades were all between 97 and 100 percent. At the age of eleven, he entered Newark High School, but an injury and his family's move to New York required him to terminate his studies at midyear. The next year he entered the graduating class of New York's Public School No. 35; upon his graduation, he gave the salutatory address and was awarded a silver medal for composition. He was then thirteen years old — too young to go to college — so he studied by himself for another year before entering Madison (now Colgate) University. At Madison, where he remained for two years, his scholastic record was excellent (an average of 4.74 out of a possible 5.00), and at Brown, to which he transferred, he also did well, being elected to Phi Beta Kappa and graduating third in his class. He graduated first in his law class at Columbia, and when he took the New York bar examination, he received the highest grade ever given up to that time — 99½ percent.[10]

In his Notes, Hughes minimizes his early childhood academic accomplishments. He acknowledges that he was somewhat precocious but denies that he was a prodigy, attributing his precociousness to his environment — the atmosphere of his home and the constant stimulus of his parents. The atmosphere was a loving one and parental expectations were extraordinarily high.[11] The fact that he had received most of his precollege education at home was important because he could move as quickly as his abilities permitted him and could explore subjects that interested him most. Furthermore, being an only child, he matured intellectually and socially in a world of adults. Even when he began school, his classmates

[10]Merlo J. Pusey, *Charles Evans Hughes*, 2 vols. (New York, Macmillan, 1951), I, 11–23.

[11]See Catherine M. Cox, *The Early Mental Traits of 300 Geniuses*, vol. II: *Genetic Studies of Genius*, ed. Lewis M. Terman (Stanford, Stanford University Press, 1926). An intensive analysis of 20 of the biographies in Cox's study of men who had I.Q.'s of more than 160 showed that the typical development pattern included as important aspects: "(1) a high degree of attention focused upon the child by parents and other adults, expressed in intensive educational measures and, usually, abundant love; (2) isolation from other children, especially outside of the family; and (3) a rich efflorescence of fantasy as a reaction to the preceding conditions." Harold G. McCurdy, "The Childhood Pattern of Genius," *Horizon*, II (May 1960), 33–38.

were always from three to five years older, thus providing intellectual and social challenges that accelerated maturity and instilled self-confidence.

Hughes had a photographic memory. As a child he memorized easily, and later in public life he could deliver a long speech practically word for word after having read it only a few times. He could "read a paragraph at a glance, a treatise in an evening, a roomful of papers in a week." [12] Zechariah Chafee characterized Hughes's mind as being powerful rather than exploratory.[13] His mind was powerful in the sense that it was highly retentive and strongly analytical, that is, logical, the kind of mind that is usually a step or two ahead of another in an argument or discussion, precisely the kind of mind that almost certainly guarantees success in school and at the bar.[14] The quality of his mind was directly related to his selection as counsel in the gas and insurance investigations in 1905–06 and his success in them.

Hughes's extraordinary memory not only impressed those around him; it also allowed him to rely less on others and to make his judgments based on his own examination of the record. The night after President Warren G. Harding's inauguration, Hughes took home with him the Department of State's files on a bitter boundary dispute between Costa Rica and Panama which threatened to precipitate open warfare on the Isthmus. He spread the papers around him and by the time the Senate confirmed his nomination as secretary of state the next day, he had reached a decision and was ready to carry it out. His subordinates and the press assigned to the department never ceased to marvel at the manner in which he could plumb the depths of any issue. As governor of New York he conducted his own public hearings on the incompetence of an official he wished to remove from office and who had invoked the protection of the Republican state organization. He began his public career as counsel for the state legislative committee investigating the gas companies in New York City the same way. He dominated the investigation by mastering the details of the gas companies' operations. What was said of him as chief justice applies to the rest of his public career. When he gave his views, "he somehow exuded complete preparation and conveyed the impression that

[12] Edwin McElwain, "The Business of the Supreme Court as Conducted by Chief Justice Hughes," *Harvard Law Review*, LXIII (1949), 9.

[13] Zechariah Chafee, Jr., "Charles Evans Hughes," *Proceedings of the American Philosophical Society*, XCIII (1949), 279.

[14] "You just didn't talk unless you were sure of your ground, because that gimlet mind of [Hughes] was there ahead of you." Felix Frankfurter, "Chief Justices I Have Known," *Virginia Law Review*, XXXIX (1953), 902–903. One drawback of knowing "that gimlet mind" would be there ahead of you was that it inhibited some subordinates and turned them into yes-men. See Hyde, "Hughes," pp. 233–234.

anyone who disagreed with him had better know *all* the facts and know them well."[15]

III

A strong sense of duty instilled by his parents dominated Hughes all of his life. Duty meant two things to him: he had to do worthy things, and he had to do them well. Early in his life, he saw duty first in relation to God — "God's glory is my only aim" — and then his parents — "Whatever I do, wherever I go, when the question of right or wrong comes up, it is decided by what Pa or Ma will say if I did it." Vocationally, duty pointed young Hughes toward the ministry. Hughes said that he had not thought much about a vocation when he was in college but took it for granted that if he did not enter the ministry, he would teach. In his senior year at Brown, when classmates said that law was the ideal profession for him, he wrote his parents: "Now I know that I could do well in law, but the profession is repugnant to me." Later the same year, when the notion was again suggested, the idea fascinated him. He took a teaching position his first year out of Brown but with the understanding that he could simultaneously read law in a lawyer's office. The next year he enrolled at Columbia Law School.[16]

As a lawyer, Hughes felt it was his duty to take worthy cases, and duty was important in bringing him into public life in the gas investigation. Although he had doubts about his adequacy for the investigation, he felt it would have been "cowardly" of him to reject this call to public service. Duty again prevailed when he was asked to conduct the insurance investigation. While he was involved in the investigation, the Republican Party sought to nominate him for mayor of New York. In declining on the ground that he had to finish the investigation, he said: "If I were free, however, to take a nomination, it might seem to be my duty to do so against the wishes and the interests of my family." When he was mentioned for the governorship of New York, he said he did not desire the office and was not a candidate, but he would not declare himself out of the field because that might put himself "forever beyond the possibility of rendering a public service." When he was nominated, he wired party leaders: "I shall accept the nomination without pledge other than to do my duty according to my conscience. If elected, it will be my ambition to

[15]McElwain, "Business of the Supreme Court," p. 14; Bertram D. Hulan, *Inside the Department of State* (New York, McGraw-Hill, 1939), pp. 35–36, 130–132, and 148–149; William Phillips, *Ventures in Diplomacy* (Boston, privately printed, 1952), p. 113; Interview with Mr. and Mrs. William T. Gossett, Mar. 11, 1969. For Hughes's own version of these exploits, see Notes, chapters 10 and 11.

[16]*Ibid.*, p. 49; Pusey, *Hughes*, I, 31, 36, 60.

give the State a sane, efficient and honorable administration, free from taint of bossism or of servitude to any private interest." [17]

His acceptance of the presidential nomination in 1916 had the same ring to it. He was "torn between two profound desires, one to keep the judicial ermine unsullied, and the other not to fail in meeting what might be a duty to the country." In his telegram to the Republican convention, he said: "I have not desired the nomination. I have wished to remain on the bench. But, in this critical period in our national history, I recognize that it is your right to summon and that it is my paramount duty to respond." [18]

Practical politics was repugnant to Hughes, just as, years before at Brown, he had said law was. Yet it, too, fascinated him. The fascination apparently goes back to his boyhood when he used to listen to his uncle, Carey Simpson Connelly, who was active politically in Ulster County, discuss New York politics, which to young Hughes "seemed . . . a world of extraordinary cunning." [19] If he was to participate in politics, it had to be on his own terms. The office or nomination had to be offered. He would not seek it, because to seek it would mean he would have to become involved in repugnant politics, the politics of the fray; but a nomination offered, such as the governorship of New York, or the presidency in 1916, was not so much an opportunity to exercise power as a duty to perform a public service, though, of course, it was both. In many ways, the Supreme Court was the ideal place for Hughes, for the Court was supposed to be above politics, and because of its great power, it offered a magnificent opportunity for worthy public service. There Hughes could grandly satisfy the claims of duty within him.

Strong claims of duty, however, did not deprive him of the satisfaction of a job well done or the thrill in undertaking a challenging assignment.

[17] *Ibid.*, I, 149, 172, and 173. Hughes refused the mayoralty nomination because he felt "he was being simply pulled out of the investigation. . . . Everything he had stood for in the public estimation would be pulled down, and his character before the people would no longer be established." Memorandum by Henry C. Beerits, "Entry into Politics and Election as Governor," pp. 2–3, in the Papers of Charles Evans Hughes, Library of Congress. During this period, Hughes was convinced that he was being of service to society in his law practice. His experience in the gas and insurance investigations and as governor led him to believe that service was connected with public office. He accepted this amplification of his duty but the added responsibilities depressed him. See E. J. Ridgeway to Hughes, Apr. 27, and Hughes to Ridgeway, May 14, 1910, Hughes Papers.

[18] Notes, pp. 180, 181, n. 6. Ironically Hughes's public image, which had fit him so well as a judge, did not at first sit comfortably on his shoulders as a candidate for the presidency. The New York *Evening World*, June 13, 1916, commented, "The celerity with which Charles Evans Hughes has ceased to be the Supreme Court Justice and became Busy Charlie the Candidate is bewildering to the country and in the view of many, far from pleasing."

[19] Notes, p. 17.

A good example is Hughes's reaction to the cablegram asking him to undertake the insurance investigation. He received it late one evening at an alpine retreat in Switzerland where he was resting with his family after the gas investigation. Excited by the request, he hardly slept that night and set out for the nearest railroad station at 4:00 A.M. the next day. The early morning mountain views were magnificent, and Mrs. Hughes could not help exclaiming: "Look, sweetheart, we may never see such a scene again." Hughes, lost in his own thoughts, answered: "My dear, you don't know what this investigation would mean. It would be the most tremendous job in the United States." [20]

Hughes's sense of duty probably accounts for his rather rigid interpretation of appropriate role behavior. As a Supreme Court justice, his opinions were said not to be in the style of the man; instead they were, "sober, rather lapidary, doubtless to conform to his notion of what an opinion should be, as a sonnet has its fourteen lines." [21] As a lawyer he took pains to observe the proprieties in his relationships with judges before whom he had cases. Because of this, he once responded coolly to Chief Justice Taft's warm greeting in the Supreme Court. He explained his behavior later to his co-counsel saying, "I did it intentionally as I intend to win my cases on their merits and not through friendship with the judges." [22] Such behavior contributed to Hughes's public image, and that behavior stemmed, at least in part, from his strong sense of duty.

Duty for Hughes also meant that whatever he undertook, he had to do well. Near the end of his life, he put it this way: "I inherited a continuing ambition to excel in good work and to do my job as well as could be done. I couldn't bear the thought of leaving undone anything which could be done or of not doing my particular work as well as it could be done within my limitations." Almost seventy years earlier, his mother had written to him when he was a student at Madison: "*Be thorough. BE THOROUGH. BE THOROUGH* in all you undertake." And he was for the rest of his life. Sometimes he carried thoroughness to extremes. When he was a law student, for example, he attended his regular classes during the day and private law quizzes at night, and during his senior year, he attended, for purposes of review, lectures he had heard the year before. His thoroughness, however, was important in the gas and insurance investigations; in a short time he knew as much or more about those businesses than the executives who controlled them, and thoroughness was also important in

[20] *Ibid.*, pp. 121–122; Pusey, *Hughes*, I, 142.

[21] Frankfurter, "Impact of Hughes," p. 148. Frederick Bernays Wiener, however, singled out Hughes's opinions as examples of highly effective argumentative style. "There is," Wiener wrote, "something powerful and inexorable about a Hughes opinion." *Effective Appellate Advocacy* (New York, Prentice-Hall, 1950), p. 68.

[22] Pusey, *Hughes*, II, 635.

his work in the State Department and the Supreme Court. Indeed, it was Hughes's thoroughness coupled with his intelligence that separated him from practically all the lawyers in New York when he was selected to conduct the gas investigation.[23]

In his effort to be thorough in all he did, Hughes drove himself mercilessly — sometimes to the edge of endurance. He candidly admits in the Notes that at times he was on the brink of nervous collapse. In preparing for the bar examination, which he passed with a near perfect score, he wore himself out and had to take a long vacation in order to recoup his strength. As a young lawyer, hard work had so impaired his health that he felt he had to give up legal practice. He taught law for two years at Cornell, where he regained his health, and then returned to practice in New York. But thereafter he again worked himself to the brink of nervous and physical exhaustion and periodically took long vacations, usually in the Alps, to calm his nerves and restore his strength. During the gas investigation he said to his wife in exasperation: "It is too much. I simply can't go on." In 1910, when President Taft told Hughes it was his duty to seek reelection as governor of New York, Hughes answered: "I do not dare to run the chance of breaking down mentally."[24]

IV

Hughes was unusually self-sufficient, and his relations with others, with only a few exceptions, were characterized by detachment. Herbert Hoover referred to him as the "most self-contained man I ever knew," adding that Hughes "simply had no instinct for personal friendship that I could ever discover." [25] That is not to say that Hughes lacked friends. On the Supreme Court he had friendly relations with a number of his colleagues, but those relationships were more cordial than intimate. His relations with Justice Holmes were, in his words, "of the happiest sort." [26] Holmes regarded him as a good friend, and when Hughes left the Court in 1916, the Magnificent Yankee said he would "miss him consumedly." [27] What drew Holmes and others toward Hughes was the quality of his character. Learned Hand once said of him: "You might differ with him as

[23] *Ibid.*, I, 39, 95.

[24] Notes, p. 127; Archie Butt to Mrs. Lewis Butt, Mar. 21, 1910, in Archie Butt, *Taft and Roosevelt: The Intimate Letters of Archie Butt*, 2 vols. (New York, Doubleday, Doran & Co., 1930), I, 309.

[25] Quoted in Betty Glad, *Charles Evans Hughes and the Illusions of Innocence: A Study in American Diplomacy* (Urbana, University of Illinois Press, 1966), p. 109.

[26] Notes, p. 172.

[27] Holmes to Pollock, June 12, 1916, in Mark DeWolfe Howe, ed., *Holmes-Pollock Letters*, 2 vols. (Cambridge, Harvard University Press, 1941), I, 237.

radically as you chose; you might believe that he had gone astray; but to question the sincerity and purity of his motives betrayed either that you had not understood what he was after, or that your own standards needed scrutiny." [28] Justices with disparate constitutional views and different personalities — McReynolds and Frankfurter, Roberts and Black, Cardozo and Van Devanter, Reed and Douglas — all offered him their friendship as well as their esteem. Two of them — Roberts and Douglas — went so far as to say that Hughes had been like a father to them. Yet, with perhaps the exception of Holmes, none of his colleagues were close to him. Throughout his public life, he had no close personal or political advisers, no Colonel House to lean on, no favorites, no intimate confidants. He would listen to others, but he always reserved decision for himself. Speaking of Hughes as chief justice, Justice Roberts said: "He neither leaned on anybody else for advice nor did he proffer advice or assistance to any of us. I am sure that this calculated course greatly strengthened his position and authority with his brethren." [29]

With his family — first his parents and later his wife and children — Hughes was less self-contained. They fulfilled what affective needs he had. "There is no doubt of my need of you," he wrote to his wife during the third year of their marriage. "You are my 'strong tower.' Without you I feel helpless . . ." To her he told all. He confessed weakness: "I lack *nerve* — wifie — *confidence, cheek* — I could [do] so much if I had it." He confessed love: "I want to say *mon ange — mon trésor — ma femme, la femme, la plus belle et la plus chére dans le monde.* But I will forbear, and you can dream in English all I cannot say in French." He used to read "Uncle Remus" and "Mr. Dooley" to his children, in dialect, and sometimes to their delight would imitate a cat, a lion, or monkey. When he was away from home, the children were remembered in his letters. From Switzerland, he wrote his wife one summer: "Kiss the little doddies and tell Charlie his papa is riding on the funniest 'choo-choos' — little Brownie 'choo-choos.' Tell both Charlie and Helen how much their Papa loves them." [30]

But outside the family circle, Hughes went about his work with detachment. Justice Frankfurter noticed this in the Supreme Court. When a case was decided, he wrote, it was over for Hughes regardless of its outcome; "he had no lingering afterthoughts born of a feeling of defeat . . . Intellectual issues were dealt with by him as such. As a result, differences

[28] Learned Hand, "Charles Evans Hughes," in Irving Dilliard, ed., *The Spirit of Liberty* (New York, Vintage Press, 1959), p. 168.

[29] Roberts in U.S. Supreme Court Bar, *Proceedings*, pp. 125–126

[30] Hughes to Antoinette Carter Hughes, Sept. 15, 1892; June 20, 1893; Aug. 8, 1894, Hughes Papers; Pusey, *Hughes*, I, 219.

in opinion did not arouse personal sensitiveness . . . This capacity for detachment also reflected his keen sense of humor, which it often pleased him to conceal; partly such detachment must be ascribed to great conservation of energy that saved him from crying over spilt milk." [31] Once Hughes was outvoted after a lively discussion in conference just before the justices recessed for lunch. "Without once alluding to the case," Pusey reports, "the Chief sat by the junior member who had taken the lead in opposing his view and chatted in his most fascinating manner throughout the lunch period." [32]

Hughes's self-sufficiency and detachment apparently had its roots in the adult world of his childhood. Without siblings or schoolmates his own age, he learned to live with and by himself. According to Pusey, he was content with his early solitary life, for when his parents, concerned about his lack of companionship, discussed adopting a child, "Charlie, overhearing the discussion and knowing the family's meager resources, marched into the room and said he thought it would be a mistake. It was more important, he said, to give him an education than companionship at home." [33] In the Notes, Hughes depicts himself in his youth as a solitary, detached onlooker.

Hughes's detachment was in part the basis of his aloof public image, and he was aware of this. At times — for example the ocean voyage in 1924, described by Hyde — he made an effort to be genial and affable, perhaps because he understood that that was required of him in such situations. But he was not always successful. Once he invited a group of leading New York lawyers to dinner. Nervously, they awaited their host. When Hughes arrived, he tried to put them at ease. Cocktails before and wine during the dinner helped a little, but throughout there was "a bowing, a scraping, an everlasting deference amusing to behold." [34] Of course, it may be that Hughes's aloofness in his official roles was deliberate. In regard to his service as chief justice, Frankfurter wrote that Hughes "acted on the realization that aloofness is indispensable to the effective discharge of the Supreme Court's functions." [35]

In view of Hughes's detachment, it is not surprising that he had remarkable self-control, but withal he was human. When he heard that his

[31]Felix Frankfurter, "'The Administrative Side' of Chief Justice Hughes," *Harvard Law Review*, LXIII (1949), 3. Such detachment could also be ascribed to Hughes's personality. Harold D. Lasswell has written that detachment characterizes a basic political personality type. "From detached characters, useful judges, arbitrators, conciliators, diplomatic negotiators and scientists can be recruited." *Power and Personality* (New York, W. W. Norton & Co., 1948), pp. 92–93.

[32]Pusey, *Hughes*, II, 677.

[33]*Ibid.*, I, 12.

[34]John P. Frank, Book Review, *Journal of Public Law*, I (1952), 151–152.

[35]Frankfurter, "Impact of Hughes," p. 147.

twenty-eight-year-old daughter Helen was fatally ill, he broke down and wept like a child; when his wife died he also briefly lost control; and after he performed the painful duty of telling Justice Holmes that he had become too old to remain on the Supreme Court, there were tears in his eyes.[36]

V

Odd as it sounds, Hughes's political style was determined largely by his distaste for politics and politicians. This is seen clearly during his governorship of New York. He refused to bargain with members of his own party; he would not use patronage as a weapon of influence; and rarely did he threaten to use the veto to achieve his legislative program. Instead, he appealed to public opinion. This was consistent with what he took to be progressive government; it was consistent also with his sense of duty. Somehow he felt that it was unworthy to become involved in political manipulation. Furthermore, he lacked empathy with the typical party leader and preferred to go it alone. His political style was a natural outgrowth of his detachment: he saw himself as being above politics. He was, to be sure, in politics in the sense that he exercised power, but his exercise of power was somehow purified — legitimated — by public opinion. Hughes's reliance on public opinion is not surprising. He was, after all, catapulted to power by it during the gas and insurance investigations. Moreover, once he rejected prevailing political practices to achieve his goals, public opinion was one of the few sources of power available to him.[37]

Also influencing Hughes's political style was his experience as an advocate. In accepting a nomination or appointment, he wanted all the responsibility or none of it. This appears to be related to his self-sufficiency and sense of duty. Once he accepted a public position, he saw himself as an advocate of the people, defending the public interest. That was precisely his role in the investigations in 1905–06, and he retained that self-image throughout his public career. When he was secretary of state, for example, he said: "I am counsel for the people of this country." And he acted accordingly. When he met with newsmen to discuss foreign policy, David Lawrence reported, they "listened often to an argument that might have been directed to the Supreme Court or a world tribunal." [38] The notion of advocate implies adversaries, and Hughes had no difficulty in

[36]Pusey, *Hughes*, I, 402–403; II, 797; Paul A. Freund, "Charles Evans Hughes," *Harvard Law Review*, LXXXI (1967), 29.

[37]Robert F. Wesser, *Charles Evans Hughes: Politics and Reform in New York 1905–1910* (Ithaca, Cornell University Press, 1967), *passim*.

[38]Quoted in Glad, *Hughes*, pp. 121, 146.

identifying them early in his public career. They were corrupt profit seekers, political bosses, those who would stand in the way of progress. Hughes indicted them, as it were, and took his case to the people. As in law cases he had argued, he appealed more to reason than to passion, but his arguments were often phrased in moral terms. He was making his case with the electorate — justifying past political actions and seeking mandates for the future — and moral rhetoric in those circumstances was a realistic approach. But that is not to suggest that Hughes was insincere in his moral arguments; on the contrary, he gloried in them. Nothing pleased him more than letters praising his moral stance, such as the following, after his re-election as governor: "I look upon your victory as the most significant moral achievement in politics almost within my memory, certainly within recent times in America. It is a great and good thing to have done, by one's personality and one's method of conducting himself in office to have compelled an alignment and cohesion of the forces of evil, and then to have met and routed them."[39]

Hughes's moral approach served to reaffirm and exaggerate his Puritan image, but the image was effective. His political style irked a number of politicians in his own party, among them Theodore Roosevelt, but nonetheless they grudgingly renominated him for governor in 1908 and less grudgingly for the presidency in 1916.

If Hughes had been more of a politician, more of a realist, might he have accomplished more as governor and as secretary of state, and might he have defeated Woodrow Wilson for the presidency in 1916? Perhaps, but this is by no means clear. He was elected and re-elected governor on a progressive platform with the backing of a conservative Republican state machine. He got Theodore Roosevelt to endorse his candidacy both times even though Roosevelt disdained Hughes as a mugwump and gladly would have thrown his support to another candidate. He could not because Hughes was a winner. While governor, Hughes won a number of battles with the conservative legislature and neutralized the power of the Republican machine, largely through skillful use of press conferences and public disclosure of political maneuvering which traditionally had been considered behind-the-scenes.[40]

[39]C. S. Smith to Hughes, Nov. 4, 1908, Hughes Papers. After a bitter battle with the legislature, a supporter telegraphed Hughes: "Looks like you are deserted by everybody except God Almighty and the People." A. B. Humphrey to Hughes, Apr. 24, 1908, Hughes Papers. That was the way Hughes liked it. His law partner, Arthur C. Rounds, shared his views and wrote him, with reference to Hughes's victory on the bill to control racetrack gambling, "It is refreshing to see a matter like this dealt with on its merits and in a statesmanlike rather than in a political way." Rounds to Hughes, June 10, 1908, Hughes Papers.

[40]T. L. Woodruff to Hughes, Apr. 2, 1908, and Hughes to Woodruff, Apr. 4, 1908, Hughes Papers; Wesser, *Hughes, passim.*

Hughes ran a shrewd campaign in 1916, changing his tactics to suit the situation. His six years on the Supreme Court had not diminished his effectiveness as a campaigner. Except for an egregious error in California, he probably would have been elected president. The misunderstanding with Hiram Johnson was not so much Hughes's fault as it was the failure of his campaign manager. Even Hughes admitted later that had he not been swayed by feelings of personal loyalty to a friend and selected another campaign manager, he might have been president. After the election he continued to be prominent in Republican affairs. He joined with other party leaders to sign the famous Round Robin on the League of Nations, hoping to force the president to accept certain reservations to the peace treaty. His speeches during the campaign of 1920 were sharp and telling. Hughes knew how to appeal to popular sentiments and was not afraid to do so if he felt it was necessary.

As secretary of state he was extremely cautious in his political activities. He felt the public was not competent to judge the highly technical issues of foreign policy; yet he was determined to act as an advocate for the United States within the limits set by public opinion. The public was not concerned with boundary disputes in Latin America or with the fine points of petroleum concessions overseas, considered vital to American security, and in these areas Hughes was an aggressive advocate. When dealing with sensitive public issues, such as reparations, the League of Nations, and the World Court, Hughes moved carefully and slowly. Even during the fight over the World Court, when Hughes was convinced his position was morally and legally correct, he did not take his case to the people and fight to the end, as he would have done while governor of New York. He felt his role must be to educate the public to a more intelligent undertanding of the issues, not by means of impassioned speeches, but by calm and reasoned argument. The sweetest fruit of this strategy was the Dawes Plan. Whenever he could not conduct the foreign relations of the United States free from domestic political influences, Hughes demonstrated acute sensitivity to the climate of public opinion. He bowed meekly to the dictates of Congress in the Japanese Immigration Act of 1924, although he considered the measure a hindrance to amicable relations with Japan. He skillfully used American public opinion to second his challenge to the delegates at the opening session of the Washington Arms Conference, calling upon them to follow the American lead in ending the naval arms race. The public response to his moralistic appeal influenced the negotiations that followed. Hughes was using in international politics the same technique he had found so successful as governor of New York. One can criticize Hughes for a lack of crusading zeal and failure to make the American people aware of their new responsibilities in the postwar world, but given the spiritual exhaustion of the American people and their disillusionment with international crusades, it is difficult to fault Hughes for not being realistic enough. He had a sophisticated understanding of American power and of the limits imposed upon the secretary of state in its use.

Hughes also believed in the force of public opinion in regard to the Supreme Court. It is a theme that runs throughout his Columbia University lectures on the Court.[41] In those lectures he coined the expression, "self-inflicted wounds," which refers to Supreme Court decisions that resulted in loss of public confidence. Determined that the Court would maintain public confidence and not suffer "self-inflicted wounds," he used astutely his powers as chief justice to attain these ends. Perhaps the chief justice's most important power is opinion assignment. He may assign the opinion in every case in which he voted with the majority, and since Hughes seldom dissented during his first eight years as chief justice, he could, as a practical matter, choose any case he wanted for opinion. He voted with both the Court's liberal and conservative blocs during that period, but his written opinions did not divide like his votes. Most of his opinions either sustained civil liberties claims, or took a liberal view of governmental regulation of the economy. Irving Brant noticed this and challenged Hughes's reputation as a liberal. Brant's thesis was: "When Charles Evans Hughes is a liberal, he proclaims it to the world. When he is a reactionary, he votes silently and allows somebody else to be torn to pieces by the liberal dissenters." [42] A variant of Hughes's method, said Brant, was the assignment of unanimous cases to himself whether or not they were reactionary. The liberals — Cardozo, Brandeis, and Stone — then could only concur in the result and write a concurring opinion, which was in effect a dissent but not a frontal attack on Hughes, and thus he could ignore it with dignity, for the public seldom paid any attention to concurring opinions. Brant thought Hughes assigned opinions in that way as a matter of strategy to obtain public approval, exercise power, and attain definite objectives. There is perhaps more than a little truth in Brant's analysis, but another plausible interpretation is that Hughes protected and used the symbolic significance of his office to maintain public confidence in the Court. If that is so, Hughes's assignment of opinions to himself was one instance, but not the only one, of using his assignment prerogative to protect the Court.

Other instances include a series of assignments to Justice Black in cases

[41]Charles Evans Hughes, *The Supreme Court of the United States* (New York, Columbia University Press, 1928).

[42]Irving Brant, "How Liberal is Justice Hughes?" *The New Republic*, XCI (July 21 and 28, 1937), 295–298, 329–332.

upholding the rights of Negroes in the South.[43] These assignments were made, according to one of Hughes's law clerks, "with an eye to the unfortunate controversy [concerning Black's former membership in the Ku Klux Klan] which had enveloped Justice Black at the time of his appointment to the bench."[44] Another example of Hughes's opinion assignment with a view toward public opinion was his penchant for assigning, when possible, liberal decisions to conservatives, and conservative decisions to liberals. The public perhaps found it confusing to hear of Brandeis's opinion in a conservative decision and Sutherland's opinion in a liberal decision, but such assignments tended to mute criticism of the Court and reinforce the notion that law and the Constitution, not political attitudes, were the basis of the Court's decisions.

Hughes believed that unanimity of decision contributed to public confidence in the Court. Although, as one of his law clerks put it, "he did not . . . knock heads together" to achieve unanimity, he nonetheless actively sought it. Except in cases involving matters of high principle, he willingly acquiesced in silence rather than expose his dissenting views. In such cases he thought it was better to have the law settled one way or the other than express his own position in a dissenting opinion. For example, on the back of one of Stone's slip opinions, he wrote: "I choke a little in swallowing your analysis; still I do not think it would serve any useful purpose to expose my views."[45]

Hughes was also willing to modify his own opinions to hold or increase his majority, and if that meant he had to put in disconnected thoughts or sentences, in they went. In cases assigned to others, he would often suggest the addition or subtraction of a paragraph if he thought he could thereby save a dissenting vote or concurring opinion. Dissents were thus avoided in cases in which agreement seemed impossible.[46]

The high point of Hughes's public career came in 1937 when he successfully led the Supreme Court through a constitutional crisis and at the same time proved to be more than a match for Franklin Roosevelt in the Court packing fight. It was precisely the kind of political battle Hughes could wage with gusto, for he saw himself performing his duty as chief justice in repelling an unjust assault on the Court's independence, and furthermore he believed public opinion supported him. When the controversy was over, he could say with satisfaction that it "had the good effect

[43]Pierre v. Louisiana, 306 U.S. 354 (1939); Chambers v. Florida, 309 U.S. 227 (1940); White v. Texas, 310 U.S. 530 (1940).

[44]McElwain, "Business of the Supreme Court," p. 18.

[45]Confidential interview, Sept. 11, 1959; Slip opinion, Sanford v. Comm'r, 308 U.S. 39 (1939), Harlan Fiske Stone Papers, Library of Congress.

[46]McElwain, "Business of the Supreme Court," p. 19; Pusey, *Hughes*, II, 677.

of revealing the strength of public sentiment in support of the independence of the Court." [47]

VI

Hughes wrote that the Notes were not an apologia, but there are a few matters on which he seeks to set the record straight. One of them was his statement, "the Constitution is what the judges say it is." Some have quoted the statement to suggest that Hughes meant constitutional interpretation is a matter of judicial caprice. That, says Hughes, was furthest from his thought. He intended his statement to be one of respect for the judiciary, and when read in context, his intention is clear. Another is Hughes's failure to meet Governor Hiram W. Johnson in the 1916 presidential campaign. "I had been very desirous of meeting him," writes Hughes in the Notes, "and had I known he was at Long Beach when I was there, I should have seized the opportunity to greet him." [48] Hughes then explains the attempts to remedy the misadventure that quite likely cost him the election, asserting that he was without fault in the matter.

In writing of his years as secretary of state he takes issue with Walter Lippmann and others concerning events with which he was associated. Hughes is troubled by the causes of World War II, which was being waged at the time he dictated the Notes, and it is from that vantage point that he records his views of United States diplomacy of the 1920s. Two things concerned him about his appointment as chief justice — the circumstances of the nomination by President Hoover and the controversy over it in the Senate. In regard to the former, he quotes at length from later correspondence with Hoover concerning the matter to rebut published reports that the chief justiceship was offered to Hughes as a gesture on the assumption that it would be declined. In regard to the latter, he quotes Chafee, who defended him eloquently in his 1941 edition of *Free Speech in the United States*.[49]

Finally Hughes defends the Supreme Court's integrity by attempting to rebut the charge that because of President Roosevelt's Court plan the justices (or more precisely Justice Roberts) took a more liberal view of the Constitution. Hughes points out that the case in which Justice Roberts is supposed to have switched his vote — *West Coast Hotel Co.* v. *Parrish* — had been voted upon before Roosevelt announced his Court plan, and the vote was four to four, with Roberts joining Hughes, Brandeis, and Car-

[47] Notes, p. 307.
[48] Notes, p. 182.
[49] Zechariah Chafee, Jr., *Free Speech in the United States* (Cambridge, Harvard University Press, 1941), pp. 358–362.

dozo.[50] Justice Stone was ill at the time, but his liberal position was well known, and when he returned to the Court he voted with Brandeis, Cardozo, Hughes, and Roberts as expected. Another case sometimes cited to indicate that the court changed its direction because of the Court plan is *National Labor Relations Board v. Jones & Laughlin Steel Corporation*, which was decided by the same majority.[51] Hughes, who spoke for the Court in that case, argues that the principles upon which his opinion was based had been stated years before in other opinions by him. As for Roberts' vote in the case, Hughes states that he can say definitely that his position would have been the same if Roosevelt's bill had not been proposed; he concludes: "The Court acted with complete independence." [52]

VII

On New Year's Day of 1939, President Roosevelt met with Robert H. Jackson, Homer Cummings, and Harry Hopkins to discuss candidates who might be suitable to fill a vacancy on the Supreme Court created by the death of Benjamin N. Cardozo. There was some support for candidates from the west, but Jackson, who supported Felix Frankfurter, opposed them. He maintained that too much was at stake — no less than the course and direction of constitutional interpretation — to approach the appointment in terms of geography. The crucial consideration, he thought, was the prospective appointee's ability to interpret the Constitution "with scholarship and with sufficient assurance to face Chief Justice Hughes in conference and hold his own in the discussion." "Any man you would be likely to appoint from the west," he told the President, "would be possessed of an inferiority complex in the presence of the Chief Justice, who looks like God and talks like God. He would be completely unable to help give direction to the action of the Court." Whereupon FDR said, "I think Felix is the only man who could do that job, Bob." [53] Four days later Frankfurter was named to the Court.

After facing Chief Justice Hughes in conference for more than two years, Justice Frankfurter gave this private estimate of him:

> I have known or know about the leading men of my time both here and in England enough to justify me in forming a judgment. There isn't the slightest doubt that C.E.H. is among the very few really sizeable figures

[50] 300 U.S. 379 (1937).
[51] 301 U.S. 1 (1937).
[52] Notes, p. 313.
[53] Eugene Gerhart, *America's Advocate: Robert H. Jackson* (Indianapolis, Bobbs-Merrill Company, 1958), p. 165.

> of my lifetime. He is three-dimensional and has impact. And his exterior rather hides a good deal of shrewd insight and humor, and, as Holmes indicated in one of his letters to Pollock, skeptical vistas that some of his conventional formalisms might betray one into not discerning. That the settled verdict will appraise him as a great Chief Justice I have not the slightest doubt. That in a number of crucial matters he might, unlike Luther, also have done otherwise, I have also no doubt.[54]

In writing of Charles Evans Hughes, it is tempting to sketch him as larger than life, as a superman. That is a mistake. "Why not portray him," asked Alpheus Thomas Mason, "as a human being, endowed with superior gifts, titanic energy, submerged native wit, who, surmounting the regimen of theological orthodoxy, reached high rank in the roster of American statecraft?" [55] That is the way Hughes portrays himself in the Notes. The Notes are not, of course, the last words on the matters covered, but they are the first in the sense that anyone interested in understanding Hughes and his connection with important events must begin with them.

[54]Frankfurter to C. C. Burlingham, June 4, 1941, Frankfurter Papers.
[55]Mason, "Hughes," p. 19.

The Autobiographical Notes of Charles Evans Hughes

Prefatory Note[1] I shall not attempt an *apologia pro mea vita.* It is my purpose to set down objectively the facts concerning forebears and environment — the circumstances of my lot and the various efforts of professional and public life. The recital may be interesting to my children and grandchildren and possibly may be of assistance to others who may wish accurate data. Some years ago,[2] Henry C. Beerits, a graduate of Princeton, prepared under my supervision a series of memoranda dealing chiefly with the years 1905 to 1910, and 1916 to 1930. While he worked under my direction and set down what I told him by way of reminiscences, he also made his own researches, availing himself of appropriate and trustworthy sources of information, including official records. I hope that I may be able to supplement his papers, especially in relation to my early life, as to which Mr. Beerits had but little material, and as to my experiences and work as Associate Justice of the Supreme Court, which he did not attempt to describe. In connection with political campaigns and official appointments, many articles of a biographical sort have been published, but in view of the limited purpose of the writers they cannot be regarded as adequate and some of them contain inaccuracies which have been repeated from time to time and should be corrected. While I have no objection to the publishing of anything I may set down, unless the contrary is indicated, I shall write not with a view to the publication of these notes as memoirs but to provide a body of facts for reference. How far I may be able to go in carrying out this project only time will tell.

[1]November 1941.
[2]1933–1934.

Chapter I My Father and Mother

My father and mother were in strong contrast in physical appearance and temperament. Father was of the Welsh type, with black hair, snapping black eyes, and olive complexion. He was emotional, impulsive — with the Celtic warmth — generous, sociable, and with a flair for adventure. Mother was very fair, with golden hair and light blue eyes — delicate, reserved, reflective, and cautious, but of strong will. My father's impulses were subject to my mother's wise restraint. They were alike in their intellectual interests and zeal for study. They were also alike in the depth of their religious feeling, in their acceptance of the evangelical conceptions of Christian truth and in their unselfish devotion to the Church. Their love for each other, which at the outset had surmounted the obstacles raised by the differences in their early environment and in temperament, grew in strength throughout the forty-nine years of their union, as they labored together in unity of spirit for a common cause and with a profound faith. I have never known any persons more sincere in what they professed or more constantly dominated by a sense of religious duty.

My father, David Charles Hughes, was born in Tredegar, Monmouthshire, England,[1] on June 24, 1832. He was the son of Nathan Hughes, who was born in South Wales about 1780 and died about 1845,[2] and of Jane Evans (Hughes), who was born in the Vale of Clwyd in North Wales in 1788 and died in 1867. I know nothing of their forebears. I understand that Nathan Hughes was a printer and publisher and that he published a life of Howell Harris of Trevecca, the eloquent Welsh evangelist who had much

[1]Monmouthshire is an English county bordering on Wales and is associated with Wales in tradition and Acts of Parliament.

[2]My father distinctly remembered that he was in his thirteenth year when his father died. The only memento that I have of my grandfather, Nathan Hughes, is Burkitt's New Testament with "Expository Notes" published in London in 1716. My father said that he would often take this book to his father for reading at family prayers. Inside the cover appears the inscription "Nathan Hughes's Book Bought in London 1815," and below "David C. Hughes's Book, the gift of an affectionate Mother June 26th, 1848."

to do with the so-called Methodist revival which ultimately resulted in the establishment of the Calvinistic Methodist Church of Wales.[3]

I have very little information about my father's life before he came to the United States at the age of twenty-three. I do not know what schooling he had, but it is evident that he made the most of his opportunities. He became a printer and it seems that he worked at his trade at Merthyr Tydvil and for a time was employed upon a newspaper in Hereford.[4] He was very studious and read widely, devoting himself chiefly to history and biography. Speaking of his efforts at self-improvement, he was wont to quote from Bailey's "Festus":

> "I know what study is: it is to toil
> Hard, through the hours of the sad midnight watch,
>
> . . . . .
>
> Wring a slight sleep out of the couch, and see
> The self-same moon which lit us to our rest,
> Her place scarce changed perceptibly in Heaven,
> Now light us to renewal of our toils."

Brought up in a religious atmosphere, and fond of public speaking, he became a licensed preacher of the Wesleyan connection, and in 1854–1855 was on the Wesleyan Hereford Circuit.[5]

The circumstances which led my father to come to the United States are interesting. He had happened upon the *Autobiography of Benjamin Franklin* and was so impressed that he determined to leave his native land and make this country his permanent home. He had no friends — no acquaintances, no opening, no particular prospects — here. He intended to remain a preacher, but he had no promise of a pulpit. He wanted to be an American — a citizen of this Republic. He was a republican by conviction

[3]Howell Harris (1714–1773) founded a school in Trevecca and set up societies which exercised a great influence on the religious life of the people. It appears that Harris was loyal to the Church of England despite refusals to ordain him. The separation of the Calvinistic Methodists from the Church of England did not take place until after Harris' death. *Encyclopedia Brittanica*, 14th ed., vol. 4, p. 634; *Dictionary of Welsh Biography* (1908), vol. IX, "Howell Harris"; J[ohn] V[yrnwy] Morgan, *The Philosophy of Welsh History* (New York, John Lane Company, 1914), p. 139; J. F. Hurst, *The History of Methodism* (New York, Eaton & Mains, 1902), vol. 4, pp. 751 and 755. An institution founded by Harris at Trevecca was continued for some time after his death and I understand that my grandfather, Nathan Hughes, had some connection with it. I believe that it was stated some years ago, in an article in a Welsh newspaper, that my father had a copper plate of Howell Harris but I have found no trace of it. [At this point in the original manuscript, Hughes provides considerable genealogical data on his father's family. We have moved this material to Appendix I.]

[4][Reuben Richards to David C. Hughes, July 23, 1855, Hughes Papers.]

[5]This appears from the printed circular of the Hereford Circuit for that year. [*Ibid.*]

and he wished to identify himself with this country which he had come to love as he studied its history in the little printing shops across the sea. He sought here neither fame nor fortune but the privilege of participation in the efforts of a free people. Although his family strongly opposed his leaving, he was fixed in his resolve and sailed for New York on the ship *Jacob A. Westervelt*, arriving on September 20, 1855.[6]

My father spoke English fluently and accurately, with a clear enunciation and without a trace of the inflections or accent which characterize many persons of Welsh birth. He was fond of telling of his interview with the Presiding Elder of the New York Conference when he presented his letter of recommendation from Methodists in England and Wales. "Well, young man," said the Presiding Elder, "I see that you are from Hingland." "No, sir," said my father, "I am from England." "You'll do," said the Presiding Elder, and in three days my father was sent to a little parish at Vail's Gate on the slope of Storm King on the Hudson River.

As a member of the New York Conference "on trial," he was appointed to the New Windsor Circuit, Newburgh District, and there he served with "great acceptability" until December 1856.[7] It appears from the letter of commendation which he received from the Presiding Elder that he left that work "to enter school & prepare for College." He obtained the opportunity he sought in a private school in Maryland, supporting himself by teaching some branches while he studied others. I cannot recall the name or location of this school, and I do not know how long he remained there.[8] Apparently he resumed preaching, for I believe it was while he was serving a Methodist Church at Eddyville on Rondout Creek, New York, some time prior to the fall of 1858, that he met my mother, whose parents' home was then at New Salem across the Creek. With preaching and teaching, he managed to earn enough to enable him to have a year at

[6]He brought with him general letters recommending him to Methodists in the United States. In one of these, dated May 9, 1855, from Benjamin Roberts, Superintendent of the Swansea Circuit, it was stated that "had this good brother offered himself to the full work of the Ministry in his native country, he would undoubtably have been accepted and stationed on a Circuit as soon as an opening should occur." But he thought it to be "his providential call to cross the Atlantic, with a view to offer himself to the full work of the Ministry in the Methodist Episcopal Church of America." In other letters it is said that he would have offered himself to the English Conference but was afraid that he would have to wait longer than was convenient in view of the number of applicants. It may well be that probable delay in obtaining a permanent assignment in England or Wales had some influence in his decision, but I have no doubt from what he often said to me that his heart's desire was to become an American and make this country the scene of his life's work. [The letters referred to are in the Hughes Papers.]

[7][Certificate of Leon M. Vincent, Presiding Elder of the Newburgh District, Dec. 17, 1856; Resolution of the Stewards and Leaders of the New Windsor Circuit, Dec. 8, 1856. *Ibid.*]

[8]However, I remember distinctly that my father said that the school was in Maryland and that in later years he had received letters from time to time from its principal.

Wesleyan University, from 1858 to 1859, and it appears that he had gone far enough in his preparatory work to enter the Sophomore Class.[9] My father's means were too limited to permit him to remain more than a year at Wesleyan[10] and he returned to preaching. However, although not at college, he continued his studies and became quite proficient in Latin and Greek. In later years — in his thirties — notwithstanding the pressure of his duties as a pastor, he did serious work in Hebrew, aided at the outset by the instruction of a Rabbi.

It was through my mother's persuasive influence that he became a Baptist and joined the Sixteenth Baptist Church in New York City.[11] My father and mother were married on November 20, 1860, in Kingston, New York, and a few days later (November 27th) my father was ordained and assumed his first charge as pastor of the Baptist Church at Glens Falls, New York.[12]

My mother, Mary Catherine Connelly, the eldest child of William Connelly, Jr., and Margaret Ann Terpenning (Connelly), was of old American stock. She was born on November 22, 1830, in the Township of Middletown, near Margaretville, in the wilds of Delaware County, New York. Her father, a young contractor, had gone from his home, at or near Kingston, New York, with his equipment and a crew of workmen to build tanneries. My mother had two distinct lines of descent. One, on her father's side, was part Irish (or what is known as Scotch-Irish of the Protestant type, from the north of Ireland, the Ulster "Plantation"), and part English; and the other, on her mother's side, was chiefly Dutch.[13]

My mother was brought up under the influence of the traditions of thrift and self-reliance which were characteristic of her time and especially of her Dutch ancestors. As the eldest child, she was a little mother to her brothers and sisters. There were three of these,[14] Henry Cantine Connelly (born 1832, died 1914), Carey Simpson Connelly (born 1840, died 1890), and Cathalina Connelly (born 1844, died 1924) who married Alfred Von Nostrand of Kingston. Resembling her in temperament, my mother's best loved companion was her brother Henry. He became a successful

[9]From the Wesleyan University catalogue, 1858–1859, it appears that in sophomore year, besides mathematical subjects (trigonometry, analytical geometry and calculus), English literature and logic, there were other courses in Plato's *Gorgias*, Homer's *Iliad*, the Greek tragedies, and in Cicero and Plautus.

[10]A certificate of President Joseph Cummings of Wesleyan, dated June 9, 1859, indicates that my father was "honorably dismissed at his own request." [Certificate not located in Hughes Papers.]

[11]Certificate of William S. Mikels, Pastor, Sixteenth Baptist Church, New York, dated October 5, 1860, [Hughes Papers].

[12]Certificate of ordination dated November 27th, 1860. [*Ibid.*]

[13][At this point in the original manuscript, Hughes provides considerable genealogical data on his mother's family. We have moved this material, along with the material on Hughes's father, to Appendix I.]

[14]There were two other children, George Luther and Peter who died when very young.

man of business, residing first at New Salem and then at Kingston. His father's business at Eddyville, to which he succeeded, he greatly extended and his firm (Connelly & Shaffer) at one time owned extensive slate quarries. While not a practical politician, his reputation for integrity and sound judgment brought him to the State Senate where he served two terms, 1874–1875, and 1886–1887. I remember well how I was impressed by his dignified manner when I first saw him as a Senator in 1875, as he appeared in his full suit of black broadcloth. My uncle, Carey Simpson Connelly, was active in politics in Ulster County and while retaining his home there was for many years employed in the Custom House in New York City. In her early years, my mother was affiliated with the Dutch Reformed Church of which her parents were members. The latter, about 1847, joined the Baptist Church, and I understand she also became a member. Certainly in her young womanhood, and when she first met my father, she was a staunch Baptist.

My mother in her quiet way was as intellectually ambitious as my father. In her studies, she also found escape from the limitations of her environment. Taking full advantage of every educational opportunity that was open to her, she decided to become a teacher. I understand that she taught at first in the little district school in Esopus and later had a private school at Kingston. Desiring to fit herself for advanced work, she studied at two of the leading institutions then open to young women, the Fort Edward Institute and the Hudson River Institute at Claverack. She was a member of the Senior Class at the Fort Edward Institute from 1856 to 1857. Her required studies there were History, Logic, Natural History, United States Constitution, Evidences of Christianity, Kames' "Elements of Criticism," Cicero, and French and German.[15] She was at the Hudson River Institute in the year 1857–1858 where she specialized in French.[16] Returning to Kingston, she maintained a school of her own for girls.[17]

My father and mother met on her return to her home, apparently from

[15]Catalogue of Fort Edward Institute for 1856–1857, published October 1857.

[16]I have my mother's Autograph Book which shows an inscription — "Dedicatory," signed June 1857, by Joseph E. King who was President of the Fort Edward Institute. After a few pages, the Book has a sentiment signed by D. D. Owens of the Hudson River Institute, June 11, 1858. This is followed by sentiments signed by M. M. Goodenough and Mary Goodenough, teachers at the Hudson River Institute, July 6, 1858. Other signatures followed, one with a sentiment in French by her French Professor, Homer J. Doucet, who was often quoted by mother to me. Another signature is by R. C. Flack of the Hudson River Institute. When I was a student at Madison University [now Colgate University], 1876–1878, Mr. and Mrs. Goodenough were in charge of the "Female Seminary" at Hamilton, New York. Mrs. Goodenough often spoke to me of my mother's ability in her work at the Hudson River Institute.

[17]I have a book in my mother's handwriting, containing what appear to be exercises for her pupils. There is an extraordinary draft of an address to "Respected parents and friends," at the close of which she refers to "my school." I understand that she conducted this school until her marriage in the Fall of 1860.

David Charles Hughes

Mary Catherine Connelly Hughes

the Fort Edward Institute, I think about 1857. He had gone, at her father's invitation, to meet her at the station at Rhinebeck. My father always said that he fell in love at first sight. He was still to a great extent a stranger in a strange land. My mother's family, despite their well recognized old world connections through the Dutch and Irish lines, were clannish Americans and very suspicious of "foreigners." My grandmother Connelly, a positive character who dominated her household and her mild-mannered, blue-eyed husband, did not "take" to my father and made his courtship difficult. "Who was this upstart, this dark-hued Welshman?" "Who knew but that he had left a wife in Wales?" "Who really knew anything about him?" When I think of my mother's unusual reserve and caution I marvel that my father succeeded in such a hostile atmosphere. But my mother believed in him and loved him. She appreciated his sincerity and warm-heartedness and shared his aspirations and religious views. My mother's faith was like that of the Christian martyrs and like them, notwithstanding her natural timidity, I doubt not that she would have gone to the stake rather than be untrue to her religious convictions. She was my father's soul mate and they were brought together in a spiritual union which held them in the closest companionship as they pursued the same aims and cherished the same hopes.

My mother always had delicate health. She remembered that when a little girl the family doctor once brusquely remarked — "Mary, you will never make old bones." And I recall my father's rebuke, when I was about nine years old and had spoken rather rudely — "My boy, you must never speak to your mother in that way. She will not be with us very long." From that time I always regarded my mother with a certain anxiety, but she well understood the care of the body and had her little remedies for temporary ailments. She bore all the burdens of a pastor's wife with unfailing regularity and with a constant joy in the performance of duty. She belied the family doctor's prophecy and lived to be eighty-four.[18]

While my father was pastor at Glens Falls, he also served the Baptist Church at Sandy Hill (now Hudson Falls) and it was in 1863, I think, that he left Glens Falls to devote himself exclusively to the other parish. During the Civil War, he was a most earnest supporter of the Union cause, stirring the community with his impassioned speeches and losing no opportunity to denounce the "Copperheads." My mother could never forget his agitation when word came of the assassination of Lincoln. "Mary," he cried, "I could not feel worse if you had died." In 1866, he removed to Oswego, New York, and later he had pastorates at Newark (New Jersey),

[18]My mother died at my home in Washington on December 30th, 1914.

Brooklyn, Jersey City, New York City, Scranton, and again in Brooklyn.[19] He was an evangelical preacher of persuasive power and had high repute in the denomination.[20] He added largely to the membership of the churches he served, and was also a builder of churches — notably at Greenpoint (Brooklyn) and Scranton. His unvarying kindliness, his tender interest in the afflicted and unfortunate, his unflagging industry and unselfishness inspired respect and won for him many lasting friendships. My father's impetuous spirit was kept in wholesome check by my mother's caution, while her thrift made it possible to maintain the household without debt, notwithstanding my father's unquenchable desire for books, which led him to extravagances in accumulating a large library and made it necessary to endure many privations in order to make both ends meet.[21]

My father retired from active service as a pastor in 1901 but continued to preach, supplying a number of pulpits in the vicinity of New York. He made his home with me from 1901 until the end of 1906 when I removed to Albany and he remained in New York. In June 1909, he had a stroke while preaching and did not fully recover. He then came to live with me at Albany where a second stroke proved fatal. He died at the Executive Mansion on December 15th, 1909, at the age of seventy-seven.[22]

[19]He was pastor at Oswego until 1869; of Fifth Baptist Church, Newark, N.J., 1869–1874; Union Avenue (later called Manhattan Avenue) Baptist Church, Greenpoint, Brooklyn, 1874–1884; Summit Avenue Baptist Church, Jersey City, 1884–1886; Trinity Baptist Church, New York City, 1886–1889; Jackson Street Baptist Church, Scranton, Pa., 1889–1895; Pilgrim Baptist Church, Brooklyn, 1896–1901. From March 1874 to October of that year, he served as one of the secretaries of the American Bible Union in New York City. From 1895 to 1896 he made his home with me.

[20]See the tributes upon his death in the portfolio marked "In Memoriam David Charles Hughes" [in the Hughes Papers]. He received the degree of A.M. from Madison University and the degree of D.D. from Temple University, Philadelphia. He was for many years a contributor to the *Homiletic Review.*

[21]My father's largest salary was $2,000 a year (without a parsonage) and often it was in arrears. I do not know what he received on his first pastorate in Glens Falls, but when, in 1863, he left Glens Falls and devoted himself exclusively to the church at Sandy Hill, his salary was $500 with a donation or $600 without one. In Newark, N.J., his salary was $1,500 with a parsonage. In Greenpoint and later it was $2,000 without a parsonage.

When I left Washington in 1916, I had most of his books, which had come to me on my mother's death, distributed to colored ministers in Washington.

[22]In the table appended to Henry C. Beerits' Memorandum on "Ancestry and Early Life," Nos. 1–4, there are references to items in Folders filed with the Memorandum in the Library of Congress. I have not examined these papers in the preparation of my Notes.

Chapter II Childhood

There has been a dispute as to the house in which I was born in Glens Falls (April 11, 1862). No doubt it was on Maple Street. Some have insisted that it was the house still on that street, formerly No. 47, now No. 135. Others say that the house where I was born was removed from Maple Street and is now at No. 16 Center Street. I think that the latter have the better case.

An only child, I was the subject of the most watchful care and of the fondest hopes. Physically I was especially in need of that care and, but for the devotion and intelligence of my mother, who was a born nurse, I should not have grown up. I understand that I came into the world with a sound body and that I was a vigorous baby, but when I was two years old I had an attack of what was called "inflammation of the lungs" which left me in delicate health. I had about all the usual diseases of childhood and at least one that was serious — scarlet fever, when I was about ten years old. I suffered much from tonsilitis — no one in those days suggested the removal of tonsils. We lived in places where the climate was unfavorable. At Oswego (1866 to 1869) the winter winds were severe and I had chronic catarrh. In Newark, New Jersey (1869–1874), our home was near the unreclaimed meadows (marshes), and malaria, or what was locally termed "fever and ague," was prevalent. I had a whimsical appetite, and for years I did my best to resist the efforts to persuade me to eat meat and vegetables. My diet was chiefly milk, graham bread, griddle cakes and maple syrup, "johnny-cake" and honey. I was wiry and tenacious and my parents did everything possible to develop my physical strength. At Newark, my father had a structure with a horizontal bar and two flying rings erected in the yard back of the parsonage and I loved to practice there all sorts of stunts. Adjoining the parsonage (164 Elm Street) there was at that time a large vacant lot where I played baseball with the boys — "one-old cat" and "two-old cat" and over the fence was "out." We had no radio, no motion pictures, no comic strips. But we did not know what we missed. I took part in "cops and robbers" and the other modest sports of the neighborhood, and with my sled in the winter I had great fun "hooking rides" behind passing carts. In the summer I spent some time at my grandfather's fruit farm on the Hudson River where I helped in the daily work as much as a small boy could. Altogether, for one who was rather delicate, I did pretty well.

In childhood my eyes were weak. When I was five years old my mother gave me a New Testament and Psalms with large type in order that I might take my turn in reading the verses at family prayers, and when even that help was insufficient, I would recite — when my turn came — any verse that I could remember. My training in biblical lore was such that even as a child I had a fairly large repertoire. Gradually my eyes grew stronger, although at college and law school, and while teaching, I suffered frequently from inflammation. But I did not wear glasses until long after my admission to the bar and since then I have used them only for reading and writing. Despite the constant and excessive demands of professional and judicial work, I am happy to say that my eyes have continued to be strong and recent years have given no indication of any serious impairment of vision or of eye strain.[1]

I left home for college at fourteen. I was small and slender, but full of life. Systematic exercise — walks up and down the college hill at Hamilton — where for a year and a half I took meals in the town, and similar walks in Providence — kept me in good form. I recall that during all my college years I never consulted a doctor. I had colds but my mother's homeopathic remedies — with which I was always supplied (aconite, belladonna and bryonia) seemed sufficient.[2]

Along with solicitude for my physical well-being, my parents earnestly sought to supply the instruction and mental discipline by which they set such great store. I suppose that I was somewhat precocious, but I was in no sense a prodigy and the descriptions in certain biographical sketches of some of my early performances are overdrawn. The atmosphere of my home and the constant stimulus I received made my progress more rapid than otherwise would have been possible. My mother as an experienced teacher was able to practice upon me her pedagogical principles without

[1]This was written in November 1942.

[2][Aconite, or monkshood and friar's cap as it is commonly called, was used in the treatment of rheumatism, neuralgia, and to reduce swelling. When applied locally it produces tingling warmth, followed by numbness — a form of anesthesia. As it slows the heart rate and lowers blood pressure, it was used in the treatment of heart disease, hypertension and high fevers.

[Belladonna, or deadly nightshade, was used in hay fever and head cold treatments.

[Bryonia, or bryony, was used as a cathartic and diuretic.]

restraint. She believed in discipline. She encouraged me in pursuing the studies for which I seemed to have special aptitude, but I was not permitted to neglect any subject that she thought was a necessary part of a sound curriculum. I understand that I could read when I was three and one-half years old and that I memorized easily. My mother was strong in mathematics, and the most useful training I have ever had was in her exercises in "mental arithmetic." She would make me toe a mark on the floor and without changing my position do in my head the various sums she gave me. Nor was she content to limit her instruction to the "three Rs." As she had studied French, she started me in Fasquelle's *Lessons*, and while I did not get very far in French under her direction, she gave me a foundation for my later work. She also took me through a German primer.

As an experiment, I was sent to a school in Oswego, but after three or four weeks I begged to be released from what seemed to me unnecessary confinement and waste of time. It was then — when I was about six years old — that I prepared the "Charles E. Hughes Plan of Study" — of which my father, with parental pride, informed the press when I ran for Governor and the reporters sought to learn about my early life. I remember the "Plan," which I got up to prove that I could do more at home than in the school I did not like. I also remember getting up early on winter mornings and coming down stairs, before my parents were up, to begin lessons according to my schedule. I recall the great stove in our living room in Oswego — the "Morning Glory," very high and imposing, heating the room above as well — with its red coals shining through the isinglass. Another experiment in attending school was tried in Newark when I was about eight years old, but again it was soon given up and I continued my work at home with my mother until I was between nine and ten.

While my father was too busy with his parish work to give me much specific instruction, he was constantly seeking to guide my reading, for which, as I was not confined in school and generally finished my lessons in the morning, I had plenty of time. The books he gave me show his desire to excite my interest in what he thought worthwhile. When I was five years old he gave me Miss Corner's *England and Wales* — a history "adapted for youth, schools and families." [3] On my sixth birthday I received *The Wonders of Science* or *Young Humphrey Davy* — the boy "who taught himself Natural Philosophy." [4] My father thought it a fine idea to start me early in Greek and gave me some lessons. And on my eighth

[3][Julia Corner (1798–1875), author of over fifty books for juveniles, including *The History of Ireland* (London, Dean & Munday, 1840), and *The Ancient Britons* (London, Thomas Dean & Son, 1850).]

[4][Sir Humphrey Davy (Henry Mayhew), *The Wonders of Science or Young Humphrey Davy* (New York, Harper & Brothers, 1856).]

birthday he presented me with a Greek New Testament with Lexicon. I could not do much with that, but I learned the alphabet and I liked to look up words in the Lexicon. I remember that I was able, to the amusement of the family and others, to rattle off the genealogy of the first Chapter of Matthew. My efforts were aided by another Greek Testament with the English version in a parallel column and in a childish way I liked to compare the Greek and English words. In the early part of 1871, my father made a trip to Minneapolis, to attend a religious meeting, and brought back Coffin's *The Seat of Empire* which he gave me on my ninth birthday.[5] This description of the northwest thrilled me, and I resolved that when I grew up I would make my home in Minneapolis. (I cherished that notion for many years. Indeed, when I was in the law school I talked so much about it that my chum, Emerson Hadley, actually went to St. Paul where he became a member of a leading law firm — Lusk, Bunn & Hadley. My own opportunity in New York, however, was too good to lose and I remained there.)

For the days when I could not play outdoors, I had many schemes for diversion. As I had no brother or sister, I learned to play alone.[6] One of my favorite sports was "travel." In the attic in the Newark parsonage, I had a large playroom. One of my father's parishioners gave me an enormous hobby-horse, about as big as a small pony, and I rigged up a shoe-box, with a driver's seat and whipsocket, and with trunk straps for reins I set forth on my journeys which were very extensive. I loved to get hold of a travel book and pretend, with the book before me, to go with my stout steed from place to place. Especially helpful in these excursions was Thomson's *Land and the Book*, descriptive of Palestine with inset pictures, and I traveled up and down that land, reading the descriptions to aid my imagination, as they seemed very familiar in view of my Bible lessons.[7]

I liked to roam through my father's library. I knew at least the outside of the books and for a time I labored in making a catalogue of a good part of them. The library consisted mainly of theological works, commentaries, histories, biographies, and works of reference, with very little fiction. There were certain books dealing with Bible lessons which for me were "required reading." But if I found anything in the library that looked interesting I seized upon it. I read *Pilgrim's Progress* several times and

5[Carleton Coffin, *The Seat of Empire* (Boston, Field, Osgood & Co., 1870).]

6[Hughes's biographer adds the following: "As he had no brother or sister, he learned to play alone. At one time his parents thought of adopting a child to give him companionship, but Charlie, overhearing the discussion and knowing the family's meager resources, marched into the room and said he thought it would be a mistake. It was more important, he said, to give him an education than companionship at home." Merlo J. Pusey, *Charles Evans Hughes*, 2 vols. (New York, The Macmillan Company, 1951), I, 12.]

7[William McClure Thomson, *Land and the Book* (New York, Harper, 1859).]

Bunyan's *Holy War.*[8] I was fond of Chambers' *Miscellany.*[9] I discovered Shakespeare, Byron, and Tom Moore. I recall that, when I was about nine, a young Englishman (James Clare) who made his home with us for some time, gave me a copy of *Robinson Crusoe*, profusely illustrated, which he had brought from England. It was my choicest possession. My granddaughter Helen once told me that she had seen a statement in a magazine article that I had read Shakespeare when only eight years old and she wanted to know if that was true. It was true only in part. Of course I could not appreciate Shakespeare at so early an age, but I loved the stories. *The Tempest, Twelfth Night,* and *The Merry Wives of Windsor* were my favorites.

In the fall of 1871, it was decided that I should go to school and I entered the class next to the graduating class at the Tenth Ward Public School in Oliver Street, Newark, where I was duly graduated in June 1873. My chief interest in the school work was in the course in American history, taught by Mrs. Hallock, the wife of the principal. She was one of the best teachers I ever had. She seemed to give me special attention and I loved her dearly.

It was in 1871, or 1872, that our home was ransacked by a thief. I well remember that Sunday evening, when my father had gone to preach in another city and a substitute was raising money for missions. In the course of his sermon our colored maid came panting up the aisle to our pew and told my mother in a stage whisper that Mr. Hughes' cousin was in the house. As my father had no cousin in this country, my mother knew something was wrong, and, bidding me keep my seat, she hastily left the church with one of the ushers. They found the house brilliantly lighted and the "cousin" departed. He had told the maid that he would go to the guest room, the location of which he seemed to know, and would await our return from church. The maid became suspicious and ran to the church, about two blocks away. All mother's jewelry, not much of value, to be sure, but including some heirlooms she prized and the gold watch she had bought when teaching, all our silver, and the bag containing the collection taken at the morning service by our missionary friend, were gone. This thief paid special attention to the ministers of the community and told his exploits in rhyme which he sent to the local papers. In one instance — not that of our home — he was disgusted to find that the tableware he had stolen was pewter. In his rhymed narrative he said (in substance), "And what would poor Judas have thought if he had found his thirty pieces of silver to be only tin?" He was the talk of the town for a while but I believe was never apprehended. Needless to say, I was greatly excited by this episode.

[8] [John Bunyan, *Holy War* (London, W. Johnston, 1752).]

[9] [W. & R. Chambers, *Miscellany of Instructive and Entertaining Tracts* (Boston, Gould, Kendall, & Lincoln, 1802–1811).]

The happiest of the early childhood days were the few weeks in the summer at my grandfather's place. My outing began with a trip on the *Mary Powell*, the fastest and most graceful steamer on the Hudson River, leaving New York in the afternoon and reaching her berth at Rondout between eight and nine in the evening. I generally went on Saturday with my Uncle "Simmie"[10] (whose family made their home with my grandfather). I sat on deck with him and a number of his cronies from the Custom House (who also had their families up the river) and I heard endless discussions on New York politics which seemed to me a world of extraordinary cunning. Then, there were the good playtimes with my cousins. I took my part in berry-picking, but when I was nine or ten, being overcome by the heat, I was made paymaster, receiving the berries and paying the berry-pickers. Then there was the gathering of apples, a chore I never liked. But it was fun to drive with my grandfather in the late afternoon to Rondout Creek where the fruit was put on the steamer for New York. I recall that my father, who had been much on horseback in his first parishes, and prided himself on his horsemanship, wished me to learn to ride and sent the saddle he had used to my grandfather's place. So I saddled "Billy," the trusted family horse, and galloped about on the dusty country roads. Best of all, there was a rustic seat under an apple tree at the far end of the orchard which lay on the crest of a knoll commanding an extensive view up the river. I never tired of that charming scene. Immediately below was the mouth of Rondout Creek with its busy boats, the most of which I learned to know as well as the larger steamers which called across the river at Rhinebeck. The river teemed with life, always interesting, but I loved the river itself, with its broad sweep and majestic serenity, and the view of the rolling upland toward the Berkshires on the East end of the Catskills to the North — the wonderful heights, as they then seemed to me, full of mystery and legend. On the warm summer days, whenever I had a chance, I would sit and watch the river in a sort of enchantment.[11]

In the summer of 1873 I had a memorable experience. An advance of the necessary funds (on extraordinarily easy terms) by one of my father's best friends, Leonard W. Cronkhite, of Sandy Hill, at whose home we frequently visited during my father's August vacations, made it possible for us to take a trip to Europe. This was primarily in the interest of my mother's health, but my father was very anxious to go, as he had not seen his relatives since his coming to this country in 1855. We sailed in June on the steamer *City of Antwerp* of the Inman Line. We were ten days at

[10] Carey Simpson Connelly.

[11] When, a few years ago, I drove by Port Ewen where my grandfather had lived, I was shocked by its changed appearance. No longer was it the familiar rural community. The fence in front of my grandfather's place and the stately fir trees on each side of the walk to the house and other fine trees on the lawn were gone. It seemed a run-down and forlorn place and my favorite haunts had been made into building lots.

sea and my father and I spent much time at chess. My father was a good player but because of his work he had very little time at home for the game. He had taught me its rudiments and I liked to tackle some of the simpler chess problems. Naturally we had much talk of the country I was about to see for the first time. Despite my father's antecedents, he was so completely American and my upbringing was so dominated by American thought, that I never had any sense of being identified with his family abroad. I remember that on the steamer I fought over the American Revolution with an English boy, and when I visited Wales, the families of my father's brothers and sisters seemed entirely foreign to me, although I became very fond of my Uncle John. Landing at Liverpool, we went directly to Abertillery, Monmouthshire, where my Aunt Jane lived. Later we journeyed to North Wales, to the home of my Uncle John. Then we set out for London where we spent a couple of weeks. We had lodgings in King Street, not far from Guild Hall. From London we went to Paris and then returned to Wales before sailing for home.

My enjoyment of this journey was beyond words. I devoured the guide books and my parents let me plan many of our sight-seeing excursions. These left an indelible impression and when I again visited Europe as a young man, London and Paris seemed very familiar. The steamer on which we returned to New York was the *City of Richmond.* I believe the record time was then seven days, made by the *City of Brussels,* of the same line, and it was expected that the *City of Richmond* would better it. But it was her first trip and she had a good deal of engine trouble, slowing down from time to time, or even stopping, in a way which made the passengers nervous. We approached Nantucket Shoals in a dense fog and there was some anxiety which culminated in an absurd incident. Despite the unpleasantness of the night, a gay party had a farewell champagne supper and one of them, a young actress, who had taken a little too much, got into the wrong stateroom. After disrobing in the dark, so as not to disturb her companion, she aimed at the top berth and happened to grasp its occupant by the beard. She ran from the room screaming with terror, and forthwith the gangsway to the staterooms, which led off from the dining saloon, were filled with frightened passengers in their night attire. There were immediately all sorts of rumors of a terrible accident. I thought we might be going down and I shall never forget that scene. We were soon relieved, but we did not know the reason for the commotion until the next morning.

In September 1873, I entered the Newark High School. It was an excellent school and if I had been permitted to stay there for the full four years' course I should have been thoroughly prepared for college by 1877. But in a few months, in January 1874, I had an accident while playing "red lion" in the school yard during recess, being thrown against a stone pillar and badly hurt. That ended my attendance there, as my father about the same time resigned his pastorate in Newark. My chief recollection of the High School is that we started Latin under John L. Heffron, a tall, handsome young man, recently graduated from Madison University, now Colgate.[12] He was a fine teacher. Later, he took up medicine, and, after studying in New York and Germany, settled in Syracuse. He was soon made professor in the College of Medicine of Syracuse University and for many years was its Dean. I saw him but once after leaving Newark, and that was when I had the delightful surprise of meeting him at the Colgate Commencement in 1909 when he received the degree of Doctor of Science.

My father accepted appointment as one of the secretaries of the American Bible Union, which had its office at 32 Great Jones Street, New York, and we moved to that City in the early part of 1874. The office of the Union was on the first floor of a four-story and basement brownstone residence, and we made our home there. We needed but few rooms and the rest were rented to lodgers, my mother taking care of the house and acting as landlady. This move sadly interrupted my schooling. There was then no public high school in New York that I could attend. Graduates of the public schools entered the College of the City of New York (formerly called the New York Free Academy) which had a five years' course — an "introductory year" before the freshman year. The College did not admit students before they were fourteen years old, so I could not seek admission. There seemed to be nothing for me to do but to enter the graduating class of a public school in the following September. At that time, the most famous of the public schools (for boys) was No. 35 on 13th Street near Sixth Avenue. It had won its distinction under Thomas Hunter, an eminent teacher who was long its principal.[13] Sometime before 1874, he had left the school to become the head of the Normal College for Girls, now known as Hunter College, but the fame of the school was

[12][John Lorenzo Heffron (1851–1924) practised medicine in Syracuse from 1882 until his death. He joined the faculty of the College of Medicine in 1883 and served as Dean from 1907–1922. He was a member of many local and professional organizations, including the American Medical Association and the New York State Medical Society.]

[13]In the sketch of Thomas Hunter in the *Dictionary of American Biography* I find this statement: "Number 35 under him became known throughout the city, not only for its scholarship but also for its discipline. Many of his 'boys' became leaders in all walks of life, and always to his training did they attribute much of their success. The Thomas Hunter Association, organized in 1897 and composed of the graduates of the school, bears eloquent testimony to this fact." The alumni of old "No. 35," embracing graduates after Thomas Hunter left, had annual dinners for many years. [Hunter (1831–1915) began his teaching career at P.S. 35 in 1850, the year he emigrated from Ireland. He was principal from 1857 to 1870. He started the Normal and High School in 1869 to train teachers and served as its president from 1870 to 1906. In 1914 the Board of Education changed the name to Hunter College of the City of New York.]

maintained under his successors. The school attracted students from all over the City. I remember that my seat-mate and most intimate friend lived on Madison Avenue near 44th Street. In September 1874, I took the entrance examination and was admitted to the graduating class, A First.[14]

From the early Spring of 1874 until the following September (save for some summer days at my grandfather's place) I had nothing in the way of amusement save to roam about New York and this was a constant joy. I had previously visited the City only occasionally, going with my father once in a while when he attended the Ministers' Conference on Mondays. I had been especially interested in the crush of traffic on lower Broadway when we were sometimes held up for fifteen minutes or more at Liberty or Cortlandt Street by the jam of buses, trucks and other vehicles. This, with irate policemen and swearing drivers, was an exciting scene. Now, actually living in the metropolis, I was free to see all its wonders. Great Jones Street, so oddly named, was really the part of Third Street which lay between Broadway and the Bowery. The neighborhood to a considerable extent was still residential. Lafayette Street had not been cut through, and from Astor Place to Great Jones Street was known as Lafayette Place and had a number of commodious homes as well as the Astor Library. On the corner of Lafayette Place and Great Jones Street, next our house, was the church building which had recently been St. Thomas's, then removed to Fifth Avenue. This building bore an enormous sign with the words "Moral Amusements." Across Lafayette Place and on the western corner of Great Jones Street, was a large mansion occupied by the Columbia Law School. Many a time I climbed up the iron fence which surrounded it to see Professor Dwight,[15] with the white pitcher of water on his table, lecturing to the law school students.

Great Jones Street was an admirable starting point for my excursions. No one interfered with my wanderings and armed with a street directory I was in no danger of getting lost. I made trips to every part of the City, from Great Jones Street to the Battery on the south and as far as Central

[14]There were four divisions of the graduating class, A First, A Second, A Third, and A Fourth. At the time I entered the school the teacher of A First was Charles Gates, who later became principal; the teacher of A Second was Mr. Oddie, known as a strict disciplinarian and somewhat eccentric who justified his name; the teacher of A Third was Charles P[rospero] Fagnani [1854–1940], who later was an eminent professor in the Union Theological Seminary; and the teacher of A Fourth was Charles E[dward] Lydecker [1851–1920], whom I knew, when I was Governor, as an officer of the Seventh Regiment and president of the National Guard Association. [Lydecker was a member of the Council of United States Military Service Institute, a founder of the National Security League, and a member of the Navy League.]

[15][Theodore William Dwight (1822–1892), Maynard Professor of Law, History, Civil Polity and Political Economy at Hamilton College, 1843; appointed to the faculty of the Columbia Law School, 1858; member of the New York State Commission of Appeals, 1873.]

Park on the north. I was fond of walking and the distances were covered without much difficulty. When I was tired of walking, I would jump on the tail-end of an empty truck and ride joyously with dangling legs. Any part of New York that had a bad reputation was particularly interesting. I wandered about Chatham Street, the Five Points, Cherry Hill and various places that were notorious. The Bowery was a fascinating place and little escaped my curious eye. On Broadway, around the corner from Great Jones Street, stood the Grand Central Hotel, one of the leading hotels of the City, where but a short time before Stokes had shot Jim Fisk.[16] I regarded it with awe. The stretches of the lower East Side, then predominantly Irish, became very familiar. I went to Sunday School at an old Baptist Church on Stanton Street, east of the Bowery, an institution which already seemed sadly out of touch with the neighborhood. I loved to sit in the small parks. Union Square was a beautiful park with fountain and trees. Madison Square was also a delightful spot, but best of all to my mind was Stuyvesant Square and broad Second Avenue with its spacious residences and shade trees. Central Park, then a sylvan retreat of the "horse and buggy" age, was a dream of beauty, and when I had a visiting cousin we would make a day of it, investigating its by-paths. I have known New York through all the transformations of the past sixty-eight years but the memory of the old town as I first became intimately acquainted with it stands out most vividly. After we left New York, in the fall of 1874, to reside in Greenpoint, Brooklyn, I remained a pupil at No.

[16][Edward S. Stokes (1841–1901) shot Colonel James Fisk, Jr. on the night of January 6, 1872. Fisk died the next day, exactly one year after Stokes had been arrested for embezzling funds from the Brooklyn Oil Refining Company in which he and Fisk were partners. Fisk was said to have exposed Stokes because the two men were vying for the affections of Helen Josephine Mansfield. Stokes was acquitted of the charge, and after the trial he went to live with Miss Mansfield. Fisk accused the couple of trying to blackmail him and Stokes countered by suing Fisk for libel. The case was heard first on November 25, 1871, and then postponed to January 6, 1872. In the January session, both Stokes and Josie Mansfield were humiliated by Fisk's lawyers and, on the same day, the Grand Jury indicted the pair for attempted blackmail. That night Stokes followed Fisk to the Grand Central Hotel and shot him. Stokes was tried three times. The jury could not reach a decision the first time. After his second trial, he was sentenced to be hanged, but the Court of Appeals set aside the conviction. At his third trial, Stokes was convicted of manslaughter. He served four years of a six-year sentence in Sing Sing Prison. After his release, in 1876, he went to California, then returned to the East, where he died in 1901. Josie Mansfield left New York City for Boston, then traveled in Europe, and ended in a Catholic nursing home in South Dakota, where she was when Stokes died. See R. W. McAlpine, *The Life and Times of Colonel James Fisk, Jr.* (New York, New York Book Company, 1872) and Robert H. Fuller, *Jubilee Jim: The Life of Colonel James Fisk, Jr.* (New York, The Macmillan Company, 1928). Fuller was Hughes's secretary when the latter was governor of New York, 1906–1910. His book contains an epilogue by Hughes praising his former secretary. Two sensational contemporary accounts of the incident are: George Lippard Barclay, *Life, Adventures, Strange Career and Assassination of Col. James Fisk, Jr.* (Cleveland, Great Western Publishing Co., 1872); and *Life, Trial and Conviction of Edward Stokes* (Philadelphia, Barclay & Co., 1873).]

Charlie Hughes, about eleven years old

Hughes as a freshman at Madison University, 1876

35 and I continued to use every available opportunity for explorations of the City. I distinctly remember seeing workers near the polling places on election day with greenbacks in their hands, marshalling the voters.

Greenpoint at that time was like a village. It was the seventeenth ward of Brooklyn but was somewhat detached as there was a considerable stretch of undeveloped land between Greenpoint and the part of Brooklyn called Williamsburgh. It was a community of modest homes, with self-respecting families of moderate means. For the boys and girls, there were the pleasures of a small town — with plenty of room for play. The churches were flourishing. The Sunday school of my father's Church had 1000 members and its rival was that of the Presbyterian Church with about the same number. The May Walk, of the Sunday school children and young people, then held separately in Greenpoint, was a leading event of the year and the Sunday School excursions in June — with large barges — to some pleasant resort on the Sound or the Hudson River, were very popular. Then the boys had abundant opportunity for swimming in the East River and were undisturbed as they left their clothes on the docks and swam *sans* trunks. The more venturesome would swim in the late afternoon to get the swells of the Sound steamers starting on their way to Fall River and Providence.[17]

New York was easily reached by the 10th Street and 23rd Street ferries.[18] In good weather, I usually walked from the 23rd Street ferry at Avenue A to my school at 13th Street and Sixth Avenue carrying my books and lunch box. But there was always available the "bob-tail" horse-car which started from the 23rd Street ferry and ran across town to Union Square and then on 14th Street, within a block of the school. At the best, it was a long journey and I had to rise early, as Chapel began at 8:30 and in the Winter there were frequent delays due to ice in the ferry slips. Before we moved from New York, I had become so attached to No. 35 that I did not mind these trips and I would not hear of starting at another school in Greenpoint.[19] Consequently, I saw little of the Greenpoint boys and my best friends were in New York. Whenever possible, I went skating with them in Central Park. I was very fond of skating and seized every opportunity to enjoy it. At that time along the west side of the Park, on Eighth Avenue, there were shanties of squatters, with their chickens, goats and pigs. Along the east side of the Park on Fifth Avenue, there were but few houses — I recall but two — on the corners of 62nd and 64th Streets. So there was a great stretch open to the sweeping winds, and whether or not the building up of the City has had anything to do with it, it seems to me that there were then more days of skating than in recent years.

When I entered No. 35, I found that I was going over much that I had already studied. We went further in mathematics. We did not attempt Latin. Our teacher, Mr. Gates, was a middle-aged man who did excellent

[17] I did not join them in this sport as I did not know how to swim.

[18] Our home in Greenpoint at first was at 109 Oak Street and later, from May 1875, to May 1884, at 127 Milton Street.

[19] It is astonishing what treacherous memories many excellent persons have in relation to what they think have been their associations with those who have become prominent. What was first a mere possibility or surmise becomes, with much repetition, a fact definitely recalled. Thus when I suddenly emerged into notoriety, in my forties, I had letters from those who remembered that they were classmates of mine in Greenpoint in a school I had never attended. Then there were those who told me to my face what I had said to them on occasions in years past — things I never thought or could have said. Others think they have seen or met me in places where I have never been. It was worse after I grew a beard. Frequently men of about my height and build, meeting me casually, have said with apparent pleasure that they had been mistaken for me. I recall that once — many years ago — there was a piece in a newspaper about an altercation in a street car, in which I was supposed to have taken part. It was another man with a beard.

At least once, the mistake worked in reverse. Soon after I became Chief Justice, as I was walking back to the hotel where I was then stopping, I heard a quick step behind me and a young man passed, eyeing me closely. He slowed up and when I overtook him, he said — "You know, you look like Chief Justice Hughes." I said — "Yes." He said — "Are you Chief Justice Hughes?" I said — "Yes." He gave me a sharp look and said — "Oh no, you aint" and walked off.

work and delighted us with his occasional talks, when we put aside our books and learned of the great world outside and his philosophy of life. Other teachers came in once or twice a week — a French teacher with purple hair, who amused us, but whose teaching came to practically nothing, and a lecturer on chemistry, who was almost toothless and not easily understood. There was a terrible hour, once a week, in drawing — a terror to me as I had not the slightest talent for that. I toiled longer over the required sketches than on anything else, but to no purpose, and in view of my futile efforts my father had me excused from that course.

My chief interest was in writing. Early in the term, Mr. Gates directed us to bring in an essay on "Bones." That was a stumper for me, but after hard labor I produced something which stood the test. We were invited to put in voluntary essays. At my father's suggestion, I wrote one on the "Elements of Success." This pleased the authorities and I was asked to read it in Chapel. That was the beginning of a series. I was ambitious in my choice of subjects, such as "Mental Culture," "Human Limitations," "True Manhood," "Happiness and its Constituents," and "Light Reading and its Consequences," the last being often mentioned in the biographical sketches that have been published. These boyish efforts reflected the countless admonitions I received at home and the talks of Mr. Gates. What I wrote about "Light Reading" had a special significance at the time in my mind and in that of my schoolmates. Certainly, I never thought of Shakespeare, or Byron, or Moore, to whose works I had been devoted, as "light reading." Rather I was thinking chiefly of the sort of stuff which was found in the sensational weeklies of the time, such as the *New York Weekly* and similar publications which many of the boys devoured during the lunch period. Our teacher had frequently remonstrated with them and I took the matter up by way of emphasis. At any rate, so far as what I said could be related to fiction generally, it represented but a temporary phase. It was not long before I was reveling in the works of the great novelists. The very next year, when I was at home preparing for college, I found a volume of Smollett in my father's library and I became absorbed in the adventures of Peregrine Pickle and Roderick Random. And when, at fourteen, I arrived at college and had the run of the college library, I fell upon the English authors with an insatiable appetite.

But at twelve, an impressionable boy, I was still under the dominating influence of my home training. Not only did I have the preachments of my parents, but I had often accompanied them to various meetings of church associations and other gatherings and I thus frequently listened to discourses on moral and religious subjects. I had early been encouraged to take notes and I had many well-filled note books. I remember that when we visited London in 1873, we went twice to hear Charles Spurgeon and I made my notes on his sermons. My father made it a point to take me occasionally to hear a good lecturer and I recall the eloquence of Henry Ward Beecher, which held me spellbound. I remember also hearing Wendell Phillips deliver his famous lecture on the "Lost Arts." Then there was the family table where I listened not only to the talk of my father and mother but sat in silent appreciation of the words of wisdom of the visiting grown-ups, usually preachers. It was natural that when I first tried my hand at compositions in the public school I should select subjects akin to those on which I had heard so much. The school gave me "merits" for these compositions, all of which I read in Chapel. My chief competitor won his "merits" by his declamations. He was R. Floyd Clarke [1859–1921], who later made his mark in the Columbia Law School where he won the first prize in 1882. He had an honorable career at the New York Bar. Another classmate was Harry G[eorge] S[tebbins] Noble, who became President of the New York Stock Exchange.[20] At Chapel, Clarke declaimed "The Battle of Ivry" and other choice pieces with fine effect. As a result of my contributions, the school gave me on graduation, in June 1875, a silver medal marked "For Composition," and I was assigned the "Salutatory" at our Commencement. I wrote this on the subject of "Self-Help," inspired by my reading of Samuel Smiles.

Our Commencement was an affair of distinction. It was held in the old Academy of Music (14th Street and Irving Place). The Graduating Class, with its four divisions, marched from the school to the Academy in martial array, having been drilled for this purpose by Mr. Lydecker in the old Twenty-Second Regiment Armory. At the Academy, the Class sat in tiers on the stage, while our parents and friends filled the boxes and orchestra seats, and the general public the balconies.

I thus found myself at the age of thirteen, graduated at a public school for the second time but unable, because I was under age, to enter the College of the City of New York with my classmates who with the five years' course would get their A.B. in 1880. I resolved that I should graduate from some college at the same time and with that in view I began my college preparatory work at home. To that I shall refer later.

During these early years I have described, I was subject not only to an exceptional intellectual stimulus but also to a constant and rigorous religious discipline. It was much too constant and rigorous, for in the end it largely defeated its own purpose by creating in me a distaste for religious formalities, although I have always recognized their benefit to those who set store by them and I have been careful not to give offense by unwelcome manifestations of my feelings with regard to conventional procedures and expressions. But it should be emphasized that my parents'

[20][Harry George Stebbins Noble (1859–1946) was president of the Exchange from 1914–1919. He was the author of *The New York Stock Exchange in the Crisis of 1915* (1915); and *The Stock Exchange: Its Economic Function* (1933).]

insistence on formal religious exercises was based on sincere and deep convictions. As my mother had no one to assist her after the first year or so of my babyhood, I was early taken to the church services.[21] My earliest recollection is that of an exciting event when I was about two years old. I was with my father when he drove his cream-colored mare, Nellie, to the residence of Mrs. Charles Stone in Sandy Hill and Mrs. Stone brought out a little rocking chair for me and placed it in the buggy.[22] This was for my use in the gallery on Sunday mornings when my mother sang in the church choir.[23] From that time on, so far as I was physically able, I attended church services and my duties in this respect increased steadily with the years. Sunday was a day set apart for services and devotions. Anything resembling sport or even pleasure was tabooed.

It was the fondest hope of my parents that I should enter the ministry and I was early "dedicated." Their chief concern was that as soon as possible I should apprehend religious truth as they understood it, and whatever precocity I had was utilized for that purpose. My childish peccadilloes were evidence of the sinful nature of which I partook with the rest of humanity, and I was constantly warned of the necessity of subduing my evil inclinations, lest they "grow with my growth and strengthen with my strength," as my mother was wont to say. It was natural that when I was caught in a grievous fault I should have a conviction of sin. I readily absorbed the doctrines I was taught, and when at the age of nine I was admitted to membership in the Church, the Deacons who examined me were amazed — as I was later informed — at the "mastery" I displayed of the tenets of the denomination. As I look back upon that training at home, in the light of subsequent views and experiences, I realize that what interested me most was the dialectic rather than the premises. In that period, as soon as it was practicable, I also assumed certain duties of leadership. At Newark, I organized a boys' club which for about a year met regularly at the parsonage and I addressed the club from time to time. I took an interest in my father's classes for the Sunday school teachers and prepared references for his syllabi.

But with all this unusual sort of activity for a small boy, I retained a healthy love of play and frolic as I have already indicated and I was always

[21]For a time my mother's cousin Kate Van Nostrand was my devoted nurse. She married Calvin Van Leuven and lived in Port Ewen, New York. [Samuel] Burhans *Genealogy*, [*:Descendants from the First Ancestors in America — Jacob Burhans, 1660, and His Son Jan Burhans, 1663, to 1893* (New York, printed for private distribution, 1894).] No. 11701.

[22]Mr. and Mrs. Charles Stone were lifelong friends of my father and mother and we frequently visited them when we went to Sandy Hill in the summer. Mr. Stone left my father $5000 in his will.

[23]That little chair is still in the family. All my children and my son's children have used it and it is now in my son's home. [After Charles Jr. died, the chair left his household and its whereabouts today are unknown.]

eager for new experiences. A year or more before I left home for college, my spirit had begun to flutter in its cage. I recognized my parents' sincerity — I responded to their warm affection, I would not wound them for the world — but I became restive at required attendance at so many meetings and wished greater freedom. Then I began to question my father about the problem of evil and I wanted to know how what I observed in the ways of nature and of men could be reconciled with the goodness, the omniscience and the omnipotence of the Creator. Despite these disturbing thoughts I still had a deep religious feeling and I was more inquiring than rebellious. I also became increasingly conscious of internal difficulties in the church administration due, as I imagined, to the shortcomings of church trustees which were fully discussed at the family table. Tiring of the routine of services and observing my father's pastoral troubles, I concluded that I would not enter the ministry. My parents hoped that I would have a different, and in their eyes a truer, vision of opportunity and duty as I matured. But in this they were destined to be disappointed.

On my graduation from No. 35, my thought had turned to New York University, which had a regular four years' course and, as I understood, admitted qualified students at fourteen. I thought I could prepare for admission in a year of home study. In my rambles about the city, I had often visited Washington Square and observed the dignified building of the University. The idea of entering there became very agreeable. I had then no notion that it would be possible for me to have a college course away from New York.

The summer of 1875, however, marked a turning point. On our visit in August to Mr. Cronkhite's home in Sandy Hill, I had the good fortune to meet his nephew and namesake, Leonard W. Cronkhite, 2d, who had just finished his sophomore year at Madison University, now Colgate. While much older than I, he made me his companion and thrilled me with his pictures of the delights of college life on the hill at Hamilton. I became enthusiastic for a similar opportunity. Why should I not have it? I thought it all over and determined to try to persuade my parents to let me leave home. My arguments were plausible. I got a catalogue from my friend and was ready to prove that I could prepare at home during the following year for the entrance examinations. The expenses were light, especially in view of the reductions in room rent and tuition in the case of ministers' sons. My friend Cronkhite, without that advantage, got along on an allowance from his Uncle of $300 a year. Then, was not Madison University a Baptist institution, with many studying for the ministry? Was not Hamilton a safe and wholesome place, and did I not need the invigoration of life in the country, among the hills? I would be so careful, so obedient! My father, with the memory of the simple college life he had known at Wesleyan, sympathizing with my desire for the adventure, soon capitulated. My mother was not satisfied. She could not bear to think of her "little boy" (for I was not only young but small for my age and slight), with his tendency to colds and sore throat, being away from her constant and tender care. But I was determined and carried the day.

So on my return home, about the end of August, I set about preparing for Madison. My father now took me in charge. He did not have time to teach me regularly but he could supervise my study and occasionally hold recitations. My enthusiasm was unbounded and the thought that I was definitely going away to college was an unfailing stimulus. Of course, I missed the drill and thoroughness of a course at a preparatory school, but I could make my own pace and lost no time in school exercises. At first I found it very hard going. But what I had learned in the three months in Latin in the Newark High School, in the fall of 1873, had given me a good start, and I had worked at home on Caesar's *Commentaries* after we had moved to New York in 1874. So, in my own imperfect way I was able to race along rapidly. From September 1875 to June 1876, I did my lessons in Latin and Greek grammar and prose composition, and in addition to brushing up on Caesar, I read six books of the *Aeneid,* four *Orations* of Cicero, and three books of the *Anabasis.* No doubt my translations were very "free" but they served. In the English subjects and mathematics I had comparatively little to do in order to complete my "preparation."

In June 1876, my father took me to Hamilton for the entrance examinations. With one exception, I took the regular written examinations which I passed without difficulty. The exception was in Greek, in which I had, for some reason unknown to me, a separate and private examination. By appointment, I went to the home of Dr. N. Lloyd Andrews, professor of Greek, and to my surprise he took me into his library, handed me an *Anabasis* and pointed out various passages.[24] He left me for a few minutes and then put me through an oral examination, which satisfied him. Perhaps, because of my extreme youth, he sought to try me out in order to see whether it was worth while to let me enter. Anyway, I was duly matriculated, selected my room in old West College (I believe it was No. 39), observed with wonder and admiration the Commencement exercises and returned home the happiest of boys.

In the following September, I went back to Hamilton to enter the freshman class and a new life began. As my mother often said — her "little boy left home and never came back." It was a different youth, with a broadened outlook, who visited his parents in the later vacation periods.

[24]Newton Lloyd Andrews (1841–1918) graduated from Madison in 1862 and became Professor of Greek there in 1868. He served as Dean of the Faculty from 1880 to 1895, and as acting president, 1890–95. From 1895 to his death he was Professor of Greek and Lecturer in the History of Art.]

Chapter III College Life

It must be difficult for those who have had the advantages of college life in recent years to realize how meagre was the physical equipment of the typical rural college of the eighteen-seventies and how much it lacked in ordinary conveniences. I suppose the colleges had not changed much in this respect since the years before the Civil War and that they continued to be about the same until the improvements in the latter part of the nineteenth century and the great expansion in the twentieth. Certainly the physical conditions at Madison, when I entered in the fall of 1876, were of the most primitive sort. We led the simple life, taking little or no account of its limitations.

The College was delightfully located on a hill overlooking the lovely village of Hamilton. There were three main buildings — two dormitories (East and West College), and "Alumni Hall" which contained the recitation rooms, library, chapel, and a large hall at the top for Commencements. Some distance beyond was the building which housed the Theological Seminary. Below the hill, across what was then a tree-less meadow and on the edge of the town, was the preparatory school known as Colgate Academy. The dormitories were of the severest style of architecture. The halls were of the bleakest description. The rooms were in suites of two, a small study, with one large window and window-seat, and an adjoining cubicle. There was no central heating or lighting. Most of us had a small sheet-iron, cylindrical stove in one corner of the study. There was no running water and of course no baths. We got our water from an outside pump near the dormitory and in cold weather the ice about the pump would be several inches thick. We heated the water we needed in small tin pails on the top of our stoves. We bought our coal which was kept in bins lining the halls. The dormitories had no toilet facilities.[1] There were no servants to take care of our rooms and we at-

[1]The latrine was a little stone out-house at the far end of the campus, with the rudest accommodations.

tended to that, after a fashion. The students took their meals in the town, which made it necessary to take long walks, going down and up the hill three times a day. This was exercise enough for most, and what remained of a gymnasium on the campus was little used. This was a barn-like building, uncared for and terribly cold in winter; it boasted of a bowling alley, flying rings and a pair of parallel bars.

The students furnished their own rooms. My furniture came from home and gave me what was necessary without any attempt at luxury. In my study I had a round deal table with a black oilcloth cover, which served as a desk; a lounge, two straight-back chairs and one camp-chair, and a small book-case. But I was filled with pride and happiness as master of my little domain, unconscious of lacking anything which a college-man could rightly expect. I confess, however, that when my father left me, just before the term began, and in the evening the students arrived in the stages from the railroad station and clustered about the dormitory steps cheering and singing lustily "The Bull-Dog on the Bank" and "The Son of a Gambolier," my heart sank and I felt lonely and unprotected as I wondered what these gay and boisterous youths would do to the little freshman when they discovered him. I soon revived; I found that I was well received and I quickly entered into all the joys of our common campus life.

At first I took my meals with a family which had come to Hamilton from Greenpoint.[2] But, desiring to be more with the boys, I soon joined an eating club which was the general practice. A group of students, fifteen or twenty, would arrange with a landlady to cook their meals, one of the group acting as steward and the total expense being equally divided. This was a very economical plan; and my outlay for meals averaged between two dollars and a half and three dollars a week.

The number of students was small. That year there were about eighty-five in the College and thirty-five in the Theological Seminary. The Academy had about one hundred. Most of those in college had the ministry in view, but this did not seem to affect their spirits and perhaps added to their zest in singing "Pharaoh's daughter on the bank, Little Moses in the pool," "Come landlord fill the flowing bowl" and "We'll never get drunk any more," or in occasionally engaging in predatory nocturnal adventures in the nearby apple orchards. But the drinking was all in their songs. I believe that none of the students drank anything more intoxicating than hard cider, and of that we had plenty. If there were any saloons in Hamilton, I did not know of them. Many of the students smoked; more did not.

[2]The son of this family, Ralph W. Thomas [1862–1920], one of my best friends in Greenpoint, entered Colgate Academy when I entered college. He became professor of oratory [public speaking and rhetoric] at Colgate and served in the New York State Senate from 1910 to 1914. [He was New York State Tax Commissioner, 1915–1919.]

The number of good students was relatively large and some of them were of outstanding ability. The leader in the College, who became the valedictorian of the Class of 1877, was David Call, a young man of unusual promise. On graduation he became professor of Greek at Des Moines University, but death soon cut short his career.[3] The leader of the Junior Class was Benjamin S. Terry, who, after a short period of preaching, studied abroad, taught at Colgate, and ultimately became professor of English History at the University of Chicago.[4] At the head of the Sophomore Class was Albert Perry Brigham, who, also leaving the ministry, became professor of Geology at Colgate and won high distinction as an author of standard works on Physical Geography.[5] In my own class, 1880, were George A. Williams, who became professor of Greek at Kalamazoo College, and Edward F. Waite, for thirty years or more an eminent judge in Minneapolis.[6]

A large part of the student life was in the Societies. There were chapters of two national fraternities, Delta Upsilon and Delta Kappa Epsilon, and a local society, the Adelphian, which later became a chapter of Beta Theta Pi. I was at once "rushed" by Delta Upsilon and the Adelphian. My friend Cronkhite was a member of the Adelphian and some of his society brethren went to extremes in their insistence. They contended that I should be entering on slippery paths if I joined either of the fraternities and went so far as to try to hold a prayer-meeting in my room in the interest of my soul. But I was attracted by the scholastic standing of Call, Terry and Brigham, all of whom were members of Delta Upsilon, and by the obvious good fellowship of others of that chapter, and I joined it with much gratification at the opportunity.

These early days were also marked by the political excitement of the presidential campaign. My father had subscribed in my name for the Semi-Weekly *Tribune*, which I read with avidity and in that way I kept

[3]When I was teaching at Delhi, New York (1881–1882), Call wrote to me asking if I would accept a position on the faculty at Des Moines. I declined to consider the suggestion as I had then determined to take up the law.

[4][Benjamin S. Terry (1857–1931) received his Ph.D. from the University of Freiburg, 1892, and joined the faculty of the University of Chicago that same year.]

[5][Albert Perry Bingham (1855–1932) served as Associate Editor of the *Bulletin* of the National Geographical Society, and from 1911–1913, was Examiner in geography for the New York State Education Department.]

[6][Edward F. Waite (1860–1949) was with the U.S. Pension Bureau 1880–1897 and, later, Superintendent of Police in Minneapolis. His judicial career spanned the years 1904–1941. He was interested in social work and wrote many articles on the subject. In addition, he was lecturer in the Department of Sociology, University of Minnesota, 1926–1934.

[George A. Williams (1853–1918) taught for forty years in New England and Michigan. He was the author of several textbooks which were widely read. He was appointed to the chair in Greek at Kalamazoo in 1902 and taught there until his death. One of his four children, Maynard Owen Williams (1888–1963), was a famous world traveler and frequent contributor to *National Geographic* magazine.]

posted on political events here and I was almost equally interested, because of my trip to Europe, in foreign affairs, keenly following the London correspondence of George W. Smalley. As most of the students leaned to the Republican Party, we had a Hayes and Wheeler campaign club and I shall never forget my exciting experience when we drove to Morrisville and with a band and torches marched in a parade, finally standing in the open for a couple of hours while we were harangued by the speakers of the evening. Returning to Hamilton in the early morning hours, we rang the chapel bell and I felt that I was duly initiated into politics.

There were about ten professors in the college faculty. The president was Ebenezer Dodge [1819–1890], a Baptist preacher of considerable influence in the denomination. He was quite aloof from the students and I do not recall having the privilege of speaking to him, as I left Madison before I reached his courses. The ablest professors, in my view, were N. Lloyd Andrews, professor of Greek, our beloved "Kaì Yáp," and James M. Taylor, professor of mathematics.[7] The latter was an ideal teacher, helpful, precise and thorough. I was well prepared in mathematics and I had no trouble with my work under him. In Latin and Greek, however, I at once realized, when I plunged into Livy and the Orations of Lysias, how imperfect had been my home preparation and I had to apply myself with the greatest diligence to make up for my lack of drill in grammar. The other members of my class had been through the regular courses of preparatory schools and some of them had even taught before entering college in order to pay their way. I well remember how hard I worked during the first term to make up for my deficiencies, but I succeeded fairly well and I believe that my marks were high. After I overcame the difficulties which beset me at the beginning, I took the courses easily and found that I had abundant time for reading. The library was small but adequate for my purposes. On my first visit I was thrilled by the sight of the shelves of English literature and I soon began to devour Scott, Dickens, and Thackeray. Sunday gave a wonderful opportunity. We had dinner about three in the afternoon and no supper, and I would often curl up by my stove and read from four or five o'clock until one or two in the morning.

Special attention was given to elocution. In this, the influence of our neighbor, Hamilton College (at Clinton) was marked. The Hamilton prize orations were eagerly sought at Madison as material for declamations in the Royce prize contests which were held in Commencement week for each class. In freshman year, after various try-outs, four were selected to compete for the Royce prize. Then, in sophomore year, four others were

[7][James M. Taylor (1843–1930), was a Fellow of the American Association of Arithmetical Sciences and the author of several texts on mathematical subjects.]

chosen for that class competition, and in junior year another four were selected. There were two prizes for each class, and the six winners in the class competed at the end of senior year for a final prize. There was much rivalry in the Societies for college honors and the upper classmen drilled the most promising members of the lower classes. In Delta Upsilon, we had essays, declamations and debates in our weekly meetings and thus we had abundant opportunity for training. I was one of the four chosen from my class for the freshman year Royce contest at Commencement. I had a rousing declamation dealing with a cavalry charge in the Civil War. I should like to have a picture of myself, a small boy shouting, "Come on, old Kentucky, I am with you!" This cry of the cavalry commander seemed to stir the audience. I was fortunate enough to win the second prize.

There were few social privileges. There was a "Young Ladies' Seminary" in the village and the boys made good use of the opportunities it afforded. Delta Upsilon, as a non-secret fraternity, had its "private-publics" ("public," because others than members were admitted and "private" because the admission was on invitation) when the members showed their skill in song and speech. This was a chance to escort the "Sem-Girls." There was no theatre in Hamilton, but there was a good-sized hall where from time to time there were concerts and lectures. The College had a distinctly religious atmosphere. The students were expected to attend church, and in the Baptist Church seats were set apart in the gallery for the "theologues" and the college classes. At the first recitation on Monday morning, one was expected on roll call to answer whether he had attended church as well as chapel. (Some of the more zealous would answer, "Church, twice, Chapel"). But as I have already indicated, the lively spirit of the students triumphed over all attempts at artificial restrictions.

At that time it was regarded as a traditional obligation of the freshmen and sophomores to show their ingenuity and defiance of college authority by various pranks. The chapel bell would be rung at unseemly hours. There was a tradition that on some fine morning the janitor should find his cow tethered in the hall leading to the chapel. The authorities wisely paid no attention to such antics. I had no hand in them save in the instance already mentioned when we rang the chapel bell on our return from the political rally in the Hayes campaign.

There were, however, certain affairs in which I was happy to have a part. In the fall, when we learned that a successful foray had been made on near-by farms and some of the boys had acquired a store of apples or butternuts, we would raid their rooms and steal their ill-gotten supplies. In the winter, it was the special delight of a few of us to get sleds and slide down the hill, and thus going swiftly over the path through the meadow make the theologues, returning from prayer-meeting, scatter into the snow-banks. We had snowball fights — class fights and free for all. In my freshman year we had a unique affair. There were large stoves on either side of the chapel but for several days, despite our remonstrances, there was no fire on our side. We took action. About two o'clock on a bright night we took the stove down from the chapel and, using the janitor's ladders, we managed — not without difficulty — to place the stove on the top of the coal shed back of Alumni Hall, with a sign "Out after Coal." We hid the ladders and for most of the next day our stove made known its request. This amused not only the students but the Faculty, who seemed to enjoy the joke and made no reprimand. In the spring, it was the practice for a group of students in one class to camp for a night or two on an island in an artificial lake (a feeder of the canal) not far from Hamilton. Such an expedition was the signal for those of another class to make a night attack and steal the boats of the campers. These harmless escapades gave an outlet for our boyish zest. And I particularly prized these adventures which gave me a happy sense of freedom from the discipline to which I had been subjected at home.

Our only athletic sport was baseball. Our Varsity nine had close games with its principal rival, that of Hamilton College. We had class nines and one game, in which when sophomores we played the freshman nine, had tragic incidents. The catcher, who had no protection whatever, took a foul tip on his nose and was put out of commission. Soon after, our best pitcher, pitching a straight ball, was hit by the batter in a tender spot and retired in agony. Then, attempting to play third base, I had a tooth knocked out in stopping a swift grounder. But the survivors won.

The beginning of my sophomore year was marked by an event which to me was of outstanding importance. The Delta Upsilon fraternity held its convention at Madison (October 1877). The president of the fraternity was E. Benjamin Andrews, then, as the young president of Denison University (Granville, Ohio), at the beginning of his distinguished career.[8] His address at the convention made a profound impression upon me and with his vigor, directness and scholarly attainments he seemed to embody my ideals. The gathering of fraternity men from many colleges was also a stimulating experience. We had our business meetings in the chapter rooms at the top of the corner building in the "Brick Block." The literary exercises were in the Baptist Church, and there was a promenade concert at the village hall and a banquet at the Park Hotel.[9] Between meetings we

[8][E. Benjamin Andrews, 1844–1917] was a very popular professor at Brown University and Cornell University and the most popular president of Brown (1889–1898).

[9]I recall that there was no dancing. The boys and the "Sem-Girls" and others from the village walked about finding their pleasure in conversation and flirting.

entertained the delegates in our rooms in the most informal manner, playing cards and talking about our college experiences.

The college work in sophomore year was not too engrossing and I had plenty of time for extra-curricular activities. I took up whist, to which from then on I was a devotée. Card-playing had been tabooed at home, but now I thought it the best of all diversions and I learned to play many games. Once in a while I would have a good game of chess with an upper classman who roomed near me and was an expert player. Toward the close of the sophomore year, I began to smoke, but this was limited to a few convivial occasions. These followed the formation of a class society to promote good fellowship and incidentally to prepare the "mock program" with which the sophomores were expected to enliven the "junior exhibition." These humorous leaflets, distributed to the audience at the exhibition, were aimed at the peculiarities and frailties of the members of the junior class, but it was all in good sport and with none of the ribaldry and offensiveness which characterized the scurrilous sheets circulated at some institutions.[10] The meetings of our class society were held on the top floor of the old Eagle Hotel and we wound up our evenings of mirth and song with a late supper, when raw oysters and cider measured the extent of our dissipation. But I did not permit my college work to suffer because of these outside interests. I was still ambitious to maintain high standing in my class and I also kept up my reading in English literature and devoted considerable time to history.

At sixteen, I was growing fast and branching out. As I approached the end of my second year, although I enjoyed the life at Madison, I began to wish for a more liberal atmosphere and for wider opportunities. It occurred to me that I might go to a larger college. I surveyed the field and concluded that Brown University, with its Baptist tradition, which would appeal to my parents, and with the privileges of city life at Providence, would give me what I wanted and would be the best I could ask for. I began corresponding with Professor [William Carey] Poland at Brown to learn the requirements for admission.[11] I found that the curriculum at Brown was more advanced than at Madison and that the students in the corresponding class at Brown had gone further than I in certain subjects. They had entered college on French and had taken French courses in both freshman and sophomore years. They had also begun German. At Madi-

[10] I am sorry to say that especially scurrilous papers were circulated at Brown, to the disgust of most of the students. The practice was stopped by the expulsion of the culprits.

[11] [William Carey Poland (1846–1929), was Secretary, Commission of Colleges in New England for Admission Examinations and Director of the Museum of Fine Arts at Brown, 1893–1915. He served also as lecturer in the history of art at Boston University and the Rhode Island School of Design and, from 1896 to 1907, was president of the latter organization. He was the son-in-law of Professor Albert Harkness of Brown.]

son, we had merely started French in sophomore year and I had not gone much beyond the elementary lessons which my mother gave me when I was very young. Then the sophomores at Brown had a half-year in mechanics which I had not studied at all. It was evident that to enter the junior class I should have to devote the entire summer vacation to hard study with little prospect even then of covering the ground adequately. Professor Poland thought it very unwise that I should make such a hurried effort merely to stay in the corresponding class and graduate at eighteen. He strongly advised that I should enter the sophomore class and have the advantage of three years at Brown, which would give me a more solid foundation for my future career and still enable me to graduate at nineteen. He thought that early enough. Much as I disliked the idea of apparently going back a year, I recognized the good sense of his suggestion and decided to follow it. But there was still the question of expense. My entire outlay at Madison (exclusive of clothes which were bought at home) was about $250 for the first year and not more than $275 for the second. The expense at Brown would be more.[12] But I was promised a scholarship of $60 a year and a reduction in room rent and tuition. I went over the whole matter with my parents who gave their consent.[13]

So, in September 1878, I went to Providence and in view of my record at Madison was admitted to the sophomore class without examination.

[12]It turned out to be more, amounting to about $350 in my first year at Brown and somewhat more in my second year, and ran to nearly $500 in my senior year.

[13]I recently (December 16, 1944) received a letter from Dr. Everett Case, president of Colgate University, suggesting that I leave a portion of my library to Colgate, to serve, possibly in a special room, as an aid to the study of political science, jurisprudence and public affairs. I replied that while I appreciated most cordially the friendly spirit which prompted this suggestion and had a delightful remembrance of my happy days at Colgate, I could not grant the request. I informed him of the disposition of my papers and books, saying that I did not have such a set of books as I would consider adequate for the purpose suggested and that the various sorts which I did have, of permanent value, would appropriately go to my children.

The correspondence between Dr. Case and his father-in-law, Owen D. Young, in relation to this suggestion (copies of which Dr. Case enclosed with his letter to me) indicated the understanding that I had left Colgate and had gone to Brown because my family had removed to the East. To avoid misapprehension, I stated in my letter to Dr. Case that this was a mistake and that my family had lived in Brooklyn during the entire time I was in college.

A day or two later I received a letter from an alumnus of Colgate, Lt. (j.g.) Owen D. Connolly, stationed in the South Pacific, saying that a story had been circulated when he was in college that I was "the leader of a group who brought a cow into a class room" and that as a result I had been requested to leave the college. Of course there was no truth in this fantastic story and so I informed Mr. Connolly. I do not think a cow was ever brought into a class room; at least I never heard of such a thing as having happened either in my time or earlier.

I left Colgate, against the expressed desire of members of the faculty that I should remain, simply because I wished for various reasons, which I have stated in this section of my Notes, to go to Brown.

I did not take special examinations for rank. In leaving Madison I felt emancipated from rivalries for college honors and I had the notion that it would be delightful to follow my bent without any concern for marks.[14]

I was delighted with the location of the College on the "high and pleasant hill," and accustomed as I was to life in New York and Brooklyn, I found it very agreeable to be once more in a city. At the outset, with a chum, Cornelius W. Pendleton, who had also come from Madison, I took a room in a boarding house and it is interesting to note that for a very good room and excellent board we paid $6 a week apiece.[15] This, however, was more than we wished to pay, and we also desired to live on the campus. As soon as one was available, we took a room in Hope College.[16] The college buildings consisted of the familiar row on the front campus — Hope College, Manning Hall, University Hall, Slater Hall and Rhode Island Hall, with the library building (then new) on the corner of Waterman and Prospect Streets, and a small building used as a chemical laboratory on the farther side of the middle campus. Sayles Hall was built while I was in college and was first used by our class in June 1881. The president's house stood opposite the front campus on the corner of College Street, now the site of the John Hay Library, and on the opposite corner was a small school not connected with the University. The recitation rooms were in University, Rhode Island, and Manning Halls, and on the second floor of Manning Hall was the chapel, attendance at which was compulsory.

Hope College, the upper floors of University Hall, and Slater Hall were the dormitories. There were no suites except in Slater Hall (then just opened and thought to be luxurious) and the single rooms were generally occupied by two students. There was no central heating or lighting. Many of us had "Franklin" stoves with open grates. Each room had two closets, in one of which we kept our coal and in the other our wash-stand and clothes. There was no running water, or baths, but there were adequate toilet facilities on the lower floor of University Hall. The College supplied

[14]Later, when I was one of the editors of the *Brunonian*, I wrote a satirical article decrying the marking system.

[15][The room was at 171 Congdon Street. Pendleton served in the California House 1893, 1895 and 1901. He was a member of the State Senate 1903–1907; and thereafter until his retirement, the Collector of Customs for the Los Angeles District.] Pendleton [1859–1936] on graduation, went to California, studied law and practiced for many years in Los Angeles. He was at one time [1901] Speaker of the House of Representatives in the California Legislature.

[16]For the rest of sophomore year we roomed on the first floor of Hope College and in junior and senior years on the second floor at No. 22.

The charge for our rooms was very small — with the allowance both Pendleton and I had as ministers' sons, I have forgotten the amount — and our board cost about $3.50 a week. The largest amount I paid for board was during part of my senior year when I boarded in one of the best places in Providence at a cost of $4.50 a week.

servants (whom we called "slaves") to take care of our rooms and these were kept in good order. Many of the students came from Providence and lived at their homes.

There were about 250 students, and they were a jovial lot with an abundance of college and class spirit. At the very beginning of the college year, the sophomores and freshmen had their football match. This was a traditional contest in which all the members of the classes were expected to join. The classes marched down College Street on their respective sides, with songs and cheers, and out to the grounds selected, where they indulged in a rough game, really a class fight, which could be called football only because a football was used and there were goals. That was followed, in a few days, by a cane-rush, when a lusty freshman surrounded by his classmates would appear on the middle campus with a stout cane and it became the duty of the sophomores swiftly to gather and take the cane by force. No freshman was to be allowed to carry a cane. This was indeed a free-for-all fight. From time to time, an unpopular freshman would be hazed. In fall and spring, bonfires, although strictly forbidden, would be lit on the middle campus and the students would sing and dance about them with boisterous delight. The president, Ezekiel Gilman Robinson, from his citadel across from the campus, kept a watchful eye on the eruptions of the students.[17] This tall, gray-haired gentleman of great dignity, was of athletic build and could run like a deer. When there was an unseemly noise, or a bonfire, "Zeke," as he was called, would suddenly appear and would chase the disturbers who scattered in all directions at his approach. Occasionally he would catch one and act at once as both policeman and committing magistrate. The students held his physical prowess, as well as his intellectual vigor, in high respect. There were more decorous activities, notably when the students would gather on the chapel steps after supper and sing their glees. This amiable practice was not only permitted but encouraged.

There was no college gymnasium; some of the students used the gymnasium of the Young Men's Christian Association in the city. The athletic sports were football and baseball, chiefly the latter; the baseball grounds were on what was called the "back campus." There was some attention to track athletics. At an earlier day, Brown had a crew and there was still an old boat-house on the Seekonk River. My class, in their freshman year, had a class crew, perhaps the last of which the College could boast.

Brown had a strong faculty. Such men as J. Lewis Diman, John L. Lincoln, Albert Harkness, and Alpheus S. Packard would have been dis-

[17][Ezekiel Gilman Robinson (1815–1894) was president of Brown from 1872–1889.]

tinguished in any university faculty.[18] Alonzo Williams was an excellent teacher in the modern languages.[19] Nathaniel Davis, in mathematics, had already shown conspicuous ability.[20] The students were brought into direct contact with these and other professors and there was no reason to complain of lack of competent guidance in the various courses. The president was a powerful directing force.

In my time, the college year was divided into two terms. In the first semester of sophomore year, the class had a course in geometry and calculus, which I had already studied at Madison. I asked to take an examination and to be relieved from attendance on that course. The request was granted and I passed the examination, as I was told later, with a perfect mark. Being excused from mathematics in that semester, I started at Brown with very light work. This enabled me to devote myself to the French which my classmates had taken in freshman year. I was able not only to keep up with the class but soon I was one of those who volunteered for extra work. The volunteer would read a given play or selection and discourse upon it to the class. In view of what I had read at Madison, I found the Latin and Greek in sophomore year quite easy and I thus had an unusual amount of leisure, not only for my French studies but for general reading. I read a great deal, especially in English literature. I browsed in the University Library and also drew many books from the excellent Public Library in Providence.

I used my freedom in other ways. Before going to Providence, I had never visited a theater and the opportunities I now enjoyed were eagerly seized upon. I saw good plays and not a few that were poor. During my college years, I had the privilege of seeing Edwin Booth in "Hamlet," Lawrence Barrett in "Richelieu," Joseph Jefferson in "Rip Van Winkle,"

[18][J. Lewis Diman (1831–1881) was a clergyman and educator. He joined the Brown faculty in 1864 and served until his death.

[Albert Harkness (1822–1907) was educated at Brown and at various German universities. He was founder of the American Philological Association and its president, 1875–1876. He was the author of more than twenty Latin and Greek textbooks and dictionaries.

[John Larkin Lincoln (1817–1891) was at Brown from 1844–1890. He was one of the first members of the American Philological Society.

[Alpheus Spring Packard (1839–1905) was professor of zoology and geology at Brown from 1878 until his death. He was the author of many books, including *Guide to the Study of Insects* (1869); *Life History of Animals* (1876); and *Observations on the Glacial Phenomena of Labrador and Maine* (1891).]

[19][Alonzo Williams (1842–1901) attended Brown after fighting in the Civil War. Upon graduation he joined the Brown faculty and, with the exception of four years spent teaching at a local secondary school, he served until his death.]

[20][Nathaniel French Davis (1847–1921) graduated from Brown in the same class with Alonzo Williams but did not join the faculty until 1879. He served continuously until his retirement in 1915.]

and Mary Anderson in "Ingomar." Opera also came to Providence; my first opera was "Aida" with Clara Louise Kellogg and Annie Louise Cary. There was good light opera, notably the "Chimes of Normandy," and in the early part of 1879 the campus resounded with the catching airs of "Pinafore." There were, of course, various variety shows. In cards, while I knew about all the popular games, my favorite was still whist which I took more seriously, playing with those who were expert. I smoked more than previously and enjoyed our occasional gatherings at one of the beer gardens patronized by the students.

There were several fraternities but, so far as I can recall, no fraternity houses as yet. I joined the chapter of Delta Upsilon and found there a delightful and profitable companionship. One of the leaders in the College as well as in the fraternity — a member of the class ahead of mine — was William H. P. Faunce who became one of my best friends.[21] Our weekly chapter meetings were largely taken up with debates in which two of the members would assume the burden of leading and their chief and rebuttal speeches would be followed by a general discussion. In these, I frequently took part with a good deal of earnestness.

Despite my new experiences, my increasing liberality of thought, and my love of a good time, I had by no means lost my religious feeling or my interest in religious subjects. Occasionally, at my father's request, I prepared a synopsis for his expository articles in the *Homiletic Review*. Church attendance was no longer compulsory at Brown and I did not care for the preaching at the First Baptist Meeting-House. But there were two eminent pulpit orators in Providence, Dr. A. J. F. Behrends at the Union Congregational Church, and Dr. David H. Greer at Grace Episcopal Church.[22] These I liked to hear. During one season, Dr. Greer devoted his Sunday afternoon discourses to the history of the English Church and these I found most interesting.

In the second semester of sophomore year, I had more classroom work as we took up mechanics, but I was not overburdened. I finished my first year at Brown with a feeling of deep satisfaction. True, I was a little disappointed in my Greek courses, for while Professor Harkness (of Latin

[21]After a brilliant career in the ministry, W[illiam] H[erbert] P[erry] Faunce [1859–1930] became president of Brown University and served with distinction for about thirty years (1899–1930). [He was president of the World Peace Foundation, trustee of several educational institutions and author of many books including *What Does Christianity Mean?* (1912) and *Religion and War* (1918).]

[22][Dr. Adolphus Julius Frederick Behrends (1839–1900) spent most of his career as pastor of the Central Congregational Church in Brooklyn, New York. He lectured at the Yale Divinity School, and the Hartford, Andover, Union, Crozer, and Rochester Theological Seminaries.] Later Dr. [David Hummell] Greer [1844–1919], after a most successful pastorate at St. Bartholomew's, became Bishop of New York [on the death of Bishop Henry Potter, July 21, 1908].

Grammar fame but Professor of Greek) was a great scholar and a most gracious and careful teacher, he kept hammering away at construction and I felt that we did not fully enter into the spirit of the classics we were studying. In our Latin courses there was a notable contrast. Professor Lincoln embodied the Latin spirit and his familiar talks gave us a sense of the most charming companionship. Everyone loved "Johnny Link." On the whole, and excepting the Latin courses, I felt that I had profited more from my extra-curricular reading than from the classroom. But this did not disturb me as I especially prized the large opportunity to follow my own inclinations.

I returned from the summer vacation to enter junior year (1879–1880) with the liveliest expectations and these were not disappointed. In the first semester we had good courses in astronomy, chemistry and physics, but German had my special attention and I sought to become no less proficient in that language than in French. In the second semester, I had a thrilling experience as I came under the instruction of Professor Diman in political economy. He did not use textbooks or dictate his lectures. He talked to us with freedom, brilliancy and lucidity, and left us to take our notes as best we could and to consult the books he recommended. With his stimulus to thought and research, I felt that I was lifted into a new and exalted sphere of intellectual activity.[23] I may add that Professor Diman was a freetrader and I left college fully persuaded by his arguments, but later I thought them less securely based than I imagined them to be when under the spell of his expositions. In junior year, we also had advanced work in rhetoric and English, calling for many essays which I based on my reading and prepared easily with no little zest.

My diversions were about the same. As to these, I did not feel in the least cramped, as I had already found — in my first year at Brown — that by a little tutoring and helping some of the boys in the class below who were behind in their work, I could easily earn enough to cover the outlays for my modest pleasures without drawing on the amounts received from home. I had become a baseball "fan." Providence had a good nine in the national league of that day and I attended the league as well as the college

[23]In my Historical Address at the Sesquicentennial of Brown University (October 1914), I spoke of him as follows: "Professor Diman was fascinating in his exhibition of intellectual mastery. His unusual acumen, lucidity, candor, and breadth of vision, his rhetorical skill — which gained its effects without sacrifice of accuracy or sincerity — his native dignity, and entire freedom from eccentricity and affectation, made him a prince of teachers. One was not left in a state of idle admiration, as a spectator of a brilliant performance, but was stimulated to the highest pitch of effort, and heroic endeavors in individual research supplemented the attractive labors of the class-room." "The Sesquicentennial of Brown University," published by the University, 1915, p. 190.

Professor Diman had several offers from other Universities, including a most attractive and pressing invitation from Harvard, but he refused to leave Brown.

games held there. I was fond of keeping a full score and in some way I managed to get a place in the scorers' stand. In the spring of 1880 there was an exciting season for us in college baseball, as Brown won the intercollegiate championship, defeating Harvard and Yale. Brown had a redoubtable battery, J. Lee Richmond and William H. Winslow of the class of 1880. Richmond was one of the first great left-hand pitchers. His victories made him so famous that, shortly before his graduation, the Worcester nine of the national league engaged him and his catcher to play in a game with the champion Chicago nine. A host of Brown students went to Worcester to see the game, and it was a marvel as in the nine innings not a single Chicago man got to first base.[24]

Forty-four years later, at a birthday dinner at my home in Washington (April 11, 1924), when President Coolidge, Chief Justice Taft, Secretary [of War John W.] Weeks and Samuel E. Winslow, Representative in Congress from Worcester, were present, conversation ran to baseball and I told the story of that game, adding, "That's a tall one! And I suppose you don't believe it." To my surprise, Representative Winslow at once exclaimed, "That's a true story for I was at that game." He was then in a preparatory school in Worcester.[25]

As I was approaching happily the close of junior year, Professor Lincoln surprised me one day by saying: "Hughes, why don't you take examinations for freshman year rank? You ought to do it. You will be sorry in later life if you graduate without class standing." This was a new idea, as I had been rather proud of my independence and had gone along without bothering my head about marks. Whether Professor Lincoln made this suggestion solely on his own behalf or at the instance of the faculty, I do not know. But when I made inquiries as to what would be necessary, the professors at once responded with similar advice. I found that the procedure would not be difficult. Of course, the professors had kept my record in the usual way for sophomore and junior years and I could not change that. The question was simply as to rank in the freshman year subjects. As to mathematics, Professor Greene, who had examined me in geometry and calculus and had excused me from that course in sophomore year,

[24]This put Richmond in the front rank of pitchers and on graduation he went into professional baseball, playing on national league nines. He then studied medicine but ultimately took up teaching. I did not see him after his graduation until one day in the late nineteen-twenties. As I was walking on 42nd Street in New York, I noticed a wizened little man looking at me curiously. He stopped as I approached and said, "Is this Hughes?" I said, "Yes." He said, "I am Richmond, 'eighty.' " I said, "Well, what in the world have you been doing with yourself?" He answered, "Oh, I have been teaching in a high school in Ohio for thirty years."

[25]When I was in the Cabinet, it was the practice of Secretary Weeks, Representative Winslow and myself to hold birthday dinners at our respective homes, as we were all born on the same day in April, Weeks in 1860 and Winslow and myself in 1862.

declared that I need not take another examination as he would use the one I passed as the basis for freshman year rating. In French, Professor Williams said that he would rate me on the basis of my volunteer work in sophomore year without a further examination. It turned out that the only subjects in which I needed to be examined were the Latin and Greek texts studied in freshman year and those examinations I duly passed. As a result, I was one of the five members of my class who were admitted to Phi Beta Kappa at the end of junior year, an honor deeply appreciated. There was another welcome surprise when I was awarded the Dunn Premium for the year 1879–1880. This prize was given to the member of the junior class who had the "highest standing in rhetorical studies."

During the vacations in 1879 and 1880, I spent two or three weeks at a fraternity (Delta Upsilon) camp on an island in Lake George, off Bolton. The camp had been started in 1877 by Marcus C. Allen of Sandy Hill and I had a week there at that time.[26] In those days the developments at Lake George village (then known as Caldwell) and at Bolton Landing were not dreamed of. From the rather ambitious Fort William Henry Hotel with its broad and columned veranda at the head of the lake, to Ticonderoga, there were only a few summer cottages and a scattering of modest inns along the lakeside. We went to the lake by stage or wagons from Glens Falls. The noisy facilities of airplanes, sea-sleds, motor boats and outboard motors, had not yet become available and we happily got about the lake in rowboats, much to the advantage of our health. In the evening we would sing our college songs and the patrons of the near-by inns formed an appreciative audience as they clustered about our island in their boats. Despite the changes in recent years, this lovely lake has never lost its charm, but I knew it at its best.

I returned from my vacation in September 1880 determined to devote to the studies of senior year all the energy I possessed. And they demanded it, for now we had difficult courses in medieval and modern history under Professor Diman and in psychology and philosophy under President Robinson. There was also a course in international law and I elected another in Italian. I had also been chosen as one of the editors of the *Brunonian*, the college paper which then came out bi-weekly.

There were certain distractions early in the term. In October 1880, I was appointed senior delegate from Brown to the Delta Upsilon Convention at Amherst. There I had the good fortune to meet college men of marked ability and I was spurred to new efforts as I was called upon to take a leading part in the discussions. Among the prominent men of the Amherst

[26]Allen was the son of the Allen brothers in Sandy Hill who had been prominent members of my father's church and I knew him well there and at Madison where he was a member of the Class of 1881.

chapter at that time, whom I came to know well, were Starr J. Murphy, Frank C. Partridge and William Travers Jerome. Murphy was a brilliant student who, after a few years of general practice at the bar of New York, became the personal counsel of John D. Rockefeller, giving his special attention to the investigation of proposed philanthropic enterprises.[27] Partridge became Solicitor of the State Department at Washington and then United States Minister to Venezuela and Consul General at Tangier. Later he entered upon a successful business career in Vermont and for a short time served as United States Senator from that State to fill a vacancy.[28] Jerome was destined to become famous as an able and aggressive District Attorney of New York County.[29]

While in attendance at the convention, it was my privilege to serve as chairman of a committee which sent congratulations and good wishes to the fraternity's president, James A. Garfield, then Republican candidate for the presidency of the United States. Brown students took an active part in the presidential campaign. We organized a Garfield battalion and with caps, capes, banners and torches, we marched in Providence, Bristol and Boston, returning late at night after a heavy dose of campaign oratory.

The course in history under Professor Diman was even better than I had anticipated. In connection with his lectures, he gave us each week five questions requiring much independent research. There was no end to the work that could be put into the report on those questions and I did my best. To our great sorrow, Professor Diman died in February 1881, after a brief illness. It was a hard and sudden blow and we had a keen sense of irreparable loss. When he died, the *Brunonian* had just gone to press and I well remember the night of hard labor which the managing editor, George F. Bean, and myself spent in preparing a suitable obituary article which we were able to publish with the current issue. I then turned my

[27]See [Simon and James Thomas] Flexners' biography, *William Henry Welch* (New York, The Viking Press, 1941), pp. 272 and 285; also references to Starr J[ocelyn] Murphy [1860–1921] in Allan Nevins, *John D. Rockefeller, The Heroic Age of American Enterprise* (New York, 2 vols., C. Scribner's Sons, 1940), [II, 470–472, 475–480].

[28][Frank C. Partridge (1861–1943) was Consul at Tangier, 1897–98, and president of the Vermont Marble Company, 1911–1935. Earlier he had been Solicitor in the Department of State, 1890–93, and Minister to Venezuela, 1893–94. He served in the Senate from 1930 to 1931.]

[29][For information on Jerome (1859–1934), see Richard O'Connor, *Courtroom Warrior: The Combative Career of William Travers Jerome* (Boston, Little, Brown and Company, 1963). Jerome was Assistant District Attorney for New York County, 1888–1890; Justice of the New York Court of Special Sessions, 1895–1902; and District Attorney for New York County, 1901–1909. In 1906, Tammany nearly chose him to run for governor against Hughes. William Randolph Hearst ran instead and lost. See below, chapter 10. While Hughes was governor there was an effort made to remove Jerome from office. Hughes appointed R. L. Hand as a special commissioner "to hold hearings on why Jerome should or should not be removed from office." Hand's report was in Jerome's favor and Hughes continued him in office. See O'Connor, *Courtroom Warrior*, pp. 275 and 283–284.]

particular attention to President Robinson's lectures in philosophy. In addition to these, I took a special course in the history of philosophy in which I became absorbed. I gave every hour I could spare to the collateral reading which I found to be essential.

In the midst of the second semester of senior year, one of my intimate friends had typhoid fever. We were together the night before his attack and for a time I took charge of him. We had no college infirmary and he was removed from the dormitory to a room in the house where we had our meals. We had no thought of contagion and two or three of us took turns in nursing him. In consequence, through loss of sleep in connection with very hard work, I was much run down. My eyes became badly inflamed and I felt quite sick. I was excused from classes and went home. This was the first time in my five years at college that my work was thus interrupted as I had suffered from nothing worse than an occasional cold. Fortunately, it turned out that I was not seriously ill and after a week of my mother's nursing I returned to college.

After our final examinations, I was assigned the "Classical Oration" at Commencement, which meant that I stood third in the class. My Oration was on "The First Appearance of Sophocles." I was also awarded on graduation one of the two Carpenter Premiums. These were assigned to the two seniors who, "already on scholarships, in the judgment of the Faculty, united in the highest degree the three most important elements of success in life — ability, character, and attainment." The other recipient of the Carpenter award was Charles C. Mumford, who became an Associate Justice of the Superior Court of Rhode Island.[30]

The valedictorian of our class was Walter J. Towne [1859–1928], who took up teaching and for many years was a highly esteemed teacher in the Providence schools. The salutatorian was George F. Bean, who entered the law, practicing in Boston, and at one time was mayor of Woburn, Massachusetts.[31] The fourth honor — "The Philosophical Oration" — went to William C. Ladd [1858–1908], who became Professor of French at Haverford College. The president of the class was Frederick R. Hazard [1858–1917], of the well-known Hazard family of Peace Dale, Rhode Island. He became president of the Solvay Process Company of Syracuse, New York, and an eminent leader in the industrial field. Another prominent member of the class was William Sheafe Chase [1858–1940], who became a Canon of the Episcopal Church and a noted crusading reformer.

[30][Charles C. Mumford (1860–1918), a Rhode Island lawyer, legislator, and judge, was a member of the Rhode Island House of Representatives (1893–94; 1903). He served on the Superior Court from 1905 to 1909.]

[31][George F. Bean (1857–1934) was mayor of Woburn, 1891–92, and Massachusetts State Representative, 1910.]

Hughes at graduation from Brown University, 1881

Another was J[ohn] Murray Marshall [1859–1931], the leader of the singing in Chapel and on the campus, who practiced law in Los Angeles. A classmate whom I greatly admired, and who is one of the few still living, was Morgan Brooks. He has had a distinguished career as Professor of Electrical Engineering at the University of Illinois.

Commencement was then held on the third Wednesday of June, but the commencement activities began with Class Day on the preceding Friday. That was a busy day with formal exercises in the morning, tree-planting in the afternoon, and a Promenade Concert in the evening (balls had not yet come in), followed by the Class Supper. Beginning with Class Day, the seniors wore full dress suits, "swallow-tails" and pumps, with silk hats, not only in the evening but through the entire day, and this continued until the festivities had ended on commencement night. (Gowns were worn by the speakers at the commencement exercises.) After the Concert in the evening of Class Day, that is, about midnight, the seniors escorted by their band marched down college hill and on to the Narragansett Hotel for the Class Supper. That was a convivial affair, with a few literary efforts in keeping with the occasion, among them being the Class Prophecy which I was chosen to prepare. This attempted to predict for the boys their future careers according to the notions their classmates entertained of them. In the early morning hours, about four or five o'clock, the hilarious seniors marched back to the campus and attempted, in accordance with the tradition, to have a game of baseball, to the amusement of those who had risen early to see the fun.

The days following Class Day had their special exercises. The seniors listened to the president's baccalaureate on Sunday, and on Monday and Tuesday there were the Phi Beta Kappa and alumni meetings.

On Commencement Day the academic procession formed on the campus and the Officers of the Corporation, the Faculty, the seniors and alumni, marched to the old First Baptist Meeting-House, "built for the worship of God and to hold Commencements in," and the commencement orations were heard and degrees were conferred. The alumni, with the new graduates, then gathered for luncheon and to hear the president and eminent guests speak on University affairs and the state of the Nation.

[Hughes maintained close ties with Brown University for the rest of his life. In the 1890s he served as president of the New York Alumni Association, spoke at alumni banquets in Providence and Boston, and was chosen a trustee of the University. In 1906, his alma mater honored him with a Doctorate of Laws degree. Not all of his fellow trustees approved of this action. Because of his vigorous investigation of the New York insurance companies, some of the trustees regarded Hughes as a dangerous radical and for that reason refused to attend his commencement address.[32] In 1908 Hughes was appointed to a committee selected to consider revision of Brown's 1764 charter. He led a movement to eliminate the charter's requirement that the president of the University and substantial majorities of its trustees and fellows be Baptists. Hughes was successful in committee, but the committee's recommendation was not fully realized until 1940 when President Henry N. Wriston, after conferring with Hughes, reopened the matter. Throughout his career, Hughes often spoke at the University. In 1914 he was chosen to deliver the historical address at Brown's sesquicentennial. In his speeches he fondly remembered his student days at Brown. Adopting the words of James Burrill Angell of the Class of 1849 — when Brown had but seven faculty members — Hughes told a Brown convocation in 1923 that "no college in the country furnished better training to its students."[33]

[In 1937 three generations of the Hughes family participated in the Brown commencement. Hughes gave the commencement address, his son, Charles Evans Hughes, Jr. (Class of 1909), received a Doctor of Laws degree, and his grandson, Charles Evans Hughes, 3rd, received a Bachelor of Arts degree.]

32[Zechariah Chafee, Jr., *Free Speech in the United States* (Cambridge, Harvard University Press, 1941), p. 361.]

33[Charles Evans Hughes, *Pathway of Peace* (New York, Harper & Bros., 1925), p. 279.]

Chapter IV Teaching and Studying Law

When I was writing the Class Prophecy at Brown, one of my classmates asked what I proposed to make of myself. I replied that I should probably take up teaching. He laughed, saying, "Of course, you will be a lawyer." This struck me as a novel suggestion. I knew nothing of law and I had no acquaintance with lawyers, judges or courts. My life at home had been remote from any such contacts. In college I had not thought much of a vocation, but I had rather taken it for granted that, as I did not wish to enter the ministry, I should teach. I had a vague notion that I might make enough money in teaching to enable me to study for a year or so in Germany and thus fit myself for a college position. The idea that I might become a lawyer fascinated me. I had heard that Samuel H. Ordway, the valedictorian of 1880, was making a fine record at the Harvard Law School and I thought enviously of such advantages, but I did not feel that my parents should be burdened with the expense of a law school course.[1] My uppermost thought was that I must support myself and teaching seemed to afford the best opportunity. So, on returning from college, I at once registered with a teachers' agency for a position to teach Latin or Greek in a secondary school and I obtained recommendations from my professors at Brown. I soon had several inquiries, but when it appeared that I was only nineteen, my application was immediately dismissed. One of the best chances was at the Pennsylvania Military Academy (now Penn-

[1]Ordway (1860–1914) became a leading member of the New York bar. He was chairman of the New York State Civil Service Commission and served for a time as a Justice of the State Supreme Court. When I was Governor of New York I appointed him in 1909 a member of the Commission to investigate speculation in securities and commodities.

sylvania Military College) at Chester, and I had an interview with its principal, the then Colonel Hyatt, in New York.[2] He had seemed pleased with my letters but when he saw me he exclaimed, "Why, you could never maintain discipline with my cadets!" And I could not complain, for while I had attained my full height, I was slight and looked younger than my years. I had not even begun to shave. In 1928, when the Pennsylvania Military College gave me the degree of Doctor of Laws, I had the pleasure of recounting this experience to the alumni and I observed that it was much easier to get that degree than to enter its faculty.

Despairing of obtaining a suitable chance to teach, I sought other employment. In mid-summer (1881) I had a novel opportunity. Owners of property in certain parts of Brooklyn had been heavily assessed for local improvements which were in advance of immediate needs, and their unpaid taxes and assessments exceeded the then assessed valuation of their property. The Legislature offered relief in permitting them, as I recall it, to pay that valuation in full discharge of their obligations. One of these owners undertook to act on their behalf and it became necessary to calculate the amounts of arrears. I was offered that job and I spent six weeks, working ten hours a day from eight A.M. to six P.M. at a wage of six dollars a week, in calculating interest and thus determining the total amounts due, and occasionally interviewing owners.

Just as I finished that job, I was pleasantly surprised by the offer of a position to teach Latin, Greek and mathematics at Delaware Academy in Delhi, New York. It seems that the teacher who had been selected for that post had proved unsatisfactory and there was a hurried call for a substitute. One feature of the offer was that if I desired to study law, I could do so in a good office as I should have to teach only in the forenoon. The salary was two hundred dollars for the school year with my board and room. I accepted with alacrity and at once proceeded to Delhi. On arrival on a September afternoon, I was met at the station by the principal of the Academy, James O[wen] Griffin, and I could not fail to note the shade of disappointment that passed over his face as he looked me over. After supper, he took me aside and told me that he had not supposed I looked so young — quite as young as many of his students. I felt my one chance slipping and I summoned all my powers of persuasion to induce him to give me a trial. I succeeded, and after a couple of weeks I was definitely placed. Then ensued one of the happiest experiences of my life. Delhi was a charming village nestled among the hills, and the Academy had a de-

[2][Charles Eliot Hyatt (1851–1930) was brevetted Brigadier General in the National Guard of Pennsylvania, 1923. He was president of the Pennsylvania Military College from 1888 to his death. In 1966, the Pennsylvania Military College was joined to the Penn Morton College to form coordinate units of the PMC Colleges.]

lightful setting in spacious grounds with beautiful trees. It was an old and honored institution of the type of many which had been established through upstate New York in the middle or early part of the nineteenth century. There was a main building with cupola and broad veranda, and a separate hall which served as a commodious dormitory. The students came from Delhi and from farms and villages in the outlying parts of Delaware County. They were of the best sort of rural stock, steady, industrious and ambitious. Professor Griffin became one of my best friends. He was a teacher of exceptional talent, who had specialized in German and had studied abroad. In later years he was appointed Assistant Professor of German at Cornell University and about 1892 became Professor of German at Leland Stanford.[3]

The Academy had all grades from the primary to full preparation for college, and the tests of proficiency were found in the thorough examinations held by the Board of Regents of the University of the State of New York, which maintained high academic standards. I taught Latin and Greek subjects and algebra and plane geometry. I also drilled the boys in their declamations. One of the outstanding students was James E. Russell, who has had a career of high distinction and is now Dean emeritus of the Teachers College in New York City.[4] Another, too young to be in my classes, was Lafayette B. Mendel who became distinguished as a scientist, being for many years Professor of Physiological Chemistry at Yale.[5] Early in the term, two young ladies of Delhi, one of whom was engaged to be married to a young businessman who was about to be sent to Belgium, wished to have a course in advanced French and I undertook that. When they asked me to teach French conversation, I demurred as I was without practice in that, but they insisted that I should try it. And so I did, using as a basis for our talks excerpts from a French translation of *The Vicar of Wakefield* which I happened to have.

In my dormitory my room was at the center of a long hall on the second floor, with the girls' rooms on one side of mine and the boys' rooms on the other. I was expected to maintain order in the hall, and despite my youth, I had no difficulty whatever.

[3][James Owen Griffin (1851–1939) taught at Cornell from 1885 to 1891 and then went to Stanford when that university opened in 1891. He served until his retirement in 1917.]

[4][James Earl Russell (1864–1945) was dean of the Teachers College of Columbia University from 1897 to 1927, when he was made Dean Emeritus. He was the author of many books on education and member of the New Jersey State Board of Health, New Jersey Milk Control Board, American Association for Adult Education, National Council of Education, and the American Psychological Association.]

[5][In addition to his teaching posts, Mendel (1872–1935) was Director of the Russell Sage Institute of Pathology, member of the advisory board of the Guggenheim Memorial Foundation, and research associate of the Carnegie Institute of Washington. He received the Gold Medal from the American Institute of Chemists in 1927.]

For the most part my afternoons were free and these and frequently my evenings were spent in the law office of William Gleason. He had been County Judge of Delaware County and was a lawyer of high repute in upstate New York. His son and partner, John B. Gleason, was a graduate of Yale of the class of 1876 — a friend and classmate of Arthur T. Hadley — and was also a graduate of the Columbia Law School. John Gleason had one of the best minds I had known and my association with him as a student in his office was very stimulating.[6]

I started my reading in law with Maine's *Ancient Law*, and followed that with Kent's *Commentaries* and the first volume of Washburn on *Real Property*, making elaborate notes. Once in a while John Gleason would prod me with questions. Delhi was a county seat and sessions of the Supreme Court were regularly held there. I occasionally had an opportunity to attend them and thus I got my first glimpses of court procedure. There were social privileges. Delhi, considering the size of the village, had an unusual number of young men of ability, several of whom were college graduates and others were in college, returning for their vacations. They readily admitted me to their good fellowship, and as an informal club we would meet on Saturday evenings for whist or other games at the American Hotel, the larder of which was open to us as the genial son of the proprietor was one of our intimates. The townspeople also were kind, and when those — and there were many of them — of Scotch descent met in honor of Robert Burns to dine and to eat the haggis I was invited to join them and to respond to a toast.

Although I found my work and my surroundings most congenial, and Professor Griffin offered me a salary of eight hundred dollars, with my board and room, for the next year, I decided to leave. I had become keenly interested in law study and I was not satisfied with the progress I was making by reading in a law office. Some of my friends suggested that I might stay in Delhi, in due course be admitted to the bar, and, practicing in an upstate community where I should be well known, I should have political opportunities. Such a prospect did not attract me. I was intent on thorough preparation in law and I wrote my father that if he could pos-

[6]John B[lanchard] Gleason [1885–1935], a few years later, settled in New York City where he had as his associate in law practice his brother, Lafayette B[lanchard] Gleason [1863–1937], long secretary of both the Republican National Committee and the Republican State Committee. [John B. Gleason was attorney for the New York Stock Exchange, 1880–1890; counsel for the New York State Inheritance Tax Board, 1915–1923; and secretary of the Republican County Committee for Delaware County, 1884–1885. His father William Gleason (1819–1894) was an early and active member of the Republican Party, and served, in addition to his judicial duties, as supervisor of the town of Delhi, New York.]

sibly see me through two years at Columbia I was sure it would pay in the end. He agreed, and in June 1882, I returned to New York with the purpose of entering Columbia Law School in the fall.

Meanwhile I looked for a job during the summer and found one which had extraordinary consequences. I answered an advertisement by one Edgar Gray, who wished a secretary. I found him a handsome and agreeable man in his forties, who was promoting the Gill Rapid Transit Company which was formed to supply New York City with a cheap cab service. He painted an attractive picture of the future of the enterprise and, apparently impressed by my qualifications, offered me a position at a salary of two hundred dollars a month, which I thought a princely sum. He indicated that I might find the opportunity so desirable that I would give up the idea of studying law and become a permanent officer of the Company. Incidentally, he wished me to make a small investment in the Company's stock so that I should feel identified with the undertaking. I did not like that idea, but being anxious for a job and thinking that I should be able to recoup out of my salary the little amount my father could put in, this did not seem to be a serious obstacle. We took the precaution of inquiring of W. Fearing Gill, the originator of the Company, and of its bankers, a reputable Wall Street firm, and their replies being entirely satisfactory as to the prospects of the enterprise, my father made a modest payment to Gray for stock to be later delivered, and I was duly employed.

At the outset Gray wished me to become familiar with the legislation under which the Company was organized and with its financial set-up. Then, he gave me his press copy letter-books to index and I soon noted that he had previously been promoting an electric light company with which one of the Vanderbilts was associated. Later, I observed that some of the letters were signed with other names although apparently in his handwriting. One day he surprised me by saying that he was sending a telegram and, as he did not wish to be known in the matter, he had used my name. Then, coming to the office early one morning I found a note addressed to me by a lady, expressing regret that I had not kept an appointment of which I knew nothing — apparently another use of my name. This greatly disturbed me and I felt that it must be stopped at once. Still the affairs of the Rapid Transit Company seemed to be in good order and I did not wish to lose my job. In the midst of my anxiety, I had an inspiration. It occurred to me to go to the Astor Library and consult the newspaper files to find out if Mr. Gray and his enterprises had been mentioned. I was soon rewarded. I found in the New York *Tribune* an account of the electric light company, which had come to grief, and that Edgar Gray was no other than William E. Gray, a notorious character.

Reading back through the files, I got his record. His father was a minister, chaplain of one of the Houses of Congress, who had been able to get a position for his son with a Wall Street banking firm. The young man, as it was charged, had raised checks and fled the country with about $300,000. After several years he was found in London, a dashing member of the Prince of Wales' set. As I recall it, he was arrested in a London street and when first taken to his lodgings at his request he contrived to escape and was not found again for a long period. Then he was discovered in Paris and arrested. It seems that he had good friends and there was much delay in his extradition. Finally he was brought back to New York, was tried and convicted, but upon appeal he obtained a new trial. When I met him, he had been, I believe, for several years out on bail awaiting trial. Although it was a *cause célèbre,* he managed as Edgar Gray, and without other disguise, to establish contacts with some of the best people of New York and to become associated with various enterprises. He became connected with the project of the electric light company and when that failed he was again exposed in the press. But again, with his extraordinary effrontery, he got in touch with influential persons among whom were those interested in the Gill Rapid Transit Company. He held a promoter's power of attorney.

With this information, I went at once to Mr. Gill and asked him if he knew Gray's record. He said that Gray had been introduced to him by General Daniel E. Sickles and was "all right." I told Mr. Gill what I had discovered. He was greatly shocked and was disgusted at Gray's taking money from my father. Promising that it would be returned, he wished me to have my father call the next morning at Gray's office when he (Gill) would come in and I would face Gray with my knowledge of his record and demand restitution. Mr. Gill particularly wanted to get back Gray's power of attorney. We met as agreed and there was a dramatic scene. I told Gray that I knew who he was and I recited the salient facts, demanding the return of the money my father had paid him. He insisted on his right to take subscriptions for stock, which Mr. Gill denied saying that it had not yet been authorized, and Gray produced his power of attorney. I asked to see it and then handed it over to Mr. Gill. As a result, my father got his money back and I left Gray's employment with my salary for my two weeks' services and with a new insight into the ways of men. Gray, I think, was never brought to retrial. I saw him once again. Some fourteen years later, when I was dining with my wife at the Hotel Victoria in London, in came Gray in evening dress escorting a handsome woman. I inquired about him at the bureau of the hotel and found that he was living there and was supposed to be engaged in an investment business.

Turning again to the study of law in preparation for Columbia, I thought that I should enter a law office, but I had no means of approaching any of the large law firms. A Brooklyn clergyman, a friend of my father, came to my aid, giving me a letter of introduction to General Stewart L. Woodford, then United States Attorney for the Southern District of New York. He took an interest in me but had no place in his office. He said, however, that he could let me have a desk in a room adjoining his own in the Federal Building and that I should thus be able to use the library of the Law Institute on the floor above. This struck me as an excellent plan and so I entered the U.S. Attorney's office in the summer of 1882 and I remained there until the following spring. When, in March 1883, Elihu Root became United States Attorney, I was the last in the line of the office staff to pay my respects, explaining that I was merely a law student, without salary, and my desk was, of course, at his disposal.

The Columbia Law School had then a two years' course. Each class, of two hundred or more, was divided into two sections, one meeting in the morning and the other in the afternoon, and the students were permitted to select the one or the other within the limits necessary to insure substantially equal divisions. Entering in the fall of 1882, I chose the afternoon section which gave me an uninterrupted morning in the Law Institute library. We began the term with Chase's *Blackstone* which was followed by a course in contracts, embracing the various subjects with which Parsons dealt in his treatise, which was used as a textbook.[7]

In the second half of the school year we studied the law of real property with Washburn's book. That year we had the good fortune to have Professor [Theodore] Dwight in both contracts and real property, as John F. Dillon, who previously had the latter course, had resigned and his place had not been filled. Professor Dwight was a teacher of remarkable powers. He had a most engaging manner and his expositions were so luminous that they were easily followed and remembered. His method was to assign portions of the textbook and hold recitations thereon, which were accompanied by his running comments with an occasional dictated note. No casebooks were used and the "Dwight Method" was frequently contrasted with the Harvard system. The advantage of the Dwight Method was that the students readily grasped fundamental legal principles, but it had the disadvantage of leaving the students with an illusion as to the extent of their knowledge and the daily drill in the analysis of cases was lacking. But it must not be supposed that Professor Dwight ignored the leading cases. On the contrary, he was profuse in citations, and if the student

[7][George Chase, *Blackstone* (Albany, Banks and Company, 1881) and Theophilus Parsons, *The Law of Contracts* (Boston, Little, Brown & Co., 1873)]. These subjects were partnerships, bills and notes, domestic relations, bailments, shipping, insurance, guaranty, damages, insolvency, etc.

followed the classroom expositions with thorough work in the library, he could master the precedents and follow their evolution. This I did, digesting in my notebooks every case Professor Dwight cited and many others to which my attention was called in reading opinions. My preliminary study at Delhi had broken the ground and I was quite ready to make the most of this sort of analytical work.

To supplement the law school course, I joined a small private "quiz," conducted by Walter Leggat and Lewis Burchard (capable young lawyers), which met two nights a week for a rapid-fire review. I also joined the legal fraternity of Phi Delta Phi which held "quizzes" and a moot court.[8] Then, one of my classmates, John S. Melcher, a graduate of Harvard College, organized a club of seven, called "The Law Club," which held a moot court fortnightly at Melcher's home. In this very exclusive club were Sherman Evarts, a son of William M. Evarts, and my old friend of Amherst, Frank C. Partridge. In this way, my evenings as well as my days were full and I was going ahead at full steam.

I still had the notion that I ought to be seeing something of office work. In the spring of 1883, a young lawyer in my father's church in Greenpoint gave me a letter of introduction to Eugene H. Lewis, the junior member of the well-known firm of Chamberlain, Carter & Hornblower. I presented the letter, but Mr. Lewis showed no interest and did not seem to remember the one who had taken the liberty of introducing me. With as much dignity as I could command I was leaving the office when, turning at the doorway, I literally bumped into Mr. Carter. That was a most fortunate bump, as it was my introduction to the best friend of young lawyers, my future partner and father-in-law.

Walter S. Carter, then turned fifty, with iron-gray hair and closely trimmed beard, had an exceptionally fine presence and a most pleasing address. Of Connecticut lineage, he went to Milwaukee soon after his admission to the bar, and in a few years removed to Chicago, where he practiced law until the great fire. He then came to New York City, representing numerous property owners who had claims against insurance companies, and he made that city his permanent home. One of his early firms in New York was Carter & Russell; Leslie W. Russell was later Attorney General of New York. That firm was followed by Carter & Eaton; Sherburne B. Eaton was later Counsel for Thomas A. Edison. Its successor was Chamberlain, Carter & Eaton, when Daniel H. Chamberlain, an able lawyer — a former Governor of South Carolina who had failed of election in 1876 — joined the firm; and that was followed by Chamberlain, Carter & Hornblower. William B. Hornblower at the time to which I am re-

[8]Some of these quizzes were held by my old friend P. Floyd Clarke, my classmate at the Public School, No. 35, and a graduate in law of the Columbia class of 1882.

ferring, a graduate of Princeton of the class of 1871 and of Columbia Law School in 1875, was rapidly rising to eminence in the profession.[9]

After our involuntary contact at the door of the office, Mr. Carter gave me a sharp glance, asked me what my business was and, when I told him I was seeking a place in his office, he led me into his private room. He then gave me a thorough examination as to my antecedents and aspirations. Mr. Carter, a man of hobbies, was just then deeply interested in German universities, as he was planning ambitiously for his son George, then a student at Yale. He drew catalogues from his desk and described courses in jurisprudence. I ventured to say that, if I were his son, I might hope for such advantages, but all that I wanted at present was to know whether I could enter his office. He then launched into an attack on the idea that one should attempt work in a law office while studying in a law school and advised me to give my undivided attention to the latter. However, he wound up by saying that if I wished to come into his office during the summer I could do so — without pay — and see the wheels go round. I eagerly accepted the invitation and as soon as the law school term ended, I became a non-salaried clerk.

Mr. Carter was perhaps the first of the New York lawyers to begin the practice of instituting inquiries in law schools to find out what students in the opinion of the professors were taking the highest rank and to bring some of them into his office. As a result, students trooped [in] from the schools to interview him and, aside from those who entered his own office, he was able to place many in other offices throughout the country. In this he was aided by a wide acquaintance with lawyers and a phenomenal memory which enabled him to remember the names — even the middle names — of everyone he had met. In January 1901, he received a remarkable tribute when about eighty of his then and former associates gave him a testimonial dinner. There were tributes from friends who could not be present, eminent judges and lawyers. One was from "Professor James C. McReynolds" of the law school of Vanderbilt University. Aside from the formal address of Mr. Hornblower, there were a number of impromptu speeches. Among the speakers was "Louis D. Brandeis of Boston." [10]

Mr. Carter was at the beginning of his congenial enterprise when I made his acquaintance, but he had been at it long enough to have

[9]In 1893, William B. Hornblower was nominated for the office of Associate Justice of the Supreme Court of the United States but failed of confirmation because of the opposition of Senator David B. Hill, who resented Hornblower's participation in an adverse report of the committee of the New York Association of the Bar which investigated the conduct of Isaac H. Maynard as a Deputy Attorney General of New York in connection with a contested election.

[10][McReynolds and Brandeis were later Hughes's colleagues on the Supreme Court.]

gathered about him a notable group of young men. When I entered his office in the summer of 1883, the managing clerk was Lloyd W. Bowers, the valedictorian of the class of 1879 at Yale, who was destined to win high distinction at the bar, becoming in the opinion of the Justices of the Supreme Court of the United States one of the best Solicitors General who ever appeared before them.[11] Bowers' immediate predecessor as managing clerk was Clarence H. Kelsey, another Yale valedictorian, of Chief Justice Taft's class of 1878, who had left the office to organize the first title company, which ultimately became the Title Guarantee & Trust Company, of which he was president for many years. Next to Bowers' desk in the clerk's room sat James Byrne, a graduate of Harvard College (1877) and of Harvard Law School (1882). He became one of the leaders of the New York bar and has served as president of the Association of the Bar of the City and also as Chancellor of the University of the State of New York. On the other side of the room sat Starr J. Murphy, my friend of the Amherst convention of Delta Upsilon. George W. Wickersham, who became Attorney General of the United States under President Taft, and Henry W. Taft, the President's brother, had recently left the office to join the staff of Strong & Cadwalader.[12]

My chief work in the office was to assist Bowers. This brought me into close association with one who seemed to me to possess not only the intellectual power, but all the other personal qualities, which would insure

[11]Mr. Carter praised Bowers so highly that Thomas Wilson, of Winona, Minnesota, a former Chief Justice of the Supreme Court of that State — a close friend of Mr. Carter — offered Bowers a partnership in 1884. After practicing in Winona for some years, Bowers became general counsel of the Chicago & Northwestern Railway Company with his office at Chicago [1893]. President Taft appointed him Solicitor General in 1909 and had it not been for his untimely death in the summer of 1910 he would probably have been appointed as Associate Justice of the Supreme Court.

[12]In the memorial of George W. Wickersham (1936), prepared by Henry W. Taft for the Association of the Bar of the City of New York, appears the following reference to Mr. Wickersham's connection with the office of Chamberlain, Carter & Hornblower:

"It was a day when young students and lawyers served in offices on what were called the 'usual terms', their only compensation being what they gained by experience. It was upon such terms that Wickersham and I were provided with desk room. But we had the opportunity to form lasting friendships with an interesting group of our contemporaries. These were:

"Clarence H. Kelsey, the valedictorian of the class of 1878 at Yale, the Managing Clerk; Lloyd W. Bowers, the valedictorian of the class of 1879 at Yale, who after a successful career at the bar became Solicitor General of the United States during the term of Mr. Wickersham as Attorney General; and James Byrne, former President of the Association of the Bar of the City of New York. A little later Charles E. Hughes, now Chief Justice of the United States Supreme Court, entered the office. Intimate association with such a group of young men at the outset of their careers, formed an episode which was not only a rich source of reminiscence, but also an inspiration for professional achievement. For myself, it established a life-long friendship with Wickersham and an association with him as a partner for thirty-five years." *A Century and a Half at the New York Bar* by Henry W. Taft [New York, privately printed, 1938], pp. 187–88.

the highest professional success. To work with him was a prized privilege. And there was plenty of work, much of it in matters which Mr. Hornblower had in charge. The latter was small and slight, rather insignificant in appearance, but he had a keen intellect, a clear voice and an incisive manner which demanded attention and secured respect. Unfortunately, he was irritable and a difficult man to work for. One incident, when Bowers and I came a cropper, stands out vividly in my memory. Mr. Hornblower was in the midst of a vexatious litigation over the assets of an insolvent firm and he was opposed by one E. Payson Wilder, a terror of the New York bar. Hornblower and Wilder were up and down in the courts, fighting savagely with motions, appeals, etc. Wilder never failed to begin his argument by saying—"My friend, Mr. Blowhorner, I beg pardon, Mr. Hornblower," which would make the latter livid with rage. On a certain Friday Mr. Hornblower, leaving for his place in the country, left with Bowers the proof of a brief which was to be printed and in readiness on Monday morning. Mr. Hornblower had a liking for emphatic printing and used italics, capitals and boldface freely. In this brief he reached the summit of his argument in an outstanding line, "And the firm paid *seven thousand dollars* in CASH." On Monday morning, the brief neatly printed was on his desk, but soon we heard his quick step down the hall and he appeared at the clerk's door so full of wrath that he could hardly speak. He pointed to the climax in his brief, which to our amazement and horror read, "And the firm paid *seven thousand dollars* in COAL." Bowers and I did not know which of us was responsible for this egregious error, whether it was due to a misreading of Mr. Hornblower's script or to a failure to catch the mistake in the print, and we both took Hornblower's unsparing denunciation with abject humility and contrition. Thenceforth, I was the most careful of proofreaders, quite sure that the mistake most likely to be overlooked would be on the title page or in some conspicuous place where it would stand out like a monument.

The summer in the office was a profitable one, but in accordance with my agreement with Mr. Carter, I left as soon as the law school opened. I was greatly cheered by his parting words, "Hughes, when you get through the law school, you can come back and I will put you on a salary." I thought my future was now secure.

In the second year at Columbia we had equity under Professor Lee who had succeeded [Judge John F.] Dillon, and torts, evidence and the New York Code of Civil Procedure under Professor George Chase.[13] I also took

[13]George Chase (1849–1924), author of several textbooks, later became dean of the New York University Law School.

[Benjamin Franklin Lee (1839–1907) was a specialist in patent law and, later, was appointed lecturer on patent law at the New York Law School.]

the course in common law pleading, not because I had any notion of practicing in other than a code state but because I wanted to be familiar with the subject. Chase did not have Dwight's magnetism and was utterly uninspiring, but he was precise and accurate and we soon came to have a high regard for him. As the seniors' hour and a half followed that of the juniors, it was the custom of many, and I was one of them, to attend the junior period by way of review of the previous year's work. In order to facilitate the taking of classroom notes, and because I thought it would help me at the bar, I had taken a course in stenography in a commercial school in the evenings during the summer, and I went so far as to obtain a diploma certifying that I could write 150 words a minute. I was thus able to take full notes of what Dwight and Chase said and these proved in my later teaching to be most valuable. But after leaving the law school, I never used shorthand. The study of the monstrosity known as the New York Code of Civil Procedure was greatly aided by a series of lectures which Professor Dwight had given on "The History of an Action," of which I obtained a copy. Although I was no longer in the U.S. Attorney's office, I continued to use the Law Institute library, and I also kept up my attendance at the private "quiz," the Phi Delta Phi meetings — I was consul of the chapter — and our Club moot courts.

In the spring of 1884 my father resigned his pastorate in Greenpoint and moved to Jersey City Heights.[14] As I did not wish to lose my residence in New York, I took a room with my classmate Emerson Hadley on West 34th Street, then a desirable street of brown-stone fronts. We had a small room on the fourth floor back, and there we crammed for the final examinations. The law school offered a prize for the best essay and the highest marks on a special examination, but I did not enter that competition, which was entirely voluntary, as I did not wish to attempt the extra effort after a hard year. The winner of the competition was J. Parker Kirlin, who attained front rank at the admiralty bar.[15] In the preceding year, Columbia had established a system of prize fellowships, one for each graduating class. The fellowship was for three years with a salary of five hundred dollars a year and the fellows were to serve as tutors in the law school. After our final examinations, and just before graduation, Professor Dwight offered me the fellowship for my class which I gladly accepted, with the understanding that it merely involved the holding of a law school "quiz"

[14]He became pastor of the Summit Avenue Baptist Church. His residence was at 39 Cottage Street and after the first year was on the corner of Cottage Street and Summit Avenue.

[15][J. Parker Kirlin (1861–1927), an authority on admiralty and international law, was head of the firm Kirlin, Woolsey, Campbell, Hicks & Keating which was counsel for Cunard Lines in the *Lusitania* case and for White Star Line in the litigation following the sinking of the *Titanic*.]

two nights a week and thus would not interfere with my plan for entering Mr. Carter's office.

Following our graduation, an examination for the bar was held in New York County. The examinations in those days called for definitions, statements of general principles, discussions of particular topics, on which one could discourse endlessly, with special inquiries as to the provisions of the general statutes of New York as, for example, in relation to future estates and as to various requirements of the Code of Civil Procedure. Our examination was a very long one — I remember writing for about seven hours — but I passed without difficulty.[16] In due course I took the oath and was admitted to the bar in June 1884.

[16]Henry C. Beerits says in his [Memorandum] that I passed "with a rating of 99 7/8." I do not know where he got that information. While I had heard that I had a very high mark, I was unable, until recently, to verify the statement.

The examiners were Edward F. Brown, William C. Beecher, and Michael H. Cardozo. The grandson of the last-named, Michael H. Cardozo IV, brought to my house, on November 6, 1944, his grandfather's original record of the bar examinations during the time he was a member of the examining committee. This record shows that I received the mark of 99 1/2. See Mr. Cardozo's letter of November 5, 1944 [in the Hughes Papers].

Chapter V Early Experiences at the Bar *1884–1887*

For the first time since boyhood, the state of my health gave me serious concern. I had worked night and day for so long that I was in bad shape. I weighed only 124 pounds with my clothes on, and following a severe cold had an obstinate cough. It was evident that I should have a good rest before taking up my duties as a law clerk. An odd chance came my way. Among my classmates in the law school were the Seligman cousins, Edwin R. A. Seligman (the distinguished economist) and DeWitt J. Seligman. The latter asked me to tutor his brother-in-law, Larry Bernheimer, during the summer so that he might pass the bar examinations in the fall. His family was to spend the summer at Long Branch and thus I could have an entire season at the seashore. I was glad to seize this opportunity, as I was so familiar with the subjects that the task of tutoring would not be onerous. As a result, I tutored for two hours a day for more than two months. It was during that time that I first met Benjamin N. Cardozo. Two of the young ladies at the boarding house at which I was stopping at Long Branch asked me to escort them to a "hop" at the West End Hotel. I did so, and while we were sitting on the veranda, up came Albert Cardozo, a friend of the young ladies, with his young brother Ben — then a shy lad of fourteen, in knickerbockers — and we spent a large part of the evening together.[1] Not enjoying Long Branch, I moved to Asbury Park but returned daily on the train for my tutoring. When, in the early part of September 1884, Mr. Carter sent me a note asking me to begin my clerkship in the office, I was ready, fully restored to health and in good spirits.

There had been certain changes in the firm of Chamberlain, Carter & Hornblower. The junior partner, Eugene H. Lewis, who had left to become

[1]See George S. Hellman, *Benjamin N. Cardozo, American Judge* (New York: McGraw Hill, 1940), p. 221.

a partner of Sherburne B. Eaton, had been succeeded by Lloyd W. Bowers.[2] Despite his promotion, Bowers accepted a partnership with Judge Thomas Wilson of Winona, Minnesota, and in his place James Byrne became a junior partner. About this time Robert Grier Monroe, a grandson of Mr. Justice Robert C. Grier of the Supreme Court, entered the office. The action of Bowers in leaving his promising opportunity in New York may have been influenced to some extent by a disagreeable experience which I mention because it early impressed upon me the importance of good manners on the bench. In those days, with the exception of the few who specialized in conveyancing, searching of titles and incidental matters relating to real property, the best law firms were engaged in general practice, with many cases in the courts, and the most highly prized professional opportunities in New York City still lay in advocacy. The juniors and the best of the young clerks were busy answering calendars and arguing motions. The Special Term of the Supreme Court for hearing motions, then called "Chambers," later "Part I," would be thronged with these young lawyers and they came to know each other very well. Bowers, on account of his record at Yale, already had a fine reputation. It fell to his lot to argue a motion before Justice Abraham R. Lawrence, a choleric gentleman with wavy white hair and florid complexion, who in calling the motion calendar would name only the senior member of a firm as if he had the leaders of the Bar before him; thus, *Jones v. Smith*, Mr. Evarts and Mr. Butler; *Brown v. Robinson*, Mr. Coudert and Mr. Stetson. Justice Lawrence was also fond of punctuating his utterances by the constant use of his gavel. Bowers, at the close of his argument, ventured to suggest that it was highly important that the question should be speedily decided. Unhappily, procrastination was a well-known failing of Justice Lawrence. Pounding with his gavel, the Justice shouted that "it did not lie in the mouth of a young lawyer whom he had never seen before to tell him when to decide his cases"; he wanted "the young lawyer" to know that he would not "tolerate such an innuendo by any member of the bar"; that a "more experienced lawyer" would know better than to make such an "unjust imputation," which he resented. Bowers was crestfallen at receiving this unmerited rebuke in the presence of so many of his friends and came back to the office fuming and vowing that he would never enter a New York court again. And, so far as I know, he did not.

I found Governor Chamberlain busy with speeches in support of Grover

[2][Lloyd W. Bowers (1859–1910) was a friend and Yale classmate of William Howard Taft, who warmly recommended him to Theodore Roosevelt for appointment to the Supreme Court in 1902. "One of your kind of men," Taft assured T. R. See Otto E. Koegel, *Walter S. Carter: Collector of Young Masters or The Progenitor of Many Law Firms* (New York, Round Table Press, Inc., 1953), pp. 345–353; and Henry F. Pringle, *The Life and Times of William Howard Taft*, 2 vols. (New York, Farrar & Rinehart, Inc., 1939), I, 241.]

Cleveland in the presidential campaign and later with preparation for his argument in the famous *Virginia Coupon Cases* in the United States Supreme Court.[3] The business of the firm was mostly commercial, brought into the office by Mr. Carter. He did little law work and gave his attention to managing the office, interviewing clients (whom he would generally turn over to Hornblower or Byrne) and correspondence. In the days of Carter & Eaton, the firm had a large practice in bankruptcy cases and Mr. Hornblower had won his spurs in the bankruptcy court. After the repeal of the Bankruptcy Act in 1878, the succeeding firms handled commercial cases under the state laws governing the remedies of creditors. On the failure of Grant & Ward, Mr. Hornblower became counsel for the receiver, Julien T. Davies, and the ensuing litigation took a large part of his time and made necessary the creation of a special department of clerical work. Mr. Hornblower began to be retained in important cases for the New York Life Insurance Company in whose old building at No. 346 Broadway the firm then had its office. The general run of the commercial business was left to Mr. Byrne.

In accordance with the custom of the firm at that time, I began at a salary of $30 a month with an increase of $5 every two months. But the experience was invaluable, for it was my job to assist the members of the firm in whatever was assigned to me and thus I had general office work, helped on briefs, and frequently acted as junior in cases in court. It was a privilege to be about the court house, for any morning one might see Joseph H. Choate, Benjamin F. Tracy, Frederic R. Coudert, Edward C. James, or some other distinguished advocate, ascending the stairs to one of the court rooms and one might find a few minutes to hear part of some important trial and observe a great lawyer in action. I had not only these advantages but I was soon put in charge of a hotly contested litigation in which I had to play a lone hand. One Wellenkamp, a German broker, had sustained severe injuries and was somewhat disfigured in his effort, which was successful, to save the lives of his two young children when a fire occurred in his home. While he was in the hospital, his wife went to her brother's home and, when Wellenkamp recovered, refused to return to him or even to allow him to see his children. On his behalf, I brought a *habeas corpus* proceeding to assert his rights as a father, and there followed a long and bitter controversy in which Mrs. Wellenkamp was defended by her brother. This precious pair, she a virago and he a pugnacious lawyer and glib witness, piled up accusations regardless of truth or decency against the unfortunate Wellenkamp. The case was referred to Samuel A. Blatchford, son of Mr. Justice Blatchford of the United States Supreme Court, and the hearings lasted for many months. Every detail of

[3] 114 U.S. 269 (1885).

their married life was gone into, and I had to break down the combined stories of the brother and sister by rigorous cross-examination. In this I succeeded. There was a mass of testimony and prolonged argument. The referee decided in Wellenkamp's favor, awarding to him the custody of the children, and the referee's report was confirmed by the court. In the course of the proceeding there were various motions in court which aired the matter and the case, both at its outset and later, had a good deal of publicity. The children, boy and girl, were well cared for by their father, and years later I had the pleasure of hearing from the daughter who was happily settled, I think, in Chicago.[4]

While during this first year (1884–85) I was thus busily engaged in office work, I held quizzes four nights a week. Two of these were in virtue of my fellowship at Columbia and were held in a spacious room of the law school building on East 49th Street to which the school had moved from Great Jones Street the year before. Two other evenings were given to a private quiz which I had established at the request of about a dozen seniors. This was held in a room which I hired for the purpose from a proprietary school in East 44th Street. As I was living with my parents on Jersey City Heights, I had a long journey after the quizzes (each of which lasted for two hours), taking the elevated railroad to Cortlandt Street, then the ferry to Jersey City, and then a horse-car for twenty-five minutes more to the Heights. In consequence of all this work, I felt in the mid-summer of 1885 that I should take a good vacation and the firm agreed with me. I had done very well financially during this first year. The office paid me about $500, another $500 came from my fellowship, and a like amount from my private quiz. I was allowed by the firm 50 percent of the fees of my own business and I had managed to make almost another $500 in that way, so that my total income for the year amounted to nearly $2000.

I decided on a trip abroad. The old State Line running to Glasgow had a rate of $75 for first-class passage over and return. Of that I took advantage and I sailed for Glasgow on the *State of Nevada*. My companion on the voyage was Mr. Carter's son, Colin S. Carter. We parted at Glasgow and I journeyed to Oban and thence to Inverness; then to Edinburgh and through the Trossachs. From Scotland I proceeded to Wales, visiting my Aunt Jane Jones in South Wales and my Uncle John Richard Hughes in North Wales, and thence I went across the St. George's Channel to Dublin and north to Belfast, taking my return steamer, the *State of Pennsylvania*, from Larne. As the sea voyages were long, my stay in the British Isles was short but every moment was enjoyable and I returned to work with abundant zest.

In those days, most of the lawyers, even young lawyers like myself,

[4]Wellenkamp was poor and these services were rendered without prospect of adequate, if any, compensation. The firm was willing that I should give my time to the case.

wore silk hats and frock coats, at least when they were in attendance at court. This was considered the proper attire of a gentleman of the bar. But, worse than that, it was the style in that summer to wear gray top hats, and, so accoutered, I made my journey to Scotland. Standing in the rain on a vessel in Loch Katrine, I fell into conversation with a Scotchman who informed me that gray top hats could be seen at the races and sometimes in the House of Commons. That somewhat relieved me, as I had come to think I was the only man in Great Britain who possessed one.

On my return voyage, my stateroom companion was a young Englishman, Gerard Murray, and this casual meeting brought me into a highly sensational affair. Murray was on his way to the University of Virginia in company with his brother, an Episcopal clergyman living in that state. They were of a good English family; their father held the position of "keeper of the petty bag" of the Court of Chancery. Young Murray soon told me his story. He was in love with the daughter of a tavern-keeper at Brighton but his family disapproved the match and, having failed in an attempted elopement, he was shipped to America to finish his medical education. He swore that he would marry his girl. And so he did. In the fall he suddenly appeared at my office, saying that he had been informed that the young lady was sick; that his prospective mother-in-law had sent him money for the voyage and that he was going over to get married and to bring his bride to America. As he knew that he would be cast off by his family, he wished me to get him a job. In a few weeks he reappeared. He had brought his wife to New York and placed her in a boarding house. As he was going to Charlottesville for his books and clothes, he asked me to come and see his wife so that I would know her and could give any assistance she might ask for while he was away. Accordingly, I called upon her on my way to Columbia for my quiz and found her a slip of a girl, apparently unsophisticated. But it turned out that she was thoroughly bad and married Murray merely to get away from home. On the voyage, while Murray was seasick, she had formed an acquaintance with a well-to-do merchant and, shortly after Murray left for the South, she disappeared. As a telegram that Murray had sent her was returned with the word that she was not found, he hurried back to New York. We put detectives on her track and she was discovered in a house of ill repute to which the merchant had taken her. Murray visited her, and, as she claimed, threatened to kill her. This he denied, although he admitted that, overcome by his feeling of disgrace, he had tried to persuade her to join him in committing suicide. He was arrested, sent for me, and I appeared on his behalf. There was a sensational hearing in the police court and the case attracted much public attention. Murray was held for trial, but De Lancey Nicoll, then Assistant District Attorney, after talking with Mrs. Murray, agreed with me that the case should not be tried. The girl's mother was sent for, the case was *nolle prossed,* and mother and daughter returned to England. Six months later Murray was taken suddenly ill and died.

Aside from this break in my routine, I went about my duties as usual. During a part of the second year of my fellowship at Columbia [1885–86] Professor Chase asked me to take the regular course in Common Law Pleading in place of my quizzes. I was reluctant to do this, as I felt that I knew little about the subject, but he insisted. My hour was from five to six in the afternoon and while I taught that course I was relieved of my evening duties. For the rest of the law school year I had my quizzes as usual. I also had another private quiz, two nights a week, for a group from the new senior class.

Two new men, graduates of the Columbia Law School, had come into the office, Ethelbert Dudley Warfield (who became president of Lafayette College) and Charles B. Storrs, a Yale man of considerable prominence.[5] In December 1885, Storrs accepted an offer to teach in the law school of the University of Tokyo, Japan, and the firm gave him a dinner at old Delmonico's. Standing with Mr. Carter, who was receiving the guests, was Antoinette Carter, his younger daughter. That was our first meeting. Of course, I did not imagine that this tall, attractive young lady of twenty-one was to be my partner for life, a relation which has made all my other privileges seem trivial in comparison. I had but a word with her, but at the dinner table, to which I escorted Mrs. Thomas Wilson of Winona, I happened to catch Miss Carter's eye when we both saw the same joke which others seemed to miss, and a certain understanding was then and there established, although it was some time before this ripened into the love that has never failed.

It was during that year that Governor Chamberlain withdrew from the firm to practice alone, and Chamberlain, Carter & Hornblower was succeeded by Carter, Hornblower & Byrne. I was made junior member or fourth man. The custom, however, was to put the junior on a salary, without a share in the firm's profits, outside his separate business, and this, which had been the rule with Bowers and Byrne, was continued with me. So I went along on the usual terms, but the bi-monthly increase brought my salary for the second year up to nearly $900. My own business increased, as I began to write briefs from time to time for other lawyers. Eugene H. Lewis had me write briefs in two or three important cases.[6] He

[5][Ethelbert Dudley Warfield (1861–1936) was president of Lafayette College and Wilson College, Chambersburg, Pennsylvania.]

[Charles B. Storrs (1859–1931) spent most of his professional life in New Jersey, serving in the state legislature, 1893–1895, and as judge of the Orange County District Court, 1896–1906.]

[6]See below, note 9.

also asked me to join the staff of Eaton & Lewis, and Turner, Lee & McClure, a large firm (counsel for the Farmers' Loan & Trust Company), offered me a position with a salary more than twice as large as that I was receiving. I also had offers of partnerships with young lawyers. But I fully appreciated the special opportunity I had with Carter, Hornblower & Byrne for taking part in important work, an opportunity which was constantly enlarging, and to be the ostensible junior in a firm with excellent standing meant more to me than larger compensation.

In the summer of 1886, I took another trip abroad. This time I went with Colin Carter on the Dutch Line, sailing on an old vessel, the *Zaandam,* to Amsterdam. The voyage took fourteen days, but the passage was continuously smooth, there were only seven first-class passengers, all men, and we had a joyous time. After going about Holland, we journeyed to Paris and London, returning from Rotterdam on the *W. A. Scholten,* another old vessel, which was crowded and uncomfortable. I think that she went down not very long after.

In London, I noted in the morning paper that Parliament was assembling and I announced to Colin Carter that I would try to get in. He laughed, thought it idle to attempt that on the opening day without a card from our Legation and refused to accompany me. Of course, there was no chance of being admitted, but encountering a "bobby" near the entrance, I had an inspiration. I asked, "Where are Mr. Parnell's headquarters?" He directed me, and I went there, presented my card which disclosed that I was an "Attorney and Counsellor at Law, 346 Broadway, New York City," and I was soon introduced to an agreeable young man who said he was on his way to the House and would take me over. He was none other than John Redmond [1856–1918], then at the outset of his parliamentary career and destined to become the leader of his party. Full of inquiries about the States and our public opinion on the Irish question, he proved a most amiable escort. He took me to the lobby of the House, pointed out some of the most distinguished members who were about, and left me with one or two of his friends, an exciting and unforgettable adventure.

On returning to New York, I decided that I could no longer endure the inconvenience of living on Jersey City Heights and I took rooms with Colin Carter at the Murray Hill Hotel, then new, with a first-class clientele, rivalling the Windsor. I did not remain there long, however, as my father accepted a call to the Trinity Baptist Church on East 55th Street, New York, and I then made my home with my parents at No. 110 East 81st Street. In this third year of my fellowship at Columbia (1886–87) I succeeded in being relieved of the course in Pleading which was given to Robert D. Petty, the prize fellow of the class of 1885. In my private quiz I now had a partner. Mr. Carter had asked me who was the best man in my quizzes. I said — Paul D. Cravath — and he became a clerk in the office.[7] He was appointed prize fellow of his class (1886) and I arranged with him to share my private quiz, so that it would require of each of us only one night a week. My relation to the students in the law school quiz continued to be most happy. That quiz was very largely attended and when I finished my three years' fellowship in May 1887, the students presented me with a handsome gold watch, an excellent timepiece, which after fifty-five years I still carry.

My share in the firm's work increased in difficulty and responsibility. I had the usual run of office matters which would fall to an ostensible junior partner, e.g., preparing pleadings, working on briefs, drawing contracts, holding interviews with clients and occasionally giving a written opinion on some submitted question. I was also quite active in court work, arguing motions and now and then trying a minor case or assisting Mr. Hornblower or Mr. Byrne in an important one. I represented the firm in a series of negotiations and legal proceedings growing out of extravagant transactions by one of the members of a western firm who was a drug addict.[8] In addition, I had some matters in which I was retained separately from the firm. I wrote the brief for Eaton & Lewis, and appeared on the argument with Mr. Lewis, in successful opposition to an application for a preliminary injunction in an interesting case presenting the question whether the case was one of which the federal court could entertain jurisdiction under the patent laws, there being no diversity of citizenship.[9] In another case, Mr. W. Fearing Gill (whom I had met in the *Gray* affair)[10] retained me in 1886 to bring suit for services rendered to a company of which he was an officer and director. This suit was tried in the fall of

[7][Paul Drennan Cravath (1861–1940) became a leader of the New York bar. A consultant to the Treasury Department during World War I, he was decorated by the Rumanian, Italian, French, and American governments. For details concerning his background and career, see Robert T. Swaine, *The Cravath Firm and Its Predecessors, 1819–1947*, 2 vols. (New York, privately printed, 1946), I, 573ff and II, *passim*.]

[8]See printed brief on successful motion in one of these cases (Rowland v. Alden [*aff'd mem.*, 45 Hun. (Sup. Ct.) 590 (1st Dep't 1887)] to set aside service of summons. *Cases and Points*, Vol. I, 2d brief.

When I left practice in 1891, on going to Cornell University, I assembled certain printed records and briefs in eight bound volumes entitled "Cases and Points." Of course, most of my work in the lower courts did not get into print.

I regret that briefs and records in connection with my later practice were not similarly assembled. [The briefs and records referred to as "Cases and Points" are in the Library of the Association of the Bar of New York City.]

[9]*Cases and Points*, Vol. I, 1st brief, McCarty & Hall Trading Co. v. Glaenzer [30 Fed. 387 (C.C.S.S.N.Y. 1887)].

[10]See above, pp. 53–54.

1887 before Mr. Justice Barrett and a jury, Mr. Hornblower assisting me. We got a verdict but met with reversal on appeal.[11]

I may mention one disagreeable experience because it again deeply impressed me with the importance of decent judicial manners. In the absence of a bankruptcy law, there was great competition between creditors. When failures were thought to be fraudulent — and this was not rare — efforts would be made, if sufficient evidence could be quickly gathered, to obtain attachments on the ground of fraudulent disposition of property. In one case, which Byrne handled, private detectives had been employed. Byrne was a most meticulous practitioner, and made a practice of putting each day's report of the detectives into affidavits. In the hurry to get an attachment, he did not take time to assemble the facts in better arranged papers, and thus had a sheaf of affidavits some of which had very slight, if any, significance. A motion to vacate the attachment on the papers on which it was granted came before Mr. Justice Van Brunt, "Sitting Bull," an excellent Judge, but overbearing and at times very rough in his treatment of counsel. The redeeming feature was that he was no respecter of persons and lawyers old and young suffered alike at his hands. It happened that I knew nothing about this particular case. Byrne had a severe cold and sent word to the office that I should argue the case. I made a hasty preparation. The counsel for the defendants was one Abram Kling, a close friend of Justice Van Brunt, his companion on summer trips. Kling at once attacked the papers, selecting affidavits of no importance and holding them up to ridicule. This appealed to Justice Van Brunt who shouted, "Who appears on the other side? It's an imposition on the court to present such papers. I'll vacate the attachment!" I rose to receive more tongue-lashing, but in loyalty to the office I did not feel that I should disavow personal responsibility for the state of the papers which I explained was due to the haste of preparation. Van Brunt's outburst aroused my fighting disposition and I insisted on being heard. I finally succeeded, in the midst of the Judge's interruptions, in pointing out certain affidavits containing admissions by the defendants which under a decision of the General Term justified the issue of the attachment. But the animosity of the Judge was so apparent and his comments so caustic that I suffered keenly. However, I held my ground, Van Brunt knew that we would appeal if we lost, and he eventually sustained the attachment. Many years after, when Justice Van Brunt was Presiding Justice of the Appellate Division and Alton B. Parker was sitting on that court, the latter told me of

[11]*Cases and Points*, Vol. 1. [Gill v. New York Cab Co., 48 Hun. (Sup. Ct.) 524, 1 N.Y.S. 202 (1st Dep't 1888). Hughes is listed as counsel for the respondent with Presiding Justice Van Brunt writing the opinion which reversed the trial court judgment and ordered a new trial.]

Van Brunt's rough treatment of a young lawyer. Parker said to Van Brunt, "That is probably that young man's first case and you have humiliated and discouraged him." "Absurd," said Van Brunt. "He ought to know better than to come here with a case like that." But Parker protested so vigorously that Van Brunt sent for the young lawyer and virtually apologized.

The work in the office was too heavy in the summer of 1887 to permit another trip abroad and my vacation was limited to two weeks which I spent at the Ocean View Hotel at Block Island. As I sat in the smoking room on the evening of my arrival, a stocky and imposing man appeared at the door and after looking about advanced toward me, saying, "Young man, do you know how to play whist?" I admitted that I had played, and he said, "Come into my apartment, we need a fourth hand." That was Mr. Justice Samuel F. Miller of the United States Supreme Court and I had what seemed to me the inestimable privilege of playing whist with him every evening during my stay. To be his partner was a tough experience. He played without signals and expected one to divine his hand without the aids which modern whist had provided. When things went wrong, he used his objurgatory vocabulary without restraint. We cut for partners every rubber and it was a joy occasionally to get the best of him. Despite his brusquerie, he had a very kindly disposition and took a genuine interest in young lawyers. One evening he said to me, "Who was that young fellow you have been walking about with today?" I said, "He is a young lawyer from New York." "Well," said he, "why does he not come up and speak to me?" "Oh, Mr. Justice," said I, "he would not wish to intrude." "Intrude!" said he, "Nonsense, he knows who I am and I do not know him and every lawyer ought to come up and speak to me. I should like to meet him." Justice Miller made many inquiries about practice in New York. Once he observed, "It is hard to make a good lawyer in New York. You try to get an injunction or an attachment or something right at the start and if you don't get it you drop the case. What we want at the bar is thoroughness." He was greatly impressed with Morawetz' book on corporations.[12] That, he said, was the best treatise that he had seen in a long time. By the way, Victor Morawetz was then a young lawyer under thirty and the production of his book in a few years after his graduation from the Harvard Law School was an extraordinary achievement. His advice in important cases was already sought and I recall being sent to him by Mr. Carter and Mr. Hornblower in connection with one of the cases brought against the New York Life Insurance Company relating to its tontine

[12][Victor Morawetz, *A Treatise on the Law of Private Corporations* (Boston, Little, Brown & Co., 1882). For information on Morawetz' legal career see Swaine, *The Cravath Firm*, I, 379–564.]

policies. On the last evening I played with Justice Miller, when I explained that I had to leave, he abundantly made up for the severe discipline to which I had been subjected by saying, "Well, Hughes, if you will practice law as well as you play whist I think you will get along."

Another privilege I had enjoyed at Block Island was in meeting Justice George C. Barrett of the New York Supreme Court.[13] He was easily the best of the New York judges, scholarly, dignified, keen, always courteous, an admirable trial judge commanding the respect of litigants, witnesses and jurors. In those days, of course, a New York judge except in rare instances was virtually the appointee of the Tammany leader. But following the Tweed and Erie scandals, the leaders would quite often select a young lawyer of outstanding ability and promise. In that way, men like Barrett, Edward Patterson, George L. Ingraham and Morgan J. O'Brien, got their positions on the bench where they made excellent records.[14] I already knew Justice Barrett, having appeared before him on several occasions, and when I met him at Block Island he was good enough to ask me to join him in an afternoon walk. He had presided at the trial of Jacob Sharp, indicted for bribery in obtaining the Broadway street-car franchise, and the Justice talked to me at length of the difficult questions which had arisen and of the basis of his rulings. These meetings with eminent judges made that vacation a memorable one.

In the fall of 1887, Mr. Hornblower and Mr. Byrne decided to withdraw from the firm. Hornblower's practice in connection with the Grant & Ward receivership and the New York Life Insurance Company had become so important and lucrative that he wished to establish a separate firm and Byrne agreed to go with him. Mr. Carter looked about for some outstanding person at the bar to take Hornblower's place. As he was considering several possibilities, Mr. Hornblower, who was still on very friendly terms with Mr. Carter, suggested to him that he should not go outside the present staff, saying, "Why not take young Hughes?" When Mr. Carter repeated this to me I was greatly surprised and overjoyed at the opportunity. But I said, "We should hold Cravath." Mr. Carter agreed. So I asked Cravath to dine with me at the famous Martinelli restaurant where we discussed the matter over a bottle of Chianti. "Cravath," I said, "this is an extraordinary chance." We would be a young firm with a good

[13] [George Carter Barrett (1838–1906) was appointed to the New York Supreme Court in 1871.]

[14] [Edward Patterson (1839–1910) became a justice of the New York Supreme Court in 1887 and was elevated to the Appellate Division in 1896.

[George Landon Ingraham (1847–1931) served on various New York State courts from 1883 to 1915.

[Morgan Joseph O'Brien (1852–1937) served on the New York Supreme Court from 1887 to 1905, in the Trial Division, 1887–1896, and in the Appellate Division, 1896–1906.]

business at the start and every opportunity for making an independent reputation instead of virtually being clerks. Then, to clinch it, I said, "We will make the firm Carter, Hughes & Cravath." Bringing his fist down on the table, Cravath exclaimed, "Make it Carter, Hughes *& Cravath,* and I'll join." And this was done. We agreed on the division of net fees of the general business — 60 per cent to Mr. Carter, 24 per cent to me and 16 per cent to Cravath. In addition, Cravath and I were to continue to have, respectively, 50 per cent of the fees from the business we might bring in. Our fourth man, an ostensible partner but on a salary, was John W. Houston, a graduate of the Harvard Law School, who had been a clerk for some time and had shown exceptional talent.[15]

During this three-year period I have been describing, closing with 1887, despite office work and my evening quizzes, I took advantage of every chance to carry out my resolve to get in a good deal of reading outside the law. Generally I had free weekends (Saturdays and Sundays) and occasionally I would have an evening when I did not have to work. There were, of course, the horsecars and elevated trains and, in the first two years of my fellowship the ferryboats, where I could read the daily papers. I maintained my interest in Delta Upsilon affairs. I responded to a toast at the banquet of the Semi-Centennial Convention in December 1884. On one occasion, I went to Easton to install a chapter of Delta Upsilon at Lafayette College. In the fall of 1886, I made a hurried trip to Hamilton to act as toastmaster at the fraternity convention held with the Madison chapter, and there were dinners in New York at which I served in a like capacity. I had practically nothing to do with politics. My first vote had been for Seth Low in the Brooklyn mayoralty campaign of 1883. I lost my vote for president in 1884 by removing to my parents' home in Jersey City after my admission to the bar and I did not again become a resident of New York until the fall of 1886. About that time I was admitted to membership in the Association of the Bar and I joined the Republican Club. In 1887, I took an active part, with other young lawyers, in the unsuccessful campaign of De Lancey Nicoll for District Attorney. Nicoll had won laurels in his work as Assistant District Attorney in many important cases,

[15][Houston later left the Carter firm to join Cravath and formed the firm of Cravath & Houston. He ended his professional life as a professor of law at Columbia University.] Other young men of unusual ability who had come into the office as clerk were Thaddeus D. Kenneson [1859–1924], later a teacher of law and a member of the firm of Kenneson, Crain & Alling; Howard A. Taylor [1865–1920] (formerly famous as a tennis player) who became a partner of Hornblower & Byrne; and Harry W[olf] Mack [1861–1938], a brilliant lawyer who became engrossed in important business interests. [According to Swaine, *The Cravath Firm,* I, 588, the firm's practice "was principally in the dry goods trade, with much collection and commercial paper litigation." For more information on the firm's business and a sample of the partners' correspondence, see Koegel, *Walter S. Carter, passim.*]

including that of Jacob Sharp, and was the rising hope of the independent bar.

During the law school year 1887–1888 I continued with Cravath our private quiz, but as I was through with my fellowship duties and I had the private quiz only one evening a week, I had the other evenings for work or diversion, principally the former.

Although I looked forward eagerly to the new opportunities, I deeply regretted the necessity of severing my association with Mr. Hornblower and Mr. Byrne. Mr. Hornblower's clarity and precision — the exacting demands he made upon his associates — and Mr. Byrne's extreme care and caution, furnished an excellent discipline, while intimate contact with men of such high character and first-rate ability gave one a constant awareness of the best traditions of the bar.

Chapter VI First Firms *1888–1891*

On January 1, 1888, the firm of Carter, Hughes & Cravath entered the legal arena with abundant zest. As Mr. Carter owned the library and office furniture, Hornblower and Byrne merely stepped out and our firm continued in the old offices in the New York Life Building at 346 Broadway. It was a proud moment when I took possession of Mr. Hornblower's room and assumed the leading role so far as the legal work of the office was concerned. In those days the office arrangements even of the best firms were very simple. Large retinues of law clerks, secretaries and various helpers, and facilities such as are now quite usual, were unknown. When I entered the office of Chamberlain, Carter & Hornblower in the summer of 1883, important court papers (when not printed) were still written by a copyist whose "copper-plate" work was greatly admired. While that was the practice, drafting was careful and there was constant effort to make the papers succinct. The firm had a single stenographer and there was but one telephone which was placed in the outer hall of the office. A second stenographer was soon added and typewriting with its temptation to prolixity became the rule. When our new firm started in 1888 we had two stenographers and a couple of law clerks, and in the late spring our clerical force was reenforced by two graduates of the Columbia Law School of the class of 1888, Philo P. Safford and Frederic R. Kellogg [1867–1935], the former being a prize fellow.[1]

I do not wish to appear as a *laudator temporis acti*, as I fully appreciate the vast improvement that has been made in legal education and the superior equipment of the young lawyers of today who have profited by the discipline of the best schools. But despite their poor preparation if

[1][Safford was Carter's nephew. He left Carter's firm in 1890 to found his own firm. Carter's biographer suggests, "Perhaps brilliant Safford felt that brilliant son-in-law Hughes provided enough relationship in the office." See Otto E. Koegel, *Walter S. Carter: Collector of Young Masters or The Progenitor of Many Law Firms* (New York, Round Table Press, Inc., 1953), p. 110.]

tested by present standards, the outstanding lawyers of the eighteen-eighties would seem, at least in the field of advocacy, to be unsurpassed. William M[axwell] Evarts [1818–1901] was then approaching the close of his distinguished career, and Joseph H[odges] Choate [1832–1917], James C[oolidge] Carter [1827–1905], William Allen Butler [1825–1902], Frederic R[ené] Coudert [1832–1903], Wheeler H[azard] Peckham [1833–1905] and other leaders were in their prime. If we have regard to the prestige of the legal profession, it was a golden age of the bar. Roused by the scandals of the Tweed regime, public-spirited lawyers had founded in 1871 under the leadership of William M. Evarts and Samuel J[ones] Tilden [1814–1886], the Association of the Bar.[2] In the eighteen-eighties, the great leaders of the bar were generally in attendance at the meetings of the Association and took part in discussions which were as stimulating as any forensic battles. I recall in particular the debate over the advisability of the codification of the common law, James C. Carter being the leading opponent in challenge to the author of the proposed code, David Dudley Field [1805–1894], and his earnest supporters.

The giants of the profession were retained in the more important litigations and dominated the legal scene. Their firms were entrenched financially and socially, having as regular clients the large moneyed institutions and transportation companies. These highly privileged firms seemed to hold in an enduring grasp the best professional opportunities and to leave little room for young aspirants outside the favored groups. But I thought little of that, being intent on the day's work with the single ambition to do it well. And as I look back over the years, nothing is more striking than the gradual disappearance of leaders and their onetime associates, and the emergence of new leaders and groups in the constant fructification of the bar. If the young lawyer sees to it that his work is of the best and if by intelligence and industry he stands well in his own generation, he can afford to await his share of the privileges and responsibilities which to that generation are bound to come.

In the time to which I am now referring, the field of commercial law had its special opportunities. That was the field in which Mr. Hornblower had made his mark and it was the one in which our new firm had its best chance of success. In Mr. Carter's clientele, there were leading houses in the dry-goods business, importers, jobbers and commission merchants, and they had many claims against insolvent debtors. There was no bankruptcy law and the state insolvency law was rarely resorted to. Failing

[2][The Association was organized in 1870, not 1871. Hughes probably was referring to the several committees formed and meetings held by the same men in 1871 to rouse public support for the fight against Tweed.]

debtors usually made general assignments for the benefit of creditors.[3] These were voluntary, although subject to certain statutory regulations relating to their provisions and administration. In the trade of a great metropolis there would always be those who would devise schemes to defraud creditors and the credit departments of the large business houses had to be constantly on the alert to detect them. Insolvent debtors in disposing of their property frequently resorted to fraudulent preferences and if these were embraced in a general assignment, the assignment itself would be set aside.[4] Shrewd and unscrupulous lawyers would aid debtors in contriving means for the concealment of property and for separate transfers to relatives and friends on pretended claims, and these would often be followed by a general assignment, itself without preferences and perfectly fair on its face. Creditors with the assistance of counsel would seek to discover and set aside such transfers, and if they could be shown to be so connected with the general assignment as to make the latter a part of a single fraudulent scheme, the assignment as well as the anticipatory transfers would be held invalid.

Law practice in representing creditors was thus in a highly competitive field and called for agility as well as resourcefulness. As soon as a failure was announced the race was on. If facts showing a fraudulent disposition of property could be readily discovered, it might be advisable to sue out an attachment. If the attachment held against attack, judgment could be speedily taken for an undisputed debt, execution levied, and the validity of the alleged fraudulent disposition could be determined in litigation between the claimant of the property on the one hand, and the sheriff and his indemnitors on the other, the latter acting at the creditor's instance and the creditor's counsel usually taking charge of the case. If sales had been induced by fraudulent representations and the goods were still on hand, the sales could be rescinded, the goods replevied, and the issue of fraud could be determined in the replevin suit. If remedies by attachment or replevin were not feasible, creditors might hurry their claims to judgment and, on the return of execution unsatisfied, creditors' bills in equity could be brought to set aside a fraudulent transfer. In pursuing that remedy, creditors would have equitable liens dating from the commencement of their suits. If, on the return of execution unsatisfied, creditors did not have evidence to justify charges of fraud, such evidence could be

[3] [A general assignment for the benefit of creditors is a transfer by the debtor of all his property to a third party, the assignee, who usually sells the property and distributes the proceeds to the creditors of the debtor.]

[4] [A preference is the favoring of one creditor over another, usually by paying one creditor to the neglect of the other creditors.]

sought in examinations of the debtors and others in proceedings supplementary to execution under the applicable statute. In all these proceedings it was only the diligent creditor who was rewarded. The difficulty was that fraud would not be presumed but had to be clearly proved, and the courts were averse to setting aside general assignments with the result of "giving the worm to the early bird."

I may here say a word as to the organization of the State Supreme Court at that time. Prior to the Constitution of 1894, the appellate branches of the Supreme Court were the General Terms, with three Judges sitting, and the scope of their jurisdiction enabled them largely to dominate the legal work of their respective departments.[5] In the First Department Mr. Justice Van Brunt was for many years Presiding Justice of the General Term, with Justice Daniels (from the western part of the State) and Justice Brady as associates.[6] Justice Van Brunt, able and severe, dominated the court as Justice Brady usually agreed with him, so that the General Term was considered almost a one-man court. This led to one of Joseph H. Choate's witticisms. At a bar dinner when Justice Brady came in late, Choate welcomed him with the salutation, "See the concurring hero come!" Whatever success one might have below, there was always the General Term and Van Brunt to reckon with. And it was a stiff ordeal. When in 1896 the Appellate Division, with five Judges sitting, was substituted, Van Brunt's executive capacity as Presiding Justice was still available, but his control of decisions was considerably diluted, to the relief of lawyers who admired Van Brunt's ability but did not want too much of it. I must add, however, that, aside from the single experience which I have already mentioned, I had no occasion to complain of my treatment by Justice Van Brunt. But it was not exactly a joy to argue in his court.

Our new firm started under good auspices. I had already been in contact with most of Mr. Carter's commercial clients and they were not only content to continue with the new firm but brought in other clients. We had not only the sort of creditors' business I have described but other important activities in relation to contracts and general litigation. I tried several jury cases, which were not especially important but afforded a valuable experience. In attacks upon assignments and fraudulent trans-

[5]In New York City the Superior Court and the Court of Common Pleas (prior to their abolition by the Constitution of 1894), which had in many matters a virtually coordinate jurisdiction with the Supreme Court, also had their General Terms of three Judges.

[6]The General Term of the Supreme Court for a long period was generally so constituted, but from time to time other Associate Justices would be assigned to it. [Charles H. Van Brunt (1836–1905) actually was junior to John R. Brady (1822–1891) in terms of service on the State Supreme Court. Brady was elected to the Supreme Court in 1869. Van Brunt in 1883. Charles Daniels (1825–1897) was from Buffalo. He was first elected to the Supreme Court in 1863.]

fers, we had our ups and downs.[7] In one case, in which we were successful in the difficult task of upsetting a general assignment without preference, there was an unusual incident. Attachments had been sustained at Special Term by Mr. Justice Barrett but were set aside by the General Term.[8] While these proceedings were under way, an employee of a brokerage house brought me information of a purchase of shares of stock by the debtor shortly before his assignment. The stock had not been scheduled or delivered to the assignee. The debtor was examined in supplementary proceedings without a disclosure of this information and his testimony covered his affairs so completely as to leave no room for a reasonable explanation of the stock transaction consistent with good faith.[9] A creditors' bill was brought in 1888, a motion for a bill of particulars was successfully resisted, and although a long period elapsed before the case was tried, our knowledge of the stock purchase was not discovered.[10] On the trial, after the debtor had been examined, the evidence of that transaction, which the debtor had carefully concealed, was produced to his dismay and his feeble effort to escape the necessary inferences was without avail. There was conflicting evidence as to other fraudulent transfers but this one clinched the case for the creditors, and the assignment, as a part of a fraudulent scheme, was held invalid.[11] That success, with its dramatic feature, was quite a feather in our cap.

Another case brought in the early part of 1888 (relating to the owner-

[7]We lost the Rindskopf case, which had been tried by Mr. Hornblower and Mr. Byrne in 1885, and the decision against them had been affirmed by the General Term in 1886. I was unsuccessful in 1889 in seeking a reversal in the Court of Appeals (Seymour v. Rindskopf [41 Hun. (Sup. Ct.) 646 (1st Dep't 1886), *aff'd mem.*, 116 N.Y. 659, 22 N.E. 1134 (1889)], *Cases and Points*, Vol. II.) In the long litigation over the affairs of Halsted, Haines & Co., the general assignment was set aside and we obtained a recovery against a fraudulent transferee of the net avails of the transfer (Bank v. Richard H. Halsted [56 Hun. (Sup. Ct.) 530, 90 N.Y.S. 852 (1st Dep't 1890, modified, 134 N.Y. 520, 31 N.E. 900 (1892)], *Cases and Points*, Vol. IV), but failed in a zealous effort to recover from preferees who had valid debts but who had received payment pursuant to the fraudulent assignment (Bank v. Laura P. Halsted [unreported], Peyser v. Myers [56 Hun. (Sup. Ct.) 175, 9 N.Y.S. 229 (1st Dep't 1890)], *Cases and Points*, Vol. IV).

[8]Fleitman v. Sickle, Caeser v. Sickle [147 Hun. (Sup. Ct.) 633 (1st Dep't 1888)], *Cases and Points*, Vol. I.

[9][Besides the debtor, Isaac Sickle, Hughes also examined Herman Cantor, the assignee who received Sickle's property. Probably suspecting collusion between Sickle and Cantor, Hughes secured a contempt order against Cantor when he refused to answer questions or produce documents relating to Sickle's financial dealings immediately prior to the assignment. In re Sickle, 52 Hun. (Sup. Ct.) 527, 5 N.Y.S. 703 (1st Dep't 1889).]

[10][By the use of a bill of particulars, Sickle attempted to force Hughes into disclosing his knowledge of property that Sickle had fraudulently withheld from his creditors. In Passavant v. Cantor, 48 Hun. (Sup. Ct.) 546, 1 N.Y.S. 574 (1st Dep't 1888), Hughes was able to defeat this application for a bill of particulars and thus avoided disclosing knowledge of the stock until a more dramatic time at trial.]

[11]Passavant v. Cantor, [62 Hun. (Sup. Ct.) 623, 17 N.Y.S 37 (1st Dep't 1891)], *Cases and Points*, Vol. I. See also, In re Sickle, 52 Hun. (Sup. Ct.) 527, [5 N.Y.S. 703 (1st Dep't 1889)].

ship of a deposit with the *Consolidated Stock and Petroleum Exchange*), while involving but a small amount, was of special importance to me as I had the privilege of trying it before Justice Alton B. Parker, who was destined to be Chief Judge of the New York Court of Appeals.[12] He was an excellent presiding judge in both trial and appellate courts, a man of fine presence and courtly demeanor, invariably kind to young lawyers. Our friendship which began with that trial continued unbroken until his death.

On March 12, 1888, occurred the great blizzard. The evening before (Sunday) I had walked from my father's church on 55th Street to our home on 81st Street in a light rain. The next morning I was surprised to find that there had been a heavy fall of snow which had blown above the stoops of the houses. It was bitter cold when I started for the office, the streets were impassable to vehicles and few persons were about. As no trains were running on the Third Avenue elevated, I proceeded to Second Avenue. There I found an elevated train which took me to Chatham Square, and thence I made my way to the office on Broadway. No one else had arrived and as it was apparent that it was not a day for business I thought I had better get home as soon as possible. There were neither cabs nor buses and the trains had stopped, so I proceeded to walk up Broadway. Those who were doing the like walked in single file through the snowdrifts. Stopping to rest at hotels on the way, I got as far as 23d Street and concluded that I would not attempt to go further than the Murray Hill Hotel. Fifth Avenue between 23d and 40th streets was a wild scene. There were no vehicles and almost no pedestrians. The wind was blowing a gale and the drifts not only covered the street but the lower parts of the dwellings. There was no place to stop on that leg of the journey and it was all I could do to finish it. I arrived at the Murray Hill almost exhausted and remained there for a couple of days while the City sought with difficulty to renew its life.

In May 1888, my parents removed from the apartment on 81st Street to the three-story and basement brownstone house, 129 East 62d Street. As I was now relatively prosperous, I became responsible for the rent which I recall was $1,200 a year.

It was to that house, in the following December, that I took my bride. I confess that I had been adverse to paying special attention to Mr. Carter's daughter while I was a subordinate in the office, but with my independence as a member of the firm and with good prospects, I could no longer

[12]The case was Hanscom v. Hendricks in which Judge Parker's decision in my favor was affirmed by the General Term and the Court of Appeals. 123 N.Y. 664 [26 N.E. 750 (1890)], *Cases and Points*, Vol. I. [Alton Brooks Parker (1852–1926) was the unsuccessful Democratic candidate for President in 1904.]

suppress my feelings. The summer of 1888 brought us frequently together and in the fall we were engaged. Our marriage followed on December 5th. It was a simple ceremony at Mr. Carter's home in Brooklyn (176 Brooklyn Avenue) at which my father and Reverend E. H. Dickinson, the husband of Mr. Carter's elder daughter, officiated and only members of the family were present. As we were leaving the house, Mr. Carter said, "Hughes, you'll find that Nettie is a good person to live with." That was the most masterly understatement of which Mr. Carter was capable. Our cup of happiness was full at the beginning and has been full and overflowing ever since. In all my privileges and responsibilities, in good times and bad, in success and defeat, in joy and sorrow, we have had a perfect union of minds and hearts. Whatever I have accomplished has been made possible by that strong, unselfish, ever radiant spirit, constantly at my side. Our wedding trip was only for a fortnight and about ten days of that we spent in Washington. Although I tried to conceal my plans, Mr. Carter guessed correctly and telegraphed Judge Thomas Wilson [1827–1910] (then in Congress) that we would arrive at the Arlington Hotel, and there we were greeted. I recall that one of our fellow passengers on the train was Mayor Hugh J. Grant of New York and it was to him that I had the privilege of first introducing my "wife." [13] In Washington we drove about in the one-horse "victorias" then common, and went by steamer to Mount Vernon. We visited the Supreme Court where I was able to point out Mr. Justice Miller, my erstwhile partner in whist. In the old court room in the Capitol, I often in later years looked to the seat in one of the niches at the rear and pictured the young couple who gazed upon the court with such interest and reverence, without imagining that one day I should sit upon that Bench. I have frequently been asked if I did not cherish such an ambition and I have answered, "Not for an instant." Of course, I was fully aware of the special combination of circumstances which would make such an appointment possible, and aside from that my aspirations were more modest and I never gave it a thought. I dreamt of nothing more than a reasonable measure of professional success.

While I think it fair to say that my work helped to hold the clients and increased the firm's business, I had little business that I could properly

[13][Hugh J. Grant (1853–1910) achieved notoriety in 1890 as the result of a State Senate investigation of Richard Croker and Tammany Hall. It was alledged that Croker had made Grant Sheriff of New York in 1885 in return for a share of the spoils of the office, and that Grant had made two payments to Croker of $5,000 each. The money was handed to Croker's young daughter. Grant admitted handing the money to Croker's child, but claimed it was a gift to the girl. She was his godchild and he said he took his responsibilities in the relationship very seriously. See Willis Fletcher Johnson and Ray B. Smith, *Political and Governmental History of the State of New York*, III, *Consecutive History, 1856–1896* (Syracuse, The Syracuse Press, Inc., 1922), pp. 355–356.]

Charles Evans Hughes and Antoinette Carter Hughes soon after their marriage

call my own as distinct from that of the firm as I had hardly any acquaintances in business circles save those that I had made through the office. Cravath was in a very different position. One of his uncles was Caleb H. Jackson, an associate of George Westinghouse. Mr. Jackson soon began to bring Westinghouse business into the office, and within a year or so we were almost swamped with it. At the beginning there was difficult litigation brought by a former Westinghouse employee, who claimed to have been wrongfully dismissed and had established a competing concern.[14] But the most important matters grew out of the situation of the electric light companies which were engaged in furnishing electric current for light and power by means of overhead wires strung on poles in the city's streets. These were defectively insulated and serious accidents occurred. This was the situation in the fall of 1889 when the municipal authorities took action which threatened a destruction of the overhead system. The companies had erected their poles and strung their wires with proper authority and, under the legislation for the placing of electrical conductors underground, only a small part of the city had been supplied with subways. In order to preserve their properties and to obtain a reasonable opportunity to repair their overhead lines, the companies brought suit against the municipal officials to secure an injunction. Our firm was employed by a company controlled by Westinghouse and we retained Joseph H. Choate as counsel.[15] One of the other companies retained James C. Carter.[16] In our suit, I drew the papers and prepared the brief, and on the motion for injunction I had the privilege of opening the case, stating the facts and the questions involved. Naturally the case had the greatest public attention because of the dangerous condition of the electric wires on the public streets. In this delicate situation, I observed particularly the difference in bearing and method of approach between Joseph H. Choate and James C. Carter. The latter, in his most authoritative manner, bore heavily on the legal rights of property and was not as persuasive as Mr. Choate, who skillfully presented the practical problem of supplying current to consumers and the earnest efforts of the companies to remedy as promptly as possible the defects in their lines. An injunction was issued at Special Term which gave the companies but a short breathing spell, as the General Term, not unexpectedly, sustained the right of the municipal authorities to remove wires which were not adequately repaired and constituted a

[14]Johnson v. Union Switch & Signal Co. [9 N.Y.S. 655 (Super. Ct. N.Y.C., 1890), *appeal dismissed,* 125 N.Y. 720, 26 N.E. 455 (1891)], *Cases and Points,* Vol. III.

[15]United States Illuminating Co. v. Grant [55 Hun. (Sup. Ct.) 222, 7 N.Y.S. 788 (1st Dep't 1889)], *Cases and Points,* Vol. III.

[16]Mount Morris Electric Light Co. v. Grant [55 Hun. (Sup. Ct.) 222, 7 N.Y.S. 788 (1st Dep't 1889)], *Cases and Points,* Vol. III.

public nuisance.[17] The importance of securing suitable subway facilities was apparent. These the Westinghouse interests sought to obtain through arrangements with a new company which was granted authority by the municipal board to supply subways. This action by the board was challenged by another electric light company (which had contracts with an existing subway company) in a suit brought by Elihu Root and also in a taxpayer's suit.[18] The Westinghouse concerns were not parties to these suits but Wheeler H. Peckham was retained and appeared in support of the municipal board. I was given the task of assisting in the preparation of Mr. Peckham's briefs. He was successful at Special Term but the General Term reversed in the taxpayer's suit, holding that the contract between the board and the new subway company was invalid. The proceedings in relation to the building of subways were very complicated and the questions difficult, and I thus had the advantage of gaining considerable experience in a new field.

My contacts with Mr. Choate were especially stimulating. When I would appear at his home in the early morning, eager and tense after a long night of labor, I would find him in his library reading some literary work and serenely looking forward to the heavy tasks of the day without a suggestion of strain. His invincible calm in difficult situations, his easy mastery of his cases, and his unvarying geniality and air of complete confidence, won my admiration. I also profited by his advice. At one time, he commented on the mistake of accustoming one's system to more physical exercise than it was feasible for a busy professional man to take. His advice was to find some method of moderate daily exercise, which would not take much time and would be just enough to keep one fit despite hard day and night work. Walking, he thought, was the best and most convenient form of exercise for a professional man. I have long followed that advice.

I recall on another occasion, when I was under severe pressure, he pointed out the great importance of being able quickly to relax and to find some agreeable resource. "Hughes," he said, "if you don't get your fun as you go along, you will never have it."

Through his wit and the confident way in which he used his talents in forensic contests, Mr. Choate was allowed great liberties by admiring judges. The extreme length to which he went in his cross-examination of Russell Sage in the *Laidlaw* case has often been commented on as a notable instance of a great lawyer being permitted to overstep all reason-

[17]United States Illuminating Co. v. Grant, 55 Hun. (Sup. Ct.) 222 [7 N.Y.S. 788 (1st Dep't 1889)].

[18]Manhattan Electric Light Company v. Grant, 56 Hun. (Sup. Ct.) 642 [9 N.Y.S. 942 (1st Dep't 1890)], *Cases and Points*, Vol. IV. Armstrong v. Grant, 56 Hun. (Sup. Ct.) 226, [9 N.Y.S. 388 (1st Dep't 1890)].

able limits.[19] In another case, bearing upon the honesty of the transactions of a fur trader, I understand that Mr. Choate constantly referred to him in the course of the trial as a "skin merchant." Mr. Choate occasionally turned his biting wit on judges as well as on his opponents. In a long trial before a Justice who found it difficult to rule on questions of evidence, Mr. Choate and Colonel James had argued, rebutted and surrebutted, until neither could say more, and as the Justice leaned forward on the bench with his head in his hands, unable to decide, Mr. Choate arose and in his blandest manner inquired, "Is your Honor still thinking?" Lawyers opposing Choate in a jury trial often found it difficult to escape the notion that they belonged to the underprivileged.

Cravath's business developed so rapidly and was so distinct that the

[19][Laidlaw v. Sage, 73 Hun. (Sup. Ct.) 125, 25 N.Y.S. 955 (1st Dep't 1893), *aff'd*, 2 App. Div. 374, 37 N.Y.S. 770 (1st Dep't 1896), *rev'd*, 158 N.Y. 73, 52 N.E. 679 (1899). William R. Laidlaw, Jr., a stockbroker's clerk, brought suit against the noted financier Russell Sage (1816–1906). On December 4, 1891, Sage was confronted in the antechamber of his office by Henry F. Norcross of Boston who threatened to blow up the building if Sage did not give him $1,200,000. At that moment, Laidlaw entered the room, making a routine delivery. Sage greeted him warmly, threw an arm around him and drew him back into the office. Norcross detonated the dynamite, obliterating himself and seriously injuring Laidlaw. Sage escaped without major injury. Laidlaw sued Sage for $50,000 damages accusing him of having used Laidlaw as a shield against the blast. (*New York Times*, December 5, 1891, p. 1; December 25, 1891, p. 3; June 6, 1893, p. 1.) The case was dismissed from the state Supreme Court on the grounds that the plaintiff failed "to show that Sage by his action removed Laidlaw from a position of safety to a position of danger . . . There was not a safe spot in the room." (*New York Times*, June 7, 1893, p. 8.) Laidlaw appealed this decision to the General Term of the Supreme Court which decided the suit had been wrongly dismissed and ordered a new trial (73 Hun. (Sup. Ct.) 125), which was held in March 1894. The verdict rendered in the second trial was in Laidlaw's favor, awarding him $25,000 with the usual 5 percent added by the presiding judge. Sage appealed the decision (80 Hun. 550). A third trial, in January 1895 resulted in a hung jury. In the fourth trial, June 1895, the jury awarded $40,000 to Laidlaw. After much legal haggling and appeals by the defendant Sage, the verdict was upheld in 1896 by the Appellate Division of the Supreme Court, which was reversed by the Court of Appeals. (*New York Times*, February 12, 1896, p. 14; March 11, 1896, p. 14.)

[Hughes's comments on Choate's behavior were prompted by the way in which counsel for the defense abused Sage and fairly ran the courtroom. At one session, Choate spoke to the judge with reference to the packed galleries, "Your Honor will soon have to charge 'gate money.' " At one point, Sage answered Choate in a muffled voice and the latter cried "Louder, if you please! Just imagine yourself on the Stock Exchange making a bargain." When Sage stated that he had acted upon the advice of his attorneys, Choate remarked, "Don't do any barking when you've got a dog to do it, eh?" (*New York Times*, March 30, 1894, p. 8.) Choate insulted and berated Sage without letup throughout the second, third, and fourth trials. In each case the judge permitted him to dominate the proceedings. Even the defense attorneys seem to have been cowed by him. There is no record of strenuous objection to Choate's tactics. The Court of Appeals, however, harshly admonished the trial court for allowing the cross examination of Sage to go beyond "the legitimate bounds of a proper cross-examination." (158 N.Y. at 102–104, 52 N.E. at 689–690.) For additional examples of Choate's behavior see *New York Times*, January 18, 1895, p. 9; January 19, 1895, p. 8; January 22, 1895, p. 14; June 14, 1895, p. 9; June 18, 1895, p. 1.]

firm established a branch office for him in the Equitable Building at 120 Broadway. I was busy at both offices, trying to carry on with the commercial business at the old office, while at the same time writing briefs and otherwise assisting Cravath in his Westinghouse matters. This finally proved to be an impossible task and we agreed on a dissolution of the firm. Cravath formed a new firm — Cravath & Houston — while Mr. Carter and I continued together with Frederic R. Kellogg, under the firm name of Carter, Hughes & Kellogg.[20] Kellogg was a brilliant lawyer who achieved a leading position at the bar. Our fourth man was Edward F. Dwight [1862–1903], a nephew of Professor Theodore W. Dwight, and a prize fellow of the class of 1889 at the Columbia Law School.[21] Our new firm had plenty of work.

An important case, a hangover from the days of Chamberlain, Carter & Eaton, came to its climax in the New York Court of Appeals in 1890. It involved the question of the duty, owing by the promotors of a corporation to the subscribers for its shares, to account for secret profits. The suit was brought in 1880. On the trial in 1883, in which Mr. Hornblower appeared for the plaintiffs, the complaint was dismissed. That judgment was affirmed by the General Term. The case in the Court of Appeals was on the books of our firm, but Mr. Hornblower retained his interest in it, as a member of the old firms, and made the argument. I prepared the brief.[22] We were successful in securing a reversal of the judgment. The Court of Appeals held that the promoters of the corporation occupied before its organization a position of trust and confidence toward those whom they induced to invest in the enterprise and were liable for damages.[23]

Several cases in the Court of Appeals, in which I wrote the briefs and made the arguments, were heard in 1891.[24] In one of these, the court

[20][Houston withdrew from active practice in 1899 and became a professor of law at Columbia. Cravath joined the firm of Seward, Guthrie & Steele.]

[21][Dwight's career was cut short by ill health. At his death, Hughes said of him, "I have never been associated with a man . . . who so unqualifiedly commanded my esteem. I never knew a more indefatigable and conscientious worker. In the course of years, as I observed how unremittingly he toiled, he became to me the personification of devotion and duty, and I never think of the qualities of persistency and fidelity, but (his) life at once seems to me, as their best illustration." Quoted in Koegel, *Carter*, p. 400.]

[22]Brewster v. Hatch [42 Hun. (Sup. Ct.) 659 (1st Dep't 1886), *rev'd*, 122 N.Y. 349, 25 N.E. 505 (1890)], *Cases and Points*, Vol. VIII.

[23]Brewster v. Hatch, 122 N.Y. 349, [25 N.E. 505 (1890)].

[24]Carroll v. Sweet [5 N.Y.S. 572 (Super. Ct. 1889), *rev'd*, 128 N.Y. 19, 27 N.E. 763 (1891)], *Cases and Points*, Vol. VIII; Saint Nicholas Bank v. State National Bank [59 Hun. (Sup. Ct.) 383, 12 N.Y. 864 (1st Dep't), *rev'd* 128 N.Y. 26, 27 N.E. 849 (1891)], *Cases and Points*, Vol. VIII; Gilman v. Tucker [13 N.Y.S. 804 (Super. Ct. 1891) *aff'd*, 128 N.Y. 190, 28 N.E. 1040 (1891)], *Cases and Points*, Vol. VII; Matter of Stonebridge, [59 Hun. 626, 13 N.Y.S. 770 (1st Dep't) *aff'd mem.*, 128 N.Y. 618, 28 N.E. 253 (1891)],*Cases and Points*, Vol. VI.

sustained the view, for which I had contended, that a section of the Code of Civil Procedure, relating to the title to real property sold on execution, was unconstitutional as depriving the owner of his property without due process of law.[25]

I was so busy as a member of the firm of Carter, Hughes & Cravath that I had very little time for vacations. In the summer of 1888, I had one week. In 1889, my wife and I spent most of the summer at Lake Mahopac and while there I went back and forth each week-day. I managed to get two weeks, however, for a trip to the Adirondacks where we stopped at the old Miller House on the Lower Saranac. It may be worth mentioning, as indicating the general ignorance on the subject, that the hotel had a large number of tubercular patients and no one seemed to think that any special precautions were necessary.

In the spring of 1889, my father gave up his pastorate in New York and accepted a call to Scranton, Pennsylvania.[26] Our son, Charles Evans Hughes, Jr., was born on November 30, 1889, and we decided that we should look to the establishment of a permanent home. We thought Brooklyn might be most desirable and rented a house on the Park slope, No. 117 St. John's Place. We moved there early in 1890. In the summer of that year we took a little cottage at Siasconset, Nantucket, and I obtained a holiday of about three weeks, in addition to a few week-ends.[27]

Still looking about for a permanent residence, we decided that the upper west side of Manhattan was preferable to Brooklyn, and early in 1891 we bought the house at No. 318 (I believe it is now 320) West 88th Street, near Riverside Drive. That is, we bought the equity subject to the building loan. This was a very attractive residence which we decorated and furnished to our complete satisfaction. But we were destined not to remain there long.

In truth, despite a gratifying degree of professional success and an excellent outlook, I was nervously depressed because of the steady grind to which I had so long been subject. One thing that greatly disturbed me was that I was unable to obtain life insurance. I was thoroughly examined and no particular defect or ailment was found. As I was informed, I was rejected solely because of underweight.[28]

It was about that time that my old friend Professor James O. Griffin, one-time principal of the Delaware Academy at which I had taught, paid me a short visit. He was then an Assistant Professor of German at Cornell

[25]Gilman v. Tucker, 128 N.Y. 190, [28 N.E. 1040 (1891)].

[26]The Jackson Street Baptist Church.

[27]It was at that time that I grew a full beard. There were no safety razors and I disliked shaving. In accordance with the custom of the day, I had kept a shaving cup at a barber shop, but I thought it rather a nuisance to go there regularly.

[28]I weighed only 127 pounds, with my clothes on, excepting coat and vest.

University. He asked me if I would consider a professorship, that is, of law. I said that I would jump at the chance. Bearing this in mind, when Professor Francis M. Burdick of the Cornell Law School resigned to take a chair at Columbia, Professor Griffin mentioned my name to the Cornell authorities. President Adams asked me to come to Ithaca for an interview. I did so and was offered a full professorship in the Law School, which I accepted. This action greatly distressed Mr. Carter. He thought it absurd.[29] He pointed out my professional opportunities — even the prospect of what he termed "opulence." That did not attract me. While I naturally enjoyed receiving the fruits of my work, I had labored just as hard in cases involving small amounts, or where we were not paid at all, as in others. It was the nature of the questions involved, the interests of the clients, and especially the opportunities for advocacy, which had appealed to me. Now I was tired, and the offer of an academic retreat, affording what I thought would be abundant time for study and reading, was so attractive that I could not refuse it. My wife, with her unfailing loyalty and unselfish interest in my well-being, strongly supported me in this decision, and in September 1891, we gave up our new home in New York City and took up our residence in Ithaca.

The firm of Carter, Hughes & Kellogg was dissolved and Mr. Carter brought in an able young lawyer, George M. Pinney, Jr., the business being continued under the firm name of Carter, Pinney & Kellogg.[30]

On the eve of my departure for Cornell, the firm gave me a luncheon at the Lawyers' Club and presented me with a copy of Lord Campbell's *Lives of the Chief Justices* and *Lives of the Lord Chancellors*, of England.[31]

[29][On May 26, 1891, Griffin wrote Hughes that he had had an interview with Dean Boardman and Professor Hutchins, Acting Dean of the Law School, and both wanted to know more about Hughes and his plans. He said the salary would be $3,000. "The cost of living," he added, "is, of course, small as compared with N.Y. I have a very pleasant home which I rent for $300.00 per year, and the best house on the street can be obtained for $450.00. And the cost of table is very reasonable. If you dare consider so small a salary, come up and see us. I can assure you that you have never seen a more *beautiful* place than our campus at present. Cornell's future is great, and is assured." On June 6, Griffin informed Hughes that the law faculty was unanimous in recommending Hughes's appointment, but the law professors and the president did not want to make the nomination unless there was at least a chance of his accepting. "All the N.Y. men, Pres. Dwight included," wrote Griffin, "say that *you will not accept*. May I assure them that you will? The place is yours if you will accept, and you need have no hesitancy in getting the *ball* rolling with Mr. Carter." Collection of Regional History and University Archives, Cornell University. On June 9 Hughes accepted Cornell's offer.]

[30][George Miller Pinney, Jr. (1856–1921) later became district attorney of Richmond County, New York, and a member of the New York Charter Commission.]

[31][John Campbell, *The Lives of the Chief Justices of England from the Norman Conquest till the Death of Lord Mansfield* (London, J. Murray, 1849–1857); *The Lives of the Lord Chancellors and Keepers of the Great Seal of England, From the Earliest Times till the Reign of King George IV* (London, J. Murray, 1847–1869).] The inscription is dated September 21, 1891.

Note by the way. What benefit does a young lawyer gain from observing the methods of his elders, the leaders of the bar? I hardly think that anyone of common sense would seek to emulate the sparkling wit of Joseph H. Choate or the charming pleasantries of his rival, Frederic R. Coudert. He would know that there are gifts which belong to one's native endowments and are not to be had by laborious effort. Nor would he be likely to think that he could successfully imitate the profundities of James C. Carter. He would realize that while he could aim at equanimity, clarity, and force, he must succeed, if at all, by being himself.

The first and most obvious benefit he would derive by watching the leaders in action would be in improving his technique. I think that young lawyers in their first experiences in court work are more troubled by the little details of correct procedure — governed by unwritten laws — than by the large problems of their cases. It is by observation and practice that one can become at ease in the court room, knowing what to do at any turn of a case and never being thrown off balance by the unexpected which generally happens. This cannot be learned in a law school or taught by lectures, save in the most elementary way. Observing the manner in which experienced lawyers work, the smoothness of their performances, soon gives one the pattern of expertness and the assurance which goes with the "know how."

I have often thought that the observant and intelligent neophyte learns almost as much by seeing what he should avoid as by watching skillful operations which look so easy that one may be more entertained than cautioned. This benefit he can gain any day by noting the shortcomings of many practitioners. He learns to be courteous, but never obsequious, always the gentleman. He learns how important it is to keep one's temper, never to appear nervous or to lose poise; never to be petty, wordy, repetitious; to know when to keep still; to express himself candidly, concisely, always going directly to the point; to use a rapier rather than a club; to have one's papers so arranged that whatever may be needed will be immediately at hand so that he does not have to fumble; to be so well prepared that he is ready for any emergency; not to be tied down by brief or memoranda and always to show spontaneity as well as alertness. Obvious departures from these standards carry impressive lessons to the observer.

I may add a word as to one's demeanor in an appellate court. Some judges do not treat counsel fairly. They are impatient; not content to permit counsel to develop his case; ask questions unnecessarily, not for the purpose of enlightenment, but to break counsel down and try to make him admit that he has no case. Of course, when a case is poorly presented, without adequate appreciation or discussion of essential points, questions from the Bench may be necessary to bring the argument into proper line. But judges sometimes abuse their prerogatives and the advocate must learn to take their sins with a good grace. If a question is asked, it is almost always better to answer it at once than to say, "I will come to that later," and leave the judge unsatisfied. One should be careful as to his manners during his opponent's argument. A "poker face" is a good asset. I remember that a learned and distinguished lawyer who appeared before the Supreme Court was accustomed to make such grimaces during his opponent's argument that one of the Justices would pile up his records on the Bench in front of him so as to hide the disagreeable spectacle. Whispering to associate counsel, while an opponent is presenting his case, or apparently gloating over the latter's difficulties, are breaches of decorum which are unpleasant to witness and bring a lawyer into disfavor.

Chapter VII Teaching Law

I went to Ithaca with a sense of emancipation. The setting of the University on the hill — "far above Cayuga's waters" and "reared against the arch of heaven" — proved a constant charm. We were unable to get a house on the campus and for the first year we lived on State Street, about half way up the hill. There was no trolley line at that time and the only public conveyances from the town to the campus were lumbering buses. I preferred walking, and going up and down the rather steep hill was good exercise. The air was exhilarating and I soon found myself gaining in vigor and thoroughly enjoying life.

We formed many friendships in the University circle. I believe that — being only twenty-nine — I was the youngest full professor but we were received with the utmost cordiality and without any suggestion of condescension on the part of our elders. Indeed, the most outstanding members of the University faculty, although considerably older than I, were young men. But I viewed them in the light of the scholarly reputations they had already won, and I never thought of them as young. For example, there was Jacob Gould Schurman,[1] Dean of the Sage School of Philosophy, who was only thirty-seven;[2] Benjamin Ide Wheeler,[3] head of the Greek

[1][Jacob Gould Schurman (1854–1942) was born and raised in Canada, studied in Europe and began his teaching career at Acadia College. He came to Cornell in 1886, as Professor of Philosophy and became president of the university in 1892, serving until 1920. In 1899, he was appointed President of the first Commission to the Philippine Islands; in 1912–1913 he was Minister to Greece and Montenegro. During World War I he served on the New York State Food Commission. After resigning from his post at Cornell, he served as Minister to China, 1921–1925, and Ambassador to Germany, 1925–1930.]

[2]I am speaking of 1891 when I went to Ithaca.

[3][Benjamin Ide Wheeler (1854–1927) studied philology and linguistics in German universities and, in 1887, joined the faculty at Cornell. He was appointed president of the University of California in 1899 and served for twenty years. Among his scholarly works were *Analogy and the Scope of Its Application in Language* (1887); and *Alexander the Great: The Merging of East and West in Universal History* (1900).]

Department, of about the same age; Liberty Hyde Bailey,[4] of the Department of Agriculture, who was four years younger; James Laurence Laughlin,[5] Professor of Political Economy, who was forty-one; Harry Burns Hutchins,[6] Associate Dean of the Law School, who was forty-four. These men, already of note, were really on the threshold of distinguished careers. Dr. Schurman in the following year became President of Cornell; Dr. Wheeler, a few years later, became President of the University of California; Professor Hutchins became Dean of the Law School, and then President of the University of Michigan; Professor Laughlin soon went to the University of Chicago to head its Department of Political Economy; Professor Bailey became one of the most distinguished of the country's agricultural experts.

The agreeable social intercourse among the members of the faculty and the leading residents of the town gave opportunity for relaxation. Andrew D. White[7] still had his residence on the campus, and in the town, Henry W. Sage [1814–1897] and his sons had large mansions in which they gave generous entertainment. Mr. Sage had moved from Brooklyn to Ithaca in order to give more direct attention to the finances of the University which prospered by his foresight and unremitting care. On the campus, the professors had frequent dinner parties which were simple, but conducted with *savoir faire,* and afforded the most delightful contacts. Some of us became close companions, playing whist from time to time in each other's homes, trudging about the campus in daily walks, or bowling in the excellent alley of the Town and Gown Club.

The University encouraged the professors to acquire homes on the campus, renting plots at a nominal sum and lending about one-half to

[4][Liberty Hyde Bailey (1858–1954) was a prolific writer of popular and technical books on various aspects of botany. He was editor of the *Rural Science* and the *Garden Craft* series and author of many bulletins of the agricultural experiment station of Cornell. He organized the nature study and extension work at the University. From 1903 to 1913 he was Dean of the College of Agriculture at Cornell.]

[5][James Laurence Laughlin (1850–1933) was at Cornell only briefly after teaching at Harvard and before going to Chicago where he taught until his retirement in 1916. He was an aggressive advocate of the principles of sound money. At his death, the *New York Times* editorialized, "With a knowledge of economic theory and history possibly unequaled among American teachers he was for half a century a continuous and unsparing fighter against the recurrent popular mania for greenback inflation, free silver coinage or depression of the money standard." (November 30, 1933, p. 32.)]

[6][Harry Burns Hutchins (1847–1930) left a post as Professor of Law at Michigan to become Dean of the new law school at Cornell in 1887. He returned to his Alma Mater, Michigan, in 1895 to be Dean of the law school there. He succeeded to the presidency of the university in 1910 and served until 1920.]

[7][Andrew Dickson White (1832–1918) was the first president of Cornell, 1867–1885, and one of its major benefactors. He also had an active diplomatic career, serving as Minister to Germany, 1879–1881; Ambassador to Germany, 1897–1902; and President of the Peace Commission to the Hague, 1899.]

two-thirds of the amount needed to build a modest but commodious house. I had a few thousand dollars saved from my law practice and bought the house which had been built by Professor William Gardner Hale,[8] who left Cornell to become head of the Latin Department at the University of Chicago. I got the house (No. 7 East Avenue) which had an especially fine room for a library, at a bargain, and we moved there at the beginning of the summer of 1892. We were thus able to enjoy all the advantages of campus life.

The physical equipment of the Law School was meagre. During my first year the classes were held on the top floor of Morrill Hall. A new law school building was in course of construction — Boardman Hall[9] — and was ready in the fall of 1892 providing ample quarters for the school of that day. There were about two hundred students in the Law School,[10] an earnest lot who set no limits to their efforts to make the most of their course. The faculty was small but painstaking and full of zeal. The titular Dean of the School was Judge Francis M. Finch [1827–1907], of the New York Court of Appeals, who was not only an efficient judge but possessed exceptional literary skill which gave distinction to his opinions. It was Judge Finch who wrote the college song, "Far above Cayuga's Waters." Professor Hutchins, Acting Dean, was a careful student of the law and handled the administrative work with tact and dispatch. The oldest member of the law faculty was Professor Charles A. Collin, an expert in corporation law. At that time he was also legal adviser to Governor Hill and at great inconvenience, in travel back and forth, spent his weekends at the Executive Chamber in Albany. An able Associate Professor was William A. Finch [1855–1912].[11]

Supplementing the regular courses were special lectures. One course was given by Judge Finch on the statute of frauds and fraudulent conveyances; another by Daniel H. Chamberlain on constitutional law.[12]

[8][William Gardener Hale (1849–1928) taught at Cornell from 1880–1892 and at Chicago from that year until his retirement in 1919. He was the author of numerous Latin textbooks and for many years editor of the *Classical Review*.]

[9]Now the Law School is housed in a commodious new building — Myron Taylor Hall — the gift of Myron C. Taylor of the Class of 1894, who has had a most distinguished career in the field of industry. [See Harry Henn, "The Cornell Law School — Its History and Traditions," *New York State Bar Journal*, XXXVII (1965), 139.]

[10]The total number of students in the University was then about 1600.

[11][Other members of the law faculty during 1892–1893 were Moses Cort Tyler, Herbert Tuttle, and Brainard G. Smith. See *Cornell University Announcement of the School of Law*, p. 4 (1892–93). The 1891–92 announcement does not mention Hughes although he also taught that academic year. A copy of the Law School Announcements for all years is available at the Cornell Law School Library, Myron Tyler Hall.]

[12][Daniel Henry Chamberlain (1835–1907) fought in the Civil War for the Union and then settled in South Carolina (1866–1877). He was elected governor of South Carolina in 1874 and served until 1876. Thereafter he practiced law in New York with Walter S. Carter, William B. Hornblower, and others. See above, p. 56. He died in Charlottesville, Virginia.]

Judge Alfred C. Coxe, of the United States District Court, lectured on shipping and admiralty, Albert H. Walker [1844–1915] on patent law, John Ordronaux [1830–1908] on medical jurisprudence, Judge Irving G[oodwin] Vann [1842–1921], of the New York Court of Appeals, on insurance, and Goodwin Brown on extradition.[13] I had many subjects — "Elementary Law," contracts, agency, partnership, "Mercantile Law" including bills and notes, suretyship, sales, etc., and evidence.[14] To cover all this ground, I had to teach not less than fifteen hours a week. In addition I held moot courts, and in my second year I gave considerable time to graduate students who were taking advanced work in my subjects. While I used textbooks, I insisted on the study of cases, and the leading cases were analyzed and discussed in the classroom.[15] Because of my tutorship at Columbia and my practice in commercial law, I was well up in the law of New York. And I determined to make up the deficiencies in my legal training by taking by myself a course in the Harvard casebooks. In that way I went through the casebooks of Langdell, Ames and Thayer. Whether or not the students were benefitted by my teaching, I got the advantage of a self-conducted but thorough post-graduate course which in my later practice proved to be invaluable. During my first year, I was offered a professorship at the Northwestern University Law School and also one at the New York Law School which had been started by Professor Chase after he left the Columbia faculty. I declined both offers, as teaching in a city law school had no attraction for me. If I was to live in a city it was clear that I should prefer to practice rather than to teach.

In my second year at Cornell, as Herbert Tuttle, Professor of Interna-

[13][Goodwin Brown (1852–1912) held various administrative positions in New York, including State Commissioner in Lunacy. He was instrumental in establishing a system of state care for the insane.]

[14][Cornell U. *Announcement of the School of Law*, pp. 9–11 (1892–93). A copy of all examination papers given on those subjects for the years Hughes taught at Cornell are available at the Cornell Law School Library.]

[15]For a generous reference to my teaching, see article by Justice Harry L. Taylor in the *Cornell Law Quarterly* for December 1940, [Vol. 26], pp. 2–3. Justice Taylor was a member of the Class of 1893 at the Cornell Law School; he served as Justice of the Supreme Court of New York from 1914 to 1927. [Justice Taylor wrote (p. 3): "It cannot be said that Mr. Hughes was not well cast in the part of professor. He bore himself with dignity but without aloofness. There was nothing of the frivolous about him; he was constantly 'on the job.' He created in all of us respect for his extensive and (so far as we could judge) accurate learning, his uncanny memory and his ability to 'put over his messages.' He never produced in us any feeling of doubt as to his genuineness or as to his desire to help us on our way to become lawyers. He grew in favor with his students as their experiences with him progressed. He was especially happy in his conduct of oral examinations of each of us privately at test times. When one left him after such a session it was a feeling that here was a man not only capable but kindly, a man truly desirous of assisting us to develop ourselves, not a bogey man looking for a chance to 'bust' someone. The result of all this finally was a deep-seated regard for the man as well as the professor. Something which had been growing until it was ripe and thoroughly felt and understood by us all."]

tional Law, was away on his sabbatical vacation, the authorities asked me to take the University course in that subject.[16] I could not persuade them that I was too unfamiliar with international law to justify such an assignment, and with much misgiving I set myself to that new task. It meant devoting all the time I could spare from my other courses to a study of international law, but as it was in an entirely different field it proved to be a most satisfying diversion. Little did I dream that many years later I should find that year of special and exacting study a highly important, if not an indispensable, preparation for my service in connection with our foreign relations.

In the midst of my second year, thoroughly settled as we were in our home on the campus, I was faced with a difficult problem. The firm of Carter, Pinney & Kellogg was about to be dissolved, and Mr. Carter and Mr. Kellogg were insistent that I should return to New York and resume my old position. From a financial standpoint, the offer was a tempting one. I had been unable to live on my salary. The standard salary of a full professor at Cornell was then $3000 a year. Our family had been increased by the birth of our daughter Helen on January 11, 1892. I had been unable to sell our house in New York, and carrying that property for some time without a tenant had largely depleted the balance of my savings which remained after the purchase of our home in Ithaca. I saw that soon I should have to retrench to the point of serious inconvenience or should need a larger salary, which I knew it would be difficult to get as the University wished to maintain its salary scale without discriminations. Again, congenial as were my surroundings and work at Cornell, I was disappointed in the failure to have the opportunities for general reading and study to which I had looked forward. Far from being an academic retreat, I found Cornell to be a hive of industry, and aside from the occasional and enjoyable evenings I spent with my colleagues, my life was one of constant toil; in truth, I was about as busy with my courses as I had been with my practice in New York. Moreover, I had regained my nervous poise in the invigorating air of the hill country and I was in sound physical condition. I had obtained life insurance without difficulty, wiping out the black mark I had received in my previous rejection. So far as health was concerned, I could resume professional practice without anxiety. My wife, who had borne the burden of our frequent moves, did not shrink from another if it seemed best. Then, there was not only the professional opportunity in New York, but, Mr. Carter urged, the duty to provide a larger measure of protection for my family than was possible

[16][The course in international law was open to law students but was taught in the School of History and Political Science. *Cornell U. Announcement of the School of Law,* pp. 18, 20 (1892–1893).]

with the limited insurance I was able to carry. On the other hand, I did not wish to give up teaching. I was free from the worrisome demands of clients and was spared the effort to perform miracles on their behalf.

The University through President Schurman and Professor Hutchins made a strong appeal to me to remain. During the winter holidays, while I was in New York holding interviews with Mr. Carter and Mr. Kellogg and was about to make a decision, Professor Hutchins telegraphed me that the Trustees of the University had agreed to raise my salary to $4000. I could live comfortably on that and, deeply gratified by this evidence of my standing with authorities, I was inclined to keep on with my professorship. But the arguments *pro* and *con* were so evenly balanced that it took but a slight matter to turn the scale. And that little difference President Schurman unwittingly provided. He had also come to New York, and when I went to see him full of the idea that I should accept his offer, he surprised me by not telling me of the action of the Trustees. Evidently he did not know that I knew of it and thought that in view of my interest in teaching he could persuade me to remain at the old rate. I was so put out by his failure to meet me frankly and offer me the increase which the Trustees had authorized, that I decided to accept the offer of the firm. And when President Schurman later got around to making the proposal of the increase in salary, I was already committed and refused it. I have often thought how changed my life might have been had I remained at Cornell.

I left Cornell at the close of the school year in 1893 and in the following September we removed to New York.[17] I did not, however, entirely sever my connection with the Law School. I gladly accepted an invitation to become one of the special lecturers and for several years I spent a week at Ithaca delivering a course of lectures on "Assignments for the Benefit of Creditors."[18] I also delivered these lectures at the New York Law School until the enactment of the Bankruptcy Law of 1898, and from that time until about 1901 I gave a course in Bankruptcy Law at the latter school. It was in that period that I delivered several lectures in the evening, under the auspices of the New York Law School, to young lawyers on the "Trial of Cases." I enjoyed these opportunities, but with the increase in my practice, I had to give them up.

[17]We made our residence at No. 329 West End Avenue.

[18][Hughes is listed as a Special Lecturer on "Assignments for the Benefit of Creditors" at Cornell for the academic years of 1893–1894 and 1894–1895. See Law School Announcements for those years. A copy of these lectures delivered at Cornell is available at the Cornell Law School Library.]

Chapter VIII Practice Again *1893–1905*

While I was in Ithaca, the firm had removed to No. 96 Broadway, the old Schermerhorn Building, which was torn down when the present Surety Building (No. 100 Broadway) was erected. But before I could resume regular office duties there, I had an important retainer which took me to the far West. The economic depression in 1893 put many railroads into the hands of receivers. As soon as my retirement from Cornell became known, I was retained by Rowland Hazard of Peace Dale, Rhode Island, to look after his investment in the bonds of the Oregon Pacific Railroad. This was a small line which was projected to run from the coast in Oregon across the Cascade Mountains to Boise, Idaho — a grandiose scheme for the development of a port on the Pacific and the resources of Eastern Oregon. Its promoter was one T. Egenton Hogg, a plausible person who persuaded some of the most conservative investors in the East, including such men as John I. Blair,[1] George S. Coe [1817–1896] and Rowland Hazard, to buy $15,000,000 of the Oregon Pacific bonds. The project was not carried out. The road in 1893 was described by a disillusioned bondholder as running from a snowbank on the Cascades to a mudhole on the Pacific. Hogg had secured his appointment as receiver and had induced the bondholders to take receiver's certificates to the amount of several hundred thousand dollars. I was sent out in June 1893 to make a careful examination of the situation. I did so, remaining several weeks at Corvallis, Oregon, where the railroad crossed the Willamette Valley, and I reported that the road, as a separate enterprise, could not pay expenses unless it was extended to certain points at a cost of several million dollars. In its then condition, it was not worth anything like the amount of the receiver's certificates. On

[1][John I. Blair (1802–1899), at one time president of sixteen roads, owned more miles of railroad than anyone else in the country; he died with a fortune estimated at $70,000,000. His best known lines were sections of the Union Pacific, the Chicago and Northwestern, and the Delaware, Lackawanna and Western. He founded the Wall Street banking house of Blair and Company to look after his interests.]

my report, the receiver's certificate holders, who were also largely the bondholders, organized a committee which sent me out in December 1893, with another lawyer, Fabius M. Clarke of New York, to bid in the property at the foreclosure sale. The court had fixed $200,000 as the upset price and this amount, and no more, were we authorized to bid. This was with the idea that the certificate holders and the bondholders, if permitted to purchase, would pay off all current obligations, that is, to labor and supply creditors, and would put up the necessary funds to extend the line and give it a chance to earn its operating expenses and something on the investment. We bid in the property at the upset price, but the community had been so filled by Hogg with inflated notions of the value of the railroad that the confirmation of the sale was violently opposed, although, with the prospect of the investment of new money, it afforded the only promise of protection to the community through a solution of the road's difficulties. Our clients, who were not very optimistic at the best, were unwilling to go on in the unfriendly atmosphere created by the opposition, and we asked to withdraw our bid. Accordingly, the sale was not confirmed and the certificate holders and bondholders decided to take their losses and give up the enterprise. I observed at the time that the court would never see again as much as $200,000 for the railroad as it stood, and this proved to be so. I understand that sometime later the road was sold for $100,000 and ultimately became a part of one of the Pacific railroad systems.

T. Egenton Hogg, who devised the original scheme and induced the Eastern conservatives to part with their money, was an interesting individual of the promoter species. Adroit with his patrons and violent with his opponents, he had his way until he was carried down with the crash and even then he defied the facts, still insisting that his railroad was a potential gold mine. He was the hero of an interesting Lincoln story. Hogg told me that in his younger days in Illinois he had once engaged a rig to take him to Springfield from a nearby town. The landlord of the inn where he was stopping told him that one of the guests, a lawyer, wanted to go to Springfield but could find no conveyance. "Would Hogg take him?" Hogg agreed, and they drove to Springfield together — he and Abraham Lincoln. On arriving at Springfield Lincoln thanked Hogg and said, "If I can ever do anything for you, let me know." Some years later in the early days of the Civil War, Hogg, who was an ardent sympathizer with the Confederates, was arrested in Baltimore for hauling down a Union flag and was put in jail in Washington. He insisted upon seeing the President and finally succeeded in having his card taken to the White House. Mr. Lincoln sent for him and asked him "what scrape he was in" and what he wanted. Hogg said with passionate emphasis, "I want to go

South." "What for?" said Lincoln. Said Hogg, "I want to save my country." Lincoln turned to his desk and wrote on a card addressed to the commander of the defenses of Washington: "Pass the bearer T. Egenton Hogg through the lines. He is going to save his country. A. Lincoln."[2]

In connection with this railroad matter I had my first opportunity to see the far West and I made the most of it, visiting Portland, Tacoma and Seattle, seeing the great pine forests of Oregon as I went over the projected line of the railroad and journeying by the Siskiyou pass to San Francisco. The communities I visited were in the depths of the depression. There was no market for the best properties. Lawyers in Washington and Oregon who had gone to new settlements with the brightest prospects found themselves in a wretched plight. It was a dark outlook and one would have been bold indeed to have prophesied the prosperity which awaited the Northwest in the coming years.

On my return to New York, I plunged into the office work. There had been changes in personnel. Arthur C. Rounds [1862–1928], a graduate of Amherst and of the Harvard Law School — with a keen mind and thoroughly trained — had joined the staff shortly before I went to Ithaca and was now one of the strong pillars of the firm. Randell J[ames] Le Boeuf [1870–1939],[3] had become managing clerk on his graduation from the Cornell Law School in 1892, and when I returned to practice I brought to the office George W. Schurman [1867–1931], a brother of President Schurman, who had been one of my graduate students. I had been impressed with his special aptitude for legal work, an impression which was more than justified by his future career. With him, together with Rounds, it was my privilege to be associated for many years.

During the period 1894 to 1904 I was a hard working lawyer in private practice. The bar felt the effect of the depression of 1893 (which continued for a considerable time thereafter) but it did not diminish the volume of

[2]I have recently come across the sequel to this story. It appears that Hogg in his effort "to save his country" engineered a scheme to seize a merchant vessel in the Port of Panama for the purpose of converting her into a Confederate cruiser. He was caught, tried by a Military Commission on May 22, 1865, convicted, and sentenced to be hanged. The reviewing military authority affirmed the conviction but commuted the sentence to imprisonment for life. Department of the Pacific, G.O. No. 52, June 27, 1865. This appears in a footnote in the recent opinion of the Supreme Court in the saboteurs' case, Ex parte Quirin [317 U.S. 1, 32, n. 10 (1942)], decided October 29, 1942.

Following this up, I have found that Hogg was released by order of President Johnson, dated May 3, 1866. See volume entitled *War of the Rebellion. Official Records of the Union and Confederate Armies*, Series II, Vol. VIII, Prisoners of War, etc., Serial No. 121, p. 905. In that order Hogg is described as Thomas E. Hogg, but I find from "Archives" that his middle name was Egenton and there is no doubt that he was the Thomas Egenton Hogg who promoted the railroad to which I have referred in the text. He was an ambitious and daring character.

[3]He soon began practice in Albany and was highly successful. During my term as Governor I appointed him Justice of the Supreme Court to fill a vacancy. [Subsequently, he was elected to a fourteen year term in his own right.]

work in our office. Fees were necessarily lower than in more prosperous times and were not always easily collected. There was a general revival of legal business in the latter part of the nineties and, at that time and in the succeeding years, many lawyers made large fortunes in connection with the corporate organizations and mergers which were incident to industrial and commercial expansion. Our firm did not have that sort of work, but its business of the ordinary professional type did increase in importance. Throughout the entire period I am describing, apart from the usual office practice, I had a great deal of court work, trying both jury and equity cases. Many of these did not reach appellate courts but I was quite busy in the latter and appeared in a number of cases in the New York Court of Appeals.[4] Favorable comments by judges upon my work, as I was informed, brought me clients who were involved in serious controversies and hotly contested and difficult litigation. One of these clients was

[4]American Sugar Ref. Co. v. Fancher, 145 N.Y. 552, [40 N.E. 206] (1895), *rev'g* 81 Hun. (Sup. Ct.) 56, 30 N.Y.S. 482 (1st Dep't 1894); Robinson v. Passavant, 147 N.Y. 714 [42 N.E. 725 (1895), *aff'g* 73 Hun. (Sup. Ct.) 138, 26 N.Y.S. 128 (1st Dep't 1893)]; Todd v. Gamble, 148 N.Y. 382, [42 N.E. 982 (1896), *aff'g* 74 Hun. (Sup. Ct.) 569, 26 N.Y.S. 662 (1st Dep't 1893)]; Sickles v. Herold, 149 N.Y. 332 [43 N.E. 852 (1896), *modifying* 15 Misc. 116, 36 N.Y.S. 488 (C.P. Gen. T.), *aff'g* 11 Misc. 583, 32 N.Y.S. 1083 (C.P. 1895)]; Baily v. Hornthal, 154 N.Y. 648 [49 N.E. 56] (1898)[*aff'g* 1 App. Div. 44, 36 N.Y.S. 1082 (1st Dep't 1896), *motion for new trial denied* 89 Hun. (Sup. Ct.) 514, 35 N.Y.S. 437 (1st Dep't 1895)]; Stokes v. Stokes, 155 N.Y. 581 [50 N.E. 342 (1898), *aff'g* 11 Misc. 716, 34 N.Y.S. 1149 (Super. Ct. 1895)]. (James C. Carter made the argument [in the Court of Appeals]; I wrote the brief.) Jacquin v. Boutard, 157 N.Y. 686 [51 N.E. 1091] (1898) *aff'g mem.* 89 Hun. (Sup. Ct.) 437, 35 N.Y.S. 496 (1st Dep't 1895)]; Talcott v. Wabash R.R., 159 N.Y. 461 [54 N.E. 1 (1899), *rev'g* 89 Hun. (Sup. Ct.) 492, 35 N.Y.S. 574 (1st Dep't 1895)]; New York Life Ins. Co. v. Viele, 161 N.Y. 11, [55 N.E. 311 (1899), *aff'g* 22 App. Div. 80 47 N.Y.S. 841 (1st Dep't 1897)]; Blanchard v. Jefferson, 162 N.Y. 630, [57 N.E. 1104 (1900), *aff'g* 13 App. Div. 314, 43 N.Y.S. 512 (1st Dep't 1897)], Stokes v. Polley, 164 N.Y. 266 [58 N.E. 133 (1900), *rev'g* 30 App. Div. 550, 52, N.Y.S. 406 (1st Dep't 1898)]; Young v. Farwell, 165 N.Y. 341 [59 N.E. 143 (1901) *aff'g* 30 App. Div. 489, 52 N.Y.S. 283 (1st Dep't 1898)]; Schumacher v. New York, 166 N.Y. 103, [59 N.E. 773 (1901), *aff'g* 40 App. Div. 320, 57 N.Y.S. 968 (1st Dep't 1899)]; Stokes v. Hoffman House, 167 N.Y. 554 [60 N.E. 667 (1901), *aff'g* 46 App. Div. 120, 61 N.Y.S. 821 (1st Dep't 1900)]; In re Hart, 168 N.Y. 640 [61 N.E. 1130 (1901), *aff'g* 61 App. Div. 587, 70 N.Y.S. 933 (1st Dep't 1901), *aff'g* 33 Misc. 12, 67 N.Y.S. 1123 (Sur. Ct. 1900)]; Ives v. Ellis, 169 N.Y. 85 [62 N.E. 138 (1901), *rev'g* 50 App. Div. 399, 64 N.Y.S. 147 (1st Dep't 1900)]; Richardson v. Hinck, 169 N.Y. 588 [62 N.E. 1100 (1901), *aff'g mem.* 48 App. Div. 531, 6 N.Y.S. 1073 (2nd Dep't 1900)]; Stokes v. Stokes, 172 N.Y. 327, [65 N.E. 176 (1902), *rev'g* 49 App. Div. 302, 63 N.Y.S. 887 (1st Dep't 1900), *rev'g* 28 Misc. 58, 59 N.Y.S. 801 (Sup. Ct. 1899)]. (John G. Milburn made the argument; I wrote the brief); Hoffman House v. Foote, 172 N.Y. 348 [65 N.E. 169 (1902), *rev'g* 50 App. Div. 163, 63 N.Y.S. 784 (1st Dep't 1900)]; Levy v. Passavant, 175 N.Y. 482 [67 N.E. 1084 (1903), *aff'g* 67 App. Div. 619, 73 N.Y.S. 1139 (1st Dep't 1901)]; Robinson v. New York & T.S.S. Co., 177 N.Y. 565, [69 N.E. 1130 (1904), *aff'g mem.* 75 App. Div. 431, 78 N.Y.S. 359 (1st Dep't), *aff'g* 36 Misc. 705, 74 N.Y.S. 384 (Sup. Ct. 1902)]; Hendricks v. Hendricks, 177 N.Y. 402 [69 N.E. 736 (1904), *rev'g* 78 App. Div. 212, 79 N.Y.S. 516 (1st Dep't 1903)]; Young v. Valentine, 177 N.Y. 347 [69 N.E. 643 (1904), *aff'g* 78 App. Div. 633, 79 N.Y.S. 536 (1st Dep't 1903)]; Dunn v. National Surety Co., 178 N.Y. 552, [70 N.E. 1098 (1904) *aff'g* 80 App. Div. 605, 80 N.Y.S. 744 (1st Dep't 1903)]; National Broadway Bank v. Sampson, 179 N.Y. 213, [71 N.E. 766 (1904), *aff'g* 85 App. Div. 320, 83 N.Y.S. 426 (1st Dep't 1903)]; People ex rel. Rosenberg v. German Housewives' Assn., 179 N.Y. 523 [71 N.E. 1138 (1904), *aff'g mem.* 83 App. Div. 642, 82 N.Y.S. 1111 (1st Dep't 1903)].

Edward S. Stokes who was in a bitter legal fight with his cousin, W. E. D. Stokes [1853–1920], and also had many troubles in connection with his ownership and disposition of the Hoffman House. The only redeeming feature of this relation, which I found highly disagreeable in other respects, was that it brought me for a time into close association with James C. Carter, who by virtue of his legal scholarship, his masterly forensic arguments, and his public spirit, was considered the leader of the American bar. His only rival in that leadership was Joseph H. Choate, whose never failing humor, adroitness and brilliant advocacy gave him the greater popular acclaim. James C. Carter had been counsel for Edward S. Stokes and I was retained to act as his junior in *Stokes v. Stokes*, which I did by writing the brief in the Court of Appeals, and drafting papers in subsequent proceedings.[5] I recall Mr. Carter's earnest advice. While I did not take part in the argument in the Court of Appeals, Mr. Carter asked me to accompany him to Albany. The night before the argument, as we were talking together in the hotel lobby, I excused myself saying that I would like to make a memorandum on certain points that we had been considering. That led to a discussion of night work, and especially of the inadvisability of hard work on the night before an argument. Mr. Carter referred to an incident, many years before, in a case in which he had been junior to Charles O'Conor. I think he said it was one of the Jumel will cases.[6] Mr. Carter was to sum up before the jury and the Judge announced that he would give each side a limited time for that purpose. As Mr.

I have not taken the trouble to look up the citations of cases in which I appeared in the lower courts.

I also was permitted by courtesy to appear as counsel in the New Jersey courts and I tried a jury case for a New York client and argued the appeal in the Court of Errors and Appeals, Gerli v. Poidebard Silk Mfg. Co. [57 N.J.L. 432, 31 A. 401 (Ct. Err. & App. 1895)].

[5]Stokes v. Stokes, 155 N.Y. 581 [50 N.E. 342 (1898), *aff'g* 11 Misc. 716, 34 N.Y.S. 1149 (Super. Ct. 1895)]. I acted for Stokes in other litigation. See cases cited in list, Note 4, [above, Stokes v. Polley, Stokes v. Hoffman House, Stokes v. Stokes, and Hoffman House v. Foote. The Court of Appeals upheld the lower court judgment against Hughes and Carter's client, Edward Stokes.]

[6][This refers to the more than twenty cases tried in various courts over a period of fifteen years to determine the distribution of the estate left by Madame Eliza Bowen Jumel. This lady, a widow of Stephen Jumel, a rich New York wine merchant who came from Haiti, married Aaron Burr after her husband died in 1832. She began life in poverty and rose to social eminence and great wealth. The Jumel Mansion is one of the historic sites in New York City. Mrs. Jumel's colorful career is described in William Cary Duncan, *The Amazing Madame Jumel* (New York, Frederick A. Stokes, 1935). The bitter litigation among her heirs, legitimate and illegitimate, is in the Appendix to Duncan's book, pp. 303–314. See also Robert T. Swaine, *The Cravath Firm and Its Predecessors, 1819–1947*, 2 vols. (New York, privately printed, 1946), I, 292–293; Bowen v. Chase, 3 Fed. Cas. 1046 (No. 1,720) (C.C.S.D.N.Y. 1870), *aff'd*, 98 U.S. 254 (1878). Carter (1827–1905) and O'Conor (1804–1884) represented Nelson Chase, Madame Jumel's stepson. They took the case on speculation and were awarded $100,000 and $75,000, respectively, by the Court.]

Carter's notes were very elaborate, he stayed up until four o'clock in the morning to condense his argument so as to fit the time allowed. He went to court the next morning and within fifteen minutes after he began his argument he lost his train of thought and found it impossible to continue. He was assisted from the court room and did not enter a court again for a long period. Mr. O'Conor stepped into the breach and summed up the case. I remember how emphatic Mr. Carter was in saying, "Hughes, never work the night before an argument." I must confess that I thought this advice a counsel of perfection and for many years I put in my hardest licks at night in preparation for trials and arguments. But finally I learned that it was much better when under severe pressure to get up early in the morning — even at four or five o'clock — and that I could accomplish much more by working when I was refreshed and vigorous than by toiling late at night.

On another occasion, I brought to Mr. Carter the papers which I had prepared upon an important motion. He examined them with care and complimented me upon their accuracy, observing that a lawyer could not be too careful in preparing affidavits in interlocutory proceedings. He spoke of an incident — I think he said it was also in one of the Jumel will cases — when he had drawn affidavits on a motion which he had handled independently. After it was over, he brought the papers to Mr. O'Conor. The latter looked at them and to Mr. Carter's surprise burst into vehement criticism. Mr. O'Conor pointed out that Mr. Carter had drawn one of the affidavits so that it casually stated the relationship of one of the persons concerned. Mr. O'Conor exclaimed, "They never could have proved it." He had thought he could succeed on that question of pedigree.

The summer of 1898 brought an exceptionally interesting experience. I went to Brussels with Frederick R. Hazard (my college classmate) to advise him in connection with the negotiation of contracts between the Solvay Process Company of New York, of which Mr. Hazard was president, and the Solvay Company of Belgium. At the time of our graduation from college, Mr. Hazard's father, Rowland Hazard, a manufacturer in Rhode Island, who strongly believed in developing American industry, had conceived the idea of introducing into this country the Solvay process for the manufacture of sodium compounds. Frederick was sent abroad to serve an apprenticeship in the Solvay works and soon took the lead in the American enterprise at Syracuse, New York, which he conducted with distinguished success. We spent about two weeks in Brussels in friendly negotiations with the Solvay people, and then went over to London to meet Ludwig Mond [1839–1909] of Brunner, Mond & Company, the leader in the alkali industry in England. I also met Alfred [Moritz] Mond [1868–1930] (later Lord Melchett) then a young man already showing business ability of the highest order. I had made a close study of the Sherman Anti-Trust Act of 1890 and the Wilson-Gorman Act of 1894 and had advised clients as to the broad reach of their provisions. An important phase of the negotiations abroad was the endeavor to avoid conflict with the policy of the United States as declared in the anti-trust statutes.

On my return from this trip I was suddenly brought into important litigation over a bond issue of the City of New York, in which our clients contested the validity of the competing bid of another banking house because of its conditional character. This was a short but spirited contest in which I had the privilege of being associated with John F. Dillon.[7] He did not take part in the argument, but we retained him as counsel in view of his great experience and eminent reputation in connection with municipal bond issues. He approved and signed the brief which I had prepared under the greatest pressure in a long night of labor. He was so expert that he needed only a glance to know that the points were well taken and the important authorities cited. It was generally understood that Judge Dillon passed upon a host of municipal bond issues, with a routine fee of $1,000 for his approval in each case, that is, in the absence of questions of particular difficulty.

It would not be worthwhile to attempt anything like a comprehensive description of my various cases, and I allude only to a few which may be regarded as being of special interest. One of these was a suit against the *New York Sun*. In the Spanish War, the *Sun* had chartered a yacht to use as a dispatch boat for obtaining war news in Cuban waters. The charterer agreed to be responsible for all loss and damage and the charter fixed for that purpose the yacht's value. The yacht was lost by stranding and the owner brought suit in admiralty against the Sun Printing & Publishing Association, the alleged charterer. The libelant's attorney, George Zabriski [1852–1931], a distinguished New York lawyer, was taken sick before the trial and I was retained to try the case. The *Sun* insisted that its managing editor, Chester S. Lord, had no authority to bind the *Sun*. I went thoroughly into that question, showing by abundant evidence the broad authority exercised by the managing editor to get the news. There were several important legal questions. The case was tried before the eminent admiralty judge, Addison Brown, and resulted in a decree against the Sun Company. The Judge made a deduction of the charter hire ($10,000) from the agreed value of the yacht ($75,000) and awarded judgment for the

[7][John Forrest Dillon (1831–1914) began his career as an attorney and then judge in his native Iowa. He was United States Circuit Judge, 8th Judicial Circuit, 1869–1879; leaving the bench to teach at Columbia Law School, 1879–1886; and then entering practice in New York City.]

remainder.[8] Mr. Zabriskie, having recovered from his illness, handled the case on appeal, which reached the Supreme Court of the United States. The final decision upheld the authority of the managing editor upon the evidence which I had introduced and sustained all the legal points I had made upon the trial, so that the owner recovered the entire amount claimed.[9]

I had another unusual case about the same time (1899–1900) in which my opponent was Henry W. Taft.[10] A group of enterprising young businessmen of Detroit, of which Henry B. Joy[11] was the leader, undertook the establishment of a beet sugar factory at Caro, Michigan. The contract for its construction was made with a German concern with a bond for fulfillment executed by Speyer & Company of New York. The work was miserably botched by the contractor and I was retained to sue upon the bond. The suit involved every detail of the manufacture of beet sugar and the preparation for trial required a minute examination of the various parts of the factory with regard to what should have been done and what was actually done, and a comparison of the results reasonably expected and those obtained. The case was tried for many months before a retired Supreme Court Justice as referee, and his death made it necessary to take the evidence again. The suit was satisfactorily settled before judgment.

In another matter — I should say about the latter part of 1900 or early in 1901[12] — I came into intimate association with former Speaker Thomas B. Reed, who after his career in Congress had come to New York to practice law. He was retained as counsel in connection with the bankruptcy of a large concern doing business in Boston and having its domiciliary seat in Maine. As I was supposed to have some knowledge of bankruptcy law, being a lecturer on that subject, I was retained to assist Mr. Reed. We spent some days in Boston preparing for the hearing in

[8]Moore v. Sun Printing & Publishing Ass'n, 95 F. 485 [S.D.N.Y. 1899].

[Chester S. Lord (1850–1933) worked for the *Sun* from 1872 to 1913. He served first as regent (1894–1921) and then as chancellor (1921–1933) of the University of the State of New York.

[Addison Brown (1830–1913) was Judge of the U.S. District Court for Southern N.Y. from 1881 to 1901.]

[9]101 Fed. 591; [2d Cir. 1900]; 183 U.S. 642 [1902].

[10][Henry Waters Taft (1859–1945) was a partner in Cadwalader, Wickersham & Taft and a major figure at the New York bar for nearly half a century. He wrote several volumes of memoirs, including *A Century and a Half at the New York Bar* (New York, privately printed, 1938).]

[11][Henry Bourne Joy (1864–1936) was president of the Detroit Union Depot Company at the time. Subsequently, he was a director of the Federal Reserve Bank of Chicago, president of the Packard Motor Car Company, and director of the United States Chamber of Commerce.]

[12]I have no records at hand in Washington to enable me to fix the date.

consultation with Boston counsel, and during that time I shared with Mr. Reed the same hotel suite. Finally we journeyed to Portland with a considerable section of the Boston bar, including Moorfield Storey[13] and George Fred Williams.[14] Mr. Reed was a delightful companion, witty and gracious, but violent in his expressed dislike of President McKinley. In the Pullman drawing room on the way to Portland — in the presence of several lawyers — he roundly denounced the President, almost going so far as to attack his personal character. The bad taste of such an onslaught was apparent and it was difficult to resist the conclusion that it was animated by some degree of an unworthy jealousy. While I had a high opinion of Mr. Reed's ability, I felt that he was not as large-minded as I had supposed him to be.

In 1902, or thereabouts, I had my first contact with Joseph Pulitzer. He was greatly disturbed by the question of the enforceability of a contract which he had made with a paper company for the supply of newsprint for the *New York World.* The company was threatening to stop furnishing the newsprint and the question was whether there was a binding contract. He had submitted that question to several leading lawyers and their opinions were conflicting. I recall that he was especially critical of the reply of Mr. Hornblower that "he was inclined to the opinion," etc. Mr. Pulitzer did not think much of that expression. Justice Edward Patterson of the New York Supreme Court, as I was told, suggested that I should be consulted, and I was greatly surprised when one day the managing editor of the *World,* [Willam] Bradford Merrill [1861–1928], walked into my office and asked for my opinion. I gave it. Mr. Pulitzer then asked me to come to Lakewood for a consultation. I did so and had an extraordinary experience. When I entered his room, Mr. Pulitzer, who was almost blind, came very close to me and passed his hand over my face in order to get some idea of my features. He then put me through a rigorous examination on all the points involved in the contract. This took an hour or so and then, as he left me, he called a stenographer and asked me to dictate what I had said. I was invited to stay to luncheon, where he sat surrounded by his secretaries and representatives of the *World.* He called upon his secre-

[13][Moorfield Storey (1845–1929), one of the last of the Boston "goo goos," was a founder and one-time president of the Anti-Imperialist League, the National Association for the Advancement of Colored People, and other reform organizations. During his career he was president of the American Bar Association, the Massachusetts Bar Association, and the Bar Association of the City of Boston. For many years, he was an overseer of Harvard College. See Mark A. DeWolfe Howe, *Portrait of an Independent, Moorfield Storey 1845–1929* (Boston, Houghton Mifflin Co., 1932).]

[14][George Fred Williams (1852–1932) was a member of the Massachusetts House of Representatives, 1889–1891, and the United States House of Representatives, 1891–1893. He served briefly as Minister to Greece, 1913–1914, and for many years was editor of the Annual Digest of the United States.]

taries for all sorts of reports and I thought that everything important in the whole world was discussed. One would have supposed that Mr. Pulitzer was sitting as the judge of all the earth, and I was vastly entertained by the way in which this man, so physically dependent, dominated all by his intellectual power. After a rest following the luncheon, he asked me to drive with him and discussed his will. I did not see him again, but from time to time his representatives brought me questions for opinions and I drafted contracts for the *World*. When I entered upon the legislative investigations, in 1905, and especially in connection with the insurance inquiry, Mr. Pulitzer was my strong supporter, although at times his editorial demands were somewhat embarrassing in their insistence. I did not, however, permit them to deflect me from what I considered my necessary course in keeping the inquiry within its proper bounds.

The *World* gave me energetic support in my campaigns for Governor, and Mr. Pulitzer paid me the compliment of naming me in a codicil to his will as one of the trustees of the stock of the Press Publishing Company, which controlled the *World*.[15] When I was appointed Associate Justice of the United States Supreme Court, in 1910, I informed Mr. Pulitzer that I could not serve as trustee, as I did not see how it would be compatible with my position as Justice of the Supreme Court to engage in the direction of the policies of the *World*. Mr. Pulitzer strongly objected to the withdrawal of my name, and on his death, in October 1911, I found that I was still named as one of the trustees and also that Mr. Pulitzer had provided that I should receive a fee of $100,000 for my service in that capacity, which was twice the amount he fixed for the other trustees. I was still of the view that I should not accept the appointment and I at once renounced it.

Another interesting professional connection in the early nineteen-hundreds, which I may mention as indicating the variety of my cases, was with David Belasco [1854–1931]. I represented him in successful opposition to an effort to enjoin him from producing "The Music Master" with David Warfield, and I was consulted by him from time to time in other matters.

Early in 1904, I was counsel in a case in the New York Court of Appeals in which my opponent was former Governor David B. Hill.[16] In an adroit oral argument, Governor Hill went out of his way to make one of the most barefaced attempts to flatter the court, some of the judges being his

[15]James Wyman Barrett, *Joseph Pulitzer and His World* [New York, Vanguard Press, 1941], pp. 203 and 292.

[16]Young v. Valentine, 177 N.Y. 347 [69 N.E. 643 (1904) (note 4, above). David B. Hill (1843–1910), prominent in the New York Democratic Party since 1868, was governor for three terms, 1885–1891, and then a United States Senator, 1891–1897.]

intimate friends, that I have ever witnessed. In illustrating one of his points, Governor Hill spoke of the characteristics of the style of the opinions of the judges then sitting in the court, complimenting each of them in turn rather profusely. I think this must have disgusted the judges. Anyway, I won the case.[17]

It was in 1903–1904 that I was retained to prepare an opinion on the validity of the charter of a railroad company seeking a local franchise.[18] The leading counsel was John G. Johnson,[19] the undisputed leader of the Pennsylvania bar (and by some considered the leader of the American bar), with whom Mr. Hornblower was associated. I prepared the opinion which was signed by Mr. Johnson, Mr. Hornblower and myself, and I made the argument upon the legal points involved before the local authorities.

In the latter part of 1904, James W. Alexander [1839–1915], president of the Equitable Life Assurance Society, in his controversy with James Hazen Hyde, retained a number of lawyers to assist him in an effort to mutualize the insurance company.[20] Bainbridge Colby was the regular counsel for

17[Between 1894 and 1904, Hughes argued 25 cases before the New York Court of Appeals. "These cases," Edwin McElwain wrote, "involved questions of contract law, sales, bills and notes, wills, evidence, and in general almost every phase of 'private' law . . . Fifteen were won and nine lost for an average of .625." "The Business of the Supreme Court as Conducted by Chief Hughes," *Harvard Law Review*, LXIII (1949), 8, n. 6.]

18The New York, Westchester & Boston Railway Company.

19[John G. Johnson (1841–1917) represented many of the principal corporations of the country in state and federal courts. He declined the offer of appointment to the United States Supreme Court tendered by Presidents Garfield and Cleveland and rejected President McKinley's offer of the attorney generalship.]

20[Beerits adds: "When Henry Baldwin Hyde, founder and president of the Equitable Life Assurance Society of the United States, died in 1899, he left his son, James Hazen Hyde, a youth of twenty-three, 'custodian of a billion dollars of life insurance, caretaker of the savings of six hundred thousand policy holders'; and young Hyde 'became, as symbolized by the vignette which his father had ordered to embellish the heading of policy contracts, "protector of the widow and orphan," to the number of three million; became autocrat over an organization, the fortunes of several thousand employees, and master of four hundred million dollars of assets with all their ramifications of power and prestige.' Young Hyde was an aesthetic dilettante with extravagant tastes. James W. Alexander, President of the Equitable, and trustee of the younger Hyde's estate until he should reach thirty, saw, in the influence of rival financiers over young Hyde, a great menace to the Equitable. Much concerned about the future of the company, he set about a movement to make Hyde surrender the control he enjoyed as owner of a majority of the stock, and to carry out the original purpose of the Equitable as stated in a clause in its charter — namely, that it be mutualized . . .

["Alexander's effort was successful, and young Hyde, after much public humiliation, sold his stock for $2,500,000, and moved to Paris, whence he never returned.

["Mr. Hughes was very busy on this matter from December 1904 until March 1905. The important thing in the whole episode, as far as it concerns him, is the fact that he was chosen as counsel with such eminent members of the bar. It is very significant of his professional standing at the time that he was brought into this, for there were no personal relations that influenced his being retained." "The Gas and Insurance Investiga-

the Equitable, and William D. Guthrie,[21] William N. Cohen,[22] Adrian H[offman] Joline,[23] William B. Hornblower, and myself, were retained as special counsel to aid Mr. Alexander. This effort required much study, preparation of opinions and constant consultations as to advisable steps. I was engaged in it from December 1904 to March 1905 when I gave up that retainer on becoming counsel for the legislative committee appointed to conduct the inquiry into the affairs of the corporations supplying gas in New York City. With that employment I entered upon a new career.

During this period of professional activity (1894–1905) I did not have the privilege of arguing cases in the Supreme Court of the United States. But when I virtually left general practice for the legislative investigations, I had three cases which were on their way to the Supreme Court and which I had expected to argue.[24] They were reached in the Supreme Court when I was Governor and of course I took no part in them at that time.

So far as my professional engagements permitted, I was active in Bar Association affairs. As a representative of the American Bar Association, I attended a meeting of the Montreal Bar Association and spoke at its banquet.[25] This gave me the opportunity to form the acquaintance of leading Montreal lawyers and several Canadian judges.

---

tions," pp. 2–3. The quotation in Beerits' Memorandum is taken from Mark Sullivan, *Our Times: The United States, 1900–1925*, 6 vols. (New York, Charles Scribner's Sons, 1926–1935), III, p. 30. For further information on the struggle for control of the Equitable, see R. Carlyle Buley, *The Equitable Life Assurance Society of the United States, 1859–1964*, 2 vols. (New York, Appleton-Century-Crofts, 1967), I, 539–699.]

21[William D. Guthrie (1859–1935) argued the income tax, California irrigation, Illinois inheritance tax, oleomargarine, Kansas City stockyards, and the Oregon school law cases in the United States Supreme Court. He taught at the Columbia Law School from 1909 to 1922.]

22[William Nathan Cohen (1857–1938) was a justice of the Supreme Court of New York, 1897–1898. During World War I, he was chairman of the Draft Board and later chairman of the Ocean Advisory Commission of the United States Shipping Board which sat as a court to determine the compensation to be made to owners of vessels requisitioned by the United States Government.]

23[Adrian Hoffman Joline (1850–1912) was the director of numerous corporations and senior member of the firm Joline, Larkin, and Rathbone. He was perhaps known more widely as a bibliophile and was the author of *Diversions of a Book Lover* (1903), *At the Library Table* (1909), etc.]

24I was counsel in the case of White-Smith Music Publishing v. Apollo Company [139 Fed. 427 (C.C.S.D.N.Y. 1905), *aff'd*, 147 F. 226 (2nd Cir. 1906), *aff'd*, 209 U.S. 1 (1908)], involving the question whether perforated records of musical compositions for mechanical players were "copies" within the protection of the Copyright Law, and I had appealed to the Supreme Court from the decision of the Circuit Court of Appeals. See 139 Fed. 427; 147 Fed. 226; 209 U.S. 1. I had also been retained by Edward R. Finch (later Judge of the New York Court of Appeals) to argue the appeal to the Supreme Court in New York ex rel. Silz v. Hesterberg [211 U.S. 31 (1908)], presenting the question of the constitutional validity of certain provisions of the New York Game Law. See 211 U.S. 31. There was also an office bankruptcy case which was on its way to final decision in the Supreme Court; I do not recall the names of the parties.

25I think this was in 1895 or 1896.

In 1898, I was appointed a member of a special committee of the New York State Bar Association to report upon the revision of the Code of Civil Procedure. The committee submitted its report at the annual meeting of 1899.[26] We emphasized the necessity for revision and stated the objects to be accomplished. It was many years before these objects were appreciably attained but it may be worthwhile to state them as they appeared to us over forty years ago. They were said to be: (1) to simplify the practice so as to render it less technical and cumbersome, and more flexible; (2) to separate procedure from details relating to court officers by eliminating from the Code what might be termed administrative law; (3) to distinguish between such matters of procedure as relate to jurisdiction and the like, and the details of general practice, by placing the former in a statute and leaving the latter to be provided by rules of court; (4) to place the various provisions of substantive law which have crept into the Code in their proper positions in the statutes relating to cognate topics; and (5) to take such action as should avoid the constant changes in procedure and amendments from year to year by legislative action. We made more specific recommendations with respect to several matters and appended to the report illustrative Articles.[27]

At the annual meeting of the Association, in January 1905, I read a paper on "Arrest and Imprisonment on Civil Process."[28] I took the position that the existing law of New York on this subject was unsound in principle; that the remedy it afforded was of slight value; that while it was ordinarily ineffective as a remedy for the *bona fide* enforcement of just demands, it was easily made a means of extortion and oppression in the case of the ignorant and friendless poor and was a ready instrument of blackmail. I gave a number of illustrations.

From 1898 to 1900, I was a member of the Committee on Admissions of the Association of the Bar of the City of New York, and in 1905 I was elected a member of the Executive Committee of that Association to serve from 1906 to 1908.

There were several changes in my firm. About 1896, Frederic R. Kellogg left the firm to form another connection and Edward F. Dwight took his place. The firm name became Carter, Hughes & Dwight. In 1901, Mr. Dwight was stricken with a fatal illness, and he died in 1903. George W. Schurman had left the office to become an Assistant District Attorney under William Travers Jerome, and after Mr. Dwight became incapacitated, Mr. Schurman returned to us and with Arthur C. Rounds we formed the firm of Carter, Hughes, Rounds & Schurman. My senior

[26]New York State Bar Association, *Annual Report*, XXII (1899), pp. 170–193.
[27]*Ibid.*, pp. 194–251.
[28]*Ibid.*, XXVIII (1905), pp. 151–181.

partner and father-in-law, Walter S. Carter, died in June 1904,[29] and the business was continued under the firm name of Hughes, Rounds & Schurman until I retired, at the end of 1906, on my election as Governor.

During the period covered by this [chapter], I had varied interests apart from my vocation. I was active in the affairs of Brown University. I served as president of the New York Alumni Association and became a member of the Board of Trustees of the Corporation of the University. In the mid-nineties I spoke at the mid-winter banquet of the alumni in Providence (at which I had the good fortune to meet President Eliot of Harvard) and also at the banquet of the New England Association in Boston.

When my college friend William H. P. Faunce became pastor of the Fifth Avenue Baptist Church, about 1889, I became a member, and on my return to New York City from Ithaca I resumed an active relation with that Church. The name was somewhat misleading as the church building was not on Fifth Avenue but a short distance west on 46th Street, the explanation being that the Church had originally acquired lots on the Fifth Avenue corner but on account of economic difficulties (I think in the seventies) it had to dispose of these lots and build on the adjoining property. The name gave rise to an amusing incident at one of the meetings of the Baptist Association. Dr. Robert S. MacArthur, the popular pastor of the Calvary Baptist Church, had taken exception to the naming of churches after places and called attention to the misnomer in the case of the Fifth Avenue Baptist Church. The then pastor of the latter, Dr. Thomas Armitage, a noted divine, observed in reply, "The Fifth Avenue Baptist Church is a great deal nearer Fifth Avenue than the Calvary Church is to Calvary!" Soon after I rejoined the Church, Dr. Faunce asked me to take a Young Men's Class in the Sunday School. I had retained my early interest in the study of the Bible, although that interest now lay more in the critical and literary study than in the rather narrow routine of the Sunday School. While at Cornell, at the request of some of the seniors and graduate students, I had conducted a course on Sunday afternoons in the Old Testament prophets, with special reference to their place in the evolution of religious thought. I accepted Dr. Faunce's invitation with the understanding that instead of following the scheduled lessons I should be at liberty to take the class through the Gospels in the study of the teachings of Jesus. This I did for several years until the pressure of professional work made it necessary for me to keep my Sundays, so far as possible, for needed relaxation. The class went on under the

[29]See Memorial, New York State Bar Association, *Annual Report*, (1905), p. 453.

leadership of John D. Rockefeller, Jr. and became widely known as the Rockefeller Class.[30]

Meanwhile, I was elected a trustee of the Church and served in that capacity until 1905 or 1906. The elder John D. Rockefeller was President of the Board and took a deep interest in the affairs of the Church. He was unassuming in his bearing and particularly agreeable in his intercourse with the church members. He was always affable and occasionally asked me to join his golf parties at Pocantico Hills. But I had no business dealings with him or the companies in which he was interested. That is, aside from one matter which he asked me to take up on behalf of one of the active workers in the Church, a young woman who was having trouble with her partner in the operation of their private school. That service I performed *gratis*.[31] I mention this because of the assumption by the Hearst papers, when I was chosen as counsel in the Gas Inquiry, that as I was a trustee of the Church and an acquaintance of Mr. Rockefeller, I had business relations which would interfere with the impartial and adequate discharge of my duty, an assumption, as events proved, wholly without basis. I was always jealous of my independence, and while I did not look forward to public office or even public employment, when these came I was free to enter upon them not only without any conflicting obligation but without any sense of embarrassment because of church, social or business relations.

Mr. Rockefeller was very fond of a good story. I recall one that he enjoyed telling. A Swede in his employ, a recent immigrant, found his way into a Salvation Army meeting on the Bowery. One of the Army lassies sat down by him and said, "Wouldn't you like to work for Jesus?" The Swede stiffened and shook his head. She was not to be put off. "Why wouldn't you like to work for Jesus?" Again the Swede shook his head, saying, "I have a very good yob with Rockefeller."

My relation to the Church brought me into prominence in the Baptist Social Union of the City, and for two or three years I was its president and presided at its dinners. At one of these, I invited Booker Washington, the Negro leader in education, to be our principal guest, and to my surprise some of the good Baptists were critical of my action and especially of our escorting Mr. and Mrs. Washington to seats at the guest table. I

[30]See *Church Monthly, The Riverside Church*, N.Y., April 1944, pp. 110–112.

[31]In Mr. Beerits' Memorandum ("Gas and Insurance Investigations," pp. 5–6) it is said that Mr. Rockefeller made no offer to recompense me for my service, although I gave it at his request and made reports to him from time to time as to the progress of the case. That is true, but in fairness it should be added that I made no suggestion that I expected payment and I have no doubt that he thought it quite appropriate that I should give my services when I was so active in church work, and he felt no obligations in the matter.

thought this criticism ridiculous and ignored it. It, of course, amounted to nothing, save as it indicated an inveterate prejudice on the part of some who would be supposed to be least likely to entertain it.

While I maintained my Baptist connection, I had long since ceased to attach importance to what many regard as the distinctive tenets of the denomination. Rather, I cherished the noble tradition of the Baptists as protagonists in the struggle for religious liberty.[32] I wished to throw what influence I had to the support of Christian institutions, and so far as the dogmas of the creeds were concerned I saw nothing to be gained by leaving the Church in which I had been brought up and joining another denomination.

Throughout this period my political activities were very limited. I voted the Republican ticket in State and National elections and I attended primaries in my district. On Election Day I was assigned by the Republican Committee to take charge of legal work for the protection of those entitled to vote, the prevention of fraud, etc., in certain areas generally on the lower East side. I actively supported the local fusion campaigns and independent candidates for judicial office. I attended meetings of the Social Reform Club. In the latter part of the period I was frequently named as one of the vice presidents of political meetings. But I was not asked to make political speeches and made none. There were not wanting suggestions that I should be more active in politics, but I was too busy to do more unless it was in some worthwhile matter and that opportunity was not offered. I recall, however, that at one time a leader in the Republican County Committee asked me why I did not come more frequently to the Republican Club, observing that they might wish some day to make me a candidate for the New York Supreme Court. I said that I had no political ambition and did not wish that or any other office. I also remember that I was once called on the telephone by one who was very close to President Roosevelt and asked whether I would consider accepting a federal district judgeship. I immediately said "no," that, with my family obligations, at the salary then paid, I could not afford to take such a position.

While it sufficently appears that I was very busy in many ways, I was not brought into public notice and my name rarely appeared in the newspapers. I remember well — and it seemed very amusing in later years — remarking to my wife as we sat together in the evening looking at the papers, and noted the absence of my name in connection with an important matter in which my associates were mentioned, "My dear, you must know that I have a positive genius for privacy." I little thought how

[32]See my address, on April 22, 1922, on "Roger Williams," published in the volume of my addresses, *The Pathway of Peace* (New York, [Harper & Bros.,] 1925), p. 267.

soon that would change and that for thirty-seven years I should be under the spotlight of publicity.[33]

DIVERSIONS, EXERCISE AND VACATIONS

My wife and I were very fond of the theatre and whenever my work permitted we seized the opportunity to see a good show. There was no lack of performances of the first quality. Aside from the famous stars of the period, with their separate companies, there were stock companies, notably the Daly company with Ada Rehan, John Drew and George Lewis, and the Frohman company with Herbert Kelcey and Georgia Cayvan, whose productions were a never-failing delight. Musical comedies still had standards of decency, and such inimitable comedians as Francis Wilson, De Wolf Hopper, and Jefferson De Angelis, afforded the best of light entertainment. Occasionally we would go to the opera, though my wife and son went more frequently than I, availing themselves of the afternoon performances.

In the nineties, bicycling was the well-nigh universal diversion. On a pleasant evening the Boulevard (upper Broadway) would be crowded with hundreds of bicycles so that it was almost impossible to cross the street. My wife and I were very fond of bicycle trips and whenever possible we made long excursions on holidays. I recall that in one autumn I wheeled every morning, weather permitting, before breakfast, from our residence on West East Avenue to Grant's Tomb and back. But I found that this did not agree with me and I had to be content with our outings. In the late summer of 1899, I took up golf, and from that time on I seized every chance to play on a Saturday or holiday.[34] I was not a good player, but my zeal was boundless. It is well illustrated by the fact that on one Washington's birthday, as I remember, I played with red balls in the snow. It was not until 1901 that I began regular setting-up exercises, on arising in the morning.[35]

But I needed more than exercise to overcome the fits of depression

[33][In this connection, Beerits comments, "He was well known at the bar, especially with the junior members of the bar. During the three years in which he had conducted rapid fire quiz class at Columbia in the evenings, he had come in contact with five or six hundred young men who settled in New York to practice law. These men were approximately Mr. Hughes's age and had, for the most part, achieved a good standing at the bar. To the newspapers and the general public Mr. Hughes was not known, however, until his work in the gas investigations." "The Gas and Insurance Investigations," pp. 1–2.]

[34]At first I was a member of the Scarsdale Golf Club and the Englewood Golf Club. Later I joined the Nassau Country Club.

[35]I followed Swoboda's lessons. At first I took the full course, but after a time I made a modest selection which gave me what I needed in about ten minutes and these exercises I kept up until 1939.

which often followed exertions in difficult cases. A good deal of my professional work seemed to be unrequited drudgery and I needed periods of complete freedom, with joyous and uplifting experiences. These I got in frequent trips abroad.

It was in 1894 that I discovered Switzerland. I had had no real vacation since 1891, as I spent the summer of 1892 in Ithaca working on my courses and the summer of 1893 in the Oregon Railroad affair. The office and court work in the following year had pulled me down and it was evident that I should have a few weeks of freedom. Nothing would answer the purpose so well as a trip abroad. Mrs. Hughes could not go on account of the children but felt it advisable that I should get the benefit of an ocean voyage. So, while the little family was sojourning among the Connecticut hills, I took passage on a Dutch steamer for Boulogne. After a day in Paris, I left for Lausanne and I shall never forget the thrill as for the first time I caught a view of the Alps from the pass over the Jura. I spent thirteen days in the mountains — walking over the passes — and then went directly to Boulogne and sailed for home. I was gone a bare month, but no outing had ever done me so much good, a reinvigoration in body and spirit. It gave me what perhaps has been my only hobby, walking in the mountains. Of course, I was never a mountaineer but I did all that a sedentary man, with a young family dependent upon him, should attempt.[36]

In the following winter, I happened upon Amelia Edwards' book *Untrodden Peaks and Unfrequented Valleys* and was filled with the desire to visit the Dolomites.[37] This I did in the summer of 1895, spending a brief holiday there and in the Engadine.[38]

[36]I recall how I spent the thirteen days. From Lausanne, I went by the Lake to Geneva and then to Chamonix. On the diligence from Cluses where the train journey ended at that time, I fell in with a young Londoner who proved to be a good companion. When we arrived at Chamonix the clouds overhung the mountains and this was so on the next day, but nevertheless we walked up to Montanvert, crossed the Mer de Glace, and then walked up on the other side of the Valley to Elègére in a thick fog. We remained at a little inn there overnight. At five o'clock the following morning the sky was beautifully clear and I had from that point of vantage my first view of the Mont Blanc range in the sunshine. We immediately returned to the valley and set out for Martigny, walking over the Col de Balme. There I left my friend and, taking the train to Leuk, I proceeded on foot over the Gemmi pass to Kandersteg. From there I proceeded by diligence to Spiez and by boats to Interlaken and Matringen. Thence I walked over the Grimsel pass (in a snowstorm) to the Rhone Glacier. I then went by diligence over the Furka pass to Andermatt and Goeschenen and on to Altdorf and Fluelen; thence by the Lake to Lucerne, and then by train via Basel to Boulogne. Thirteen glorious days!

[37][Amelia Edwards, *Untrodden Peaks and Unfrequented Valleys: A Midsummer Ramble in the Dolomites* (London, Longmans, Green & Co., 1873).]

[38]I went through Germany to Innsbruck and Cortina d'Ampezzo. From Cortina I walked over the passes to Caprile, Canazei, St. Ulrich and Botzen (now Bolcano). Thence I proceeded to Merano; and then by diligence over the Stelvio pass to Bormio and Tirano; and over the Bernina pass to Pontresina in the Engadine, where I had many delightful excursions.

Naturally, I was most anxious to have my wife enjoy these beautiful scenes and in 1896 we were able to go together, as we arranged to leave our children with my parents at a well-kept farm in Chesham, New Hampshire, where my wife had stayed the year before. As it was Mrs. Hughes's first trip abroad, we went by way of Liverpool to London and then to Paris. After a few days there, we proceeded to Lausanne and Geneva; thence to Chamonix, Zermatt, the Rhone Glacier, Interlaken, Lucerne and back to Paris.[39] In 1897, I went to the Alps once more, but alone, making my headquarters in Pontresina which I liked best of all, because of the high altitude of the valley and the many delightful excursions that could easily be taken in the vicinity.[40] In 1898, there was no chance of another trip abroad, and we took a cottage at Twilight Park in the Catskills. This was of such easy access that I could count on weekends with my family, to which we were expecting an addition before the end of the summer. That event happened on August 11th — much earlier than we expected — and took me off guard. I had run up to Canada for a few days and learned at Quebec of the new arrival. I hurried to Twilight Park to make the acquaintance of my daughter Catherine, but had hardly done so when I was summoned to New York to handle the litigation over the City bond issue to which I have referred. That was soon over, as it was an injunction suit, swiftly begun and terminated. But I had no sooner returned to my family than I was asked by Mr. Hazard to go with him to Belgium for the Solvay negotiations. We were gone just thirty days — the month of September — and on my return the regular office work was resumed.

We went to Twilight Park for the summer of 1899. In June, I had to go to London to take depositions in a will case. When those were finished, I made another trip to Switzerland. I went from London direct to Geneva and then to Fayet and St. Gervais to make the tour on the southern side of Mont Blanc. I walked over the Col du Four and the Col du Bonhomme, passed through L'Alleé Blanche, directly below the great massive of Mont Blanc, and by the Lac de Combal to Courmayeur, which lies across the Mont Blanc range from Chamonix. I then proceeded to Aosta and Valtournanche. From there I walked over the Theodule pass to Zermatt. On the way I stopped at the Alpine hut on the side of the Theodule Glacier and from there made the ascent of the Breithorn — for me a memorable climb. Starting about two-thirty in the morning, my guide and I crossed the glacier under a starlit sky. We reached the summit in time to see the glorious sunshine — which already illuminated the world of peaks — gradually

[39]From the Riffelalp above Zermatt we walked to the Gorner Grat (there was no railway at that time), and on the way to the Rhone Glacier we climbed the Eggishorn. While at Interlaken we visited Mürren and Grinderwald.

[40]From Pontresina I went over the Maloja pass to Italy, visiting the Italian Lakes.

fill the valleys. We returned to the Alpine hut and then had a tiresome walk to Zermatt. Leaving Zermatt, I went across the Rhone Valley and walked up on the other side to Belalp near the Aletsch Glacier where Tyndall had his villa. From Belalp there were interesting excursions on the glacier. Then I returned to the Rhone Valley and went up to Sass Fée. That was the end of what was perhaps my best trip. I returned home early in August.[41]

In 1900, there was no opportunity for a long outing. Our family was settled for the summer at Mt. Menagha near Ellenville (in Ulster County, New York) and my wife and I had a two weeks' holiday on the Maine coast. In 1901, I was able again to go to Europe, and as our children were left in the care of my parents at Mt. Menagha, my wife and I made the trip together. This time we sailed to Bremen and visited Hamburg, Berlin, Dresden, Prague and Vienna. We then made our way via Salzburg to Munich and Innsbruck, and thence to Thusis and the Engadine. From there we journeyed to the Italian Lakes and then had the thrill of our first visit to Venice. In 1902, I had the pleasure of taking my son to Europe for the first time. We visited London, Paris and Switzerland (Chamonix and Zermatt), saw something of Germany (especially Nuremburg) and Belgium, sailing home from Antwerp.[42]

In the summer of 1903, we turned to the delights of Maine. We took a camp on Moosehead Lake, on the western side about ten miles north of Kineo. We were near Williams Stream where we had good fishing even in mid-summer. Across the lake from our camp lay Northeast Carry (then much traveled by campers) which led to the beautiful west branch of the Penobscot River. I had the month of August with the family and my son and I made the most of it in our excursions. We visited Lobster Lake, climbing Spencer mountain. We had an excursion of two weeks on what was called the Allagash trip, going by canoes and carries via Chesuncook, Chamberlain, Eagle, Churchill and Umsaskis lakes and the Allagash river to Fort Kent. Returning by train to Norcross, we proceeded by canoes and carries to the foot of Mt. Katahdin. With the hope of fair weather, we started to climb the mountain and succeeded in reaching the summit, although we had to make the last part of the ascent in a driving rain. We then found our way back to our camp on Moosehead, rewarded and invigorated, despite a great deal of bad weather, by this intimate acquaintance with the Maine woods.

I had no chance for an outing in 1904. That was a hard summer. Mr.

[41]In the following month, we moved to No. 570 West End Avenue where we lived until I went to Albany.

[42]On our way to Germany we stopped at Strasbourg and had an unusual experience in ascending to the top of the spire of the Strasbourg Cathedral.

Carter died in June, and the reorganization of our firm kept me in New York, with only an occasional weekend with the family who in the early part of the summer were at Chocorua, New Hampshire, and in the latter part at Twilight Park in the Catskills.

Throughout this period of over eleven years of practice, I had no serious illness. In the winter I almost always had a severe cold and twice I had a mild attack of grippe. The latter kept me away from the office for only a few days, and I suppose that during the whole period I did not lose a total of two weeks on account of being confined to the house. I was still slight, but this was an advantage in the hours of exercise in the Alps. In the nineties, if on my return from Europe, having enjoyed to the full the pleasures of the table as well as the various excursions in the mountains, I weighed 140 pounds (with my clothes on) I thought it a substantial gain. It was not until 1901, when I began my regular morning exercises, that I steadily gained in weight. By 1903, I weighed 153 pounds (with my clothes); by 1905, 160 pounds; and by 1907, 165 pounds. I finally got to my present weight, 173 pounds (stripped, before breakfast) and that I have kept as my average weight (occasionally a little more or less) for over twenty years.

Our family also enjoyed good health during the period I am describing. My wife was always vigorous, a perfect helpmeet, attending most efficiently to all the demands of the household; an ideal mother, not only loving, but even-tempered, understanding and capable, guiding without friction the development of our children. She was the Queen of our home, which under her gentle sway was ever a place of rest and happiness.

Our children had the usual childish ailments but nothing serious. Our son entered the primary department of the Collegiate School (an old Foundation affiliated with the Dutch Reformed Church) on West 77th Street. He went straight through the entire course under excellent teachers and was ready for college at fifteen, entering Brown University in the fall of 1905. Our daughter Helen attended a Girls' School near our home (St. Agatha) and our daughter Catherine had a couple of years at the same school, until we removed to Albany at the end of 1906.

The Gas and Insurance
Chapter IX Investigations *1905–1906*

There is little that I can add to the Beerits' Memorandum.[1] The records of both investigations, and the reports which I prepared for the respective legislative committees, are in printed volumes.[2] The voluminous clippings as to the insurance investigation, in bound volumes, attest the close public attention which it received throughout the country.[3] There are also numerous magazine articles, relating to the insurance inquiry, and my part in it, in the *Fuller Collection.*[4]

I think that Judge William N. Cohen was the one who originally suggested to Governor Higgins that I should be selected as counsel for the Gas Committee. He was a prominent Republican, had served as Justice of the New York Supreme Court (by appointment to fill a vacancy) and had an intimate knowledge of my work at the bar. Many years before, when he was a member of the firm of Hoadly, Lauterbach & Johnson, of which George Hoadly (formerly Governor of Ohio) was the head and Cohen was the trial lawyer, I had crossed swords with him in a hotly contested litigation. I had succeeded in a creditors' suit against a client of Cohen's firm, and while Governor Hoadly argued the case in the Court of Appeals, Cohen bore the brunt of subsequent suits which I brought for other

[1]Beerits' Memorandum, "The Gas and Insurance Investigations," Hughes Papers. [Where appropriate, material from the Beerits Memorandum is used to supplement Hughes's account.]

[2]*Report of the Gas and Electric Light Investigation Committee* (Albany, 1905), and *Report of the Insurance Investigation* (Albany, 1906). [The report actually was issued in three parts: *Testimony Taken Before the Joint Committee of the Senate and Assembly of the State of New York To Investigate and Examine into the Business and Affairs of Life Insurance Companies Doing Business in the State of New York* (seven volumes); *Exhibits Accompanying the Testimony* . . . (two volumes); and *Report of the Joint Committee* . . . (Albany, Brandow Printing Company, 1906).]

[3][In the Hughes Papers.]

[4]In the New York Public Library.

creditors against the same defendant.[5] The law had been settled by the Court of Appeals, but with other plaintiffs there was a renewed and bitter controversy over the facts, involving the analysis of somewhat complicated accounts.

It was evident that the legislative inquiry, in order to lay a basis for a fair legislative rate for supplying gas in New York City, would require an examination of the financial setup of the companies, their practices, and all the factors entering into the cost of production. Judge Cohen strongly urged that I should be entrusted with that difficult duty, and it seems that others joined in the recommendation. I did not know of this intervention, and I was greatly surprised when Senator Frederick C. Stevens, the Chairman of the Joint Committee of the Legislature, called upon me and asked me to undertake the job. I demurred. I knew nothing of the gas business, I had little or no confidence in the integrity of legislative investigations, and I feared that, with the great financial interests involved, the investigation would be thwarted in some way and I should be in a position of apparent responsibility and debited with a conspicuous failure in a matter in which there was intense public interest. Senator Stevens was insistent. I found that, while he was active in politics, he had the reputation of being a man of independence and complete integrity. He had large means; as Job Hedges put it, he was "desperately solvent." He assured me that I should not be "called off" and would be allowed to make a thorough inquiry without political hindrance. That still left the question whether I was competent for such an undertaking, having had no experience in legislative investigations, I distrusted my capacity and I hated the idea of work where the public eye would be upon every step, with the newspapers keen on the scent for any political intriguing and the Hearst press ever ready to make sensational charges. I felt, however, that it would be cowardly to refuse; that there was a public service of importance to be rendered and that if I went at it with the single purpose of doing a thorough professional job, that atitude would be recognized and in some way I should get through. So I went ahead with what I found to be a task even more difficult than I had anticipated. But Senator Stevens was true to his promise and I was not hindered by political interference. I shall not comment on the result, which I leave to speak for itself.[6]

[5]Baily v. Hornthal, 154 N.Y. 648 (1898). ["Cohen was especially impressed by the Chief's ability to analyze the partnership's exceedingly complex accounts and then explain them in simple terms to court or jury." Edwin McElwain, "The Business of the Supreme Court as Conducted by Chief Justice Hughes," *Harvard Law Review*, LXIII (1949), 8, n. 7.]

[6][Beerits, "Gas and Insurance Investigations," pp. 4 and 8, says that Hughes at first refused Stevens' offer and that the latter left. "He soon came back again, however, and

As the Legislature had started the inquiry late in the session, there was an urgent demand for speed so that the hearings of the Committee were held virtually without interruption and the report was prepared under severe pressure. I spent several days at Albany in conference with members of the Legislature and then returned to my regular practice, to which meanwhile I had not been able to give any attention. I badly needed a holiday, but was unable to get away and my wife, with my son and two daughters, left for Europe in June without me. I joined them sometime later at Nuremberg. From there we went to Cortina, where I had delightful excursions, including a bicycle trip with my son to Belluno, on the way to Venice. From Cortina we drove to the Pusterthal and thence on the other side up the mountains to Heiligenblut, near the Gross-Glockner.

It was in that remote spot, and in the evening after a long day's trip to the Gross-Glockner glacier, that I was almost stunned by receiving a telegram asking me to become counsel for the Joint Legislative Committee, which was to investigate the life insurance companies. On account of my connection with President Alexander of the Equitable, in his controversy with Mr. Hyde, I did not feel at liberty to act. I was too far away to be sure of adequate cable facilities, so leaving Heiligenblut in the early hours of the morning, I made haste to get to Munich. I recall that as we were driving from Heiligenblut to the Pusterthal, my wife tried to draw my attention to the extraordinary beauty of the morning scene, but despite my love of the mountains I was too deep in thought of the terrific responsibility of trying to handle an insurance investigation to give heed to anything else. And when Mrs. Hughes chided me, saying that we might never see such a scene again, I exclaimed, "My dear, you don't know what this investigation would mean. It would be the most tremendous job in the United States." In answer to my telegrams, I received assurances from all concerned that I should be free to act without any restriction or em-

---

said that the more he thought about it, the more he thought that Mr. Hughes was the man to take charge of the investigation. He assured Mr. Hughes that he would be untrammeled in his conduct of the investigation." According to Beerits, Hughes then thought "more seriously" of the job and "finally told Senator Stevens that he would undertake the work upon the condition that it would be purely a professional matter for him, with no political influences involved. Senator Stevens agreed that he should undertake the work on this basis. When asked by newspaper men what led to Mr. Hughes's selection, Senator Stevens replied: 'It was purely a Diogenes search, and we found an honest man. Furthermore, I think it will be conceded that we obtained one of the most eminent as well as one of the most able attorneys.' " (Quotation taken from the *New York Journal*, March 24, 1905.) As to the report, Beerits says, "The report which Mr. Hughes submitted to the Legislature was considered a model, and was made the basis for much constructive legislation. It was followed by the creation of a commission to regulate gas and electric companies, and the fixing of an eight-cent rate for gas."]

barrassment.[7] So I at once arranged for passage home, and arriving about the middle of August, I set to work in preparing for the investigation, which began its public hearings early in September and continued them until December 30th. There was no time for adequate preparation. The *World* was hammering away and the Committee was impatient to have the public hearings begin.[8] There had been an inquiry by the Superintendent of Insurance directed at the Equitable controversy, but I realized that the dispute with Hyde was only a phase of a much broader situation and that the investigation must deal comprehensively with all the companies and with whatever abuses had grown up in the life insurance business. The newspaper representatives, particularly those of the *World*, had been busy, but I found that the information they had gave hardly any definite leads or clues of importance and that I must make my own plans and get the facts from testimony and corporate books and papers. The time for rumors and the sensational reporting of conjectures had passed, and now evidence must be produced and the actual situation fully ascertained in a responsible manner. I tried to formulate a general outline of procedure for my own guidance and I had subpoenas issued for records and books, and obtained transcripts of many accounts. But the public hearings had to be started with only a modicum of material, aside from what was contained in the annual published reports.

I chose as my general assistant, Matthew C. Fleming, an able lawyer (a graduate of Princeton of the Class of 1886), who had been one of my aides in the gas investigation, and for actuarial help, Miles Merander Dawson, who was in an independent position with considerable actuarial experience.[9] I found, however, that the Committee had chosen an associate counsel, James McKeen [1845?–1910]. He was a lawyer of integrity and excellent standing at the bar (considerably older than I), and was sup-

[7][Beerits' account, "Gas and Insurance Investigations," p. 13, is somewhat more detailed: "Mr. Hughes first replied that he wasn't free to accept, since he had been connected with the effort to dislodge Hyde from control of the Equitable. He received a reply saying that that fact offered no obstacle. He then called Armstrong to see Hornblower, Cravath, Alexander, and others in order to make sure that he would not be disqualified from taking charge of the investigation by reason of his connection with the Alexander case. He was assured, in reply, that he was in a perfectly free position to undertake the work. He cabled that it must be understood in advance that he was to have a perfectly free hand in conducting the investigation. Upon being informed that this condition was accepted, he agreed to take charge of the investigation."]

[8][To describe the muckraking campaign, Beerits, "Gas and Insurance Investigations," pp. 10–12, quotes Mark Sullivan, *Our Times: The United States, 1900–1925*, 6 vols. (New York, Charles Scribner's Sons, 1926–35), III, 49–51.]

[9][Matthew C. Fleming (1865–1946) was a member of Osborn, Fleming & Whittlesey and general counsel of the Phelps Dodge Corporation.]

[Miles Merander Dawson (1863—1942) wrote prolifically on the subject of life insurance. His works include: *The Business of Life Insurance; Elements of Life Insurance;* and *Workingmen's Insurance in Europe.*]

posed to have had some connection with the Mutual Life Insurance Company and to be familiar with insurance affairs. I learned that some of the Committee had desired him to be counsel and had agreed to my selection with the understanding that he would be associated with me. However, Senator William W. Armstrong, the Chairman of the Committee, advised me that I was expected to take full charge of the examination of witnesses, and this I did. But I found that it would be impossible to do this and to make the necessary preparation, so as to keep the hearings going, if I had continually to advise with Mr. McKeen. So I soon was playing a virtually lone hand, with Fleming who worked with me at home in the evenings. I recall in particular that when Emory McClintock [1840–1916], the well-known actuary of the Mutual, took the stand, Mr. McKeen asked to conduct his examination. I readily assented for I had no desire to monopolize the inquiry to the apparent disregard of my associate and had only deferred to the strongly expressed wishes of the Chairman of the Committee. After Mr. McClintock's examination had proceeded for some time, Senator Armstrong called me to the bench and said that the Committee wished me to take up the examination and thereafter to examine all witnesses. Mr. McKeen was advised of the Committee's desire and readily assented. I think in truth that considering the way in which the investigation was developing he was quite willing, if not glad, to have me take full responsibility.

The sensational disclosures which came out in the testimony were generally as much of a surprise to me as to others. I would plan for a day's work, but almost invariably something would soon be developed in the course of the examination of witnesses which would give a lead that had to be followed up at once, and in so doing new and important facts would be elicited. These revelations were headlined by the press and were very disquieting to the companies.[10] That disquiet had a certain reflection in the Committee itself. On one occasion, when a disclosure had political significance, the Committee asked me to meet them in the morning before

[10] [Beerits, "Gas and Insurance Investigations," pp. 14–15, says these revelations "resulted in a popular interest throughout the nation that, with the exception of presidential campaigns, has almost no parallel, in times of peace, in the history of our country." Mark Sullivan, *Our Times*, III, 54, describes Hughes's methods and the results they produced: "Without ever heckling a witness, permitting every sweating financier to make such explanation or excuse as he could improvise; without seeming to be a cross-examiner at all, as unemotionally as a teacher finding a mild enthusiasm in leading a child to concede the irrefutable verities of mathematics, with no violence of gesture or words, in a voice that was only saved by its virile timbre from being a monotone, Hughes by the sheer clarity and power of his mind made every newspaper reader understand what had gone on. As undramatic himself as an adding-machine, he brought out such a series of dramatic revelations as had the effect, on the public, of a tumbling cascade of sensations."]

the hearing, and one member complained that the Committee never knew in advance what would be the course of the examination. Would I not let them know so they could be prepared? I showed them how impossible this was. But some members were insistent, intimating that after all it was the Committee's investigation. I at once said that I understood that; that I was only their counsel; that as such I would receive their explicit instructions which I would obey or I would at once resign as counsel and tell the public the reason why. One of the Committee, Senator William J. Tully, walked over and took his position beside me, saying, "I am with Mr. Hughes." Others followed suit. I had no further trouble.

In accordance with precedent, the Committee did not allow counsel to appear for witnesses or cross-examine them. I felt that this put upon me added responsibility to see that the inquiry was conducted with absolute fairness. Almost all the witnesses were officers or important employees of the companies, and I was careful to give them the opportunity to make any pertinent statements they wished in explanation or defense. The phalanx of distinguished counsel for the companies were in the front row close to me and to the witnesses, and whenever counsel desired a question asked or an opportunity given for a particular explanation by witnesses, they let me know and I was glad to accede to their suggestions whenever these were relevant. Presidents and leading officers of the companies explained at length their attitudes and views. But there was no getting away from the facts.[11]

Beerits refers to the unhappy situation in which John A. McCall, President of the New York Life Insurance Company, found himself in being unable to make a satisfactory accounting for the disbursement of a large sum shown by a mysterious account contained in a special book (separate from the regular books of the company), the existence of which was ascertained in a hunt for the disposition of the avails of what were "non-ledger assets." [12]

[Beerits refers to a disbursement of $235,000 for which McCall could not account. He also mentions an item for $48,000 which, it turned out, had been a contribu-

[11][For a description of the investigation from the point of view of the counsel for the Equitable Life Assurance Society, see Robert T. Swaine, *The Cravath Firm and Its Predecessors, 1819–1947*, 2 vols. (New York, privately printed, 1946), I, 756–766. The background for the scandal and the investigations, from the industry viewpoint, is in R. Carlyle Buley, *The Equitable Life Assurance Society of the United States 1859–1964*, 2 vols. (New York, Appleton-Century-Crofts, 1967), I, 603–699. Other, less detailed accounts are Shepard B. Clough, *A Century of American Life Insurance: A History of the Mutual Life Insurance Company of New York, 1843–1943* (New York, Columbia University Press, 1946), chap. 12; and Marquis James, *The Metropolitan Life: A Study of Business Growth* (New York, The Viking Press, 1947), chap. 9.]

[12]The facts are detailed in the *Report* of the Committee, pp. 51, *et seq.* [Beerits, "Gas and Insurance Investigations," pp. 16–19.]

tion by the company, through George W. Perkins to Theodore Roosevelt's campaign fund.

["One of the most dramatic episodes of the entire investigation was the revelation of the New York Insurance Company's contribution to the Republican campaign fund.

["Mr. Hughes in the course of the investigation had uncovered many things indicating systematic corruption in Albany. He had great difficulty, however, in tracing down these facts. It was exceedingly difficult to determine just what the companies' disbursements were spent for. For example, the Mutual, in connection with the Equitable, maintained at Albany a house — promptly designated by newspapers as the "House of Mirth" — where their agents kept close watch upon the Legislature and exerted pressure to prevent the passage of bills unfavorable to the companies; and the disbursements for leasing this house were hidden by being placed under the accounts charged to stationery. Moreover, the companies placed some items under non-ledger assets, which were not admitted as assets in figuring the solvency of the companies; and they had a way of going into syndicates and underwritings that was very perplexing.

["In examining the accounts of the New York Life Insurance Company, Mr. Hughes came across some Erie stock that the company carried as a non-ledger asset. He could not find out what had happened to the money that was paid for this stock when the company sold it. He sought evidence on this point, and finally some men connected with the company produced a card which simply contained balancing items recording the sale of the stock, but did not explain the real problem as to what had been done with the money. In one corner of the card were the letters H.B.O.; they were relatively inconspicuous and ordinarily would have passed unnoticed. Mr. Hughes, however, asked what they meant, and was told they signified the Hanover Bank Office.

["When he found that the company had an office there, Mr. Hughes at once insisted upon seeing the books from that office. He was told that the books would be brought. All during the afternoon, however, the books did not arrive, and towards the end of the afternoon Mr. Hughes went to the Chairman of the Committee and said that he felt that he should make a public statement concerning the fact that the company had failed to submit for examination the books which he had requested. The Chairman suggested postponement and assured him that the books would be brought. Mr. Hughes said that he would wait until the following morning. That night it seemed that everyone of importance in the State had members of the investigating committee on the wire.

["The next morning members of the Committee asked him what he wanted in these books. He replied that he did not know just what he would want in them, but that he wanted to see the books. He said to the investigating committee that he was their counsel and he would take their instructions; or, if he felt that he could not comply with their instructions, he would resign and tell the public why he had resigned.

["Finally, the books were brought in. In examining them, Mr. Hughes found a disbursement of $235,000 that could not be accounted for. For information on this point, he called in John A. McCall, President of the New York Life Insurance Company. McCall was a former Superintendent of Insurance and a man highly respected by all, and when it became evident that he could not give an exculpatory explanation, the public felt a distinct shock. He made a most pathetic exhibition on the witness stand, and the whole episode led directly to his premature death.

["Near the end of the book that Mr. Hughes was examining was a record of a disbursement of $48,000. He asked who knew about this item and was told that George W. Perkins did. Mr. Perkins was called to the witness stand, and began by saying that he wanted to make a statement before being questioned. He then told the story of his life, dwelling upon the principles which had motivated him. After this the examination began with respect to the company's transactions and the items in the account. The hearing was adjourned for luncheon, and Mr. Perkins took advantage of the opportunity to speak to Mr. Hughes privately.

[" 'Mr. Hughes,' said Perkins, 'you're handling dynamite. That $48,000 was a contribution to President Roosevelt's campaign fund. You want to think very carefully before you put that into the evidence. You can't tell what may come of it.'

[" 'After lunch,' replied Mr. Hughes, 'I'm going to ask you what was done with that $48,000; and I expect a candid answer.'

["So when the examination was resumed, Mr. Hughes asked his question, and Mr. Perkins explained what had been done with the money. The revelation caused a tremendous sensation, and the newspaper men ran for the nearest telephones."]

The revelations ruined McCall, but apparently he cherished no resentment against me. Haley Fiske, President of the Metropolitan Life Insurance Company, in an address before an annual meeting of the Association of Life Insurance Presidents, says, in referring to the investigation: "Mr. McCall told me not long before he died that Mr. Hughes had been eminently fair; and there could be no better witness quoted."[13]

The responsibility of the investigation weighed heavily upon me. I was determined to make it as thorough as possible, but despite demands of newspapers, I refused to permit it to be led off into inquiries which were not germane to the insurance business as such. I knew that if I did, the inquiry would be smothered by politics and nothing of value would be accomplished. It was my aim to disclose such abuses as there were in the insurance business and seek to provide for their correction, while at the same time maintaining the credit of the companies, with respect to their fundamental soundness and their ability to meet their obligations, and the public esteem and confidence in which the essential life insurance enterprise had been held. At times I felt the responsibility almost too heavy to bear and the work too exacting to be continued. I remember that

[13]See address "Fifty Years of Life Insurance," by Haley Fiske (December 4, 1925), p. 5. [Copy in the Hughes Papers.]

occasionally at night I would feel worn out and utterly depressed and would exclaim to my wife, "I can't see any end to this. It is too much. I simply can't go on." But after a night's rest I would start again.

So the inquiry continued until the end of the year 1905, when the public hearings were closed. I took two or three days' rest with a trip to Montreal and returned to begin writing the report. Someone had proposed to the Committee that there should be no report and Mr. McKeen supported this proposal. "The testimony had shown the facts, let it stand. Why summarize it?" But I insisted that a comprehensive report must be made. The testimony covered many thousands of pages and there were a host of exhibits. The newspaper accounts, though voluminous, had given and could give no systematic review of the whole situation. It was necessary to have a report to provide the appropriate and adequate basis for legislation, and it was due to the companies as well as to the Committee and the public that a fair and complete summary of facts and conclusions should be presented in an authoritative manner. In this, as well as in all other matters, I had the full support of Chairman Armstrong.

My view was accepted by the Committee and, with Fleming's assistance, I proceeded to draw up the report which I found a very laborious task, taking about six weeks of day and night work. It gave the salient facts as to the respective companies, the practices found to exist, the evidence which supported each finding, and the recommendations for legislation.[14] Then in conference with the Committee, and with the actuarial assistance of Dawson, I prepared the various bills to carry out the recommendations and went to Albany to explain them to members of the Legislature and the legislative correspondents. The enactments of 1906 followed.[15]

[14]A pamphlet copy of the Report is in the folder marked "Insurance Investigation" [in the Hughes Papers].

[15]These enactments are summarized in a popular way by Mark Sullivan in *Our Times*, III, 67. [Beerits, "Gas and Insurance Investigations," p. 20, refers to Sullivan's account of the investigations in *Our Times*, III, 27–68. The bills had to do with requiring insurance companies to pay their dividends annually, limiting the annual business that a company could write, forbidding campaign contributions, setting required standard forms of policies, and requiring full publicity in company reports.]

Chapter X The Governorship *1907–1910*

Immediately after the insurance investigation, I was retained in important matters and I looked forward to an agreeable and profitable professional activity as counsel in worthwhile cases. I had no desire to engage in politics. Apart from that, I had no notion that the party leaders would wish me to run for office. There were two reasons for this: one was that I had turned down the Republican nomination for Mayor of New York in the preceding October. The nomination was made after I had absolutely refused to allow my name to be considered and with the purpose, as I believed, to pull me out of the investigation and I knew that, in consequence of the embarrassment the leaders felt I had caused the party, they had been very sore. Further, in the insurance investigation I had shown the failure of the State Insurance Department, which was under Republican control, vigilantly to protect the interests of policy holders, and there was a feeling that I had exposed the party organization to public criticism. When President Roosevelt had said (when I saw him in May 1906, in connection with the coal investigation which he had asked me to undertake) that I would have "two votes for Governor in the next Republican Convention, mine (his) and Loeb's," I thought it only a pleasantry and that even the President could not persuade the Convention, dominated by the State leaders, to nominate me. Occasional rumors that I might be nominated I did not take seriously.

[The circumstances are described in Beerits' Memorandum, "Entry into Politics and Election as Governor." [1]

["After the gas investigation, when, as a result of Mr. Hughes' report, a commission to regulate the gas and electric utilities was established, Governor Higgins asked Mr. Hughes to be chairman of this commission, but Mr. Hughes declined.

["In September 1905, public interest in the insurance investigation was very

[1] [Beerits' Memorandum, "Entry into Politics and Election as Governor," pp. 1–9.]

keen. At this time there was considerable question as to who was going to be the Republican candidate for Mayor in the coming election in New York City. There was talk of giving Mr. Hughes the nomination, and a committee came to him with the suggestion. He replied that he would not hear of it. There was a little talk in the papers at this time to the effect that the real purpose in nominating Mr. Hughes would be to pull him out of the investigation, in order to prevent a cataclysm in the insurance world. After his talk with the committee, Mr. Hughes thought that he had put a stop to the movement in his favor, and gave it no attention.

["On the evening of Friday, October 6th, in order to gain a little relief from the steady toil of the investigation, he went to the theatre with Mrs. Hughes. After the theatre, they stopped for something to eat, and then between 11:00 and 12:00 o'clock, walked to their home at 570 West End Avenue. As they rounded the corner at 87th Street, they found that the street in front of the house was filled with cabs, and that the stoop of the house was filled with people. They soon discovered that Mr. Hughes had been nominated for Mayor that evening.

["A committee was there to notify him of his nomination — a committee consisting of Herbert Parsons, the County chairman; Julius Mayer, Attorney-General of the State; Senator Page, who had been Mr. Hughes's backer in the gas investigation; Ezra Prentiss, a member of the insurance investigation committee; and several others. Mr. Hughes took them upstairs to his library. He told them that he could not accept the nomination.

["They protested strongly. They pointed out that he was the one man who could be elected by the Republican party, and that it meant a great deal for New York City. They insisted that he could continue with the investigation without interruption; that he would not have to campaign; that his character before the people was esablished.

["Mr. Hughes replied that, if he accepted the nomination, everything he did would be attributed to a political motive. Under this situation, he would have to campaign in order to save his character. And he couldn't campaign and continue the investigation at the same time. It was too patent that he was being simply pulled out of the investigation. While the members of the committee might not be asking him to accept the nomination for that reason, nevertheless the people would think that that was the real reason why he had been nominated. Everything he stood for in the public estimation would be pulled down, and his character before the people would no longer be established.

["The committee asserted strongly that it was his duty to the Republican party to accept the nomination. They said that if he did not run for Mayor, George B. McClellan, the Democratic Mayor then in office, would be re-elected by a large plurality, as a result of which he would be elected Governor in 1906, and probably President in 1908. The Democrats would then be in control, and Mr. Hughes, who by refusing to run for Mayor would have made this possible, would be responsible for the whole welfare of the country. They pointed out that even if Mr. Hughes was defeated, he would prevent McClellan from being re-elected by such a large victory as to carry him by its momentum into the Governorship.

["Mr. Hughes replied that he was not able to penetrate the future as clearly as they felt they could, but that right then in the present he had a job and he was going to complete it. The importance of the insurance investigation to millions of people throughout the country was evident, and nothing was to be gained by any failure on the part of Mr. Hughes to perform his duty in the work of that investigation. He flatly refused the nomination.

["The committee took his refusal very hard. No one there sided with him. Mrs. Hughes, who was in the next room and could not help hearing the conversation that was being carried on in loud voices, told Mr. Hughes afterwards that she did not see how he possibly withstood the persuasion of the committee.

["Mr. Hughes thought, and the members of the committee thought, that this was the end so far as any political preferment for Mr. Hughes was concerned. He would never again be given another political opportunity. This, however, did not bother him, for he had no desire to enter public life.

["The committee, finding him adamant, said that he was doing a serious injury, and that the least he could do was to make no public announcement of his declination until Monday. Mr. Hughes agreed to wait.

["That week-end was one of the most difficult times in Mr. Hughes's life. He was swamped with telephone and telegraph appeals, insisting that he must accept the nomination. Ervin Wardman, an ardent supporter, editor of the New York *Press*, which had said in editorials that it was absolutely vital that Mr. Hughes run for Mayor, came to him bringing a message from William Randolph Hearst. Hearst sent word that if Mr. Hughes would run for Mayor, he would support him. He would either support him directly through his papers, or indirectly by running as a third candidate himself and thus assuring McClellan's defeat — whichever method Mr. Hughes thought best. Mr. Hughes' election was thus assured; but his decision to refuse the nomination was not shaken.

["On Monday, October 9th, Mr. Hughes was formally notified of his nomination, and he formally declined to accept it. In his statement to the committee he said, after referring to the arguments of the committee:

[" 'In this dilemma I have simply to do my duty as I see it.

[" 'In my judgment, I have no right to accept the nomination. A paramount public duty forbids it.

[" 'It is not necessary to enlarge upon the importance of the insurance investigation. That is undisputed. It is dealing with questions vital to the interests of millions of our fellow-citizens throughout the land. It presents an opportunity for public service second to none and involves a correlative responsibility. I have devoted myself unreservedly to this work. It commands all my energies. It is imperative that I continue in it. You have frankly recognized that it must continue unembarrassed and with unimpaired efficiency. But it is entirely clear to me that this cannot be if I accept the nomination.

[" 'You know how desirous I have been that the investigation should not be colored by any suggestion of political motive. Whatever confidence it has inspired has been due to absolute independence of political consideration. It is not sufficient to say that an acceptance of this nomination, coming to me unsought and despite an unequivocable statement of my position, would not deflect my course by a hair's breadth, that I should remain, entirely untrammelled. The non-political character of the investigation and its freedom from bias, either of fear or favor, not only must exist, they must be recognized. I cannot permit them, by any action of mine, to become matters of debate.

[" 'There are abundant opportunities for misconstruction. Doubtless many abuses will remain undisclosed, many grievous wrongs to which the evidence points from time to time may be found unsusceptible of proof; many promising clues will be taken up in vain. Were I with the best of intentions to accept the nomination, it is my conviction that the work of the investigation would be largely discredited; its motives would be impugned and its integrity assailed. To many it would appear that its course would be shaped and its lines of inquiry would be chosen, developed, or abandoned as political ambition might prompt or political exigency demand.

[" 'Such a situation would be intolerable. There is but one course open. The legislative inquiry must proceed with convincing disinterestedness. Its great opportunities must not be imperilled by alienating the support to which it is entitled or by giving the slightest occasion for questioning the sincerity and single-mindedness with which it is conducted.' "

[Beerits describes Hughes's meeting with Roosevelt as follows:

[President Roosevelt was much impressed with Mr. Hughes's conduct of the investigation, and in the spring of 1906 he asked Mr. Hughes to accept an appointment as special assistant to the Attorney-General, to take charge of the coal inquiry, the purpose of which was to check the combinations in restraint of trade and illegal practices of corporations. Mr. Hughes accepted this appointment.

["Mr. Hughes had never met President Roosevelt nor had any relations with him prior to the insurance investigation. In the course of the investigation it fell to Mr. Hughes's lot to bring out the corporation contributions to Roosevelt's campaign fund. He dealt with this matter only in so far as it affected the insurance companies. Although some felt that it hurt the administration, it really did not, and the President certainly felt no hostility toward Mr. Hughes for having disclosed the contributions.

["In the investigations Mr. Hughes referred to a man whom the President was considering for an appointment. The President wrote to Mr. Hughes and asked whether the reference that had been made to the proposed appointee reflected upon him and proved him to be an undesirable man to appoint to the position in question. Mr. Hughes answered the question very carefully, pointing out that the facts that had been disclosed had not been of such nature as to make such an appointment inadvisable, and that he knew of no reason why the President should not make the proposed appointment. The latter was very much pleased with Mr. Hughes's answer and said that Mr. Hughes had met the request for information in fair and impartial manner and had proved that he was not in the least vindictive.

["On the day after Easter, 1906, Mr. Hughes went to the White House, at the President's request, and there took place their first meeting. From the White House Mr. Hughes went to see Attorney-General Moody to talk over the prospective coal inquiry. Moody said that Secretary Taft was going on the Supreme Court in the fall and that he was anxious to complete the inquiry before that. (This shows what was then in contemplation, and what was not achieved.) When Mr. Hughes returned to the White House, President Roosevelt and Mr. Loeb, his secretary, were standing by a window watching the Easter Monday egg rolling on the lawn. As Mr. Hughes was leaving, the President said to him 'In the next Republican Convention you will have two votes for Governor — mine and Loeb's.' "]

In order to recuperate from the strain of the year, I went to Europe with my son for a holiday and, returning in September, I found that there was a strong movement to bring about my nomination [for governor.] Herbert Parsons, the Republican committeeman for New York, had come to the conclusion that I was the most available candidate, and Governor [Benjamin B.] Odell, [Jr.], the State leader who had been responsible for my nomination for Mayor, had so declared openly. Whatever opposition this movement would have had was quelled by President Roosevelt.[2] The campaign against William Randolph Hearst and my election as Governor followed. All the other candidates on the Republican ticket were defeated. (November 1906).

My course as Governor, the recommendations I made to the legislature and my administrative action, and my relations to the party leaders, were the subject of constant public discussion from every point of view. These are a part of the history of the times.

Beerits' Memoranda cover the ground very fully and give references to source-material in publications and correspondence. I have no desire to go all over it again in detail. I shall refer to only a few matters, leaving the rest to Beerits' narrative.[3]

The explanation of my difficulties with the party leaders is a very simple one. I had always been a Republican, and I had complete sympathy with the proper aims of party organization, as it was natural I should have in view of my zeal for efficient methods in every line of work. But the Republican party had been in power in New York State for many years and its control, through the party leaders, of the administrative departments had become suspect. The insurance department was regarded as faithless to its trust and the Railroad Commission was under attack. The charge that financial interests had obtained a grip upon the various depart-

[2][Beerits, "Entry into Politics," p. 10, says Roosevelt sent the following message to the convention at Saratoga, "I think that Mr. Hughes is the strongest candidate before the convention. We need just his qualities in the coming campaign."]

[3]Beerits' Memoranda, "First Term as Governor"; "Renomination and Re-election as Governor"; "Second Term as Governor." [Material from these memoranda is included wherever relevant. The source material to which Beerits refers consists of New York City newspapers and Hughes's public papers as governor, *The Public Papers of Charles Evans Hughes*, 4 vols. (Albany, J. B. Lyon Company, 1908–1911). Perhaps the most important matters left to Beerits are the unsuccessful fight to limit horse racing, the direct primary bill and various efforts to regulate the use of public resources of the state. These issues are discussed and analyzed in Robert F. Wesser, *Charles Evans Hughes: Politics and Reform in New York, 1905–1910* (Ithaca, Cornell University Press, 1967), *passim*.]

ments was widely believed and the time was ripe for a general "housecleaning." It was realized that this was not likely to be had if the Republican "bosses," so-called, remained in power. I think it was generally assumed that the party faced defeat in the State unless I were nominated. And my availability was due solely to the fact that I had won credit for an independent position. In short, the party relied upon me to win the election because of the public conviction that I would give a clean and efficient administration in the interest of the people, that is, as I expressed it in accepting the nomination, without any "taint of bossism or servitude to any private interest." Throughout the campaign I gave explicit promises to that effect. And that is why I was elected even against Hearst, who incarnated, to a great degree, the demand for a change and resorted to the most sensational appeals.

[Beerits explains why Hughes felt it his duty to accept the nomination:

["In 1905 William Randolph Hearst had been an Independent candidate for Mayor of New York. On election day he was polling a great many votes; then for an hour the returns stopped coming in, and after some delay the official announcement was made that Mayor McClellan had been re-elected by a slight majority. Hearst was not able to check up the votes and took legal proceedings for a recount. Those who had voted for him, and thousands who had not, believed him entitled to a recount of the votes. There was a wave of popular sympathy in his favor, and the Democratic party nominated him for Governor, fearing that any regular candidate nominated by it would run third in the election.

["The Republican State Administration had been largely discredited and public scandals had been disclosed. Governor Higgins was an honest and able man, but not only was he not in good health but there was a general feeling that he could not be re-elected. There was growing opposition to the domination of State administration by a coterie of Republican leaders, the so-called "bosses." If Hearst was to be defeated, it was essential that the Republicans nominate for Governor a candidate who could enlist the support of the people as a whole. Mr. Hughes was popular with the people, who had been greatly impressed with his work in the gas and insurance investigations. When this popularity was coupled with President Roosevelt's recommendation, the bosses who were opposed to Mr. Hughes because they feared his uncompromising integrity surrendered, and he was nominated by the convention. Since the possibility of defeating Hearst depended upon his acceptance, Mr. Hughes accepted the nomination as a clear call to duty, thus giving up the distinguished and profitable career that lay before him in his cherished profession as a result of his sudden eminence.

["On October 2nd President Roosevelt stated, in a letter to Mr. Hughes: 'The situation is certainly very serious in New York, and we must get out the reserves of decent citizenship in order to upset the apostates of unrest and their huge and misguided following. Hearst will of course use money like water and with shameless corruption wherever he gets a chance. You doubtless remember how Flower, in his campaign for Governor, bought up the interior counties and cut down the Republican vote up State almost to the vanishing point. The Democrats have not now the corrupt and unscrupulous but able up State machine they had in those days under the leadership of Hill; nevertheless I earnestly hope you will thru Woodruff see to it that our up State leaders are thoroughly on the alert and watchful about any such move by Hearst's people to cut down our vote in the Republican counties, either by downright corruption or by an unrebuked and uncontradicted appeal to envy and hate. I regard your triumph as of more consequence than anything else at stake in this election.' "

[On October 5, 1906, Roosevelt told Hughes,

[" 'My dear Sir, I feel that you are fighting the battle of civilization. If you were an ordinary time-serving politician, if you had the slightest taint of subserviency to the great moneyed interests, I would not give a rap for your success. But you are an honest, fearless, square man, a good citizen and a good American first, and a good Republican also — a Republican who believes in Abraham Lincoln's principles. You believe in reforming the relations between the Government and the great corporations as drastically as is necessary to meet the needs of the situation; but you believe in having it done in a spirit of sanity and justice. If I were not President I should be stumping New York from one end to the other for you. As it is I cannot do much of anything save to hope that my own record and the way I stand towards these questions will help and not harm you.' "][4]

I stated my attitude in my Inaugural Address:[5]

The growth of our population and the necessary increase in our charitable and correctional work, the great enterprises under State control — our canals, our highways, our forest preserves — the protection of the public health, the problems created by the congestion of our population in our great cities lead to a constant extension of governmental activity from which we cannot have, and we would not seek, escape.

This extension compels the strictest insistence upon the highest administrative standards . . . The essentials of our liberties are expressed in constitutional enactments removed from the risk of temporary agitation. But the security of our government despite its constitutional guarantees is found in the intelligence and public spirit of its citizens and in its ability to call to the work of administration men of single-minded devotion to the public interests, who make unselfish service to the State a point of knightly honor.

If in administration we make the standard efficiency and not partisan advantage, if in executing the laws we deal impartially, if in making the

[4] [Beerits, "Entry into Politics," pp. 11–14; these and other letters from Roosevelt dealing with the campaign are in the Hughes Papers.]

[5] *The Public Papers of Charles Evans Hughes, 1907*, pp. 6–9.

laws there is fair and intelligent action with reference to each exigency, we shall disarm reckless and selfish agitators and take from the enemies of our peace their vantage ground of attack.

But some of the influencial Republican leaders apparently thought that all this, like my speeches, was just "campaign talk." Others, who gave me credit for sincerity in the exaltation of the campaign, thought that, now that I was elected and on the threshold of a political career, I should have sense enough to be tractable and my noble sentiments could be conveniently and profitably laid aside. At any rate, the party leaders were determined to have their way, so far as possible, and when it was found that I meant to keep my pre-election promises and that I would not be subservient to the well-established organization control, they resolved to demonstrate their power.

The issue was presented at the very outset in an incident Beerits describes. A vacancy had occurred in the office of State Superintendent of Elections for the Metropolitan District and the leaders had persuaded Governor Higgins in the last days of his term to appoint one [Lewis M.] Swasey. Governor Higgins had asked me about the matter, but I knew nothing whatever about Swasey, and too busy with my message and pressing demands to give it attention, I refused to approve the appointment or to commit myself in any way, leaving the Governor to act on his own judgment. As it was a recess appointment, it would fall unless I sent the name to the Senate within twenty days after taking office. When I made the necessary inquiries, I found that Swasey was the ordinary sort of district leader in Brooklyn, a mere tool of the machine and not in any way qualified for the office. Timothy L. Woodruff, Republican State Chairman, backed Swasey vigorously and Herbert Parsons supported him. I informed them that I did not consider Swasey to be qualified and could not appoint him, but that I should be glad to appoint anyone else whom they would recommend provided he was a fit man for the place. But they would not listen to this and insisted on Swasey. Meanwhile, the press had become interested and treated the affair as a test whether my administration was to be "unbossed." Suspicion had been aroused because I had been Woodruff's guest, for a few days' rest after the election, at his camp in the Adirondacks. This was pursuant to an invitation which I had accepted during the campaign with the understanding that several independent Republicans, such as President Schurman of Cornell, would be there. But they did not come and I found myself surrounded chiefly by the party leaders and many thought that I had been "taken into camp" in more ways than one. Beerits describes the final interview with Woodruff and Parsons when I stood my ground and Parsons observed as they left that he thought "they would find a way."[6] I did not realize what he meant by this cryptic remark until later when they obtained President Roosevelt's support. Meanwhile, I had tried to find a good man whose party standing was such that the Senate could not well turn him down, and I selected William Leary, who was suggested by Job E. Hedges, was an organization man, and had the endorsement as fully qualified of independents upon whom I felt I could rely. On the very day when I was about to send his name to the Senate, President Roosevelt's message endorsing Swasey was brought to me. I deeply regretted this useless and foolish action of Woodruff and Parsons in bringing the President into the affair but I felt that I must adhere to the course I had definitely taken. Leary's appoinment was hailed as a sign that I would not take orders and that I had started my administration with the determination to be Governor in my own right. Woodruff and Parsons were much put out, but I had given them every chance to save their faces and they had quite needlessly made an issue and brought their trouble upon themselves.

With respect to the principal administrative departments, I made a good start. The Superintendent of Banks had resigned, and I secured the service of Charles Hallam Keep who had been Assistant Secretary of the Treasury and was highly qualified. In answer to my inquiry, President Roosevelt endorsed him. To the important office of Superintendent of Public Works I appointed Senator Frederick C. Stevens, who was by all odds the one best fitted for that place by reason of his business experience, and his integrity and independence of character. I had formed a high opinion of Senator Stevens during my service as counsel for the Legislative Committee, of which he was Chairman, in the gas investigation in 1905. I confess that I did not fully realize the bitterness of the hostility to him on the part of certain organization leaders in the western part of the State, but this in any case could not outweigh his outstanding qualifications. While his nomination caused a little flurry of talk, he was at once confirmed by the Senate.[7] As another highly important step in the improvement of the State administration, I recommended to the Legislature the creation of the Public Service Commissions, and this involved the abolition of the discredited Railroad Commission.

But I struck a snag in connection with the Insurance Department. Otto

[6]Beerits' Memorandum, "First Term as Governor," pp. 4–5.

[7][Stevens headed a political faction opposed to State Assembly Speaker James J. Wadsworth and the appointment was seen by some politicians as an insult to the Speaker. Beerits points out ("First Term as Governor," pp. 6–7) that in appointing Stevens, Hughes further alienated the bosses by rejecting their candidate for the job. Frank Simonds, Albany correspondent of the New York *Evening Post* referred to Hughes's appointment as a "revolution" in New York politics. (January 15, 1907, p. 1.)]

Kelsey had been appointed Superintendent in the preceding May, after the insurance investigation. He was honest but ineffective. Though he had been in office for over seven months, and Senator Armstrong and I, in an interview with him shortly after his appointment, had stressed the necessity for making changes, he had utterly failed to clean house. It was plain enough that if the State supervision were not more wide-awake and competent, we should have, despite the new laws, a recurrence of evil practices. To prevent this recurrence, there was an especial need for more thorough examinations of the companies. The Report of the Insurance Committee had shown how inadequate the previous examinations had been. The Mutual Life had been examined as late as 1903 and the New York Life in 1904, and the Chief Examiner had reported that these examinations had been exhaustive. He had not even hinted at the abuses which the insurance investigation disclosed and he had given the companies a clean bill of health. The Committee's Report had specifically pointed out that most of the evils disclosed "would have been impossible had there been a vigorous performance of the duties already laid upon the Department, a vigilant watchfulness in the interest of policyholders, and a courageous exercise of the powers which the statute confers." [8]

When I took office in January 1907, I found that Kelsey had failed to purge the Department of its delinquent personnel and it was evident that he was wholly without the executive capacity, independence and courage which were necessary to put the Department on the sound footing which would restore it to public confidence. Knowing that Kelsey had the strong backing of the party leaders, I sought quietly to obtain his resignation, offering to find another position for him better suited to his temperament and capacity. But he refused to resign. I then talked to his organization friends, asking them to persuade him to resign in order to avoid the scandal of keeping him in a place for which he was so conspicuously unfitted. But the leaders determined to back Kelsey, feeling confident that they could keep him in office as under the statute he could not be removed without the consent of the Senate.

Finding myself balked in this way and feeling a special responsibility in relation to the Insurance Department, of which I had learned so much, I took an unusual course. I knew that if I recommended Kelsey's removal, there would be a stiff fight and it would be contended that my charge of remissness and inadequacy was unfounded. I felt that the exact situation in this respect should be brought clearly to public attention, and accordingly I called Kelsey before me in the Executive Chamber and publicly examined him as to his official action, or lack of action, in view of

[8]Report, Insurance Committee, February 22, 1906, pp. 346–356.

the conditions in the Department as shown by the Report of the Insurance Committee.[9] I then sent a special message to the Legislature containing a full review of the matter and asked for Kelsey's removal.[10] There was a long and bitter contest which resulted in the defeat of my recommendation by a close vote, but I won strong public support as my effort to improve the administration in this important Department was fully understood. In the following August, charges were filed against Kelsey and I appointed Matthew C. Fleming to investigate them and generally to examine into the affairs of the Department. On his report, I sent the Legislature, in February 1908, a recommendation for Kelsey's removal from office, but again the recommendation was defeated.[11] After my re-election in the fall of 1908, Kelsey resigned and I appointed, in February 1909, William H. Hotchkiss, of Buffalo, Superintendent of Insurance.[12] He was a man of outstanding ability and character and gave an excellent administration.

Of course, throughout my administration, in both terms, I made a host of appointments upon the recommendation of the party leaders. I was always glad to do this, and I did it, whenever they recommended men of such ability and character that I was confident there would be no successful interference with the faithful and efficient discharge of official duties. I had strong support from able and leading Republicans in the Legislature; Alfred R. Page and George B. Agnew, of New York City, Harvey D. Hinman, of Binghamton, and others in the Senate, and John Lord O'Brian, of Buffalo, and others in the Assembly. O'Brian, a wise and staunch friend, did much to help me establish good relations with the organization in Erie County.[13]

My appointment of Charles Hallam Keep to the Public Service Commission left a vacancy in the Banking Department. The financial panic in the fall of 1907 created a particular exigency and I sought the best available man in the State. Through the aid of A. Barton Hepburn [1846–1922], a most able and public-spirited banker, I was fortunate enough to bring to the State service Clark Williams of New York City [as State Superintendent of Banks], thoroughly qualified by experience and of the highest

[9]Kelsey's testimony appears in my *Public Papers*, 1907, pp. 315–361.

[For a detailed discussion of the episode, see Wesser, *Charles Evans Hughes: Politics and Reform in New York, 1905–1910*, pp. 124–145. For a sample of newspaper comment, see the *New York Times*, February 21, 1907, p. 5; May 2, p. 5; and May 4, p. 9.]

[10]*Ibid.*, pp. 249–256.

[11]*Public Papers*, 1908, pp. 177–185. [At this point Beerits, "First Term as Governor," pp. 15–21, quotes extensively from Frank Simonds' articles in the New York *Evening Post* during February 1907, and from Mark Sullivan, *Our Times*, III, 281–288.]

[12]*Public Papers*, 1909, p. 197.

[13]See the generous article by John Lord O'Brian, "Charles Evans Hughes as Governor," *American Bar Association Journal*, July 1951, p. 412.

ability and character. In November 1909, on the death of the State Comptroller, a vacancy arose, which, though the office was elective, I was able to fill by appointment until January 1, 1911. I appointed Clark Williams and there ensued a very important reform in the administration of the State finances. In passing upon the legislative appropriations of the session of 1909, I had suggested that there should be provided some permanent method of comparative examination of departmental budgets and proposals for appropriations in advance of the legislative session so that the Legislature might be aided by preliminary investigation and report in determining with just proportion the amounts that could be properly allowed. I submitted specific recommendations for budget-making in my annual message at the beginning of the session of 1910.[14] Clark Williams as Comptroller proceeded to classify and tabulate the State expenditures and thus for the first time we had an adequate analysis of outlays and this was followed by the preparation of budgets in harmony with my recommendation.

Following the panic of 1907, I appointed a Commission of eminent bankers to consider and recommend desirable changes in the laws relating to banks and trust companies, and as a result desirable amendments were enacted. I also recommended and secured legislation for the prompt and economical liquidation of insolvent banks and insolvent insurance companies under the supervision of the Superintendents of Banks and Insurance, respectively.[15]

I suppose that the emphasis I laid on efficency in administration was influential in bringing about the presentation of charges against John F. Ahearn, President of the Borough of Manhattan, New York City, for neglect of duty, especially in relation to the shocking condition of the streets of the Borough and the administration of the Bureau of Public Buildings and Offices. As it was not shown that Ahearn was personally corrupt, the case was highly important as a precedent and I presided in person at the hearing in the Executive Chamber. Ahearn was represented by able counsel and voluminous evidence was taken. I sustained the jurisdiction of the Governor in such a case, and, finding the charge of inexcusable neglect of duty fully proved, I removed the Borough President.

[14]*Public Papers*, 1910, p. 39.

[Clark Williams (1870–1946) was an officer of the United States Mortgage Company and Managing Vice President of the Columbia Trust Company before his appointment by Hughes. After retiring from office in 1911 he became President of the Windsor Trust Company and the Industrial Finance Company. He served on the executive council of the American Bankers Association, was Vice President of the New York State Chamber of Commerce, and President of the National Association of Supervisors of State Banks. In 1934 he wrote an autobiography, *The Story of a Grateful Citizen*, 2 vols. (New York, privately printed, 1934).]

[15]*Public Papers*, 1908, pp. 17, 241, and 20–21, 1909, pp. 52, 164.

Later, Louis F. Haffen, President of the Borough of the Bronx, New York City, was removed on charges of misconduct which I sustained on the report of Wallace Macfarlane [1857–1928] whom I appointed Commissioner. Proceedings were also taken for the removal of Joseph Bermel, President of the Borough of Queens, New York City. Making no answer to the charges, he resigned his office. There were many other proceedings for the removal of public officers, resulting in the dismissal of the charges or removal, according to the evidence.[16]

In the early part of my first term, I established the practice of having a morning hour in which I sat in the large Governor's room, seeing all who might wish to present some information or request. I found that this greatly expedited my work and the room was so spacious that those waiting their turn were comfortably placed and out of hearing of what was said at the Governor's desk. One day, as I turned from one visitor to greet another, who had not been introduced, I sensed at a glance that the latter was recently out of prison. I said, "When did you get out?" He answered, "Yesterday." I said, "Where were you?" He said, "At Auburn." "What were you in for?" I asked. He said, "For burglary." "How long?" said I. "Ten years," said he. "Was that your first term?" I asked. "No, I had another for six years for grand larceny." "Well," I said, "you seem to have spent most of your adult life in jail and as soon as you are out you come to the Governor's office. What do you want?" Said he, "I want to make a complaint." He then proceeded to describe certain conditions at Auburn Prison. When he left, I asked Colonel [George C.] Treadwell, my military secretary who was taking care of the visitors, how it happened that when heads of departments, Senators, Assemblymen, etc., were waiting to see me an ex-convict could come right up to my desk without an introduction and engage me in conversation. "Why," said Treadwell, "A convict! I thought he was a member of the Legislature."

Sometimes after, at a public dinner in New York, I told this story, of course without mentioning any names, and I at once received a sharp letter from my visitor who thought he would be recognized, and he reprimanded the Governor for making his case public.

During both terms as Governor, while I was endeavoring to enforce the essential standards of official conduct, my work was largely concerned with legislative measures — in promoting those which I had recommended, and in dealing with the host of bills passed by the Legislature, many of which I disapproved.[17] There was no lack of sensational episodes. I shall not attempt to review them or my various activities during the four

[16] [For information on these incidents, see] *Public Papers*, 1907, pp. 267–286; 1908, pp. 193–4, 211, 213; 1909, pp. 239–250; 1907–1910, Titles "Complaints," "Removal Proceedings."

[17] [*Public Papers*, 1907], Title "Vetoes."

years in relation to legislation, being content to leave these to my "Public Papers" and Beerits' Memoranda.

I may, however, refer to the Public Service Commissions Act, which marked a new era in administrative regulation in the State of New York. It brought me at the beginning of my public career to the close study of administrative agencies, their necessity and appropriate sphere of action. We were then, with the increased powers of the Interstate Commerce Commission, and the Wisconsin and New York Acts, at the threshold of the extraordinary development which for the past twenty five years has been the most important feature of the political history of the nation and the States.

It was a distinct shock to the corporate interests concerned when I proposed that the Public Service Commission should have clearly defined powers, embracing the authority "to act upon its own initiative as well as upon complaint; to pass upon the issue of stocks and bonds; to examine properties, books, and accounts; to require detailed reports in prescribed forms; to prescribe reasonable rates; to require adequate and impartial service; to provide for the safety of employees and for the protection of the public; and generally to direct whatever may be necessary or proper to safeguard the public interests and to secure the fulfillment of the public obligations of the corporations under its supervision." There was also to be provision for suitable inspections by the Commission so that it might be "in a position to take action on behalf of the people without the formal institution of proceedings by complainants." The corporation guilty of disobedience to the orders of the Commission and all officers and other responsible persons were to be visited with appropriate penalties. And the Commission was to be entitled to institute legal proceedings for the enforcement of these orders and such proceedings should have suitable preference in the courts. I concluded that the Legislature "should thus provide, within its constitutional power, adequate means for the entirely just and impartial regulation of these important public enterprises."

While the corporations and their legislative henchmen were determined to make impossible the conferring of such an aggregation of powers, they found it difficult to challenge effectively any of them in view of the manifest advantage in having the interests of the public competently safeguarded. And as the debate went on, the ground of opposition appeared more and more to be lacking in substance.[18] Finally there was

[18][Beerits comments in "First Term as Governor," pp. 28 and 33–34:

["It is difficult today to appreciate fully the situation in the Legislature at that time. Good men did not dare to call their souls their own. Eight or ten men controlled the Legislature, and they were in turn controlled by the corporations. With this situation it seemed quite impossible to get through the Legislature a bill that met with as much energetic opposition from the corporations as did the Public Service Commission bill. The only way by which the opposition could be dislodged was by an appeal to the public

emphatic insistence on two points, relating (1) to the Governor's power to remove commissioners and (2) to "court review."

I had insisted, when the bill was drawn, upon giving the Governor power to remove for neglect and inefficiency as well as for malfeasance, and that this power should not be limited by requiring the consent of the Senate. This, it was contended, would put the commissioners under the Governor's control; on the other hand, the duty lay with the Governor to see that the laws were faithfully executed and the removal of commissioners who failed to give proper and efficient service was a suitable incident to the discharge of that duty. To secure the flexibility and adequate attention to details, made possible by the creation of an administrative agency, and at the same time to avoid the evils of a mere bureaucracy, we must look to the Executive who should stand before the people as responsible for the quality of administration. I may note that Elihu Root gave me his strong support and wanted the bill passed, as he said, with the power of removal in it.[19]

With respect to "court review," there was the plausible argument that the corporations affected should have the right to contest in court the orders of the Commission. I insisted that this review should be limited to the questions whether the Commission had acted within the limits of its statutory authority and whether either statute or order transcended constitutional bounds. In either of these cases there should be full judicial review. But the opposition was not content with this and sought review by the courts of the findings of the Commission, although these were not arbitrary but supported by evidence, and thus to have all the questions of fact passed upon by the courts. This, of course, would not only lead to inordinate delays and gravely impair the usefulness of the Commission, but would turn into the courts a multitude of factual controversies, overwhelming the courts with hosts of details with which it was the appropriate function of an expert administrative body to deal.[20]

---

that was able to stir up public sentiment to such a pitch that it was stronger than the influence of the corporations in the Legislature . . .

["Governor Hughes's appeal to the people in behalf of the Public Service Commission bill was successful. He so dramatized the issue between the people and the corporations that public sentiment was aroused to a degree where the leaders in the Legislature decided that in the interest of the party the bill had better pass. In June the Legislature voted in favor of establishing a system of regulation of public service corporations along the lines proposed by Governor Hughes. This plan served as a model in other States."]

[19]I dealt with this question in my speech at Glens Falls, April 5, 1907, in the volume entitled *Charles Evans Hughes, Addresses* (1908), pp. 115–122. [See Root to Hughes, May 1, 1907, Hughes Papers.]

[20]In considering this question in my speech at Utica, April 1, 1907, I said, after referring to the constitutional protection of property rights: "A different question is presented when it is urged that *all* orders of the commission should be reviewable by the courts regardless of the question whether the commission has exceeded its authority or any

It was in discussing this question in a speech at Elmira that (speaking extemporaneously and in the circumstances Beerits describes) I made the remark, which has frequently been quoted, that "the Constitution is what the judges say it is."[21] This remark has been used, regardless of its context, as if permitting the inference that I was picturing constitutional interpretation by the courts as a matter of judicial caprice. This was farthest from my thought. I was not talking flippantly or in disrespect of the courts, but on the contrary with the most profound respect. I was speaking of the essential function of the courts under our system in interpreting and applying constitutional safeguards, and I was emphasizing the importance of maintaining the courts in the highest public esteem as our final judicial arbiters and the inadvisability of needlessly exposing them to criticism and disrespect by throwing upon them the

---

constitutional privilege has been ignored. There is no occasion for such a broad provision for court review unless it is desired to commit to the courts those matters which do not involve the question of deprivation of property without due process of law or without just compensation, but are matters which might appropriately be decided by the Legislature or by an administrative commission. To provide a right of appeal to the courts from every order of the commission not only invites delay and an unnecessary multiplicity of proceedings, but has for its object the substitution of the judgment of the court for the action of the commission. To give the court power to hear such appeals, to take evidence, and to reverse or to modify the orders of the commission comes simply to this: that the court becomes in effect the ruling commission, and the commission created by the Legislature is simply a board to take evidence and make what are, in effect, recommendations. It may be said that the corporations would not necessarily avail themselves of the right of review in all cases. But it is not sound public policy for the Legislature to create a board whose effectiveness will depend on the option of the corporations."

[21]Beerits' Memorandum, "First Term as Governor," pp. 29–30.

[John B. Stanchfield was to speak after Hughes, but the Governor insisted that he speak last. Beerits' account goes on to say:

["Mr. Stanchfield was a former Mayor of Elmira who had been prominent in the Legislature and had been a candidate for governor. He had long been one of the most prominent lawyers in up-State New York, and was known as a leading trial counsel in New York City. At the meeting that night he spoke first, under the changed program, and it was soon obvious that he was there to rip up the Public Service Commissions bill. He said that he was not there under retainer of any railroad or utility, but was speaking simply as a citizen, and then proceeded to make a very strong and able attack against the bill.

["When he finished, Governor Hughes arose to defend the bill. He threw aside his prepared speech, and started his address with the statement that was to be quoted again and again during his administration. 'In distinction from my learned friend,' he asserted, 'I am here under a retainer. I am here retained by the people of the State of New York, to see that justice is done, and with no disposition to injure any investment, but with every desire to give the fullest opportunity for enterprise and with every purpose to shield and protect every just property interest. I stand for the people of the State of New York against extortion, against favoritism, against financial scandal, and against everything that goes to corrupt our politics by interference with the freedom of our Legislature and administration. I stand for honest government and effective regulation by the State of public-service corporations.'

["This idea caught the interest of the people, and from then on Governor Hughes had them with him."]

burden of dealing with purely administrative questions. These questions, I observed, were "close to the public impatience" and "the people were going to insist on having administration by officers directly accountable to them."

In view of the frequent quotation of the statement to which I have referred, I give here the pertinent context:

> I have the highest regard for the courts. My whole life has been spent in work conditioned upon respect for the courts. I reckon him one of the worst enemies of the community who will talk lightly of the dignity of the bench. We are under a Constitution, but the Constitution is what the judges say it is, and the judiciary is the safeguard of our liberty and of our property under the Constitution. I do not want to see any indirect assault upon the courts. And I tell you, ladies and gentlemen, no more insidious assault could be made upon the independence and esteem of the judiciary than to burden it with these questions of administration, questions which lie close to the public impatience, and in regard to which the people are going to insist on having administration by officers directly accountable to them.
>
> Let us keep the courts for the questions they were intended to consider. When questions of property rights are involved, the constitutional right to hold property and not to be deprived of it without due process of law is involved; when, under the guise of regulation or authority to supervise railroad management, there is an assumption of arbitrary power not related to public convenience; when there is a real judicial question — let the courts have it and every good citizen will stand aside and hope to see it decided fairly and with even-handed justice.
>
> When you deal with matters of this sort you may be sure that there will be a variety of questions, which, whatever the fact may ultimately be proved to be, can by astute lawyers be said to involve such judicial matters, and there will be abundant opportunity for review of everything that should be reviewed. But to say that all these matters of detail which will be brought before the commission — matters requiring men to give their entire attention to the subject, to get their information in a variety of ways, to have hearings of those interested, and to deal with questions from a practical standpoint — should, at the option of the corporations, be taken into court, is to make a mockery of your regulation. And, on the other hand, if that policy should succeed, it would swamp your courts with administrative burdens and expose them to the fire of public criticism in connection with matters of this description from which I hope they will be safeguarded.[22]

[22]Speech at Elmira, May 3, 1907, in *Charles E. Hughes, Addresses* (1908), pp. 139–141.

While on this subject, I may refer to what I said a few years later with respect to "administrative agencies" in an address before the New York State Bar Association. After referring to the change in point of view, owing to "abounding activities and facility of intercourse" and the disposition in the exercise of governmental control to utilize freely whatever powers the people found at their immediate command, caring little for former divergencies of political theory, I observed:[23]

> Complaints must be heard, expert investigations conducted, complex situations deliberately and impartially analyzed, and legislative rules intelligently adapted to a myriad of instances falling within a general class. It was not difficult to frame legislation establishing a general standard, but to translate an accepted principle into regulations wisely adapted to particular cases required an experienced body sitting continuously and removed so far as possible from the blandishments and intrigues of politics. This administrative type is not essentially new in itself, but the extension of its use in State and Nation constitutes a new departure. The doctrine that the Legislature cannot delegate its power has not been pushed so far as to make needed adaptation of legislation impossible, and reconciliation has been found in the establishment by the Legislature itself of appropriate standards governing the action of its agency. The ideal which had been presented in justification of these new agencies, and that which alone holds promise of benefit rather than of hurt to the community, is the ideal of special knowledge, flexibility, disinterestedness and sound judgment in applying broad legislative principles that are essential to the protection of the community and of every useful activity affected, to the intricate situations created by expanding enterprise. But mere bureaucracy — narrow, partisan, or inexpert — is grossly injurious; it not only fails of the immediate purpose of the law and is opposed to traditions which, happily, are still honored, but its failure creates a feeling of discouragement bordering on pessimism which forms the most serious obstacle to real improvements in the adjustment of governmental methods to new exigencies.

Success in obtaining the passage of the Public Service Commissions' bill and other important measures against strong opposition, and the spirit and purpose of my administrative policies, had won such public acclaim that in 1908 there was a movement to bring about my nomination as the Republican candidate for the Presidency. I was neither surprised nor disappointed at the failure of this movement. It was said that having been

[23]Addresses, New York State Bar Association, January 14, 1916.

elected Governor of New York in a severe contest and having a considerable measure of popularity, I was the logical candidate. And I suppose that if the President had not sought to influence the choice, the chances would have been very much in my favor. But I had no ambition to be President. This may seem strange to those who are dazzled by the glamour of high office or are avid for political power. I had been close enough to pomp and power to be without illusions. I fully realized the vast responsibilities of the Presidency, and while I would meet them unflinchingly if the lot fell upon me, I did not wish them and would not seek them. Apart from that, I thought the position of a successor of Theodore Roosevelt would not be an attractive one. I was sure that, although out of office, he would still desire to have a dominating influence and that he would have a large following which would make the way of his successor hard. Nor did I think that with his temperament and enjoyment of the strenuous life and especially of political activity, he would long be content to remain out of office. In all probability he would be at least a receptive candidate four years later. Further, I had no doubt that he would put forth all his strength to secure the nomination of Mr. Taft — a most worthy selection — and it was idle to think that I could be nominated. I could not, however, refuse to my earnest supporters the use of my name, but I did refuse to take any active steps to further my candidacy, contenting myself with a statement, which I had been earnestly urged to make, of my views on national questions — a statement which President Roosevelt blanketed by a highly sensational message evidently timed for that purpose.[24] That annoyed my friends more than it did me.

In referring to my relations to President Roosevelt, Beerits mentions an unfortunate incident which occurred in the spring of 1907. He quotes at

[24]Beerits' Memorandum, "First Term as Governor," pp. 58–63. [Beerits takes his material from Mark Sullivan, *Our Times: The United States, 1900–1925*, 6 vols. (New York, Charles Scribner's Sons, 1926–35), III, 297–304. Beerits also discusses Hughes's abortive candidacy on pp. 46–57, where he quotes at great length from Oscar K. Davis, *Released for Publication* (Boston, Houghton Mifflin Company, 1925), pp. 45–68, to show that Hughes refused to work for the nomination, but that he was the "popular choice." Beerits implies that Hughes was not chosen because he would not sell himself to Roosevelt; Taft did. Beerits even implies that Roosevelt knew that Hughes was the better man, but that Taft was available — that is, Taft would follow Roosevelt's leadership. A recent study of the election offers evidence to support Beerits' contention. See Alfred Donald Sumberg, "A History of the Presidential Election of 1908" (University of Wisconsin Ph.D. dissertation, 1960), p. 178. Even after he had chosen Taft to succeed him, Roosevelt "feared" Hughes's popularity and recognized him as Taft's most dangerous competitor. Hughes was said to be Taft's "most dangerous opponent until the very moment the presidential nomination was made." Sumberg, "Presidential Election of 1908," pp. 238–241. For a sample of newspaper comment on Hughes's candidacy, see the *New York Times*, May 27, 1907, p. 5; August 27, p. 3; November 11, p. 5; and December 23, p. 3.]

length Mark Sullivan's statement in *Our Times* which gives an accurate account of the facts.[25] This deals with the removal by the President of Archie Sanders, the holder of a Federal office at Rochester, "as a means of reproving the opposition to Hughes' reform programme." It is true that I had no knowledge of the fact that Superintendent Stevens had suggested this removal to the President. Stevens acted without my authorization, direct or indirect. If I had known that such a suggestion was contemplated I should have opposed and probably prevented it for the reasons which Mark Sullivan states. And when I was asked by the newspaper correspondents if I had requested Sanders' removal, I had to say that I had not. The difficulty arose from the way in which the President's action was treated by one of the newspaper correspondents who implied that Roosevelt's "help was a detriment to Hughes, that it was resented by Hughes's friends."

This correspondent is identified by Beerits as Frank Simonds. Mark Sullivan describes him as one who "actually had been, but now was not, the closest to Hughes, in his particular confidence, and reflecting his most personal attitude." And again as one "who in the recent past had been 'closest to Hughes', but who had 'broken with him some weeks before and was not now seeing him'." This requires a word of explanation. Frank H. Simonds was an able and brilliant correspondent who had represented the New York *Tribune* during the insurance investigation. Later he represented the New York *Evening Post*, a strong supporter of my administration. Simonds was sympathetic with my administrative policies and his articles gave a trenchant account of my efforts and the character and schemes of the opposition. He was shrewd in his guesses and analysis and managed to give the impression that he was in my intimate confidence. This irked some of the other correspondents. I held press conferences twice a day, when in Albany, in the morning especially for the afternoon men and in the afternoon especially for the morning men. I had the good will of almost all the correspondents and this to a considerable extent resulted from the belief that I was fair to all and played no favorites. This was true, and I was scrupulous to give none an "inside track." I was no more intimate with Simonds than with Palmer Gavit, Louis Howe, Louis Seibold, and many others.[26] I saw them all, talked to them frequently, and

[25]*Our Times*, III, 282–288. [Beerits, "First Term as Governor," pp. 21 and 45, feels that this incident turned Roosevelt against Hughes.]

[26][John Palmer Gavit (1868–1954) did newspaper and social work in Hartford before going to Albany as the correspondent of the Associated Press. Later he was chief of the Associated Press bureau in Washington, 1909–1911, and Washington correspondent of the New York *Evening Post*, rising, finally, to become managing editor, vice-president and director of that paper until his retirement in 1922.

answered their questions as fully as I could. But Simonds, as I have said, created the impression by his manner of writing and his predictions that he was the "closest." One day he went too far, in attempting to predict what I was to say in a speech I was about to deliver. He had no basis for this and was wrong in his guess. But the article was written as though it had been inspired by me. At my press conference, after the first edition of the *Post* reached Albany, but which I had not yet seen, one of the correspondents produced the paper and asked me if I had given this advance information to Simonds. I was surprised and compelled to say that I had not, and that the prediction was mistaken. Simonds was deeply offended and left the Executive Chamber to which he did not return for a long period. That constituted the "break" to which Mark Sullivan refers. I greatly regretted this incident, as I admired Simonds' ability and appreciated his support, although its air of coming from one enjoying a confidential relation, which was not the fact, had been at times embarrassing.[27]

I shed no tears over the failure to receive the Republican nomination for the Presidency. While I refused the request of Mr. Taft, which the President endorsed, to take the nomination for Vice-President, I was glad to give earnest support to Mr. Taft both in my Youngstown speech and in campaigning for him in the Middle West.[28]

I was disinclined to become a candidate for a second term as Governor. Physically, I had been living on my reserves and I was nervously worn. Financially, I was making large inroads upon my savings — our family had been increased by the birth of our daughter Elizabeth in August 1907, and with four children (a son in college) and also my father and mother to support, my expenses were about twice my salary.[29]

[Louis McHenry Howe (1871–1936) was a reporter for the New York *Herald* at the time. Subsequently, he was secretary to Franklin Roosevelt from 1915 to his death. For a study of Howe's relationship with Roosevelt, which contains useful information on his years in Albany, see Alfred B. Rollins, Jr., *Roosevelt and Howe* (New York, Alfred A. Knopf, 1962).

[Louis Seibold (1866–1945) also worked for the New York *Herald*. Later in his career he was a correspondent at the Paris Peace Conference and wrote the first interview in the White House with a President of the United States (Woodrow Wilson) in 1920, for which he was awarded a Pulitzer Prize.]

27Mark Sullivan, in a footnote, refers to an interview he had with President Roosevelt in which the latter mentioned humorously a letter he had written to me introducing John L. Sullivan. *Our Times*, III, 288–289. I do not recall that letter, but I do recall that Sullivan came to see me and that I had a delightful talk with him, which, as I remember, he described with some enthusiasm in one of his newspaper interviews.

28Beerits' Memorandum, "First Term as Governor," pp. 64–70; see my Memorandum, *Speeches*, pp. 2–3. [This is reprinted below as Appendix II. On the Youngstown speech, see the *New York Times*, September 7, 1908, p. 5.]

29The salary of the Governor was then $10,000 a year. While the State provided a day and night man to guard the Executive Mansion, a gardener and cleaners, I bore the other

But my supporters were strongly insisting that I must run again in order to consolidate the public gains which they were good enough to attribute to the sort of administration I was trying to give. In the summer of 1908, when I was debating this question in my mind, Dean Hutchins, of the Law School of the University of Michigan (my old associate at Cornell) came to me at the instance of the Trustees of the University to see whether I would entertain an offer of the presidency on President Angell's prospective retirement. I had visited Ann Arbor on February 22, 1907, and had received a most cordial greeting when I addressed the students. I felt, however, that I should stick to the law and return to practice if I did not run again. It soon became apparent that it would seem like leaving in the lurch those who had been so generous in their support if I did not permit my name to be used as a candidate for renomination. Accordingly, I announced that I would run. This was very unwelcome news to the opposition leaders in the party and it took the great influence of Elihu Root and the virtual demand of the President to insure my renomination. In that relation, there was much talk about my having been unfair to the organization — a baseless charge, as the fact was that certain leaders had determined to destroy me politically and had failed to do so. President Roosevelt and others seemed to take some stock in the charge, but it became clear to them that I was so strong with the people that it would be inadvisable to turn me down. As Mr. Roosevelt himself put it years later, "the bosses, the machine leaders, took a man for whom they did not care, because he was the only man with whom they could win." [30]

I should add that my speeches at Youngstown and in the Middle West lessened somewhat the opposition to me in this organization, as they seemed satisfactory evidence that, after all, I was a good Republican. These speeches had pleased both the President and Mr. Taft, and the President gave me the most cordial and thorough-going support during my campaign for re-election. Beerits describes the campaign and quotes from several letters of President Roosevelt.[31]

In my second term, I stressed the importance of reform in the nominating system. The primaries, with their selection of controlled delegates to

---

household expenses including the cost of the page receptions and dinners which it was customary to give. When I went about the State making speeches, unless the occasion was distinctly a State affair, I paid my own expenses including the outlays for stenographic reports.

[30]Theodore Roosevelt, *An Autobiography* (New York, Macmillan, 1913), p. 301.

[31]Beerits' Memorandum, "Renomination and Re-election as Governor," pp. 8–14. [The letters by President Roosevelt are in the Hughes Papers, Box 2. Roosevelt was confident Hughes would defeat his opponent, Lieutenant Governor Lewis Stuyvesant Chanler. Aside from reproducing Roosevelt's letters, Beerits recounts one incident during the campaign in which Hughes answered so effectively a series of questions put to him by Chanler that he forced Chanler on the defensive.]

Reform governor

the district and State conventions, made the nominations practically a matter of appointment by the party bosses. The delegates usually could be counted on to do as they were told and the wishes of even a majority of the rank and file of the members of the party could thus be disregarded. The bosses, in turn, were often the tools of special interests. This seemed to me a travesty of representative government. Take my own case: there was no doubt of the general sentiment of the party members in favor of my renomination. It was pronounced, shown by the press and the opinions expressed by eminent Republicans. But if the President and Mr. Root had not brought strong pressure, the bosses would have controlled the convention and the party members would have had to vote for the candidate thus selected or for the ticket of the opposing party, or many of them might prefer not to vote at all.

In my first term, I had recommended the adoption of a permissive system of direct nominations, but in my second term I proposed a mandatory system. I did not desire to weaken the party, but to establish representative government within the party; not to deprive it of the benefit of the necessary leadership, but to make that leadership more responsive to the opinion of the party members. I did not approve the direct primary as it was maintained in other States, permitting voters of another party to enter the primary and perhaps determine the choice. In New York, we had an enrollment system which established the right to vote in the respective party primaries, and I desired that these enrolled voters should be able to select the candidates they wanted. I did not entertain the illusion that any method would induce party members to vote in a primary if they had no special interest in the outcome, but I wished them to have the say whenever the occasion was such that their interest was aroused. If the organization leaders backed the candidate the voters wanted, it would not be necessary for them to vote their concurrence, but I thought they should have the chance to oppose the leaders' choice and present to the primary an opposing candidate. And if they had that opportunity I thought that whenever there was a real demand within the party for a particular candidate, the party leaders would name him rather than run the risk of being turned down. My plan was worked out with the special assistance of the Young Republican Club of Brooklyn.[32] As John Lord O'Brian had recently put it, it was designed "to compel the leaders themselves to seek renomination on the same ticket with the men whose nomination they advocated." [33]

[32]Beerits' Memorandum, "Second Term as Governor," pp. 4–9. See, also, my speech in Indianapolis, ["The Fate of the Direct Primary"] November 18, 1920, published in *National Municipal Review*, Vol. 10, No. 1 (January 1921), pp. 23–31. [A copy of this speech is also in the Hughes Papers.]

[33]*American Bar Association Journal* (July 1941), p. 413.

[Beerits described the plan and Hughes' attitude toward it as follows:

["He entertained no illusion as to his ability to make men over. He realized that in public affairs one has to count on the general apathy of the people, unless a matter touches their immediate interest, in which case they will act according to that interest, despite any preaching to the contrary. Nevertheless, Governor Hughes did not see why something worthwhile could not be done to improve the primary election system...

["Governor Hughes gave a great deal of thought and consideration to the problem. He believed in the value of political parties. He believed, moreover, in the two-party system. He felt that it was impossible to manage our system of government and make it work successfully with a large jumble of parties. Primaries should be regarded as a party matter, a means of furnishing nominations for the party...

["The State should be divided into small primary districts. In each of these districts a party committeeman would be chosen by the electors of the party at a primary election. These committeemen, selected by the voters in the small districts, would meet in Assembly districts in order to select the party's candidate for Assemblyman for that district. To select candidates for Senators, a larger committee, made up of the committeemen selected in the smallest districts, would meet in the larger Senate Districts. The party's candidate for Governor would be selected at a meeting of a large committee made up of one representative from each of the Assembly districts. Thus if there were 150 Assembly districts, there would be 150 members of the committee which was to select a candidate for Governor.

["The candidates thus selected would be simply party designations, not party nominees. At a primary election there would be a vote by the members of the party as to whether the candidates thus designated should be actually nominated. At this primary the electors would be under no obligation to vote for the candidates designated by the committees, if they felt that such designations were not worthy. The electors could nominate another candidate if they wished.

["These representative bodies which we have called committees, elected directly by the party members, and having the authority to propose nominations for State offices, would formulate a statement of the party principles, or the party platform. These bodies would furnish the facilities for conference and consultation in order that fit men should be chosen to represent the party as candidates. The distinctive feature of such a body — whether or not we call it a convention is of no consequence — would be that it would consist of a directly responsible group, instead of a host of delegates selected in such manner and such number as to be without any real personal responsibility to the party voters. It would be a nominating committee, appointed by the party in convenient manner so as to charge each representative with direct responsibility.

["Under such a system the renomination of a person who had served faithfully in the Legislature would not be at the mercy of the machine, for his renomination would now depend directly upon the wishes of the party voters of his district."] [34]

[34] [Beerits, "Second Term as Governor," pp. 4–9. At pp. 15–22, Beerits describes at great length how Roosevelt was drawn back into New York politics over the direct primary fight and how Hughes skillfully maneuvered to win Roosevelt's unequivocal support. See also, Wesser, *Charles Evans Hughes*, pp. 295–301.]

I did not succeed in obtaining the legislation I sought, but the effort, I think, had a salutary effect.

In my second term, I succeeded in having the provisions of the Public Service Commissions Act extended to telegraph and telephone companies.

From the outset, I had sought to strengthen the State Labor Department. In 1909, I recommended that inquiry should be made into the questions relating to employer's liability and compensation for workmen's injuries, noting the wastefulness and injustice of the existing methods. A legislative committee conducted a thorough inquiry which resulted in two acts which I approved. One provided for an elective compensation plan; the other, a plan of compulsory compensation applicable to certain dangerous employments.[35] The New York Court of Appeals held the latter to be in violation of the due process clause of the State Constitution.[36] That was not my view. And later, the Supreme Court of the United States held that a law of this sort did not violate the due process clause of the Federal Constitution.[37] In New York, an amendment to the State Constitution was adopted in 1913 so as to permit workmen's compensation laws and under that provision a State Compensation Act was duly enacted.

Beerits refers to the various activities which lay outside my regular work.[38] During the summers, I spoke at many county fairs and I visited state institutions — the state hospitals and prisons. There were many occasions of particular interest.

It was at the Jamestown Exposition, in July 1907, that I first met Woodrow Wilson. Beerits mentions the breakfast at Henry Tucker's house in Norfolk before we went to the Exposition grounds to make our speeches.[39] Mr. Wilson was a most charming conversationalist and we had a thoroughly enjoyable time. I recall that he made some remark which led one of the ladies to express surprise, saying that she thought the President of Princeton had to be a clergyman. Mr. Wilson said that others had that notion and that the University, he feared, had lost a large gift because he had given some offense in repeating a favorite limerick in the presence of an old Presbyterian lady. We demanded the limerick and he gave it as follows:

> There was a young man of Siberia
> Whose life grew drearier and drearier,

[35]*Public Papers*, 1907, pp. 35–36; 1908, pp. 30–31; 1909, p. 34; 1910, p. 235.

[36]Ives v. South Buffalo Railway Co., 201 N.Y. 271, 317, [94 N.E. 431 (1911)].

[37]New York Central R.R. Co. v. White, 243 U.S. 188 [1917]; Mountain Timber Co. v. Washington, 243 U.S. 219 [1917].

[38][Beerits, "Second Term as Governor," pp. 26–32, mentions two sensational murder cases and a threat against Hughes's life. In the earlier sections of the memorandum, Beerits chronicles several scandals that rocked the Republican Party bosses. See especially pp. 23–25.]

[39][Beerits, "Second Term as Governor"], p. 32b.

Governor Hughes leading the New York delegation at President Taft's inauguration, March 4, 1909

So he burst from his cell
With a hell of a yell
And eloped with the Mother Superior.

In later years, when Mr. Wilson (who seemed when President of Princeton to be rather conservative, and occasionally would come to New York and I thought by innuendo somewhat disparaged my modest efforts at reform) surprised the country with the liberal measures he promoted as Governor of New Jersey, I though his limerick might be taken, in a figurative sense, to be autobiographical.

In March 1909, I attended President Taft's inauguration and rode a horse at the head of the New York troops. As I had not been on horseback since boyhood, I practiced for a few mornings at the Albany Riding Academy. But this was not adequate preparation for what proved to be the ordeal of Inauguration Day. The night before there was a fierce storm and the streets of Washington were covered with snow and ice. Immediately after the ceremony, which was held indoors, I went to a designated place southeast of the Capitol where Squadron A of the New York Cavalry was stationed. We waited for over an hour before we could take our position in the inaugural parade. The horses were very restive as the icicles dropped from the trees upon their backs. As customary, I wore a silk hat and a frock coat, with my Marshal's scarf, and thinking an overcoat too clumsy I had protected myself by a chamois vest. But my hands inside my gloves were very cold and I had to dig them into the horse's flesh to keep them from freezing. As we came down the hill from the Capitol our horses almost slid on the icy street. My horse had always been in the ranks, and it was with difficulty that he could be persuaded to take his place at the head of the procession. At the beginning he was continually trying to get back to his familiar companions in the line. But with the cheers of the crowd as we came to the large stands, he seemed to realize that this was his day and he went along at the head, proudly arching his neck and acting his part as a well-trained horse of the Commander-in-Chief should. I made my bows with all the grace I could command and managed to get through without mishap. I dismounted at 19th Street and Pennsylvania Avenue, Northwest (where the parade broke up), with a keen sense of relief. The storm was so severe that the Seventh Regiment of New York failed to get to Washington in time and President Taft gave it a special review on the next morning, asking me to join him.

In 1909, there was a series of outstanding events. I visited the Alaska-Yukon-Pacific Exposition at Seattle and spoke on New York Day. In July, we had in New York the Tercentenary Celebration of the discovery of Lake Champlain with meetings at each place of importance on both shores of the Lake, and in the fall the Tercentenary Celebration of the discovery of the Hudson River and the One-Hundredth Anniversary of Fulton's invention, combined in what was called the Hudson-Fulton Celebration, with many speeches.[40]

On my visit to Mr. Roosevelt at Oyster Bay in July 1910, on his invitation, I had a long talk with him about my experiences as Governor and he then seemed to be fully in sympathy with what I had done as well as with my objectives.[41] Later, in his library, he gave his guests a humorous description of his meeting with foreign potentates on his trip abroad, and especially of his interview with the Kaiser. He pointed to a vase, enormous but not very beautiful, which had been given him and snapped out in his inimitable manner, "A bit of German crockery; I will send it to the Germanic Museum at Harvard." Then he brought out a folio on Art, with a full-page inscription written by the Kaiser who considered himself to be the last authority on that subject. The inscription was in English dealing with the canons of art, as I recall it, and Mr. Roosevelt read it with great gusto. When he got to the signature "Wilhelm I.R." he observed with a chuckle, "slightly ungrammatical." But he added that he got one gift from the Kaiser that he really prized, a copy of the *Nibelungenlied*. "The Kaiser showed it to me," Mr. Roosevelt remarked, "and said something which I at once interpreted as an offer and immediately accepted."

During these four years (October 1906 to October 1910) I had little opportunity for diversion but I made the best of what I had. In 1907, we spent the summer (when our daughter Elizabeth was born), at the Executive Mansion in Albany. But I had a few days with my son fishing and tramping in the Adirondack woods, making our headquarters in a for-

[40][In July 1909, the University of Michigan again sought Hughes as its president. Declining to be considered, Hughes gave these reasons: "For me the work would be in an untried field, and my opinion of its importance is such that I should not care to make the experiment . . . I do not expect to hold public office after my term as Governor ends; but in the course of the professional work for which I have laboriously prepared myself, I should hope that there would be abundant opportunity for public service which might be not the less important because it was not of an official character. In short, I feel that my work has best fitted me for a sphere which I would not define too narrowly as professional, but on the other hand is quite distinct from the other sphere to which I should be introduced in undertaking the duties of a University President. There is another reason. I was born and have spent most of my life in the State of New York. The people have twice honored me with election to their highest office. So far as I can see now, my work is here. While official responsibilities will cease when my term expires, I feel that I should retain my citizenship here and my identification with the interests of the State with which I have become so closely familiar and to advance which, so far as there may be opportunity in private life, I should be ready to give my service." Hughes to James B. Angell, July 14, 1909, James B. Angell Papers, Michigan Historical Collections, University of Michigan.]

[41][These incidents are described in Beerits, "Second Term as Governor"], pp. 14–15, 17–21, 32b and c, 33–35.

ester's camp. In 1908 and 1909, we had a cottage at Saranac Inn, which was virtually an Executive office. I got away for a short walking trip, with my son and his college chum, from Lake Placid through the Indian Pass to the Tawahus Club and thence, stopping for fishing at Lake Colden, to the top of Mount Marcy. There was an interesting incident. While on the top of the mountain a party of young people joined us. One of the young ladies brought me a lot of huckleberries and I gave the party some tea and a beefsteak that we did not need. The next fall at the great campaign meeting at Madison Square Garden as I was taken through the crowd to the speakers' stand a young woman thrust out her hand and gave me a card which I read as I was waiting for the audience to quiet down and give me a chance to speak. The card said: "Good luck! We ate your steak and drank your health in the tea."

In 1909, on my way to Seattle, I drove through Yellowstone Park and, returning from Seattle by the Canadian Pacific, I stopped for a day at Banff and also for a day or two at Lake Louise. In 1910, we remained through the entire summer at Albany, save for about a week, which Mrs. Hughes and I spent at the Tawahus Club.

I resigned as Governor on October 6, 1910, and was sworn in and took my seat on the Supreme Court on the following Monday, October 10, 1910.

Chapter XI The Supreme Court *1910–1916*

The reasons which led me to accept President Taft's offer of an appointment as Associate Justice of the Supreme Court are stated in my letter of acceptance.[1]

[The President's offer came in his letter of April 22, 1910.

["I write to offer you the position of Justice of the Supreme Court of the United States to succeed Mr. Justice Brewer and I hope you will accept it. I know the reasons that suggest themselves against your acceptance and I do not minimize them. I believe as strongly as possible that you are likely to be nominated and elected President sometime in the future unless you go upon the Bench or make such associations at the Bar as to prevent.

["You are Governor of New York and have certain policies you would like to further by as much work in their support as the remainder of your term makes possible and your successor, if you resigned, would not be especially useful in that regard.

["You look forward with certainty to a professional income which will make you independent in ten years.

["1. To these suggestions, I would reply that if you prefer a judicial to a political life, you might as well take the step now.

["2. If you accept, you need not qualify as Justice or resign the Governorship until the second week of October, which would leave but two months and a half of your term remaining.

["3. The position is for life. The salary is $12,500 and will in all probability be increased at the next session to $17,500. The Chief Justiceship is soon likely to be vacant and I should never regard the practice of not promoting Associate Justices as one to be followed. Though, of course, this suggestion is only that by accepting the present position you do not bar yourself from the other, should it fall vacant in my term.

["Let me hear from you.

[1][Hughes Papers;] Beerits' Memorandum, "Second Term as Governor," pp. 38–39c. [See, also, Henry F. Pringle, *The Life and Times of William Howard Taft* (New York, Farrar & Rinehard, Inc., 1939), I, 531–533.]

["I make this offer first because I know you will strengthen the Bench as a lawyer and a jurist with a great power of application and second because you will strengthen the Bench in the confidence of the people.

Sincerely yours,
Wm. H. Taft

["P.S. Don't misunderstand me as to the Chief Justiceship. I mean that if that office were now open, I should offer it to you and it is probable that if it were to become vacant during my term, I should promote you to it; but, of course, conditions change, so that it would not be right for me to say by way of promise what I would do in the future. Nor, on the other hand, would I have you think that your declination now would prevent my offering you the higher place, should conditions remain as they are."

[In his letter of acceptance to Taft on April 24, 1910, Hughes wrote:

["So far as my personal inclinations are concerned, they lie in the direction of judicial work. My training and professional interest have been such that I should undertake this work with a personal satisfaction which no other line of effort could command in the same degree. No one could have a more profound sense of the vast responsibilities of the Supreme Court than I have, and while this makes me realize the more keenly my shortcomings, it also disposes me to welcome the opportunity to devote my life to such important service. Against such a life-work, to meet the conditions of which an adjustment could be made, I should not for a moment set any prospect of money-making at the bar.

["I trust that I should be able, however, to withstand any personal inclination and not permit it to control my decision, if it were opposed to the obligations of public duty. This is the only question which has occasioned any difficulty. But reflection has reassured me upon this point. There is no definite sphere of public usefulness, other than the place you offer, which would be open to me at the close of this year and my circumstances would permit me to accept. The opportunities of the future are conjectural. The alternative of your proposal is private practice. Undoubtedly this would permit public service in many ways, but there would also be the exacting demands of active work at the bar. Against this division of effort, and its doubtful fruition, I should have on the bench a definite field of usefulness in the discharge of a function of national government of the greatest consequence to our people and to the future of our institutions.

["The question seems to me to be really — What right have I to refuse the opportunity of public service which is now presented by you and upon what ground could justify myself in turning aside from such a plain path of usefulness?

["Your expressions regarding the Chief Justiceship are understood and most warmly appreciated. You properly reserve entire freedom with respect to this and I accept the offer you now make without wishing you to feel committed in the slightest degree. Should the vacancy occur during your term, I, in common with all our citizens, should desire you to act freely and without embarrassment in accordance with your best judgment at that time."]

My nomination by the President on April 25, 1910, was confirmed by the Senate on May 2, 1910. I reconciled my acceptance with my sense of public duty as Governor by the thought that, in accordance with President Taft's suggestion, I could remain in the latter office until the Court convened in the following October. This would enable me to serve all but a few weeks of my term. As it turned out, I had an extra session of the Legislature in June and it was July before I was relatively free. I should have resigned then and taken the long rest I seriously needed. But I had hundreds of applications for pardons pending and I did not wish to leave to my successor such an accumulation of work. So I spent the summer over a host of papers, clearing my desk so far as possible, and remained as Governor to the last possible moment. The result was that I entered upon the difficult and engrossing judicial work in October 1910, feeling tired out instead of refreshed and full of zest. It was a long time before I was fully restored to my normal vigor.

The facilities afforded to the Court were then very slender. The old court room in the Capitol, though inadequate in size, gave the Court a worthy setting and was rich in memories. Across a hall was the robing room where the Justices robed and took their lunch during sessions. Below was the conference room and library, small and cluttered, where we crowded about the conference table. As some of the Justices objected to open windows, the room became overheated and the air foul during our long conferences, not conducive to good humor.

The court room itself was not well aired. A story is told of Justice Gray[2] who was large and full-blooded. He insisted on a window being open behind the screen. Justice Brown[3] was rather frail and, feeling the draft, asked one of the pages to close the window. Justice Gray, overheated, arose from the bench and going behind the screen found the window shut. He said to the frightened page: "What damned fool told you to close that window?" "Mr. Justice Brown," said the page. "I thought so," said Justice Gray, storming back to the bench.

The Clerk's office was also most inadequate. Its entrance room and the corridor outside the court room were the only places where the members of the bar could congregate and smoke, awaiting the call of their cases. I suppose that no high court in the country had fewer conveniences.

Still, most of the Justices were loath to leave the Capitol. We could have had a new building when Taft was President, as he was eager to have one provided, but Chief Justice White[4] strongly opposed. He thought that if

[2][Horace Gray (1828–1902), former Chief Justice of the Supreme Judicial Court of Massachusetts, was appointed to the Supreme Court of the United States in 1882 and served until his death.]

[3][Henry Billings Brown (1836–1913) served on the Supreme Court from 1890 until 1906. He is perhaps best known for his opinion for the Court in Plessy v. Ferguson, 163 U.S. 537 (1896).]

[4][Edward Douglass White (1845–1921), Confederate drummer boy and later U.S. Senator from Louisiana, was appointed to the Supreme Court of the United States from the Senate in 1894. He was the first Associate Justice to be promoted to the Chief Justiceship when President Taft elevated him to that position in 1910. He died in office.]

Associate Justice of the Supreme Court, 1910

the Court sat away from the Capitol, the public would lose interest in it, a notion which seems fantastic now in view of the thousands of visitors to our present sumptuous quarters. As the individual Justices had no rooms assigned to them in the Capitol,[5] they had to obtain homes that were spacious enough to provide offices for themselves and their secretaries. The Government supplied furniture for these offices in our residences and also a working library. We had but a small allowance for clerical help; that is, $2000 a year, only enough to provide a secretary. Most of the Justices had secretaries who were lawyers, but these spent the greater part of their time in stenographic work and typewriting correspondence, memoranda and opinions. My secretaries (while Associate Justice I had three, in succession) were fine young men who had been admitted to the bar, but as I kept them busy with dictation, hating to write in longhand, they had little or no time to devote to research and whatever was necessary in that line I did myself. Occasionally, the question of providing law clerks in addition to secretaries would be raised but nothing was done. Some suggested that if we had experienced law clerks, it might be thought that they were writing our opinions. An exception was Chief Justice White who hired a law clerk and paid him out of his own pocket. Justice Holmes[6] who wrote his letters and opinions in his own hand and did not need a stenographer took each year as his secretary a brilliant graduate of the Harvard Law School and made a companion of him. Years later, after I had resigned from the Court, law clerks as well as secretaries were provided for the Justices who desired them and, indeed, with the enlarged certiorari practice after 1925, most Justices found such help indispensable. And since 1935, when the Court took possession of its new building, the Justices have had commodious offices for themselves and their clerks, with all possible conveniences.

When I was appointed, I had difficulty in finding a residence with the space needed for my family and offices. We first leased the house at 2401 Massachusetts Avenue and I had my offices in the basement. This arrangement was far from satisfactory and I soon decided that it would be advisable to put what was left of my savings into a permanent home. Former Senator John B. Henderson[7] sold me a lot on the southwest corner of Sixteenth and V Streets, Northwest, at a very low price — what it had cost him — and I built a commodious house in which I expected to live

[5] A couple of the Justices [George Sutherland and Owen J. Roberts] sometime later obtained old committee rooms in the Capitol.

[6] [Oliver Wendell Holmes (1841–1935), author of *The Common Law* (1881) and member of the Supreme Judicial Court of Massachusetts (1883–1902), served on the Supreme Court of the United States from 1902 to 1932.]

[7] [John B. Henderson (1826–1913), U.S. Senator from Missouri was author of the Thirteenth Amendment to the U.S. Constitution.]

for the rest of my days.[8] It was ready for use in November 1911, and there we remained until the fall of 1916.

During the first three months of my service on the bench, there were only seven Justices. Chief Justice Fuller[9] died in July 1910, and Justice Moody[10] was incapacitated by illness which soon led to his retirement under a special Act of Congress. Thus, I never sat in the last seat on the extreme left of the Chief Justice but took my place in the last seat on the right. Adjoining was the vacant seat of Justice Moody and next to that sat Justice Holmes. The very first day I sat, Justice Holmes leaned over and beckoned me to move up and take Justice Moody's place. I knew enough of the traditions not to make such a *faux pas,* and I tremble to think what might have happened if I had been innocent enough to follow Justice Holmes's kindly but rather thoughtless suggestion. The other Justices would have regarded me as a fresh and bumptious newcomer, and even the Chief Justices in their marble busts might have raised their eyebrows.[11]

All the Justices gave me a warm welcome. I had not known any of them personally, except Justice Harlan.[12] He had occasionally written to me in Albany, and when I came to Washington in February 1909, to deliver the address at the Convocation of George Washington University, he took me under his wing, driving me about the city in the afternoon and introducing me to Justice Brown (retired) at the latter's reception. When I came to the Court, Justice Harlan was particularly earnest in expressing his pleasure at my appointment, and during the year that I sat with him,[13] he was like a father to me.

I found the work very difficult. At that time the Court was far behind in its calendar and it was the practice to advance important cases to be heard at the beginning of each session. It was generally about January before the Court reached the regular call, and if at the end of the Term in June we had left only 150 unheard cases (which could have been argued if reached) we thought we were doing well. That was before the reform made by the Act of 1925,[14] which gave the Court in large measure, through

[8]The neighborhood was then a very quiet one. There were no buildings on the east side of Sixteenth Street between Meridian Hill and U Street.

[9][Melville Weston Fuller (1833–1910) became Chief Justice of the United States in 1888 and served on the Supreme Court until his death.]

[10][William Henry Moody (1853–1917), Secretary of Navy (1902–1904) and Attorney General (1904–1906), served on the Supreme Court from 1906 until 1910.]

[11][Hughes was referring to the marble busts of the chief justices that were on the back semicircle of the courtroom in the basement of the Senate Building. Today the room is sometimes used for hearings by Senate committees; the busts are still there.]

[12][John Marshall Harlan (1833–1911) served on the Supreme Court from 1877 until his death.]

[13]Justice Harlan died in October 1911.

[14]Act of February 13, 1925 [Ch. 229, §1], 43 Stat. 936, [as amended, 28 U.S.C. §1254 (1964).]

the certiorari practice, the right to determine in advance whether cases were of such a character as to justify their being heard. In after years, the Court was able, by virtue of this reform, to close its term every year with the record of having heard all cases that were ready for argument. This was true every year during my service as Chief Justice.

In my very first week, with the advanced cases bunched for argument, I had a heavy load. I thought, as the arguments went on, that in a month or so I might be ready to vote, and I was amazed to find that, save for some special reason for delay, it was expected that the cases heard during the week would be voted on at the Conference on Saturday. I plunged into the work and it was not long before I was able fairly well to keep up with it. But I found it advisable to do a great deal of reading outside of the demands of the cases in hand, in order to get a comprehensive view of the jurisprudence of the Court. That jurisprudence is compact, but one's study of it as a responsible Justice is distinct in its purpose and method from the sporadic review of authorities in the course of advocacy at the bar. The advocate is looking for something to support a particular argument and too often seizes upon any sentence in an opinion which he thinks will help him win his case. The jurist is studying the philosophy of the decisions and the different currents of opinion. He learns the points of view of the Justices and to read their reasoning and various *dicta* in that light. Not infrequently a sentence or phrase, or even a paragraph, will get into a majority opinion which really does not have majority support and the effect of which one or more of the majority may be desirous of destroying as soon as they get a chance. A new Justice is not at ease in his seat until he has made a thorough study of lines of cases, so that when a case is argued he at once recognizes, or by looking at a key case brings back to his memory, the jurisprudence of the Court upon the general subject and can address his mind to the particular variant now presented. That is the explanation of the ability of experienced Justices to dispose rapidly of their work, and also of the difficulties the new Justice encounters in going over ground which is more familiar to his seniors on the bench. I spent long hours at night in close study. At that time the Justices were in the center of social activity and were much in demand at dinner parties. When at the beginning of 1911, Justices Van Devanter[15] and Lamar[16] came on the bench, we had a relatively young Court and the Justices went out a great deal. The older Justices too kept up the pace. Justice Holmes was a most popular guest and an inveterate dinner-goer. I found these social affairs very exacting. I was much in demand and invitations came long in

[15] [Willis Van Devanter (1859–1941) served on the Supreme Court from 1910 until 1937.]

[16] [Joseph Rucker Lamar (1857–1916), a former justice of the Georgia Supreme Court, served on the Supreme Court of the United States from 1911 until his death in 1916.]

advance; and when I tried to limit my engagements to a couple a week, and had made these, then others of such importance that I could not well refuse would come and I would find myself going three or four nights a week. One good feature of these parties was that we could get away early, shortly after ten as a rule, and I would then return to my library to read law until one or two o'clock in the morning.

I looked forward with eagerness to the long vacation of 1911. But that gave me no relief. For President Taft had a Joint Resolution passed providing for a Commission to determine the cost of second-class mail matter, then a question of much public interest in connection with a proposal to raise the rates. The Joint Resolution provided for three members, one of them to be a Justice of the Supreme Court.[17] President Taft asked me to serve, saying that he had the Resolution passed with the intention to appoint me and did not wish to name any other Justice. I had not been consulted about this action and strongly resisted. But President Taft was insistent, arguing that it would not be a difficult task, that all the calculations had been made in the Post Office Department and that I should have able associates — President A. Lawrence Lowell of Harvard and Harry A. Wheeler,[18] a leading businessman of Chicago. So I was persuaded to undertake the task. Of course, it turned out to be a very hard one. We held public hearings during the summer of 1911. The calculations of the Post Office Department were strongly challenged and we had to take a lot of technical evidence and make our own calculations. I caught a severe cold and suffered greatly from lumbago. Through the fall while I was trying to keep up with the work of the Court I was busy over figures until late into the night. It was February 1912, before we got in our report, and it was not until the summer of 1912 that I had any opportunity for rest.

I may say a word at this point as to the practice of Presidents in appointing judges, and especially Justices of the Supreme Court, to administrative commissions. The reasons for this practice are obvious. There may be hundreds of persons well qualified for an administrative inquiry, but they may not be well known to the country or may have a disqualifying identification with politics or controversies. A Justice of the Supreme Court may be of outstanding qualifications and high in public confidence. Still, I think that the practice is bad. The work of the Court is so heavy and important that it demands all one's time and energy, and a Justice should not be drawn from it for a task not appropriately within the judicial sphere. To the extent that the administrative work cuts into judicial time,

17[J. Res. 16, 36 Stat. 1458 (1911).]

18[Harry A. Wheeler (1866–1960) spent many years with the Credit Clearing House and the Union Trust Company in Chicago. His activity with the Chicago Association of Commerce led to his participation in the founding of the United States Chamber of Commerce. He was the Chamber's first president, 1912–1913, and served a second term in 1918–1919.]

the Court is deprived of the benefit of the Justice's collaboration and sometimes this may result in an evenly divided Court. Again, these administrative commissions bring the Justice into a realm of controversy with which he should not be associated. It is best for the Court and the country that the Justices should strictly limit themselves to their judicial work, and that the dignity, esteem, and indeed the aloofness, which attach to them by virtue of their high office as the final interpreters of legislation and constitutional provisions, should be jealously safeguarded.

In saying this, I do not criticise the acceptance by Justices of the recent appointments made by President Roosevelt. After Pearl Harbor, Justice Roberts could not well decline the President's request to take part in the inquiry as to the causes of that disaster. And Justice Byrnes was especially fitted for the exacting task to which the President summoned him.[19] That task, however, was not a temporary one, like that assigned to Justice Roberts, and Justice Byrnes did well to repel the suggestion, which rumor says was made, to have his place on the bench kept open for him and he unselfishly insisted upon an unqualified resignation. I think Chief Justice Stone did the Court and the country a service by refusing appointment on the Rubber Commission, which while highly important was not of a character appropriately to demand the time and strength of the Chief Justice.[20]

Perhaps an exception should be made of international arbitrations. These call for judicial service of the most important description, and when Governments pay a Justice or Chief Justice the compliment of calling upon him to act as arbiter of an international dispute, it may be in the interest of peace and international good will that he should accept. Our Chief Justices have acted in this capacity. For example, Chief Justice White acted as arbitrator in the dispute between Panama and Costa Rica; Chief Justice Taft in that between Great Britain and Costa Rica; and I acted in the controversy between Guatemala and Honduras. But my experience in that difficult though successful arbitration made me decide never again to act in that capacity, the draft upon time and energies being too great to make such a service compatible with official duty. Justice Roberts was induced to take the umpireship in a serious controversy between the United States and Germany and, while it was believed at the outset that there would be but little for him to do at that stage of the controversy, it lasted for years in a most annoying fashion. Our Justices have too much to do to accept such responsibilities and it is hoped

[19][James Francis Brynes (1906–1972) served on the Supreme Court from 1941 to 1942. He was appointed Director of Economic Stabilization in 1942. Subsequently he was Secretary of State (1945–1947) and Governor of South Carolina (1951–1955).]

[20][For Chief Justice Stone's views on this subject, see Alpheus Thomas Mason, *Harlan Fiske Stone: Pillar of the Law* (New York, Viking Press, 1956), pp. 705–720.]

that there will be again an international tribunal inspiring such confidence that governments will be willing to submit their disputes to it and that there will be no adequate reason for Justices of our Supreme Court to undertake arbitral duties.

I confess that at the outset I found the atmosphere of the Court somewhat less agreeable than I had expected it to be. It was apparent that Justice Harlan and Justice White did not like each other. Justice Harlan was antipathetic to Justice Holmes, and Holmes to Harlan, though each respected the soldierly qualities of the other. When in conference Justice Harlan would express himself rather sharply in answer to what Justice Holmes would say, the latter, always urbane, would refer to Justice Harlan as "my lion-hearted friend." The vacancy in the Chief Justiceship was a cause of some irritation. It was clear to me that Justice Harlan desired the appointment as the crown of his judicial service; he thought that he could be appointed with the idea that it would not be long before the post could be given to a younger man. Justice White, I am sure, felt that he was entitled to the place, and through the fall he was plainly out of sorts. At that time, while Justice Harlan was presiding as Senior Justice, Justice White had little to say in conference and seemed offish. My own name was freely used in the press in connection with the vacancy. I did not, in the slightest degree, resent the President's failure to appoint me, for it was well understood between us that, despite his reference to the matter when he offered me the Associate Justiceship, he was entirely free from any commitment.[21] I felt, too, that it might well be thought that I was too young and inexperienced to deserve appointment as Chief Justice and I fully appreciated the burden it would cast upon me. However, I did wish that the President would settle the matter as I was much embarrassed by the constant use of my name. I thought that if the President was not going to appoint me he should say so frankly and proceed promptly to appoint someone else. But until the last moment many expected my appointment — both Justices Lurton[22] and Day,[23] who were close to the President, tell-

[21]See correspondence quoted in Beerits' Memorandum, "Second Term as Governor," pp. 38–39c. [Beerits quotes Archie Butt, President Taft's personal secretary, as recording the following statement by the President: "I don't know the man I admire more than Hughes. If ever I have the chance I shall offer him the Chief Justiceship." Archie Butt, *Taft and Roosevelt: The Intimate Letters of Archie Butt*, 2 vols. (New York, Doubleday, Doran & Co., 1930), I, 310.]

[22][Horace Harmon Lurton (1844–1914) had served in the Confederate army and later was a colleague of William Howard Taft on the U.S. Court of Appeals for the Sixth Circuit. Taft appointed him to the Supreme Court in 1910, and he served until his death in 1914.]

[23][William Rufus Day (1849–1923) served briefly as Secretary of State in the McKinley administration and then succeeded William Howard Taft on the U.S. Court of Appeals for the Sixth Circuit. He was appointed to the Supreme Court in 1903 and served until his retirement in 1922.]

ing me that they thought I should be appointed. On Sunday evening, December 11, 1910, I received a telephone message from the White House asking me to call on the President, but within half an hour, while I was dressing to go, word came canceling the appointment; and the next day, Justice White's nomination was sent to the Senate.

I think it is a mistake for the President to delay making judicial appointments. As soon as a vacancy occurs, especially one in the Supreme Court, the President should give immediate consideration to the appointment and make up his mind, thus avoiding the embarrassment which the vacancy occasions both to the Court and to those whose names are discussed in the press. In the fall of 1910 the Court had only seven Justices and no Chief Justice. In 1941 after Justice McReynolds retired in February, the Court was left with eight Justices until the end of the Term and several cases which were decided by an evenly divided Court had to be reargued at the next Term.

With the appointment of the Chief Justice at the end of 1910, and of Justices Van Devanter and Lamar, the atmosphere of the Court changed and we became a reasonably happy family. Chief Justice White assumed his new duties with manifest pleasure and with the most earnest desire to discharge them well. He was no longer distant or difficult. On the contrary, he was most considerate and gracious in his dealings with every member of the Court, plainly anxious to create an atmosphere of friendliness and to promote agreement in the disposition of cases. Through the six Terms of my association with him there was never a time in which he failed to show me the utmost kindliness and often he honored me with special confidences. He served with absolute fidelity, permitting neither past associations, nor differences of race or sect, to prejudice his mind or impair the impartiality of his judicial action. He had much trouble with his eyes but had an extraordinary memory for all he heard in argument. Keenly sensitive, and solicitous for the reputation of the Court, he bore his heavy burden with a troubled spirit but with unvarying steadfastness and courage. He tried to keep in good health by his daily walks to and from the Capitol, and it was a familiar scene to see him trudging along, generally with Justice Van Devanter in close consultation, and stopping every few blocks to rest his feet. In his last years, he suffered from serious physical disability but was determined not to yield his place, and with rare heroism kept at his task until the end.[24]

Justice Harlan concealed whatever disappointment he felt in not being made Chief Justice and continued his work through the 1910 Term with but little apparent abatement in his vigor. Stalwart and imposing in mien,

[24]Chief Justice White died on May 19, 1921.

somewhat overbearing yet warm hearted, he seemed to me to embody in his strength and dignity the old traditions of the Court, of such Justices as Clifford, Field, and Miller.[25] I recall that once at luncheon on conference day Harlan and White spoke of the time when Harlan had been sent to Louisiana by President Hayes, in the spring of 1877, as a member of a Commission to bring about a settlement of local controversies. The Commission was met by a delegation of which White was either the head or a member. White said that he described freely to the Commission the actual conditions in the State, and when he was through a very large man (Harlan) with a buff-colored vest rose from his seat and approached White and said, "Well, you are damned frank." That was the first meeting of these two men who were destined to be so long associated, and so influential, in the work of the Court.

Justice Harlan and Justice Holmes continued to be gentlemanly opponents. Justice Harlan thought that Justice Holmes' constitutional views were "unsound" and that his opinions had too many "obscure phrases"; while Justice Holmes thought Justice Harlan's opinions were verbose and tended to be demagogical. In the spring of 1911, Justice Harlan was disturbed by the serenity of the Court and complained to me that there were too few dissents. With a passionate outburst seldom if ever equaled in the annals of the Court, he brought his service to a dramatic conclusion. This was his oral dissent in the *Standard Oil* case.[26] He went far beyond his written opinion, launching out into a bitter invective, which I thought most unseemly. It was not a swan song but the roar of an angry lion. Almost at the opening of the next Term, he was gone.

Justice McKenna,[27] who succeeded Harlan as Senior Justice, was a mild-mannered man, always friendly. He had little to say in conference [and] was hesitant to express a definite view, often saying that he would prefer not to vote until he could "see the opinion." Justice Day was of delicate physique, in contrast to his stalwart sons, one of whom on his appearance in Court was described by Justice Holmes as "a block off the old chip." But Day was mentally very vigorous, clear in his views and precise in his statements, while enlivening our discussions with a ready wit. Justice Lurton was the typical judge of the old school, solid, experienced, deliberate and conservative. He and Day had sat with Taft in the Circuit

[25] [Nathan Clifford (1803–1881) served on the Supreme Court from 1858 to 1881.

[Stephen Johnson Field (1816–1899) served on the Supreme Court from 1863 to 1897.

[Samuel Freeman Miller (1816–1890), a medical doctor who became a lawyer, was appointed to the Supreme Court in 1862 and served until his death. He wrote the Court's opinion in the Slaughter House Cases, 16 Wall. 36 (1873). An active Republican from the party's inception, he was a dark horse compromise candidate for president at the convention of 1884.]

[26] Decided May 15, 1911 [Standard Oil Co. v. United States], 221 U.S. 1, 82 [1910].

[27] [Joseph McKenna (1843–1926), Attorney General during the McKinley administration, was appointed to the Supreme Court in 1898 and served until his retirement in 1925.]

Court of Appeals of the Sixth Circuit — which we accordingly called the "learned Sixth" — and were intimate friends. Day was proud of his service in the Department of State and was devoted to the memory of President McKinley; he never failed to give each Justice a carnation to wear on the anniversary of McKinley's birth.

The accession of Justices Van Devanter and Lamar greatly strengthened the Court. Van Devanter had judicial experience, was most painstaking and exact, and coming from the western country had an intimate familiarity with the public land laws. He was slow in getting out his opinions, having what one of his most intimate friends in the Court (Justice Sutherland) described as "pen paralysis." This difficulty increased with the years. But his careful and elaborate statements in conference, with his accurate review of authorities, were of the greatest value. If these statements had been taken down stenographically they would have served with but little editing as excellent opinions. His perspicacity and common sense made him a trusted adviser in all sorts of matters. Chief Justice White leaned heavily upon him and so did Chief Justice Taft, especially when the latter began to fail in health. When Van Devanter first came on the Court he was by no means an ultra conservative. See, for example, his opinion in *Second Employers' Liability Cases.*[28] Justice Lamar combined ability of a high order with gentleness and grace. He came from active practice where he had won the esteem of both bench and bar and no one of the Justices was more respected by his brethren. His toil broke him down and he was fatally stricken in the summer of 1915.[29]

Early in 1912, Justice Pitney[30] was appointed to succeed Justice Harlan and we thus gained a fellow worker, noted for his courage, strength of mind and conscientiousness. Justice Brandeis[31] in recent years often spoke of his high regard for Justice Pitney. In 1914, Justice McReynolds[32] succeeded Justice Lurton, and in 1916, Justice Brandeis — my old friend at the bar — took his seat the very week I left the Court. It was not my privilege to be associated with him in judicial work until I became Chief Justice.

Of all these judges with whom it was my privilege to serve during my Associate Justiceship, Holmes had the most fascinating personality. Not that on the whole he was a more admirable character, but that by reason of his rare combination of qualities — his intellectual power and literary skill, his freshness of view and inimitable way of expressing it, his enthusiasm and cheerful skepticism, his abundant vitality and gaiety of

28[Second Employers' Liability Cases]. 223 U.S. 1 [1912].

29Justice Lamar died on January 1, 1916.

30[Mahlon Pitney (1858–1924) served on the Supreme Court from 1912 to 1922.]

31[Louis Dembitz Brandeis (1856–1941) served on the Supreme Court from 1916 to 1939.]

32[James Clark McReynolds (1862–1946) served on the Supreme Court from 1914 to 1941.]

spirit — he radiated a constant charm. My relations to him were of the happiest sort.[33] His method of work was peculiarly interesting. While administrative detail was irksome to him, and as he often said he "hated facts," he was meticulous in keeping his notes of cases. In those days he was the only Justice who attempted to make comprehensive notes during the oral arguments, a difficult task. For this purpose he always used sheets of the same size (about 10 x 8 inches) and on these he put down all the important points of the case — on each side — with a brief comment. And when the argument was over, he generally could have taken his notes and at once have prepared an opinion. When he had thus grasped and assembled all that he deemed necessary for the disposition of the case, he would relax and rest quietly, sometimes, after lunch, taking a brief nap, resting his head on his hands over his desk as if in deep study. On one occasion when a prosy lawyer was going on indefinitely with tiresome repetition, Holmes woke up, and finding counsel still talking, muttered audibly, "Jesus Christ!"

His notes I think were an indispensable aid to his memory. I recall that once in a while, walking with him on our way home after arguments, I would refer to a troublesome point in a case argued two or three days before, and he would say, "Have we that point before us?" and I would have to bring it back to his mind. But when he came to conference with his sheaf of notes he was armed *cap-a-pie.* When an opinion was assigned to him, he worked rapidly and with a terrible intensity. If he received an assignment on Sunday (following Saturday's conference) he would be ready to distribute his proofsheets almost always by the next Thursday, often by Wednesday. He was miserable until his work was done. So during the recesses when most of the Justices labored on their opinions, Holmes was relatively free after a few days and could indulge his tastes in general reading. The speed with which he worked was due not only to his quickness of apprehension but to his mastery of all the fields of law. This he early achieved in preparing his notes to the twelfth edition of Kent's *Commentaries* and through the researches which underlay his monumental lectures on the "Common Law." These he completed before he was forty. And he nearly wore himself out by that achievement. Justice Brandeis told me that Holmes was so run down that some thought he would not live five years. Added to his thorough studies was his long experience on the Supreme Judicial Court of Massachusetts. Then, when he came to the Supreme Court of the United States, he was not much troubled, in view of the latitude he accorded to legislative action, by the

[33]See his friendly reference on my resignation in 1916. [Mark DeWolfe Howe, ed., *Holmes–Pollock Letters,* [2 vols. (Cambridge, Harvard University Press, 1941)], Vol. 1, p. 237. Letter to Pollock, July 12, 1916.

constitutional questions which so greatly disturbed his brethren. There were extremes, however, which even he could not stand — at least in those days — as witness his application of the due process clause of the Fourteenth Amendment to state legislation which he deemed to be utterly unreasonable and arbitrary in *Chicago, Milwaukee & St. Paul R. Co. v. Polt,*[34] and his entire agreement with my opinion as to the invalidity of certain State railroad rates, as violating due process, in *Northern Pacific R. Co. v. North Dakota.*[35]

As he wrote his opinions in his own hand, they were usually short. At the time to which I am now referring, Justice Holmes was not as popular with the bar as he became later. Lawyers complained that he did not adequately set forth the case and that his language was frequently obscure. This I learned from Chief Justice White who received letters which occasionally he would show me, and I was somewhat amused that the Chief Justice, who was none too clear in his own style, should refer to Holmes's "obscurities." Sometimes the Justices would squirm at some of Holmes's generalities, fearful of their implications, as in *Noble State Bank v. Haskell.*[36] And not infrequently they would insist on the elimination of certain phrases, to which Holmes would agree good naturedly, reporting at conference that he had the concurrence of his brethren but that the "fizz" had been taken out of his opinion.

Justice Holmes was wont to comment gaily in returning the proofsheets of opinions with which he agreed. I have preserved a few of his comments on some of my opinions, viz:

> "Yes — twice if I can get in two votes." (*Wilson v. United States,* 221 U.S. 361 [1911]).

[34][Chicago, Milwaukee & St. Paul R. Co. v. Polt], 232 U.S. 165, 168 [(1914). Writing for the majority, Justice Holmes declared unconstitutional a South Dakota law which imposed double liability when a railroad failed to offer a settlement to a plaintiff which was not equal to or greater than the amount the plaintiff later recovered in court.]

[35]236 U.S. 585 [1915]. His assent to the principles as there stated was whole-hearted. See his comment on my proof-sheet. Folder marked "Some Comments on Supreme Court Opinions" [in the Hughes Papers].

See, also, his opinion in Pennsylvania Coal Co. v. Mahon, 260 U.S. 393 [1922].

[36][Noble State Bank v. Haskell], 219 U.S. 104, 111, [*motion to file for rehearing denied,* 219 U.S. 575, 580 (1911)].

[In upholding a state law compelling banks to contribute to a general fund which protected deposits, Holmes wrote: "It may be said in a general way that the police power extends to all the great public needs . . . It may be put forth in aid of what is sanctioned by usage, or held by the prevailing morality or strong and preponderant opinion to be greatly and immediately necessary to the public welfare." 219 U.S. at 111. On rehearing, Holmes tried to explain away his earlier expansive interpretation of the state's police power: "The analysis of the police power, whether correct or not, was intended to indicate an interpretation of what has taken place in the past not to give a new or wider scope to the power." 219 U.S. at 580.]

"Clear as a bell and sound as a nut — Yes." (*Graham v. West Virginia*, 224 U.S. 616 [1912]).

"How sweet a countenance tyranny endues
What reverend accents and what tender Hu(gh)es
Such seeming modesty and justice blent
Smile at the futile claims of long dissent."

"So I expect to shut up." (*Peabody v. United States*, 231 U.S. 530 [1913]).

"Yes, with humility. I now see what you have been about when I was giving parties their constitutional right to jaw while I slept." (*United States v. Mayer*, 235 U.S. 55 [1914]).

"Wee — Mussoo — I float in a fairy bark to the bight and serenely anchor there with you." (*New York [ex rel. Kennedy] v. Becker*, 241 U.S. 556 [1916]).

"Wee — Mussoo — Ye crags & Peaks. I'm with you once again." (*Corporation Commission v. Lowe*, 281 U.S. 431 [1930]).

We did not always agree but there was never any unfriendliness in our disagreement. I was surprised by his dissent from my opinion in the peonage case, *Bailey v. Alabama*,[37] and by his narrow construction of the Food and Drugs Act in *United States v. Johnson*.[38] But I was not surprised by his dissent in the *Dr. Miles Medical Company* case,[39] as I was well aware of his antipathy to the Sherman Act and the policy it embodied. We were in accord in certain cases of special significance, notably in our dissents in *Slocum v. New York Life Insurance Company*,[40] *Coppage v. Kansas*,[41] and

[37][The majority opinion written by Justice Hughes held unconstitutional, under the 13th Amendment, an Alabama statute which authorized the jailing of a party who refused to perform a contract for personal service after accepting advance payment. In his dissent, 219 U.S. at 245, Holmes argued that refusal to perform the contract, under these circumstances, could be regarded as a crime, i.e., obtaining money by fraud, and punishment by imprisonment could be rightly imposed.]

[Bailey v. Alabama], 219 U.S. 219 [1911]. This case has been followed by a unanimous Court, since my retirement, in Taylor v. Georgia, 315 U.S. 25, 29 [1942].

[38][United States v. Johnson], 221 U.S. 488, 499. [(1911). Holmes wrote the majority opinion which held that a patent medicine was not "misbranded" within the strict interpretation of the Food and Drug Act, when the label stated the drug was effective in curing cancer. Hughes wrote a strong dissent to this opinion, 221 U.S. at 499.]

[39][Dr. Miles Medical Co. v. Park & Sons Co.], 220 U.S. 373, 409 [(1911). The case involved the validity of a price-fixing agreement between a manufacturer and his wholesale and retail dealers. The majority opinion, written by Hughes, ruled the agreement was invalid, but Holmes dissented, 220 U.S. at 409, arguing for the right of the manufacturer to determine the price at which his product will be sold to the ultimate consumer.]

[40][Slocum v. New York Life Ins. Co.], 228 U.S. 364, 400 [(1913). The case concerned the interpretation of a life insurance policy but disagreement in the Court arose over a procedural question. The appellate court had reversed the trial court judgment, which had been entered on a jury verdict, and the appellate court had directed judgment for the other party. The majority opinion, written by J. Van Devanter, ruled that the 7th Amend-

Frank v. Mangum.[42] And he was in full agreement with the pregnant doctrine of the *Shreveport Case,*[43] carrying forward the reasoning of the *Minnesota Rate Cases.*[44]

Justice Holmes's attitude toward the economic theories which underlay what has been called "social" or "progressive" legislation has been widely misunderstood. He was in no sense a crusader, nor did he share the views of the promoters of the statutes which he so readily sustained. He held them valid not because he believed in them but because he believed in the right of the legislature to experiment. Referring humorously to his action in sustaining statutes which he did not like, he would say that in his epitaph should be written, "Here lies the supple tool of power." I recall that in talking with him about certain labor acts, soon after I came from Albany, I spoke of the need of impartial and efficient administration to fulfill their promise. And he exclaimed, "I don't care anything about these fool statutes, unless they go to the *nape of the neck,*" meaning physical vigor. He prized *strength* which would count in the inevitable struggle in which the strongest, as the fittest, would win. He believed in

---

ment prohibited the appellate court from directing the judgment and the appellate court could only remand the case for a new jury trial. Justice Hughes wrote a dissent with Holmes, Lurton, and Pitney concurring. Justice Hughes felt that the guarantee of a jury trial under the Constitution did not require a new trial when the judgment is already determined as a matter of law.]

[41][Coppage v. Kansas], 236 U.S. 1, 27 [(1915). The Court declared unconstitutional a Kansas statute designed to prevent employers from interfering with their employee's union activities. Hughes, concurring in a dissent written by Justice Day (236 U.S. at 27), and Holmes in a separate dissent (236 U.S. at 26), felt the statute was within the legitimate exercise of the state police power in protecting its citizens.]

[42][Frank v. Mangum], 237 U.S. 309, 345 [(1915). Leo Frank had been convicted of murder by a Georgia court. There was considerable evidence of extremely hostile public sentiment against Frank and mob domination of the courtroom at times. The Court followed the determination of the Georgia Supreme Court that not enough undue prejudice against Frank had been shown to constitute a denial of due process of law. Holmes and Hughes, in their dissent (237 U.S. at 345), wanted federal courts to hear all the evidence of prejudice without regard to the opinion of the Georgia Supreme Court and "to declare lynch law as little valid when practiced by a regularly drawn jury as when administered by one elected by a mob intent on death." (237 U.S. at 350.)]

[43][Houston & Texas Ry. v. United States (Shreveport Case)] 234 U.S. 342 [1914].

[44][Simpson v. Shepard, et al.], 230 U.S. 352 [1913]. My opinion in the Minnesota Rate Cases was of extreme length. The arguments had taken a broad range and in view of the course of the discussion in conference, I felt it necessary to present a full review of the authorities in order to pave the way for the conclusions which won the support of the Court. I recently received a letter from a lawyer saying that his instructor in law school days had said that I "spent over a year *exclusively* for the study of, and writing his (my) opinion." That statement was quite inaccurate. I suppose it was based on an inference from the fact that the cases were argued in April 1912, and were not decided until June 1913. But these cases had extremely large records with voluminous briefs (I think that one brief on the facts had about 900 pages) and the cases were taken for study over the summer and were not assigned for opinion until the later fall. During the period in question I wrote a considerable number of opinions for the Court.

the triumph of force.[45] He admired men of power, who achieved. Men like Hill, Rockefeller and Harriman, he said, "should have statues erected to them." So far as I know, he was not interested in the charities which were making their insistent appeals in Washington, and by his will, with his patriotic ardor, he left the residue of his estate to the United States.

With all his liberality, when he thought that a case was clear according to his conception of the law, Justice Holmes scorned any suggestion at the conference table of deviating from the result the law required because it would be "unjust." He said that it was "the stinking sense of justice" that bedeviled the proper administration of the law. He was not averse to using a vulgar expression whenever he deemed it apt. His Uncle, John Holmes, who he thought was the great wit of the family, had encouraged him not to be afraid of vulgar talk. So Justice Holmes ran the full gamut of pungent utterance. He had an interesting classification of lawyers. He rated them as "kitchen-knives, razors and stings." The ordinary run of useful but undistinguished lawyers were the "kitchen-knives"; the sharper ones were the "razors"; and those whose native powers marked them as leaders were the "stings."

During the early years of my Associate Justiceship, my health was not what it had been. I lost no time in the work of the Court but I did not feel vigorous. As I have said, I was tired when I started and the extra labor in the Second-Class Mail inquiry ran me down. That was followed by the heavy demands of the Rate Cases. Social engagements took their toll. It was clear that I must adopt a new regimen. I had long felt that I should give up smoking. I had smoked in college days at Brown, and continuously from the time I was admitted to the bar, save for one period of a few months, about 1895. Inclined to be tense and high-strung, I was under the impression that I needed to smoke in order to maintain my poise. While under stress at Albany I smoked excessively. After coming to Washington, I was more moderate, and when I spoke to my physician about giving up smoking entirely, he advised against it, suggesting a rigorous limitation. One evening in the spring of 1914, as I sat smoking with the men at a dinner party, I said to myself, "I think I won't smoke again for a little while." And I have not smoked since.

Giving up smoking changed entirely my method of work. After breakfast, instead of sitting with my cigar and morning paper, I started out for a walk of half an hour. I soon found that I came back full of ideas and eager to get to my desk. In the evening, instead of indulging in a last cigar

[45]See, confirming the impressions I received from Justice Holmes's conversation, what is said in Attorney General Biddle's excellent book, *Mr. Justice Holmes* [New York, Scribners, 1942], pp. 87, 89, 125. See Charles Warren [review of Biddle's book] in *American Historical Review* [XLIX] (October 1943), pp. 71–72.

in the late hours, I went to bed. Instead of working late at night, I found that I was at my best in the morning. This gave me confidence, and when I was dealing with difficult problems I would say, "It will all clear up in the morning." And so generally it did. While I suppose that the final result was no better than in my smoking days, I worked more rapidly, with less friction, and with a much greater sense of *bien etre.* When I returned to the bar I did my heaviest work on my cases in the morning hours, rising as early as was necessary to accomplish what I set before me. And I kept to this method as Chief Justice, being always at my desk — after a brisk walk — not later than eight-thirty. Giving up smoking improved my health and increased my efficiency at least twenty-five percent.

I made but few speeches while on the Bench. Some invitations I found it impossible to refuse. On November 19, 1910, I spoke at the dinner given to me by the Lotos Club in New York City.[46] I delivered the Historical Address at the Sesquicentennial of Brown University in October 1914.[47] And I have already referred to my remarks on Administrative Agencies in my address before the New York State Bar Association in January 1916.[48]

The work of the Court during this period (1910–1916) and my part in it appear in the published opinions, which I shall not undertake to review. I leave the appraisal of that work to others.[49]

[46]Newspaper clipping of November 20, 1910, giving an account of this dinner is in "Speeches 1907–1930," [in Hughes Papers].

[47]*Ibid.*

[48]Chapter 10, "The Governorship," pp. 145–146. Printed copy [in Hughes Papers].

[49][For such an appraisal, see Samuel Hendel, *Charles Evans Hughes and the Supreme Court* (New York, Russell & Russell, 1951), chap. 2–6.]

Chapter XII 1916

Beerits' Memorandum ["The Presidential Campaign of 1916"] has described my attitude in the difficult days preceding the Republican Convention, the reasons which led me to accept the nomination, and the conduct of the campaign. I did not wish to be nominated. In view of the war in Europe, the responsibilities of the Presidency were heavier than ever and, knowing well what they meant, I had no desire to have the burden placed on my shoulders. The idea of a Justice of the Supreme Court taking part in politics, promoting in the slightest degree his selection as a candidate for the office of President, was abhorrent to me. I strongly opposed the use of my name and the selection or instruction of any delegates in my interest. I answered all inquiries to that effect. Beerits cites some instances.[1] Beerits quotes from Henry L. Stoddard, the author of *As I Knew Them*, with an important correction.[2] In his later book, *It Costs to be*

[1]Beerits' Memorandum, "The Presidential Campaign of 1916," p. 3. [Beerits set forth Hughes's reluctance to become involved in political affairs while sitting on the court and mentions several letters to prominent Republicans in which he made clear this reluctance. Beerits also lists the impressive number of polls and straw votes taken during these months which indicated preference for Hughes among Republicans.] See, also, the article by Harold L. Ickes, "Who Killed the Progressive Party," *The American Historical Review* [XLVI] (January 1941), p. 316. Mr. Ickes refers to a newspaper story that Mr. Taft had called on me on May 14, 1916, and that it was believed in some quarters that I had told him I would "accept the Republican nomination." I do not recall the rumor, but there was not the slightest basis for it. I had said nothing of the sort to Mr. Taft or anyone else. Mr. Ickes also refers to a statement by George W. Perkins, shortly after the Progressive Convention, that he knew me "very well indeed," considered me on of his "closest friends," and that he never went to Washington without calling on me. This is an extravagant statement. I think Mr. Perkins must have been misunderstood. If he called upon me in Washington I do not remember it. At most, it could have been only a brief meeting like that with many others who would call to "pay their respects." Certainly, it cannot properly be said that there was any intimacy.

[2][Henry L. Stoddard, *As I Knew Them: Presidents and Politicians from Grant to Coolidge* (New York, Harper & Brothers, 1927), pp. 446–447. Stoddard was owner and editor of the New York *Evening Mail*. Stoddard was impressed with the fact that Hughes had done nothing to win the nomination.] Mr. Stoddard was wholly in error in saying (p. 447) that I thought of resigning from the Court to resume practice. I had no such idea.

Presidential candidate with his family, 1916. Behind Hughes and his wife are Charles Evans Hughes, Jr., Helen, and Catherine. Elizabeth is seated on Hughes's lap.

President, Mr. Stoddard gives a somewhat detailed account of a conversation with me on this subject.[3]

But, despite my aloofness and my repeated protests against the use of my name, there was an insistent and growing demand for my nomination. It was thought that I was the only one who could unite the factions of the Republican Party and restore it to the place it had held before the rupture in 1912; and that this restoration was essential to the working of the two-party system. Then, the war in Europe had created a critical emergency and the conduct of our foreign affairs had been unsatisfactory. Our diplomacy had failed because of its impaired credit and of a manifest lack of disposition to back words with action.[4] Militarily, there had been a shocking neglect to provide a reasonable preparedness. There were those, quite as solicitous as I for maintaining the integrity of the judicial office, who felt that if without any encouragement on my part a genuine popular demand were voiced by the Convention in choosing me as the Republican candidate, it would be my duty to accept. Mr. Taft, who had appointed me to the Bench, was of that view. I did not discuss the matter with my brethren of the Court except with Justice Van Devanter, and while he sympathized with my efforts to oppose the use of my name as a candidate, he advised me that if nevertheless I should be nominated I could not rightly decline. Chief Justice White, at least once in referring to newspaper comment, expressed the same opinion. I think that most of the members of the Court fully understood my attitude. Certainly Justice Holmes did.[5] I was torn between two profound desires, one to keep the judicial ermine unsullied, and the other not to fail in meeting what might be a duty to the country.

I should add that, at the same time, there were certain intimations that if I remained on the bench, I should be appointed Chief Justice. Franklin K. Lane, Secretary of the Interior, took me aside at a dinner party and dropped a hint to that effect. And Chief Justice White came to me, shortly before the Republican Convention, saying that before I decided on my course he felt that I should know that he was going to retire and that if I did not resign I should succeed him. "Why," I said, "President Wilson would never appoint me Chief Justice." "Well," he replied, "he wouldn't appoint anyone else, as I happen to know." I told Chief Justice White that

[3][Henry L. Stoddard, *It Costs to be President* (New York, Harper & Brothers, 1938), pp. 110–115.] I made no notes of this interview and I cannot recall all its details. But I have no reason to question the substantial accuracy of Mr. Stoddard's report of it.

[4]See [Philip C.] Jessup, *Elihu Root,* [2 vols. (New York, Dodd, Mead & Co., 1938)], Vol. 2, p. 339. [For another view of this period, less critical of Wilson, see Arthur S. Link, *Wilson: vol. V, Campaigns for Progressivism and Peace* (Princeton, Princeton University Press, 1965).]

[5]See his reference to my acceptance of the nomination in his letter to Pollock of July 12, 1916 [Mark DeWolfe Howe, ed.,] *Holmes–Pollock Letters,* [2 vols. (Cambridge, Harvard University Press, 1941)], Vol. 1, p. 237.

I was going to do what I thought was right and that I would not be influenced by any such suggestion.

The nomination was made and in view of all the circumstances I felt that I could not refuse and, being of that mind, I should act with decision and not palter or delay. Accordingly, I at once resigned from the Court, telegraphed my acceptance, and plunged into the campaign.[6] After Colonel Roosevelt's declination, I also received the nomination of the Progressive Party. Colonel Roosevelt gave me his full support which, while earnest, proved in the latter part of the campaign to be not altogether helpful as it stimulated opposition in the Middle West where the pacifist sentiment was especially strong. However, I was measurably successful in healing the breach in the Republican Party as I received about a million votes in excess of the combined popular votes cast for Taft and Roosevelt in 1912.

In my formal address accepting the Republican nomination, I stated my views at length, more fully than would have been necessary had I not been so long absent from the political platform and immured in the Court.[7] I laid special emphasis upon what I deemed to be the serious shortcomings of the administration in the conduct of our foreign relations and the lack of preparedness. I advocated a firm foreign policy which I felt was the best assurance of peace. I did not know whether peace could be assured, but it certainly had been, and would continue to be, endangered by a course of weakness and indecision which invited a trampling upon our rights. I dwelt on the important of the "Organization of Peace," giving my views on international cooperation. What I said at that early date [July 31, 1916] is no less pertinent now [April 1943].[8]

There was a hot contest. As was to be expected the Democratic press belittled my efforts and made severe attacks. It was thought necessary that I should tour the country and I made several trips with incessant speaking.

[6]Beerits, "Presidential Campaign" (pp. 4–5) quotes Hughes's telegram to the convention accepting the nomination.

["I have not desired the nomination. I have wished to remain on the bench. But, in this critical period in our national history, I recognize that it is your right to summon and that it is my paramount duty to respond. You speak at a time of national exigency, transcending merely partisan considerations. You voice the demand for a dominant, thorough-going Americanism, with firm, protective, upbuilding policies essential to our peace and security; and to that call, in this crisis, I cannot fail to answer with the pledge of all that is in me to the service of our country. Therefore, I accept the nomination."]

[7]A pamphlet copy of this address is in [the Hughes Papers]. The slogan "American First," taken from the opening statement, did not have in 1916 the significance which it acquired by reason of its use by isolationists in the pre-Pearl Harbor days in 1940–41. Its use in 1916 was to express opposition to the divided loyalties of the so-called "hyphenated Americans." As the *New York Times* has said, "the hyphen [at that time], assumed ugly and even sinister connotations."

[8]The speech is also quoted by Beerits, ["Presidential Campaign"], pp. 25–27. In this connection, see the article (1938) by Chester H. Rowell, "If Hughes had Won," [Hughes Papers].

I had no lack of critics who said that I had been so long on the bench that I had lost whatever effectiveness I formerly had as a campaign speaker. Fortunately there were others who were more favorable. David Lawrence, a warm friend of President Wilson and his strong supporter, attended one of my meetings at Lincoln, Nebraska, apparently to see whether this criticism was justified. He was good enough to write to the New York *Evening Post* [October 17, 1916] a long and detailed description of my work on the platform. I should be happy to think that I deserved his generous appraisal.

Beerits describes my course during the campaign and various important incidents.[9] I shall not attempt to review them. The result was very close and it has often been said that I lost the election by failing to "shake hands" with Governor Johnson when we were both, for a short time, in the same hotel in Long Beach, California, on Sunday, August 20th. That failure was not due to any fault of mine. I did not know that Governor Johnson was at Long Beach. I had been very desirous of meeting him, and had I known that he was at Long Beach when I was there, I should have seized that opportunity to greet him. When on my return to Los Angeles I heard of this mischance I at once sent my train manager, Charles W. Farnham, back to Long Beach to tell Governor Johnson that I was sorry that I had failed to meet him and to ask him to preside at my meeting to be held in Sacramento. Governor Johnson refused this request. On learning of this, I had Farnham the next morning (when I was speaking at San Diego) telephone Governor Johnson suggesting an exchange of courteous telegrams between us, the text of both to be approved in advance so as to avoid any embarrassment to him. This also he refused.

My efforts and Governor Johnson's attitude are shown in Johnson's telegram to Farnham of August 21st, as follows:

> Mr. Charles W. Farnham, Long Beach Calif Aug. 21, 1916.
> Care Governor Charles Evans Hughes,
> Hotel Alexandria, Los Angeles, Cal.
> My dear Mr. Farnham your early telephone message from San Diego

[9](Beerits, "Presidential Campaign," pp. 10–13, summarizes Hughes's speaking tours, giving particular attention to two incidents, in Nashville, Tennessee, and Louisville, Kentucky, in which Hughes coped successfully with hostile audiences and won warm praise from the press. Aside from the California problem, which Hughes discusses, Beerits devotes a great deal of space (pp. 16a–16i) to the German-American issue, quoting extensively from George Sylvester Viereck, *Spreading Germs of Hate* (New York, Horace Liveright, 1930), pp. 227–228, 245–246, 252–253, to show that Hughes had never compromised himself to win the so-called hyphenate vote. For a recent study of the impact of this issue on the election, see Thomas J. Kerr, IV, "German-Americans and Neutrality in the 1916 Election," *Mid America*, XLIII (April 1961), 95–105; and Link, *Wilson*, V, 93–153.)

this morning suggesting that I wire Mr. Hughes and that he would respond as well as your suggestion last night that I go to Sacramento and there preside at Mr. Hughes meeting I have thought of most carefully. It goes without saying that I wish and have wished to extend to Mr. Hughes a most cordial and hearty welcome to California and that in view of my advocacy of him I would be very glad to present him to my fellow citizens and to state to them the reasons for my advocacy. Until now it has been rendered impossible for me to do either. The men surrounding Mr. Hughes in California and who have been in charge of his tour are much more interested in my defeat than in Mr. Hughes' election and they have made it manifest both publicly and privately that they would vote for Mr. Wilson if the commonest courtesies were exchanged between Mr. Hughes and myself. At this late day when both our itineraries are full and fixed and upon the eve of Mr. Hughes' departure from California for me even at your suggestion to wire Mr. Hughes and for him to reply or for me to preside at his Sacramento meeting would be misunderstood and misinterpreted and maliciously distorted. I have just been informed that tonight's meeting has been elaborately staged for a Booth demonstration by the very people who protest they wish Mr. Hughes' California trip wholly divorced from local candidacies. Such a thing in my behalf I would not of course tolerate or permit and I do not wish to be open even to the unjust accusation that I have attempted it. With kindest regards to yourself and Mr. Hughes and with best wishes for his success I am very sincerely yours,

HIRAM W. JOHNSON
2.32PM[10]

Governor Johnson's apprehension that the Los Angeles meeting was "staged for a Booth demonstration" (Booth being his opponent in the senatorial campaign) was utterly unjustified as he could easily have found out on inquiry. It had been arranged that at this meeting (on the night of August 21st) there should be a fifty-fifty representation of Republicans and Progressives and this arrangement was carried out, the opposing leaders sitting on the platform and uniting in the support of my candidacy.

I should add that it had been thought unwise that I should omit California in my tour of the West and that, as I was the presidential candidate of both the Republican and Progressive parties, I could confine my meet-

[10]Copy of this telegram is next to the last in a sheaf of copies of telegrams in the same folder in [the Hughes Papers]. These telegrams, save the one from Governor Johnson to Farnham, were between W. R. Willcox, Chairman of the Republican National Committee, and William H. Crocker and Chester H. Rowell of San Francisco. Those telegrams, after August 5, 1916, were exchanged while I was on my speaking tour.

ings to national issues and avoid the bitter factional fight in the State over the senatorship. I had expected to be accompanied through the State by representatives of both factions. The "men surrounding Mr. Hughes in California," to whom Governor Johnson referred in his telegram, were the official representatives of the Republican Party in California, and of course I could not dismiss them. I also had the company of representatives of the Progressive Party while I was in San Francisco, and Governor Johnson's managers could have made similar provision for my trip through the State. And, as I have said, we did achieve this unity of support at the Los Angeles meeting.

Mr. Farnham prepared a full account of the "California incident" and this is among my papers deposited in the Library of Congress. After Governor Johnson won in the senatorial primary, I sent him a cordial telegram of congratulation.[11]

Despite the misadventure in California, I still should have been elected had it not been for the effectiveness, particularly in the middle west, of the Democratic slogan, "He kept us out of war." The Democratic Convention had rocked with enthusiasm as its orator climaxed his periods with this refrain, and toward the close of the campaign Democratic speakers were especially active in spreading the notion that if I were elected Colonel Roosevelt would be the leading spirit in my administration and we should be brought into the war. The Democratic appeal was driven home during the latter part of the campaign by spreading throughout the country enormous picture-posters, giving a lurid display of the carnage of war, while on the side-lines stood a mother and her children looking on, with the legend underneath, "He has protected me and mine."

The Republican Committee was strangely lacking in appreciation of

[11]Beerits, ["Presidential Campaign"], pp. 38a–38c. See, also, [Henry F.] Pringle, *The Life and Times of William Howard Taft,* [2 vols. (New York, Farrar & Rinehard, Inc., 1939)], Vol. 2, pp. 896, 900. [Hughes refused to endorse Johnson because such a move would be dishonorable. He was very concerned to improve his image as a party regular. The Farnham report enumerates the unhappy series of misunderstandings that arose out of the ill feeling between the Johnson forces and the regular Republicans. The most critical incident occurred on Sunday, August 20, at Long Beach, California when Hughes and Johnson stopped in the same hotel and managed somehow to miss seeing one another. (See Beerits, ["Presidential Campaign"]. pp. 38d-h.) Beerits (note 64) summarizes his consideration of the entire California problem by absolving Hughes of any blame:

["In some of the arguments presented on this subject the blame for Mr. Hughes's defeat is placed upon Governor Johnson; in others it is placed upon Mr. Crocker and the Old Guard Republicans of California. Despite all arguments in support of the latter contention, the essential fact must never be forgotten that after the unfortunate failure to meet Governor Johnson in the hotel at Long Beach, Mr. Hughes did everything that was humanly possible to wipe out any offense that might have resulted from the incident. Governor Johnson flatly refused to preside at the meeting in Sacramento on Tuesday night; he refused even to send Mr. Hughes the simple telegram of greeting that was suggested; he would have none of it."]

the effect of this appeal and the situation which had developed in the middle west. Had I been warned I could have put in my time to better advantage by again visiting that part of the country before the campaign closed. One of the committee, Charles Beecher Warren, did sense the situation in Michigan and asked me to come there once more, which I did, with the result that I carried that State.[12]

I was not cast down by my defeat. As I wrote Mr. Taft, I had "no complaints and no regrets." [13] I had done my best. While of course I did not enjoy being beaten, the fact that I did not have to assume the tasks of the Presidency in that critical time was an adequate consolation. The New York *Times*, which had vigorously opposed me as a candidate, gave me a generous welcome as I returned to professional practice in New York.[14]

ADDENDUM

The death of Governor Hiram W. Johnson in August 1945, brought out many references to the campaign of 1916, with repetition of the story that my defeat was due to my "snub" of Governor Johnson. Even Mr. Ickes, while saying that it was not my fault, assumes the "snub" and insists that despite it Governor Johnson loyally supported me in the campaign.[15]

As I have shown in my Notes, I did not snub Governor Johnson. Whether or not he was justified in his feeling as to the California committeemen of the Republican organization, who accompanied me on my trip through the State, he certainly knew that I did not snub him. On the contrary, as I have said, as soon as I learned that he was at Long Beach I sent word to him expressing my regret at the failure to meet him and asking him to preside at the Sacramento meeting, and when he refused this, I suggested an exchange of telegrams of courtesy.

The New York *Times* in its issue of August 7, 1945, refers to a statement by the "new California Republican State Committee," after the "snub incident," that there was a "cordon" placed around me to prevent my meeting Governor Johnson. If there was any such effort, I did not know of it and it could have been made wholly ineffectual if Governor Johnson had seen fit to meet my wishes as strongly urged at the time. The success of the Los Angeles meeting with the conspicuous 50-50 representation of the Republicans and Progressives, shows how easy it would have been for Governor Johnson to circumvent the effort to keep us apart, if any such effort there was.

[12]Beerits' Memorandum, ["Presidential Campaign"], p. 41.
[13]See Pringle, *[Taft,]* Vol. 2, pp. 899–900.
[14]*New York Times*, November 11, 1916, p. 8.
[15]Letter of Harold L. Ickes dated August 8, 1945, printed in the *New York Times*.

Chapter XIII 1917–1921

I was fortunate in being able to sell my house when I left Washington at the end of 1916, and with the proceeds of the sale as working capital I started in my fifty-fifth year on my new career at the bar.[1]

While I received offers of professional connections promising a large income, I refused them as I was especially desirous to have the position of independent counsel. I also wished to have my son, able and thoroughly trained, associated with me. And I thought that I could best attain these objects by rejoining my old friends and partners, Arthur C. Rounds and George W. Schurman, and I did so as a member of the firm of Hughes, Rounds, Schurman & Dwight.[2]

I was at once swamped with law business, refusing almost more than I accepted. My work soon became mostly that of counsel for other lawyers and my professional income in the succeeding years was large. I had little or no trouble about fees. Very rarely was any question raised as to my charges, indeed when I was retained by other lawyers I generally left to them the fixing of amounts which would be satisfactory to their clients. Of course, I refused many cases which I thought were without merit, but I did not hesitate to take a case where the chances were against my side,

[1]I sold 2100 Sixteenth Street, Northwest, to Senator John W. Weeks, later Secretary of War. After deducting commissions, I received from the sale of the house, and some furniture, the sum of $44,438.13. In addition, I had $7500, invested in mortgages.

On removing to New York, I rented an apartment at No. 32 East 64th Street, where we resided until I went back to Washington in 1921.

[2]One offer was from Guggenheim Brothers, who wished me to take charge of their legal affairs as a part of their organization at an annual salary of $50,000, without office expenses. A more attractive offer came from Cadwalader, Wickersham & Taft asking me to take the place in that firm of John L. Cadwalader who had died in 1914.

Charles E. Hughes, Jr. (Brown, 1909) had been graduated in 1912 from the Harvard Law School where he was editor-in-chief of the Law Review. He spent a year in the office of Byrne & Cutcheon, later was secretary to Justice [Benjamin Nathan] Cardozo, then Justice of the New York Supreme Court, until the latter was assigned to the New York Court of Appeals, and then became a member of the staff of Cadwalader, Wickersham & Taft.

or the client was unpopular, if I believed that the case was such as to be justly entitled to be presented to the court.

While the pressure was heavy in my professional work, I was at the same time subject to important outside demands which considerably limited the time I could devote to my practice. Beerits' Memorandum lists a number of these activities.[3] In 1917, I became President of several organizations — the New York State Bar Association, the Legal Aid Society, the Union League Club and St. David's Society; in 1918, the Italy-America Society, and in 1919, the New York County Lawyers' Association. In addition to the requirements of these offices, I met a variety of demands for speeches, to which Beerits refers.

I may mention one meeting of especial interest which was held in the Union League Club in the latter part of March 1917. I presided, and Mr. Choate, Mr. Root and Colonel Roosevelt made speeches. We virtually declared war a little ahead of the Government. After the meeting (Mr. Choate in view of his age had gone home), Mr. Root, Colonel Roosevelt, Robert Bacon and I foregathered in the cafe where we had a long talk. Roosevelt was full of the idea that he must be assigned to a military command abroad. Speaking at length upon this subject, which was so close to his heart, he turned to Root and to me, saying, "You must see Wilson and get his consent to let me go." Then, becoming very solemn, he said with deep feeling, "I must go, but I will not come back. My sons will go too, and they will not come back." There was silence for a moment as we were impressed by his evident sincerity. But Root spoke up, with his unfailing humor, remarking, "Theodore, if you can make Wilson believe that you will not come back, he will let you go." And the tension was relieved.[4]

I was a strong supporter of John Purroy Mitchel, the high-minded, efficient and valiant Mayor of New York. For one of his patriotic outbursts he was cited by the New York State Senate for contempt, because of his reflection upon Senator Robert F. Wagner. I represented him as counsel in a lively hearing before the Senate which, after testimony and an evening of protracted and heated argument, ended in the early morning hours in a dismissal of the charges (April 1917).

A number of speeches were called forth by the war effort two of which may be regarded as of special significance at the present time. In one, before the National Conference on Foreign Relations, held at Long Beach at

[3]Beerits' Memorandum, "Activities during the years 1916–1921," with appended list of references to newspaper items relating to these. [Beerits makes a list of Hughes's activities as noted by the *New York Times* during the years under discussion in this chapter. They deal with his membership in charitable societies and his numerous public speeches. Hughes deals with all the activities of major interest.]

[4]I have seen inaccurate reports of this conversation, evidently by those who got the story at second hand.

the end of May 1917, I discussed, under the title of "The Future of International Law," the subject of post-war international organization in the interest of peace. After referring to our maintenance of the Monroe Doctrine, I ended the discussion with these words:[5]

> Is it too much to expect that our historic policy, in its essential features, should be accepted by the nations? And may we not contemplate the working out of plans for an international organization in the belief that this acceptance will in itself conduce to the peace of the world while facilitating our co-operation in its maintenance?
>
> Should we not at least postpone judgment until we know the conditions upon which we may co-operate, and shall we not at least be hospitable to the thought that America has its obligations to the world? We cannot live unto ourselves. What promise does the future hold if treaties and conventions are made only to be broken? If we can see at all into the future we know that it offers no chance for isolation to the United States. We have vast resources and extraordinary privileges and we cannot shirk our duty to mankind. Self-interest as well as a proper sense of obligation demand that we should aid in rearing the structure of international justice, and certainly that we should not make its establishment impossible by holding aloof.

In another address, before the American Bar Association at its annual meeting at Saratoga, in September 1917, I dealt with the "War Powers under the Constitution," and pointing out the breadth of the essential powers I observed that we had a "fighting Constitution"; that "The power to wage war is the power to wage war successfully." [6]

The Draft Appeals Board. In May 1917, Congress passed the draft act,[7] and at the end of July I was made Chairman of the District Draft Appeals Board for New York City. In order to harmonize the administration of the draft in Greater New York, an Appeals Board of thirty members was constituted with jurisdiction over the entire City. It had many eminent members, among them being former Chief Judge Edgar M. Cullen [1843–1922] of the New York Court of Appeals, former Presiding Justice George L. Ingraham of the Appellate Division of the New York Supreme Court, Judge Edwin L. Garvin, who was Secretary of the Board, George W. Wick-

[5] *Proceedings*, Academy of Political Science, New York, Vol. 7, No. 2 (July 1917), pp. 195–207. See also, Albert Shaw, *International Bearings of American Policy* (Baltimore [The Johns Hopkins University Press,] 1943), p. 201.

[6] The text of the address is in [the Hughes Papers and was reported in the *New York Times*, September 6, 1917, p. 1].

[7] Act of May 18, 1917, 40 Stat. 76.

ersham [1858–1936], Louis Marshall [1856–1929] and William N. Dykman.[8] The work of organizing a clerical staff to handle the immense volume of papers which poured in upon the Board was extremely arduous. At the very outset there was a vast number of cases awaiting disposition. I asked one or two of the leading banks and the New York Telephone Company to lend me some of their most efficient men to aid in this effort. These men, and Judge Garvin and myself, were nearly floored by the task, but by keeping at it night and day we managed to build up an organization which functioned smoothly.[9] I held the Chairmanship of the Board until the latter part of May 1918.

It was in the Spring of 1918 that the Italy-America Society was organized. This was due to the initiative of Colonel Edward M. House, who thought that something should be done fittingly to recognize and encourage the efforts of Italy in the War. At his suggestion, I became its President. We had a highly successful meeting at the Metropolitan Opera House on May 24, 1918, at which I presided and Newton D. Baker, Secretary of War, made an eloquent speech.

The Aircraft Inquiry. I resigned from the Draft Appeals Board to under-

[8][Edwin Louis Garvin (1877–1960) was Justice in the Court of Special Sessions, City of New York, from 1915 until 1918 when he resigned to become Judge in the United States District Court, Eastern District of New York, a post he held until 1925. He was active in behalf of New York University and the public libraries of New York City.

[William Dykeman (1855–1934) was a graduate of West Point and served in the campaign to capture Sitting Bull after the defeat of Custer. His legal activity centered in Brooklyn. He was the City Civil Service Commissioner from 1898 to 1914, and President of the New York State Bar Association in 1923 and 1924.]

[9]Beerits, ["1916–1921"], pp. 4–6. The quadruplicate signing, to which he refers, I think continued until a change in the regulations, about December 1917. [The section of the Beerits Memorandum to which Hughes refers is as follows:

["This Board held its sessions in the old Post Office Building in New York, the corridors of which were filled with large boxes of mail and with crowds of people waiting to make appeals to the Board. For a long period Mr. Hughes worked until midnight or later each night, in order to work out the problem of setting up an efficient administration for carrying out the formidable task which confronted the Board. At the same time it was necessary to start in with the work of the Board under full pressure. Its members were faced with the very difficult problem of building a wagon and riding in it at the same time. The volume of work was tremendous. The mail averaged 4,000 pieces per day. Mr. Hughes was unwilling to have a stamp with his signature there for use, since its use might mean the death of a man. Therefore, he personally signed, in quadruplicate, the papers for every man who went into the military service and for every man who was exempted from service. There were hundreds of these papers each day.

["This Draft Appeals Board was one of the most remarkable organizations of a quasi-judicial nature ever known. There were thirty members and six subcommittees and many clerks and assistants. Applications were distributed to them constantly. Subcommittees would act upon these, and when they had about fifty or so ready, they would bring the list to Mr. Hughes's desk. The committee would then gather around the desk and the reports would be passed or any questions presented would be decided. In this way they decided an average of 1,000 cases a day."]

take this inquiry. Delays in the production of aircraft were apparently inexcusable and had aroused severe criticism. President Wilson asked me to make an investigation and I undertook it with the definite understanding that I should have a free hand. For this purpose I was appointed Special Assistant to the Attorney General and was provided with offices and hearing-rooms in the Department of Justice building. I examined more than 200 witnesses and I visited and inspected the various important plants in which the aircraft and "Liberty engines" were produced. While I had charge of the inquiry, and was not interfered with, either the Attorney General (Thomas W. Gregory) or the Solicitor General (William L. Frierson), or both, were in constant attendance and kept a vigilant eye on every step taken. I had as my personal assistant a very able lawyer, Meier Steinbrink of Brooklyn, now Justice of the New York Supreme Court, who aided me with untiring industry and the utmost fidelity.[10] In order that the war effort should not be embarrassed by premature disclosures, the examination of witnesses was conducted *in camera*. I had no reason to complain of any lack of support by the Administration. I may refer to one incident. There was an understanding that no one connected with the Aircraft Bureau should leave Washington until I had an opportunity to examine him. One of the most important men in the finance department of that Bureau came to me one day with the statement that he must go to Paris as he was utterly unable to find out the extent of our commitments abroad for aircraft. I thought it ridiculous that he should have to go to Paris for such a purpose and asked for his cablegrams and correspondence. There were a great number of cablegrams but they did not give the definite information desired. I sent for Secretary Baker and explained the situation. He said that he had heard nothing of this and that he would cable at once; that if we did not get the facts we wanted forthwith an important officer would be called home. He did cable and straightway we got the facts we needed.

The investigation took several months and I submitted the results in a comprehensive report at the end of October.[11] During the investigation it was supposed that the war effort would be keyed to a great drive in the spring of 1919, but the collapse of Germany brought the hostilities to an

[10][Meier Steinbrink (1880–1967) was elected to the Supreme Court in Brooklyn in 1932 and sat on the bench until 1957. He gave considerable time and effort to the struggle against racial prejudice. He was Chairman of the Anti-Defamation League from 1946–1952, and, in 1949, participated in the establishment of the Committee for the Protection of Religious Freedom.]

[11]A copy of the report, United States Department of Justice, *Aircraft Inquiry* (Washington, U.S. Government Printing Office, 1918), and a copy of Attorney General Gregory's supplementary report are [in the Hughes Papers].

I made no charge for my services in this inquiry, being reimbursed only for my cash outlays.

end much earlier (November 11, 1918). Still, the examination of witnesses and inspections of plants uncovered many remediable causes of delay and greatly stimulated production while the inquiry was in progress.

While engaged in this investigation I had my headquarters in Washington and was absent from my law office. I had rarely been able to visit my office while I was busy on the Draft Appeals Board. I managed, however, to attend to a few legal matters of outstanding importance. Beerits mentions a hurried trip to Chicago (there and back within forty-eight hours) to argue a case before a special session of the Circuit Court of Appeals.[12] I advised the Equitable Life Assurance Society in its proceedings of mutualization and successfully defended its action against the attack by minority stockholders in the Federal Court.[13] In December 1917, I argued the first stock dividend case in the Supreme Court of the United States.[14] In May 1918, I gave an opinion in aid of the Red Cross Drive in relation to contributions by corporations.[15]

Released from the Aircraft inquiry at the beginning of November 1918, I plunged again into active practice which I continued until I took office as Secretary of State in March 1921.[16] During this period, I argued many cases in the Supreme Court of the United States, in the lower Federal courts, and in the State courts.[17] I may mention a few of particular interest. As counsel for the Commercial Cable Company and the Commercial Pacific Cable Company I challenged, in a suit against the Postmaster General, the seizure of the complainants' Atlantic and Pacific cable systems. The seizure, under a general proclamation by the President, dated November 2, 1918, was alleged to have been made after the armistice and on or about November 16, 1918, and was assailed as a wholly unwarranted and arbitrary act beyond any valid authorization. The facts showing the conditions that had obtained prior to the armistice, the priority and adequacy

12Beerits, ["1916–1921"], p. 6. This case was American Press Association v. United States, 245 Fed. 91 [7th Cir. 1917].

13Royal Trust Co. v. Equitable Life Assurance Society, 247 Fed. 437 [2d Cir. 1917]; see, also, the reference to the proceedings for mutualization in correspondence [in the Hughes Papers]. The business arrangement which made possible the mutualization is described by Harold Nicolson in his biography, *Dwight Morrow* (New York, [Harcourt Brace & Co.] 1935), pp. 152–155. [It is described at greater length in R. Carlyle Buley, *The Equitable Life Assurance Society of the United States 1859–1964*, 2 vols. (New York, Appleton-Century-Crofts, 1957), II, 800–824.]

14Towne v. Eisner, 245 U.S. 418 [1918].

15A printed copy of this opinion, dated May 9, 1918, with letter from Charles D. Norton, Chairman, Insurance Division, Second Red Cross Drive, is [in the Hughes Papers].

16My son, who had joined the firm of Hughes, Rounds, Schurman & Dwight at the beginning of 1917, enlisted in the Army as a private in the latter part of that year and I was without the benefit of his assistance until his return from France in June 1919.

17Between November 1918, and February 1921, I made twenty-five arguments (including three re-arguments) in the Supreme Court of the United States. I have no data at hand with respect to the numerous arguments in other courts.

of the service accorded to the Government, and the control and censorship exercised by the Government with the full cooperation of the complainants, were set forth in the complaints and were not denied. While the case was pending before the Supreme Court in the Spring of 1919, the cable systems were returned to the complainants and the cases became moot.[18] In the case of *Southern Pacific Co. v. Bogert,* I appeared for minority shareholders, as trustee of stock acquired through a reorganization.[19] In *Eisner v. Macomber,* the Supreme Court held that a stock dividend, evincing merely a transfer of an accumulated surplus to the capital account of the corporation, took nothing from the property of the corporation and added nothing to that of the shareholders, and hence was not subject to an income tax under the Sixteenth Amendment.[20]

The National Prohibition Cases, presenting the question of the constitutional validity of the Eighteenth Amendment, came before the Supreme Court in March 1920.[21] I was not counsel for parties to these suits as I had refused a retainer on behalf of those interested in attacking the Amendment. While I thought the Amendment unwise as a matter of policy, I took not the slightest stock in the view advanced by Mr. Root that the people had no power to adopt such a constitutional amendment if they saw fit, and I filed a brief as *amicus curiae* on behalf of twenty-one State Attorneys General in support of the provision.

In Berlin Mills Company v. Procter & Gamble Company, I made my debut in the Supreme Court as counsel in a patent case.[22]

I was also counsel in a series of cases challenging the validity of the Food Control Act of 1917 (amended 1919) which made it a criminal offense to charge excessive prices for necessaries without forbidding any specific or definite act and without setting up any ascertainable standard of guilt.[23]

In May 1917, I had given to Alexander Brown & Sons, Brown Brothers & Company, and other bond houses an elaborate opinion in support of the constitutionality of the Federal Farm Loan Act of 1916 and of the validity of the Federal Farm Loan Bonds to be issued under that Act.[24] This opinion was widely used in promoting the sale of the bonds. So when the validity of the bonds was attacked, I was retained as counsel for one

18Commercial Cable Co. v. Burleson, 250 U.S. 360 [1919].

19250 U.S. 483 [1919].

20Argued April [16], 1919, reargued October [17, 20, 1919], 252 U.S. 189 [1920].

21253 U.S. 350 [1920].

22254 U.S. 156 [1920].

23Tedrow v. Lewis, 255 U.S. 98 [1921]; Kinnane v. Detroit Creamery Co., 255 U.S. 102 [1921]; Weeds v. United States, 255 U.S. 109 [1921]. These cases were part of a group which were argued in succession. The principal opinion of the Court was delivered in the first of the series, United States v. Cohen Grocery Co., 255 U.S. 81 [1921].

24A printed copy of this opinion is [in the Hughes Papers].

of the defendants, a Federal Land Bank, and appeared at the argument in the District Court in Kansas City and also in the Supreme Court. After two arguments, the constitutionality of the statute and the validity of the bonds with the tax exemption provision, were sustained.[25]

In the opinion given to the bond houses, I discussed the meaning of the general welfare clause, upholding the view that it did not confer an independent power, nor was it limited to the subjoined enumeration of powers (as asserted by Madison), but had its separate significance as prescribing the limits of the taxing power (the view taken by Hamilton and Story) and thus by necessary implication as broadly defining the objects for which moneys raised by taxation may be appropriated by Congress. In this view, I concluded that Congress had power to appropriate moneys for the promotion of the agricultural interests of the country, and to organize banks and to provide for their issue of bonds, made tax-exempt, in order to facilitate this undertaking; and also that the banks were valid organizations as appropriate fiscal agents of the Government. The Supreme Court had not theretofore definitely passed upon the meaning of the general welfare clause with reference to the scope of the power of appropriation; nor did the Court do so in upholding the Federal Farm Loan Act. The Court sustained that Act in the view that the land banks were duly created as depositories of public moneys and purchasers of government bonds, with authority to engage in the additional activities set forth.[26] Since then, the Supreme Court has specifically construed the general welfare clause as not being a grant of an independent power, and so not limited by the other grants to Congress of legislative powers, but as simply qualifying the power to tax and appropriate.[27]

In the Spring of 1920, I was retained by the United Mine Workers to defend the coal miners who had been indicted in the Federal Court at

[25]Smith v. Kansas City Title & Trust Co., 255 U.S. 180 (1921).

[26][*Ibid.*], pp. 210, 211.

[27]United States v. Butler, 297 U.S. 1, 65–67 (1936); Helvering v. Davis, 301 U.S. 619, 640 (1937).

It has been said, I understand, that the decision in the Butler case, invalidating the exactions of the Agricultural Adjustment Act of May 12, 1933, is inconsistent with the views I expressed in my opinion given to the bond houses in relation to the Federal Farm Loan Act of 1916. This suggestion, however, fails to take account of the ruling in the Butler case that the provisions of the Act of 1933 involved more than the appropriation of money for the benefit of agriculture and were of an essentially coercive character, designed, irrespective of any relation to interstate commerce, to control and reduce agricultural production within the several States. ([United States v. Butler] pp. 70–71). There was as to this a narrow line of cleavage in the Court, as the minority opinion recognized that "The power to tax and spend is not without constitutional restraints. One restriction is that the purpose must be truly national. Another is that it may not be used to coerce action left to state control." (U.S. v. Butler, 297 U.S. at 87.)

Indianapolis for violation of the Sherman Anti-Trust Act;[28] and in October 1920, I argued the appeal of the United Mine Workers in the first *Coronado* case.[29]

The case of Senator Truman H. Newberry attracted much attention. I argued in the Supreme Court the appeal from his conviction for violating the Act of Congress which limited the amount of money a candidate for the House or Senate might expend in procuring his nomination or election.[30] The statute applied in his case to a primary election. There were two important questions involved: (1) relating to the constitutional authority of Congress to limit expenditures in connection with primaries; (2) the construction of the statute. The conviction was reversed.[31] Five Justices held the statute to be invalid as applied to a primary election. The remaining Justices concurred in the reversal because of grave error in the charge of the trial judge based on a misconstruction of the statute. As to the latter point, it may be noted that the charge of bribery had been dismissed at Newberry's trial as there was no evidence to sustain it; and as to the remaining charge of excessive expenditures, the statute had been construed by the trial judge as requiring a conviction if a candidate became a candidate or continued as such after learning that more than the amount specified in the statute had been contributed and was being expended in the campaign, even though the candidate himself made no contribution and had not caused others to contribute and the expenditures were made without his participation.

In the case of *New York v. New Jersey,* I was retained by the State of New York, on its application for an injunction against the State of New Jersey and the Passaic Valley Sewage Commissioners, to prevent the pollution of the Upper Bay of New York Harbor by the discharge of a large volume of sewage.[32] The case was argued in 1918, and after further proof was again argued in January 1921. Having regard to a provision for sewage treatment prescribed in an agreement between the Defendants and the Government of the United States, the Court decided that the evidence was not sufficiently convincing to justify an injunction and New York's complaint was dismissed without prejudice to a renewal of the suit if the operation of the proposed sewer brought about conditions which were

[28] I argued the case, on demurer, in the District Court. This case was never brought to trial.

[29] United Mine Workers v. Coronado Coal Co., 259 U.S. 344, 350 [1922]. Note, I did not take part in the reargument which took place in March 1922, after I had become Secretary of State.

[30] Act of June 25, 1910 (amended August 19, 1911), sec. 8.

[31] Newberry v. United States, 256 U.S. 232, 243–258, 270–275, 292–295 [1921]. In 1941, the Supreme Court sustained the power of Congress to regulate primary elections. United States v. Classic, 313 U.S. 299, 317 [1941].

[32] New York v. New Jersey, 249 U.S. 202 [1919].

deemed by New York to require relief for the protection of the health and welfare of its people.[33]

While I carried a heavy professional load during this period (November 1918, to February 1921), handling many important cases of which I have given but a few instances,[34] I think I may say that I responded generously to other demands. Beerits has gleaned from newspaper files such of these activities as attracted public attention, and of course there were many others.[35] I am sure that fully one-third of my time was given to matters of more or less public interest, outside my professional work.

An outstanding episode was the outrageous proceeding in the New York legislature to oust five socialists who had been duly elected. At the very outset, I protested against this proceeding and later I had the privilege of acting as Chairman of a Committee of the Association of the Bar of the City of New York which was appointed to defend the right of these members of the Assembly to retain their seats. This affair is fully described by Professor Zechariah Chafee, Jr., in his work *Free Speech in the United States* ([Cambridge, Harvard University Press,] 1941, pp. 269 *et seq.*).

Among my many speeches during this period were those at the celebration of the 50th Anniversary of Cornell University in June 1919, at the Commencement of Wellesley College in June 1920 (when my daughter Catherine was graduated), and at the Centenary of the Harvard Law School in the same month. The Harvard address has been frequently quoted from, because of what I said as to the growth of bureaucracy and my query "whether constitutional government as heretofore maintained in this republic could survive another great war even victoriously waged." [36]

[33]New York v. New Jersey, 256 U.S. 296, 314 [1921].

[34][Hughes handled an extraordinary amount of Supreme Court litigation during this period. In the weeks of October 14, 1920, and November 15, 1920, he argued six cases before the Court and won four of them. Between 1918 and 1921 and 1925 and 1929, Hughes's personal docket "included 28 full-fledged Supreme Court cases (exclusive of petitions for certiorari, etc.). The names of many of these cases have become familiar to all lawyers. Of these he won 22 and lost 16 (with some nice questions involving remands for further proceedings, etc., resolved in his favor). His average was .579, considerably lower than the .625 achieved in his earlier Court of Appeals practice, but it must be remembered that in this later period he often was called upon to resurrect cases which others had badly lost below." Edwin McElwain, "The Business of the Supreme Court as Conducted by Chief Justice Hughes," *Harvard Law Review*, LXIII (1949), 10–11, n. 9.]

[35]Beerits, ["1916–1921"], pp. 10–20, and Appendix of references. [Perhaps the most interesting of these were Hughes's speech to the Union League Club, March 26, 1919, in which he analyzed the Covenant of the League of Nations and suggested seven amendments; his letter to Senator Hale on the Covenant, proposing four reservations (*New York Times*, July 29, 1919, p. 3; ed., July 29, p. 8); and his letter to Senator Borah in which he said that Article 10 of the Covenant should be eliminated (*New York Times*, August 5, 1919, p. 3.)]

[36]A pamphlet containing the addresses at the Harvard Centenary, and a photostat copy of the report of my address in the Boston *Transcript*, are in [the Hughes Papers].

It was in the year 1920 that I sustained the greatest sorrow of my life in the loss of my eldest daughter Helen. A rare and joyous spirit, radiating happiness not only in our home but in all her associations, dedicating her life to good works, she realized my ideal of a beautiful character, and her passing in the fullness of her young womanhood — a victim of devoted service — seemed to me the saddest of life's ironies. It left a wound which has never healed.[37]

In the summers of 1919 and 1920, we had a cottage at Lake George, but with my correspondence and goings to and fro I got but little respite from work. In 1920, I gave considerable attention to politics. I declined to allow my name to be used in connection with the candidacy for the Presidential nomination. Beerits' Memorandum puts it too strongly in saying that Will Hays, Chairman of the Republican National Committee, "asked" me to act as Temporary Chairman at the National Convention and make a keynote address.[38] It would be more accurate to say that Mr. Hays put out a feeler, or made the suggestion which I at once dismissed. On my way to the meeting of the American Bar Association at St. Louis in August, I stopped at Marion, Ohio, on Mr. Harding's invitation, and issued a statement supporting his candidacy and referring in general terms to international cooperation. I took an active part in the campaign, but at the request of the Republican Committee my speeches were mainly in the

[37]Beerits ["1916–1921"], pp. 15a and 15b, gives the circumstances:

["During this period of strenuous activity, during which he was arguing his hardest cases in court and delivering many public addresses, Mr. Hughes was suffering the most terrible affliction of his life — the illness and death of his eldest daughter, Helen. A lovely girl, she had graduated from Vassar in 1914 and had then undertaken Y.W.C.A. work. After the United States entered the war, she served on the War Work Council of the Y.W.C.A. In Boston in the fall of 1918 she was stricken down by the grave epidemic of influenza, and this disease was followed by pneumonia. In January 1919, she came back to Mr. and Mrs. Hughes in New York, and during the first part of that year she had apparently recovered, and the doctors stated that she was all right. She went back to her work in April, and in June went to Vassar to her fifth class reunion. She was suddenly stricken down, however, and it was discovered that she was suffering from advanced tuberculosis. Mr. and Mrs. Hughes got a house in Glens Falls, N.Y., to which their daughter was at once taken. She never left this house, for she died the following spring, 1920. Mrs. Hughes of course remained in Glens Falls during this long period of stress. Mr. Hughes lived alone in their apartment in New York. He went to Glens Falls every Saturday, returning to New York on Sunday. For him it was a long and terrible period of much labor and little sleep, of exacting duties and the greatest anxiety.

["Although Helen was only twenty-eight years of age when she died, she had a wonderful influence with young women. A beautiful little chapel was erected by friends in her memory at Silver Bay, Lake George, the headquarters of the Silver Bay Association, and the site of annual meetings of the Y.M.C.A., the Y.W.C.A., and kindred organizations. It is a lovely little Norman structure, named the Helen Hughes Memorial Chapel, containing a beautiful organ, and it is used regularly as a place of worship — by a boys' school in the winter, and by Y.W.C.A. meetings in the summer."]

[38]*Ibid.*, p. 17.

mining districts in Ohio and Indiana. After the election, Mr. Harding requested me to visit him at Marion and this I did on December 10th. He then made me a definite offer of the position of Secretary of State and this offer I definitely accepted a few days later. The appointment was not announced until the following February when I visited Mr. Harding at St. Augustine, Florida.[39]

[39]Correspondence relating to this appointment is [in the Hughes Papers. Beerits, "1916–1921" (p. 19) describes the meeting on February 19, 1921:

["On that day, following a conference with Mr. Hughes which lasted most of the morning, Senator Harding was accompanied by Mr. Hughes at his daily audience with the newspaper correspondents at noon. Here he introduced Mr. Hughes to the press as the new Secretary of State. In answer to a question as to their discussion about diplomatic and departmental affairs, Senator Harding said: 'You must ask Mr. Hughes about that. That is going to be another policy of the next Administration. From the beginning the Secretary of State will speak for the State Department.' (*New York Times*, February 20, 1921, p. 1). Thus it was made evident that the new Secretary was to be given a free hand in directing the foreign relations of the United States. (For newspaper comment upon the appointment of Mr. Hughes see the booklet of Clippings in the Hughes Papers.)"]

Antoinette Carter Hughes, about 1916

Chapter XIV Secretary of State *1921–1925*

I met Senator Harding in 1916, when he came to New York to give the official notification of my nomination for the Presidency and presided at the meeting at which I formally accepted it. After that, I did not meet him again until my brief call at Marion during the campaign of 1920. I have already referred to my interview with him in December of that year when he offered me the position of Secretary of State.

President Harding was a most kindly man, always eager to please his old friends and to make new ones. He found it difficult to say no. To me, he was a most agreeable Chief, always accessible, anxious fully to understand each problem as it arose. I soon came to understand the limitations which were imposed upon him by the situation which had developed in the Senate in consequence of the wrangle over the Treaty of Versailles, and I sought to avoid embarrassing him by stirring up futile conflicts. I realized that I must take a full measure of responsibility when I felt definite action should be taken. I did not go to him with a statement of difficulties and ask him what should be done, but supplemented my statements of the facts in particular cases by concrete proposals upon which he could act at once, and to which he almost invariably gave his approval. Our relations were of the happiest sort. Engrossed as I was, night and day, in the work of the Department of State, I knew nothing of his intimacies with those who later abused his trust and brought his administration into disrepute.[1]

[1]See Beerits' Memorandum, "The Fall Oil Scandals," pp. 8–17.

Beerits has a series of memoranda relating to this period which deal separately with important subjects. He based these memoranda on my conversations with him, on my own papers, and on the examination he was permitted to make of the files of the Department of State. Since he worked with me, the Department has published the volumes of *Foreign Relations* [*Papers Relating to the Foreign Relations of the United States, 1921–1925,* 10 vols. (Washington, U.S. Government Printing Office, 1936–1940)] covering the years 1921–1925, so that this authoritative source of information is now available to the public. Also, a number of important books by authors of special competence have ap-

President Harding's keen desire to please and his accessibility to all sorts of visitors made his days especially arduous. Visiting the Executive Office, I usually found his Secretary's room filled with persons seeking an audience, and when I was slipped in, so that I should not be kept waiting, he would often put his arm across my shoulders and exclaim, "Hughes, this is the damnedest job!"

There was a marked change when Mr. Coolidge became President. As he was taciturn and non-committal, visitors got little advantage from a personal interview and were generally content with a word with his Secretary. Such appointments as he had he could dispose of in the morning. So that when in the afternoon I would take my telegrams or proposals over to the Executive Office, I would find the President alone, smoking a cigar and reading his papers in an atmosphere of quiet and relaxation.

When I took office in March 1921, most of the members of the Cabinet were strangers to me. I had known John W. Weeks when he was in the Senate, but not intimately. I became acquainted with Postmaster General Will Hays during my campaign tour in Indiana in 1916 and was much impressed by his executive ability and political sagacity. Without disparaging the zeal, integrity, and personal devotion of William R. Willcox, I think that if Will Hays had been the manager of my presidential campaign it would have been successful.

I had met Mr. Hoover a few times. In 1920 I had the privilege of making the presentation speech when he was awarded a gold medal for his services during World War I. And, at the request of Mr. Harding, I had urged him to accept the position of Secretary of Commerce.

Strange as it may seem to outsiders, the relations of the members of the Cabinet, while friendly, were not intimate. Aside from Cabinet meetings, they did not see much of each other, each being engrossed in the work of his own department. Of course, we met at formal dinners and at the White

---

peared. Among these are the following: *The Far Eastern Policy of the United States* by A. Whitney Griswold ([New York, Harcourt, Brace and Company,] 1938); *Elihu Root* by Philip C. Jessup ([New York, Dodd, Mead & Company,] 1938), Chap. XLVII, Vol. 2, pp. 445 *et seq.*; *Toward a New Order of Sea Power* by H. & M. Sprout ([Princeton,] Princeton University Press, 1940); *The Latin American Policy of the United States* by Samuel F. Bemis ([New York, Harcourt, Brace & Company,] 1943).

Other books referring in a more intimate way to intra-departmental affairs during my incumbency are *Inside the Department of State* by Bertram D. Hulen ([New York, McGraw-Hill Book Company,] 1939); *Diplomat Between Wars* by Hugh [R.] Wilson ([New York, Longsmans, Green & Co., 1941).

[Since Harding's private papers were opened to scholars in the 1960's, several books have been published on his administration. See: Robert K. Murray, *The Harding Era: Warren G. Harding and His Administration* (Minneapolis, University of Minnesota Press, 1969); Francis Russell, *The Shadow of Blooming Grove: Warren G. Harding and His Times* (New York, McGraw-Hill, 1968); and Andrew Sinclair. *The Available Man: The Life Behind the Masks of Warren Gamaliel Harding* (New York, Macmillan, 1965).]

House receptions, but what conversation we had on these occasions was casual. Secretary Weeks and I were born on the same day (in different years, he in 1860) and we had birthday dinners. Secretary Hoover, who was deeply interested in all matters pertaining to foreign commerce, I met quite frequently. I formed a delightful friendship with Mr. Wallace, Secretary of Agriculture, and in the summer days we frequently had a round of golf in the early morning at Chevy Chase before going to our offices.

I supposed that, of course, important matters of administration would be fully discussed at cabinet meetings. President Harding usually opened these meetings with a brief word and called on each of us in turn for whatever statement we cared to make. Vice-President Coolidge attended the meetings and spoke last, generally making a terse comment on some phase of the economic situation. After these various statements and whatever discussion they provoked, President Harding would speak briefly.

At the outset, being called on first, I described rather fully the important questions with which the State Department was concerned. But I soon found that there were too many leaks to make it safe to continue that practice and I would speak only of such matters as could immediately be made public. Then, after the cabinet meeting, I would meet the President privately. And I may say that during my entire term of office I kept the President advised by almost daily interviews of everything of importance that was done, ascertained, or proposed in departmental affairs.

Other members of the Cabinet apparently came to the same conclusion and rarely talked at length at cabinet meetings, going to the President later for more intimate interviews. An exception was [Secretary of the Interior] Albert B. Fall, who was very voluble, especially about matters that did not concern his department. He would discourse at length on foreign affairs, showing neither acumen, discretion, nor accurate knowledge. But he thought he was an authority. His flow of words without wisdom was very boring to me at least, and I think to others. I had little to do with him, but I did not suspect him of anything worse than vanity and mental indigestion.

The discussion in cabinet meetings very early came to be of a general character and was not very helpful. Each member of the Cabinet no doubt felt, as I did, that as to the pressing problems of his own Department he was the only one who fully understood them and that it was idle to attempt to detail them to others who were busy with their own affairs and not in a position to make a helpful contribution. The cabinet meetings were thus brief and often ran to a mere general and ineffective talk on the political situation.

I should add that during the time when I was especially busy with the sessions of the committees of the Washington Conference, I rarely attended cabinet meetings, but every morning early I saw the President and reported to him what had taken place the day before in the Conference negotiations.

President Coolidge gave me his confidence as fully as President Harding had given his. He asked the members of the Cabinet to continue in office and they did so. Several of us felt that he should get rid of Attorney General Daugherty, and I suggested to him that if it would help I would try to get the members of the Cabinet to place their resignation in his hands and he could reappoint those he wished to retain. "No," he said, "Don't do that, it might leave me alone with Daugherty!"

President Harding was good enough to leave to me the organization of the State Department. I chose as Under Secretaries career men who were outstanding because of their ability and diplomatic experience. At the outset, I selected as Under Secretary Henry P. Fletcher, who had served in our legations in Cuba and China and had been Ambassador to Chile and Mexico. He was a personal friend of President Harding, who was glad to appoint him, and he greatly aided me in organizing the Department. He was appointed Ambassador to Belgium in 1922 and later became Ambassador to Italy.

His successor as Under Secretary was William Phillips, also of high distinction in the diplomatic service. He had served in China and London, in the Department of State, and as Minister to the Netherlands. He left the Department in 1924 to become Ambassador to Belgium and was later Minister to Canada and Ambassador to Italy. He was succeeded by Joseph C. Grew who had a brilliant record. When he was appointed Under Secretary in 1924, he had served in Egypt, Mexico, Russia, Germany, in the Department of State, with the Secretariat at the Peace Conference in Paris, and as Minister to Denmark and Switzerland. He had negotiated the Treaty with Turkey in 1923. Later he was Ambassador to Turkey and Japan.

Alvey A. Adee, who had had a distinguished career as Assistant Secretary, was continued in office, and although impaired by age was still capable of rendering important service.[2] I secured the appointment as Assistant Secretaries of men who had been thoroughly trained and had

[2]Bertram D. Hulen, *Inside the Department of State*, pp. 27–28. Adee failed rapidly, however, and retired. He died in 1924 in his 82nd year. [For additional information on the men mentioned here, see Waldo H. Heinrichs, Jr., *American Ambassador: Joseph C. Grew and the Development of the United States Diplomatic Tradition* (Boston, Little, Brown, 1966); Joseph C. Grew, *Turbulent Era: A Diplomatic Record of Forty Years, 1904–1945*, edited by Walter Johnson assisted by Nancy Harvison Hooker, 2 vols. (Boston, Houghton Mifflin Company, 1952); William Phillips, *Ventures in Diplomacy* (Boston, privately printed, 1952); and Katharine Crane, *Mr. Carr of State: Forty-Seven Years in the Department of State* (New York, St. Martin's Press, 1960).]

won high place in the esteem of those familiar with the conduct of our foreign affairs. Later they served with distinction in our legations and embassies. These Assistant Secretaries were Fred Morris Dearing, later Ambassador to Peru; Leland Harrison, later Minister to Sweden, Uruguay, Rumania and Switzerland; Robert Woods Bliss, later Minister to Sweden and Ambassador to Argentina; Wilbur J. Carr, later Minister to Czechoslovakia; John V. A. MacMurray, later Minister to China, Estonia, Latvia and Lithuania, and Ambassador to Turkey; and J. Butler Wright, later Minister to Hungary, Uruguay, and Czechoslovakia, and Ambassador to Cuba.

And I sought to have the various divisions in the Department staffed by the most competent men. I [make special mention of] Sumner Welles in my Memorandum on Latin American Affairs.[3] He was followed by Francis White, as Chief of the Latin American Division, later Minister to Czechoslovakia. Other Chiefs of Division were William R. Castle, Jr., Western European Affairs, later Ambassador to Japan and Under Secretary of State under President Hoover; Allen W. Dulles, Near Eastern Affairs; J. V. A. MacMurray, Far Eastern Affairs (before his appointment as Assistant Secretary); DeWitt C. Poole, Russian Affairs. And we had the expert assistance of Stanley K. Hornbeck as Technical Adviser. Nor should I fail to refer to the excellent service given by Hugh R. Wilson as Chief of the Division of Current Information.[4] I cannot undertake to make special reference to all the others who served in the various Divisions, but they were trained men who deserved and had my full confidence.

The reorganization of the entire foreign service on a merit basis, in which I was deeply interested, was greatly facilitated by the passage of the Rogers Act in 1924, which has been called "the great basic charter of the modern diplomatic service." [5]

I stated my attitude with respect to the foreign service in my address before the United States Chamber of Commerce in May 1922, as follows:[6]

> The necessity for a trained staff is obvious. The notion that a wide-awake, average American can do anything is flattering to the American pride, but costs the Government dearly. In every line of effort — professional, commercial or industrial — it is thoroughly understood that you cannot obtain the necessary technical equipment through mere general experience or by reading instructions. There are thousands of

[3][See Chapter 16.]

[4]Hugh R. Wilson is the author of *Diplomat Between Wars.*

[5]Hulen, *[Inside the Department of State]*, pp. 88–89. Mr. Hulen also gives friendly reminiscenses of my work in the Department, pp. 34–37, 40–50, 198, 199, 264.

[6]"Some Aspects of the Work of the Department of State," *American Journal of International Law*, vol. 16 (July 1922), p. 361. [It is printed in *The Pathway of Peace*, pp. 250–266.]

items of necessary information which are a part of the common knowledge of men whose lives are entirely devoted to a class of work which cannot be obtained by anyone who is suddenly introduced from the outside. I have no regard for artificial technicalities and I fully understand the dangers of departmental routine, but it is a very shortsighted and foolish view which would confuse routine and expert knowledge. The patent fact is that you cannot have an efficient Foreign Service without having trained men and you cannot secure trained men without an adequate system for their selection and maintenance; and you cannot keep men who have been properly selected and trained and are invaluable to their country unless you offer reasonable opportunities for promotion.

I grant the importance of appointing men from outside the service to important diplomatic posts. It is most advisable that the country should have the opportunity to draw upon its reserves of wide experience, sagacity, and ability; that it should secure the benefit of the mature judgment of those who represent the fruition of American opportunity, culture and discipline, and thus invigorate the process of diplomacy. But it must be remembered that these men, despite their training and ability, would be helpless if they did not have the backing of trained staffs. If you are to secure the full benefit of the most distinguished service at the top you must still have your organized service in all the other grades. And, as I have said, while you cannot sacrifice the great advantage of appointments from the outside to the chief positions, it is absolutely necessary that there should be a sufficient frequency of promotions from the Service itself to the chief positions, that is, of heads of missions, so as to make possible a career warranting its pursuit by a fair proportion of the very best of our young men.

I also referred to the low salaries, to the difficulties encountered by young men without private means, and to the well-to-do young men who entered the service which in consequence was sometimes regarded as "a rich man's club." I said (p. 362):

The salaries are so low in the classified Diplomatic Service that the choice of candidates is largely restricted to young men of wealthy families who are willing and able to a considerable extent to pay their own way. It is a most serious thing to be compelled to say that a young man without means, who desires to marry and bring up a family after the American tradition, cannot be encouraged to enter upon one of the most important careers that the country has to offer. I say bluntly that no American can face the facts without a sense of humiliation, and he is compelled to qualify his boasting of our intelligence and civilization so long as this condition continues.

In the present situation there is a double harm, first in keeping out men who would invigorate the Service, and on the other hand, in creating the impression that it is a rich man's club. Let me, however, warn you against an erroneous impression. It does not follow because a man has the advantage of the background of success and wealth in his family, generally won in a hard, competitive struggle, that he is not entirely worthy of appointment and promotion. On the contrary, we have some of the finest young men of the country in our service, and we ought to be grateful that under the existing conditions they are able and content to turn aside from financial opportunities to follow an intellectual bent and seek a career of honorable service to the nation. I do not depreciate those who are in the Service, but I do decry the method which limits the selection and discriminates against the poor man of equal ability. We talk a great deal of love of our country, and I should like to see a better appreciation of what its interests demand.

We have the same difficulty in the Consular Service because of the present salary scale. It is difficult to retain the best men because of tempting offers constantly made to them by the business world.

It must be borne in mind that we have always had in this country a very large proportion of our young men of the highest ability who are strongly influenced by other ideals than those of pecuniary gain. It is because of this fact that in the past generations, while America was advancing by leaps and bounds, and vast fortunes were being accumulated, the church and the teaching profession were enriched by our best blood. But there is a limit to thc sacrifice that can be asked. There is a difference between plain living and actual poverty and distress. Further, the prospect that invites the young man of intellectual ambition is one of career, of recognition, of distinction; hence, it is of vital importance in organizing our Diplomatic and Consular Service that we should provide sufficient compensation for a decent living and hold out the hope that conspicuous ability and fidelity will be appropriately recognized.

I also referred to the need of greater flexibility in the service and to my belief that the two branches of the service called the Diplomatic and Consular should be made an interchangeable unit, saying (p. 363):

There is also the need of a greater flexibility. There has long been too great a distinction between the political interests of the Diplomatic Service and the commercial interests of the Consular Service. Both are engaged in political work and both are engaged in commercial work. You

> cannot at this time take economics out of diplomacy. If you would protect our interests on the one side you must support them on the other, and I believe that the two branches of the Service, now called the Diplomatic and Consular, should be drawn together and treated as an interchangeable unit. This would permit men to be assigned from one Service to the other and thus give a greater range of opportunity for putting men in the places where they belong as their aptitudes and special talents are revealed.

This flexibility, in establishing the unified "Foreign Service," with provision for increased salaries, was provided by the Rogers Act.[7]

While I had a free hand in organizing the Department, I had to submit to the political exigencies which to a regrettable extent dominated President Harding's selection of Ministers and Ambassadors. This is an old story. As Allan Nevins has said, with respect to Hamilton Fish, "The long suffering Secretary sometimes grew impatient as he tried to work with the tools that were given him in foreign capitals; but he realized that his was only the common lot of all Secretaries since John Quincy Adams." [8]

I did succeed in obtaining the promotion of career men and the appointment of some others, who were men of distinction, to important posts, as, e.g., Jacob Gould Schurman to China. But there were certain political appointments which I strongly disapproved. I especially opposed the appointment of George Harvey as Ambassador to England. There was no question of Harvey's ability. He was capable and astute, but his temperament, and one notorious failing, I felt made his selection inadvisable. Soon after I became Secretary, I was at a private dinner at which Harvey was a guest. He talked recklessly and it was quite evident that he was intoxicated and hardly knew what he was saying. I told President Harding of the incident and insisted that he should not be appointed as Ambassador. The President seemed to be of the same view. But, as he told me later, he took up the matter with Harvey, who burst into tears and promised to give up drinking. It appeared that Harvey on account of his great help in the President's campaign had been definitely promised the Ambassadorship and the President felt that in view of Harvey's pledge he must make the promise good. From reports I received from London, it was apparent that the pledge was not kept and as a consequence Harvey was at times unreliable. Apart from that failing, he was presumptuous. In two instances he got into a sharp conflict of veracity with Lord Curzon. And Beerits gives illustrations in connection with the negotiations for the fund-

[7]Act of May 24, 1924, c. 182, 43 U.S. Stat., p. 140.

[8][Allan Nevins, *Hamilton Fish: The Inner History of the Grant Administration* (New York, Dodd, Mead & Company, 1937), p. 654.]

The Secretary of State after a round of golf at Chevy Chase

ing of the British debt.[9] But, as Beerits says, Harvey did perform valuable service at the end of the negotiations in persuading the British Government to accept the American plan.

President Coolidge, who did not appear to be bound to the same extent by political obligations as was President Harding, was more amenable to suggestions with respect to good diplomatic appointments.

A question that is always present in the mind of the Secretary of State is how far he can make public the action he is taking. I always felt that I should be greatly relieved if I could shout from the housetops every morning everything I had done or proposed to do. But, of course, there are always communications showing the attitude of foreign governments which cannot be revealed without breach of confidence. Then, important negotiations might be seriously impeded by premature disclosures. Still, I think it clear that the Secretary should not acquire a habit of withholding information which he can properly give. His aim should be, not to see how little he can make public, but how much.

I had become familiar with press conferences when I was Governor of New York, and I was prepared to make full use of those I held as Secretary. I endeavored at least to give the background of the proceedings of the Department and so far as possible to keep the press *en rapport* with developments. Mr. Hulen, of the staff of the New York *Times*, has something to say of my efforts in that direction. I was in an especially difficult position during the Washington Conference, when my press conferences were unusually large, being attended by the representatives of foreign journals. As I was Chairman of the Conference, and engaged in all the intimate negotiations, I knew every step taken, but I could not speak freely while agreements were taking shape.[10] The press representatives of other delegations, particularly those of the British, did not feel so constrained. They were not the heads of delegations and what they said was not official. Their utterances were at times a little embarrassing. Notwithstanding the reticence I had to maintain at crucial stages in the negotiations, the Washington correspondents did not fail to appreciate my desire to keep them as fully informed as possible, and at the close of the Conference they presented me with a pair of golden shears inscribed to me "In gratitude." [11]

[9]Beerits' Memorandum, "Funding the Allied War Debts," pp. 2–5.

[One example of Harvey's maladroitness was the preparation of a speech for Chancellor of the Exchequer Stanley Baldwin, for delivery before the American and French debt funding commissions. The British Ambassador, Sir Auckland Geddes, was indignant and Mr. Baldwin astonished that Harvey would have the audacity to do this. After reading the Harvey speech, Hughes burst into laughter and told Geddes to ignore the matter, for neither he nor the State Department had known of the speech. It was, he added, merely the result of Harvey's overzealousness.]

[10]Hulen, *[Inside the Department of State]*, pp. 147–9, 130–2, 288–9.

[11]The presentation was made on March 11, 1922. See *The Pathway of Peace*, p. 245.

Chapter XV Foreign Policy Problems

In the review of the conduct of foreign affairs, which I prepared for the Coolidge campaign of 1924, I referred at the outset to the situation which confronted the Administration in March 1921.[1] I said:

> It would be difficult to imagine a worse tangle in our foreign relations than that with which the Republican Administration was required to deal when it came into power on March 4, 1921. Two years and nearly four months had elapsed since the Armistice, but we were still in a technical state of war. The peace negotiations had evoked a bitter and undying controversy. In the Far East our relations were embarrassed by suspicion and distrust, giving rise to serious apprehensions. In this hemisphere old sores were still festering. For years our relations with Mexico had been unsatisfactory. The situation was a most difficult one as opportunities for disputes lay on every hand while the chances of finding adequate means of accommodation were extremely meager. These difficulties have largely been resolved.

What I said was not intended as a reflection upon my predecessors, but merely as a factual statement of existing difficulties.[2]

[1]A copy of this pamphlet entitled, "Foreign Relations," by C.E.H., is in [the Hughes Papers.]

[2][This summary agrees, for the most part, with the priorities for foreign policy established by the Republican leadership at the outset of the Harding Administration. Senator Henry Cabot Lodge exerted the greatest influence on the incoming president. As he had been the party's foreign policy spokesman in the Senate and as he had been the architect of the successful fight against the Covenant of the League of Nations as presented by President Woodrow Wilson, he did not concern himself especially with Europe and the problems of the peace. As far as he was concerned the basic issue of the League had been settled. The rest was technical detail which the incoming Secretary of State could handle. The Harding Administration, Lodge felt, should turn its attention to relations with Japan, specifically, the dispute over control of Shantung. An obvious part of the problem in Asia was the competition in naval armaments that threatened to embitter relations between the United States and Japan. Lodge suggested that these issues might be taken up simultaneously.

THE LEAGUE OF NATIONS

I had been strongly in favor of international cooperation and had stressed both in the campaign of 1916 and later, the need of international organization in the interest of peace.[3] I was sympathetic with the proposal to create a league of nations and was anxious that a plan should be worked out which would facilitate participation by our Government. I thought it not difficult to do this, as I believed there would be widespread support for such an undertaking, if no unnecessary grounds of attack were furnished to opponents.

When the text of the proposed Covenant was first published, I saw at once that it was likely to be vigorously and successfully opposed in that form, and that amendments should be made to secure adequate American support. This was particularly true of the proposed Article X purporting to provide an immediate guaranty as against external aggression of the territorial integrity, that is, of the boundaries of the various States as these were established under the Treaty of Versailles. I thought this proposal a grave mistake. I at once called a special meeting of the Union League Club, of which I was President, for March 26, 1919, and then made an address analyzing the provisions of the proposed Covenant and suggesting amendments.[4]

In discussing Article X, I said that I regarded it as a trouble-breeder, as unnecessary and unwise, and likely to prove illusory. I said:

> This Covenant is intended to be a permanent arrangement . . . The guaranty makes no allowance for changes which may be advisable. It ascribes a prescience and soundness of judgment to the present Peace Conference in erecting States and defining boundaries which no body in the history of the world has ever possessed. Even as to the new States, it attempts to make permanent existing conditions, or conditions as arranged at this Conference, in a world of dynamic forces to which no one can set bounds. It gives no fair opportunity for adjust-

---

[Subsequent events — United States neutrality in the 1930's, the outbreak of World War II, and the creation of the United Nations — underscored for Hughes the importance of the United States relations with Europe and the League of Nations during his tenure as Secretary of State. For this reason, he begins his series of memoranda on foreign policy problems with a discussion of the League. Much of what he has to say in the memoranda on the League and on the Washington Arms Conference are reflections of the debate raging while Hughes wrote the Notes as to the causes of World War II.]

[3]See my speech in accepting the Republican nomination for President in July 1916 [in the Hughes Papers], and my address at the Long Beach Conference on international affairs in May 1917 [cited above, Chapter 13]. Beerits' Memorandum, "The Separate Peace with Germany, The League of Nations," etc., pp. 1–5, gives quotations.

[4]A printed copy of this address is [in the Hughes Papers].

ments. It is in the teeth of experience. The limitation of the words "as against external aggression" is a frail reliance; no one can foresee what the merits of particular cases may be . . .

The guaranty would be unwise even if it could accomplish its apparent purpose. But I also think that it will prove to be illusory. Should there be occasion to make the promise good, not improbably it will be insisted that it is a collective guaranty. Already, it is urged in support of the guaranty that its obligation apparently rests not upon any nation individually but depends upon united action, both as to the occasion and manner of enforcement. The general tenor of the Covenant, as well as the last clause of Article X, will be appealed to in support of this view.

Certainly, each Power will be the judge of what in good faith it should do. In the case of the United States, the guaranty will not be made good except by the action of Congress, and it will be for Congress to decide whether we are bound and what we should undertake. The course of recent debates has sufficiently indicated what the attitude of Congress is likely to be, if the resort to war pursuant to Article X is opposed to the opinion of the country. Congress not improbably will consider that it has not been put under any proper obligation to assume the unwelcome task. In such a case, the guaranty would merely serve the purpose of permitting the charge that we had defaulted in our obligation. On the other hand, if in our conception of duty, clarified by our experience in the great war, we should conclude that we should go to war to preserve the territorial integrity of another State, or in defense of liberty and civilization, we should respond with heartiness to that call of duty in the absence of Article X.[5]

I added:

I am not unmindful of the importance of making response to the importunate demand of stricken and suffering peoples that an organized endeavor should be made to prevent the recurrence of strife. I deeply sympathize with the purpose to provide international arrangements for conference, for the judicial settlement of disputes, for conciliation, and for co-operation to the fullest extent practicable and consistent with a proper regard for our national safety. But time passes rapidly, and it is not the part of wisdom to create expectations on the part of the peoples of the world which the Covenant cannot satisfy. I think that it is a fallacy to suppose that helpful co-operation in the future will be assured by the attempted compulsion of an inflexible

[5]See Philip C. Jessup, *Elihu Root*, [2 vols. (New York, Dodd, Mead & Co., 1938)], Vol. II, pp. 378–379.

rule. Rather will such co-operation depend upon the fostering of firm friendships springing from an appreciation of community of ideals, interests and purposes, and such friendships are more likely to be promoted by freedom of conference than by the effort to create hard and fast engagements.

Later, in July 1919, in response to a request of Senator [Eugene] Hale [of Maine], I proposed four reservations to the Covenant as it then stood, which I thought would afford adequate protection to the United States against commitments which otherwise would be sure to evoke successful opposition. In my letter to Senator Hale, I stated the point of view from which I thought the questions should be approached:[6]

> There is plain need for a league of nations, in order to provide for the adequate development of international law, for creating and maintaining organs of international justice and the machinery of conciliation and conference, and for giving effect to measures of international co-operation which from time to time may be agreed upon. There is also the immediate exigency to be considered. It is manifest that every reasonable effort should be made to establish peace as promptly as possible and to bring about a condition in which Europe can resume its normal industrial activity.
>
> I perceive no reason why these objects cannot be attained without sacrificing the essential interests of the United States. There is a middle ground between aloofness and injurious commitments.

In this relation it has sometimes been said that the Covenant made provision for the alteration of boundaries, etc. The reference is to Article XIX providing that the Assembly of the League might "from time to time advise the reconsideration" of treaties "which have become inapplicable and the consideration of international conditions whose continuance might endanger the peace of the world." It seemed clear to me that it was but a remote possibility that changes in boundaries might thus be obtained.

What I said in my letter to Senator Hale states the attitude which I maintained in the presidential campaign of 1920.[7] I joined Mr. Root and others in the statement made in October 1920, supporting Mr. Harding's candidacy. When I visited the President-elect at Marion in December and he offered me the position of Secretary of State, I restated my views as to

[6]A printed copy of my letter to Senator Hale, under date of July 24, 1919, proposing reservations, is [in the Hughes Papers].

[7]Beerits' Memorandum, "Separate Peace with Germany," p. 10, gives the reference to my speeches. [Also, see above, chapter 13.]

the League and Mr. Harding not only expressed no opposition but seemed to be in entire agreement. He thought that we could go through the Treaty of Versailles and decide what could be accepted, and that the Senate would ratify the Treaty with our suggested reservations.

However, when I took office, I found that the opposition to the League had become more determined than ever and that there was no prospect of obtaining ratification, whatever reservations we might propose. I was informed that if the Treaty were sent to the Senate, no matter with what recommendations as to reservations, there would be a prolonged and most bitter fight, with no prospect of ultimate success on our part, while the antagonisms aroused would seriously threaten the efforts of the Administration in other helpful directions. I was reluctant to accept this view and I did so only when friends in the Senate who were favorable to the League — known as "mild reservationists" — assured me that there was no hope of obtaining the Senate's approval of membership in the League on any terms.

Sometimes later I reviewed that situation, and my own action in the light of it, in my letter to George W. Wickersham, from which Beerits quotes at length.

["It would have been idle for the Administration to attempt the formation of another association of nations to parallel the League of Nations. One of the mischiefs of the peace treaty, as the President said in his message, was in making the League of Nations, in which it was sought to embody the great ideal of an association of nations to promote peace, 'the enforcing agency of the victors of war.' I may add that early suggestions on my part that the League might be left to perform this office while a new association on an acceptable basis not directly connected with the Peace Treaty might be formed for the broader purpose in view met with no approving response. I do not believe that there has been a time when the administration could have proposed hopefully a project for a new association of nations."

[A year earlier, Hughes had answered A. Lawrence Lowell, Chairman of the Executive Committee, World Peace Foundation, in a more testy fashion.

["The President does not think, and I entirely agree with him, that he should refer again, at this time, to his desire for an Association of Nations, as such a suggestion would not meet the criticism to which you refer but rather would tend to increase it. It seems to me that if any further reference is made to such an Association, a plan more or less definite should be proposed, and general conditions are such that it is impracticable to suggest a plan at this time. A vague reference to an Association will not, in my judgment, aid us, and I think it is much better to have the actual situation understood. We have been dealing with matters in a practical way and have accomplished a great deal. If there are those who think that they should renew a barren controversy, that is their right. Nothing good will come of it, and very likely it will stand in the way of much that might otherwise be accomplished. If, aside from doing the day's work and gradually extending the range of our helpful influence, we stop to make a proposal, we will naturally be challenged to make a definite statement and thus precipitate the very controversy which should be avoided.

["You may have noticed what is being done in connection with the old Tacna-Arica feud. There is no question of American helpfulness in all the directions in which public opinion will support the Administration. What is needed at this time is not an academic discussion, or a debate about international organizations. That will not help us. The sort of organization we have all desired depends very largely upon stable conditions. With the present lack of stability, there are certain fundamental problems that must be solved. It is not lack of machinery which stands in our way but the attitude and opinion of peoples.

["This Government is doing its full share in this matter, and, so far as the ultimate solution of the problems which really relate to the peace of the world are concerned, it makes very little difference under present conditions whether we are in or out of an Association. The difficulty lies far deeper." [8]]

I have never had the slightest sympathy with the "irreconcilables" in the Senate, but in fixing responsibility for the failure to enter the League of Nations, it seems to me that the uncompromising attitude of President Wilson, especially with respect to Article X of the Covenant, must be regarded as the proximate cause. At the outset, public opinion favored international organization in the interest of peace and there would have been, I feel, adequate support for our joining the League with a few reservations which would not have impaired its essential character. Under a leadership more sensitive to public opinion and wiser in discerning the limits of practicability, our Government would have taken its place in the League with all the promise that such a method of cooperation afforded. Instead, the President insisted on paper commitments which naturally elicited serious opposition, while at the same time they were of a sort which promised to be of little actual value in time of stress. As time went on, the controversy over these formal commitments became so acrid that the early opportunity to accomplish something worth while was lost.

[The controversy over the League produced a strong, pervasive reaction against formal international contact. In the early days of the Harding Administration officials seemed to shun all public references to international cooperation — even to the extent of limiting the courtesies of ceremonial receptions for the diplomatic representatives of foreign nations. While Hughes took pains to distinguish himself from the "irreconcilables" and others who recoiled from the very thought of international contact as if it were some foul contagion, he was affected by the climate of

[8]Beerits' Memorandum, "Separate Peace with Germany," pp. 16–18a. A copy of this letter, dated March 28, 1923, is [in the Hughes Papers; Hughes to Lowell, July 20, 1922, Hughes Papers].

opinion they created. The British Ambassador, Sir Auckland Geddes, described the inaugural festivities to Prime Minister David Lloyd George:[9]

["Possibly the most remarkable thing was the icy reception extended to the whole diplomatic corps and the way in which all the Ambassadresses and the wives of Ministers were treated. The French Ambassador, who is our doyen, foamed and even sizzled at the mouth. 'Never in his eighteen years in Washington had be been treated, etc., etc.' The reception was very much what I expected. I was even surprised to notice that if there are degrees in absolute cold, my reception was perhaps a trifle less frosty than that of the rest. There was no hostile demonstration — just a complete blank and absolute frost. The diplomatic corps is slowly recovering its equanimity. The French Ambassadress can refer to the occasion now without serious risk of apoplexy, and the Spanish Ambassadress is also feeling easier.

["Our next performance was the reception of the diplomatic corps by Mr. Hughes, the new Secretary of State. This also was a frost bound performance except as regards the British Ambassador, whose reception clearly was not personal, but national. Mr. Hughes asked after you, spoke of his Welsh ancestry and murmured of friendship and cooperation. I saw all the others received and they really needed fur coats, gloves and caps to prevent themselves from suffering from frostbite. If I had been received with the frigidity that greeted them, I should have been depressed. However, they are bearing up and now merely curse when they think of it.

["After the diplomatic reception at the State Department, we were received by the President and each Head of Mission introduced the members of his staff . . . He knew who we were anyhow, and did not confuse us with the representatives of any other Power as he did in the cases of the Norwegians and the Danes. Some of the Missions were frigidly received, but on the whole, the average temperature seems to have been a few degrees above zero.

["All this gossip is not without value if it conveys the sort of impression that the facts have made on me. Americans are 'fed up' with all other nations, although I really believe less so with the British Empire than with the rest of the world. They are for America first and no one second, but if there has to be a second let it be Britain, and third, France.

["Since we got over the formal affairs, we have been struggling to return to normalcy in our relations with the Government. Unfortunately, the Republicans have pledged themselves to the hilt not to carry on the Wilsonian policies and as they cannot think of anything else to do, we are for the moment, deadlocked. I have seen Hughes several times informally, and formally, and he is to be pitied. He is a strong man and an able one, but he knows nothing from the inside of the

[9][Geddes to Lloyd George, March 17, 1921, Lloyd George Manuscript, Beaverbrook Library, F/60/4/16.] See *Unfinished Business,* by Stephen Bonsal ([New York, Doubleday, Doran,] 1944), p. 278, Note 5. Also Herbert Wright, "The Two Thirds Vote of the Senate in Treaty Making," *American Journal of International Law,* Vol. 38, No. 3 (October 1944), p. 646.

history of the last few years and has no previous experience of foreign affairs. He is working like a Trojan to clean up the State Department . . . to systematize the work and to find out what has been going on. . . .

["As soon as I really know all the cabinet, I shall write short character sketches for your information. At present they are all new and barring Harry Daugherty, are minding their P's and Q's. But the day will come when we shall see them as they are. On first impression, I lay my money on Hughes.

["Now as to their policy — they have not any yet. Hughes is, however, I think, already sincerely convinced that Anglo-American cooperation is essential to world peace and world stability. He is, I believe, really in favor of America joining the League of Nations, but he tells me that in his opinion there is at present and in the near future, no chance of the Senate agreeing to anything of this sort. He asked me if the League could not be turned into an organ to enforce the terms of the Treaty of Versailles and if a new association of nations could not be formed outside the League. At present, we are dealing with words and wild election pledges, but soon the logic of facts will assert itself, and then the struggle will be to make the action taken look like the pledge fulfilled. I have seen that process before, and am very sympathetic but I cannot quite see how we are going to make League look like no League, and cooperation like isolation."]

I have been interested to note that this view has been accepted by those whose desire for international cooperation is not open to question. Walter Lippmann, a facile and brilliant writer, whose attempted simplification of history has led him into serious misjudgments (notably as to the Washington Conference of 1921–22) in his recent book on our foreign policy,[10] has been entirely correct in attributing the failure to obtain ratification of the Treaty of Versailles with the League Covenant, to President Wilson's insistance on Article X of that Covenant. Mr. Lippmann says:[11]

The heart of the original controversy was the famous Article X of the Covenant, which carried the commitment "to respect and preserve as against external aggression the territorial integrity" of all members of the League. Since this was taken to mean that a state in possession of disputed territory could refuse to negotiate because it was bound to be supported, Article X was looked upon as entangling the United States in wars to defend many extremely doubtful frontiers. I think I am right in saying that in the earlier stages of the Senate debate, Wilson could certainly have obtained ratification if he had been willing to eliminate

[10][Hughes is referring to Walter Lippmann, *Foreign Policy: The Shield of the Republic* (Boston, Little, Brown, 1943).] See Charles A. Beard's Comment in [*The Republic, Conversation on Fundamentals* (New York, Viking Press, 1943)], p. 289.

[11]See Mr. Lippmann's column ["How Far Inside Europe?"] in New York *Herald Tribune*, April 1, 1943, [p. 17.] See, also, column by C. P. Ives in Baltimore *Sun*, March 22, 1943. [Copies of these clippings are in the Hughes Papers.]

or amend this obligation. For extreme isolationism did not develop until much later.

This extreme isolation was, I believe, the result of a mistaken effort to carry the United States too far and too deeply into the interior affairs of the European Continent. Wilson's insistence upon the obligation of Article X forced the nation to a very bad choice; either to involve itself in every disputed European question or to withdraw from the organization of the general peace of the world. It was quite unnecessary to confront the nation with this choice. The issues which are primarily European could have been left to the European states immediately concerned, and there would have remained an immensely useful field for continuing American collaboration.

Since writing the above, my attention has been called to a statement by Judge Irvine L. Lenroot (Judge of the U.S. Court of Customs and Patent Appeals) which appeared in the *Washington Post* of March 4, 1945. Judge Lenroot is a man of ability and unimpeachable integrity, and as a member of the United States Senate from 1918 to 1927, he was intimately familiar with the proceedings in the Senate relating to the Covenant of the League of Nations. He says:

> If our country is to take the part that it should in preserving world peace, its people must make their decisions upon facts, which they are entitled to know, for a public sentiment built upon untruths is like a house built upon the sands.
>
> To illustrate how facts are being misrepresented to the American people today: They are constantly told — and millions believe it — that the Covenant of the League of Nations for which President Wilson fought was defeated by his enemies in the Senate, and that if it had not been so defeated the Second World War might have been avoided.
>
> The truth is that President Wilson himself was the cause of our failure to become a member of the League of Nations. Had it not been for his insistence that the Senate agree to Article X of the Covenant containing the promise that we would with our might and material resources preserve as against external aggression the boundaries of every nation member of the League as recognized by the Versailles Peace Conference, the Senate would have ratified the treaty containing the Covenant of the League of Nations by an overwhelming vote.
>
> I speak from first-hand knowledge upon this point for as a member of the Senate at that time I took a very active part in the contest over the ratification of the treaty as the Congressional Record will show. The day before President Wilson left Washington on his ill-fated Western

trip to seek public support for the League Covenant without reservations he invited me to the White House to discuss the matter with him. Our discussion lasted nearly an hour in which I pointed out to him that the only real obstacle to the ratification of the Treaty was Article X and that if he would agree to a reservation relieving the United States from the obligation of that article, ratification would be certain and his speaking trip would become unnecessary. He replied that he would not agree to such a reservation, for, in his opinion, Article X was the heart of the Covenant and that without it the League would be of no value in maintaining the peace of the world.

In accordance with his request his supporters in the Senate voted against ratification with the Lodge reservation and thus defeated it. I would here observe that Lord Grey, then the English Ambassador, indicated in a letter, published in the Congressional Record, that the Lodge reservations were acceptable to Great Britain.[12]

Despite our non-membership, we were able to devise means of cooperation with the League in many enterprises in which we could participate in a manner suited to the particular tasks, without becoming embroiled, in hostility to dominant American opinion, in political questions which immediately concerned Europe. I shall not attempt to review the details or method of that cooperation, which Beerits has described. Our helpfulness in important directions has been generously recognized.[13]

[12]The Charter of the United Nations Organization does not contain a provision like that of Article X of the League Covenant. See reference by John Foster Dulles to Elihu Root's criticism of Article X. After quoting Mr. Root's statement, Mr. Dulles says: "The point of view thus expressed by Root prevailed at San Francisco. The Conference abstained from seeking to legislate perpetual peace by a single Article sanctifying for all time things as they are." [John Foster Dulles, "The General Assembly,"] *Foreign Affairs*, Vol. 24, No. 1, p. 3, (October 1945).

[13]Beerits' Memorandum, ["Separate Peace with Germany"], pp. 27–29, 32d–32g. [Beerits points out that Hughes "found that there were numerous matters of a non-political character in which this country might well cooperate. Where humanitarian labors were aimed to minimize or prevent evils which could not be met adequately save by community of effort, he felt that the United States should support international conferences embracing those aims under the auspices of the League. Thus representatives of the United States Government collaborated with the committees of the League in relation to Narcotics, Anthrax, Public Health, Anti-toxin Serums, Traffic in Women and Children, Relief Work, and the Control of Traffic in Arms. Secretary Hughes made it clear that whether the United States cooperated in a particular matter with foreign countries, with or without the agency of the League, depended upon its conception of its duty and interest in relation to the matter, in the light of undertakings which could properly be made under the Constitution and with the prospect of attaining the legislation that might be necessary to carry out the desired end."] See especially article by Sir Willmott Lewis, correspondent of the London *Times*, upon the announcement (January 1925) of my resignation as Secretary of State [Jan. 12, 1925, p. 12], Beerits' Memorandum, "Activities during the years 1925–1930," pp. 9–11. [Hughes here also refers to letters and other material widely scattered through the Hughes Papers. The *Times* article is quoted below, chapter 16.]

Had we entered the League, our cooperation would have been facilitated and our representatives would have taken an appropriate part in various discussions. This would have afforded a valuable training in participation in an international organization. Most likely it would have eliminated some of the fears, as well as dashed some of the hopes, created by the prospect of that participation. I question whether, with respect to important matters especially in relation to distinctly European questions, the actual results would have been different.

There has been a disposition, on the part of some who are more zealous for their cause than careful in historical analysis, to attribute the impotency of the League, in the face of the crises which have culminated in the Second World War, to our failure to become a member, I think that this opinion is wholly unjustified.

It is unnecessary, and it would be unprofitable, in considering that question, to explore the more remote causes of the war. For there were definite actions by the aggressor powers, during the decade immediately preceding the war, which tested the League, and the course of events clearly shows, as it seems to me, that our participation in the League would not have averted war.

Certainly as to the action of Japan in Manchuria in 1931, when we consider Secretary [Henry L.] Stimson's efforts, his collaboration with the League his "seizing the initiative both in direct remonstrances with Tokyo and in the introduction of proposals at Geneva," his acting "more boldly than Great Britain or the League," the attitude of the British Government, and the final result, there is no basis for saying that this result would have been altered by our membership in the League.[14]

Nor do I find any ground for believing that our participation in the League would have prevented or stopped Mussolini's imperialistic adventure in Ethiopia in 1935 or the "undeclared war" of Japan upon China in 1937. At that time and for some time after, we were pursuing the policy

[14]See [A. Whitney] Griswold, *[The Far Eastern Policy of the United States]*, pp. 417–418, 431, 438. Also Secretary Stimson's careful review of the facts in *The Far Eastern Crisis* (New York, Harper & Brothers, 1936). Also, letter by Hugh Gibson, dated April 20, 1943, to the *New York Times*. [For more recent secondary accounts of the Manchurian crisis, see Armin Rappaport, *Henry L. Stimson and Japan, 1931–1933* (Chicago, 1963); Robert H. Ferrell, *American Diplomacy in The Great Depression: Hoover-Stimson Foreign Policy, 1929–1933* (New Haven, 1957); Robert H. Ferrell, ed. *The American Secretaries of State and Their Diplomacy, 1925–1961;* vol. XI, *Frank B. Kellogg and Henry L. Stimson* by Robert H. Ferrell (New York, 1963); Elting E. Morison, *Turmoil and Tradition: A Study of the Life and Times of Henry L. Stimson* (Boston, 1960); Richard N. Current, *Secretary Stimson: A Study in Statecraft* (New Brunswick, N.J., 1954) and "The Stimson Doctrine and the Hoover Doctrine," *American Historical Review*, LIX (1953–54), 513–542. For a discussion of the "revisionist" attacks on United States intervention in World War I and subsequent United States involvement in world affairs, see Warren J. Cohen, *The American Revisionists: The Lessons of Intervention in World War I* (Chicago, Chicago University Press, 1967).]

which Ambassador Grew has called "constructive conciliation," and continued to supply Japan with the materials which it appears she used in her war on China and in preparing for war on us. Our policy was dictated by the laudable desire to do "our very best to lay a solid foundation which would support and insure a structure of friendly relations with the Japanese Government." [15]

The immediate precursor of the Second World War was Hitler's action in rearming Germany and his subsequent aggressive measures. But Hitler rearmed in violation of [a] treaty and in the presence of Europe. There was no real secret about it. His development of Germany's air power was his boast and was well known. The European Powers could easily have stopped him but they did not. Even when he sent troops into the Rhineland, they did not oppose him. Why? I suppose that the controlling thought in Great Britain was that Germany had been harshly treated and that if she were permitted to regain her prestige and take her place again as a Great Power, she could be dealt with satisfactorily by diplomatic methods and war would be prevented. Neither Great Britain nor France wished war. And there was always the supposition that at worst there was the adequate protection in the redoubtable French Army!

Can any well-informed person, who looks at the matter realistically, believe that we should have taken a different view and as a member of the League would have thrown our weight against the policy of Great Britain and France, insisting on military action? They were immediately concerned and they, not we, had the military power to hold Hitler in check before it was too late. But they did not desire to use that power. It was in the absence of the exercise of that power that Hitler continued his aggressions and mocked at the efforts of appeasement; and when after overrunning Austria, Denmark, Norway, the Netherlands and Belgium, he invaded France, her great army crumbled. It is vain to suppose that these tragic events would have been prevented if our Government had been a member of the League!

As William Henry Chamberlain recently said:[16]

> It is often taken for granted that all would have been well with the world if we had only joined the League of Nations after the First World War. Apart from the fact that the terms of the peace settlements were glaringly at variance with the Wilsonian Fourteen Points which had been our theoretical contribution to a new world order, the actual rec-

[15]Joseph C. Grew, *Report from Tokyo* (New York, Simon & Schuster, 1942), p. 38.

[16]Address by William Henry Chamberlain as printed in the *Congressional Record* Appendix, March 25, 1943, A1524.

ord does not bear out this theory that American membership in the League would have averted war.

Canada was a member of the League. The Canadian Government, responding to the pressure of majority opinion at home, invariably tried to reduce Canada's commitments to fight under the terms of the League covenants to an innocuous minimum. There can be little doubt that the American Government would have acted similarly.

And, after all, American troops were not needed to stop Hitler when he tore up the disarmament clauses of the Versailles Treaty in 1935 and broke the Locarno Treaty by sending troops into the demilitarized Rhineland in 1936. It was not lack of physical power, but lack of will and unity of the part of France and England, that prevented the adoption of measures that would have stopped the Nazi menace at negligible cost.

This is not to say that our entry into the League with reasonable reservations would not have aided our collaboration in various enterprises of international importance. And, when the present war ends, I trust that there will be a favorable climate of opinion for international cooperation and that we shall be ready to participate in an international organization designed to facilitate united action in dealing with the grave matters which inevitably will require international adjustment, in establishing a supreme tribunal to determine international controversies which admit of judicial settlement, in providing the machinery of conciliation, and generally in taking every practicable measure to prevent or stop aggression and to assure international peace.

But the experience of the League of Nations teaches that, despite international organization, when it comes to the use of force, the Great Powers who have the force and upon whose willingness to use it reliance must be placed will act or fail to act according to the policy which they believe to be dictated by their respective essential interests at the time. Formal international organization will provide a useful mechanism to facilitate united action in the interest of peace but will not insure that action.

The charge, which has been frequently repeated, that we failed to answer or acknowledge receipt of communications from the League, I have often dealt with in public statements. It appears that during the fourteen months before I took office in March 1921, there were 33 communications received by our Government directly from the League, only 15 of which had been acknowledged or had received appropriate action by the Democratic Administration. For a time after I took office, a number of such communications were received of which I had no personal knowledge. As soon as I was advised of these communications, I had them all acknowledged, including those received before March 1921, as well as those received later.[17]

PERMANENT COURT OF INTERNATIONAL JUSTICE

I was most desirous to have our Government adhere to the Protocol establishing the Court. In earlier years I had many times stressed the importance of such an institution. In my talks with President Harding on this subject, I had found him in sympathy with my views. For practical reasons, I could not move in this direction until the Washington Conference Treaties had received the approval of the Senate.

In the Fall of 1922, in a speech at Boston, I alluded to the practicability of arrangements to permit our Government to participate in the election of Judges, so that we could give the Court our support. Shortly after, I took up the question with Senator Lodge, Chairman of the Senate Committee on Foreign Relations, and encountered no opposition on his part.

At President Harding's request, I withheld a formal recommendation until he had succeeded in disposing of certain other matters. My recommendation of February 17, 1923, President Harding's Message to the Senate, may now be found in *Foreign Relations*, 1923, Vol. 1, pp. 10–24.[18]

Beerits alludes to the question which arose in September 1921 — whether the American members of the Hague Court of Arbitration should make nominations for the election of Judges of the Permanent Court of International Justice. Beerits points out that when, later, it was asserted that I had *prevented* "the American Hague Judges from sending in nominations," I denied this, saying that the American Judges acted in accordance with their own views of propriety.[19] I had a conversation with Elihu Root, in September 1921, as to the making of nominations, to which he refers in a letter to the other members of the American group.[20] While it is true that, in response to Mr. Root's request, I stated frankly my own opinion, I was careful to say that the members of the American group should act on their own responsibility. Mr. Root, I am sure, fully under-

[17]See Beerits' Memorandum, ["Separate Peace with Germany"], pp. 32a–32c. [A recent study adopting a line of argument very similar to Hughes's is L. Ethan Ellis, *Republican Foreign Policy, 1921–1933* (New Brunswick, Rutgers University Press, 1968).]

[18]See, also, my address before the American Society of International Law, April 27, 1923, on "The Permanent Court of International Justice." A printed copy of this address [together with] my address on January 16, 1930, on the actual working of the Court, are in the Hughes Papers. [The 1923 address is reprinted in Hughes, *The Pathway of Peace* (New York, 1925), pp. 65–88.]

[19]Beerits' Memorandum, "The Separate Peace with Germany, The League of Nations, and the Permanent Court of International Justice," pp. 41–42.

[20]Jessup, *[Elihu Root]*, Vol. II, p. 426.

stood this and I am quite clear in my recollection that his action and recommendation to the other Judges were based upon his agreement with my point of view. Professor Jessup observes:

> Root had already agreed to serve on the American delegation to the Disarmament Conference. He was aware that the convening of this Conference was the first attempt of the new Administration to launch some plan along the line of international cooperation and he must have been receptive to Hughes' arguments that it would be most unwise to antagonize the Senate and risk a retaliatory battle against ratification of the results of the Disarmament Conference. But the action of Root and his three colleagues cannot be called political in the partisan sense; otherwise the two Democrats, Gray and Moore, would not have acquiesced so readily.[21]

The failure of our Government to adhere to the Protocol establishing the Court is a matter of later history which I shall not attempt to recite.[22]

My attention has been called (April 1944) to the following statement in *The Rise of American Civilization* relating to my attitude with respect to the Permanent Court of International Justice.[23]

> Encouraged by the success of the conference, the Harding administration began to show a more lively interest in other projects for the pacific settlement of international disputes. Though it continued to assume that the national verdict of 1920 had condemned the League of Nations for all time, it watched with peculiar interest the proceedings of the Permanent Court of International Justice, established under the auspices of the League and opened for business at The Hague, in February 1922. In a little while faint movements in its direction were observed in Washington. Secretary Hughes made a declaration in favor of a world tribunal standing on an independent basis. That was a concession but as nearly all the nations of the earth were operating under the League court, there was a distinct air of hauteur in an American call for *another institution* of international justice.
>
> Perceiving this *paradox*, perhaps, Harding himself then indicated a desire to participate in the *existing* World Court if it could be so constituted "as to appear and to be, in theory and practice, in form and substance, beyond the shadow of a doubt a world court and not a League

[21] *[Ibid.]*, pp. 426–27.

[22] See Cong. Rec., October 25, 1943, pp. 8773–8774.

[23] *The Rise of American Civilization* by Charles A. Beard and Mary R. Beard (New York, The Macmillan Company, 1942), Vol. 2, pp. 691–692.

> court" — adding specific conditions designed to assure the equality of the United States with other powers and to guarantee American independence of action in all circumstances. [Emphasis added by Hughes.]

This is an extraordinary misrepresentation for a competent historian to make when the facts were readily ascertainable.

To say that, after the Permanent Court of International Justice had been set up, I made "a declaration in favor of a world tribunal standing on an independent basis," that is "another institution," is grossly to misstate my position. And it is almost amusing to say that "Perceiving this *paradox*, perhaps, Harding *himself* then indicated a desire to participate in the *existing* World Court . . ."

Beerits' Memorandum gives the facts. While I was desirous to have our Government adhere to the statute establishing the Permanent Court of International Justice, I had to wait until we were through with the work of the Washington Conference and the Conference Treaties had been approved. I had no idea of proposing that another "world tribunal standing on an independent basis" should be established. On the contrary, in accordance with views which I had several times expressed to President Harding, I stated my position with respect to our support of the Permanent Court in my address at Boston on October 30, 1922, where I said:

> We favor, and always have favored, an international court of justice for the determination according to judicial standards of justiciable international disputes. I believe that suitable arrangements can be made for the participation by this Government in the election of judges of the International Court which has been set up, so that this Government may give its *formal support* to *that* court as an independent tribunal of international justice.[24] [Emphasis added by Hughes.]

It was the Permanent Court of International Justice as actually set up that I considered "an independent tribunal of international justice," and which I desired our Government to support, in the belief that we could arrange to participate in the election of judges. That would undoubtedly be an essential condition of that support.

As Beerits says, I sent a copy of my speech to Senator Lodge and shortly after spoke to him about our support of the Permanent Court and he expressed no opposition. But President Harding wished to have certain matters disposed of before making such a recommendation. Meanwhile, I had corresponded on the subject with Judge John Bassett Moore.

[24]Beerits' Memorandum, ["Separate Peace with Germany"], p. 35. The full text of the speech is in the Hughes Papers. See Reference No. 61 annexed to Beerits' Memorandum.

I was so deeply interested and fearful of too long a delay that while I was confined to the house with the grippe on February 17, 1923, I wrote my letter to President Harding recommending American adherence to the Protocol establishing the Permanent Court of International Justice. President Harding sent a copy of my letter to the Senate with his message of February 24, 1923. The conditions proposed were made after correspondence with Judge Moore and were for the purpose of facilitating our adherence.

I may also refer to my subsequent addresses, e.g., the one on April 27, 1923, before the American Society of International Law.

My whole effort and my argument in its support were addressed to the advisability, not of making a futile attempt to set up another tribunal but to arrange for our support of the Permanent Court of International Justice already established.

Because of the failure to ratify the Treaty of Versailles, I was confronted at once with two pressing questions, one relating to the Mandates, and another due to the lack of a treaty of peace with Germany.

THE TREATY OF BERLIN

As the Senate had refused to ratify the Treaty of Versailles, and there was no prospect of our being able to obtain its ratification upon a resubmission, even with reservations, it became necessary to negotiate a new treaty with Germany.

On July 2, 1921, Congress passed a Joint Resolution declaring the state of war with Germany to be at an end and reserving to the United States and its nationals "all rights, privileges, indemnities, reparations, or advantages," to which it or they had become entitled, "or which, under the Treaty of Versailles, have been stipulated for its or their benefit." [25]

Beerit's Memorandum refers to several important provisions of the Treaty the benefit of which it was important for the United States to retain.[26] There was the cession to the five "Principal Allied and Associated Powers" of the former overseas possessions of Germany. While the United States did not desire any of these territories, we should have a voice in determining their disposition. There was also the provision providing for reimbursement of the cost of maintaining the armies of occupation. Then, the Treaty provided for tribunals for the settlement of the claims of our citizens against Germany.

[25] U.S. Stat., Vol. 42, Pt. I, pp. 105. 106.

[26] Beerits' Memorandum, "The Separate Peace with Germany," pp. 19 *et seq.* [The provisions of the Treaty to which Beerits refers are those discussed by Hughes in this paragraph.]

Beerits also refers to the Conference at the White House with Congressional leaders, in which I emphasized the importance of conserving these rights and was definitely told of the impossibility of obtaining ratification of the Treaty of Versailles, no matter what reservations were proposed.

The declaration by Congress of the termination of the war was unilateral and did not take the place of a treaty of peace which would establish our relations with Germany. Still, the deliberate and thorough-going reservations by the Congressional Resolution of all the rights, privileges, etc., etc., stipulated for the benefit of the United States under the Treaty of Versailles made it necessary to incorporate these rights, privileges, etc., etc., in the new treaty in order to obtain ratification by the Senate.

There was thus created a serious problem. For, if I attempted to redraft the numerous provisions stipulating these rights and privileges, I should likely have a very difficult and protracted negotiation with Germany, and if the language used could possibly be deemed inadequate, or to have a different significance from that contemplated by the Joint Resolution, I should encounter opposition in the Senate. I hit upon the expedient of incorporating the terms of the Joint Resolution in the new treaty and of specifying, without attempting to redraft them, the Parts of the Treaty of Versailles which defined the rights, privileges, etc., stipulated for the benefit of the United States and which it was intended that the United States should enjoy. I was able to obtain Germany's assent to this course and the treaty was signed at Berlin on August 25, 1921. It was ratified by the Senate in the following October.[27] The official correspondence in the course of the negotiations will be found in *Foreign Relations* [1921, Vol. II, pp. 3–24]. In my letter to George W. Wickersham, to which reference has already been made, I stated the reasons for my action in this matter.[28]

[27]U.S. Stat., Vol. 42, Pt. II, p. 1939.

[28]Beerits' Memorandum, ["Separate Peace with Germany"], p. 22. ["Secretary Hughes wrote, in this letter to Mr. Wickersham: 'I believed that it was desirable to establish peace by the ratification on our part of the Treaty of Versailles, with all the reservations that might be deemed to be necessary. I still thought that as important rights were given to us under the Treaty we should enjoy these rights by reason of our participation in the common victory, and that any assumption of obligations which the Senate opposed could be met by reservations. However, even such an acceptance of the Treaty of Versailles was determinedly resisted and I was reluctantly forced to the conclusion that, even with the Covenant of the League excised and with other reservations relating to the parts of the Treaty defining territorial boundaries, et cetera, there would still be implacable hostility to assenting on any terms to the Treaty of Versailles. Careful study of the situation convinced me that if the Treaty of Versailles were sent to the Senate by President Harding, no matter with what suggested reservations, we should be tied up in a hopeless controversy with an indefinite postponement of the establishment of peace. You may be sure that I did not reach this conclusion until protracted examination of the situation had been made. When I did reach it, I had the alternative of allowing the state of war to continue or of negotiating a peace which would be on the simplest terms possible and would not sacrifice the just interests of this country. I took the latter course in negotiating the treaty with Germany which was signed on August 25th, 1921.'"]

The Treaty of Peace was followed by a Claims Agreement with Germany, signed August 10, 1922. Beerits gives a general description of the circumstances. The interesting negotiations are shown by the correspondence in *Foreign Relations* [1922, Vol. II, pp. 240–266].

["By the treaty restoring friendly relations with the United States, signed on August 25th, 1921, Germany had accepted, as has been seen, definite responsibility to make suitable provision for American claims arising out of the World War and within a wide field. Both the scope and the nature of her obligation were fixed by the terms of the arrangement and the annexed articles of the Treaty of Versailles.

["Secretary Hughes desired to set up tribunals for adjusting these claims in the way that such tribunals were set up under the Treaty of Versailles. That treaty provided for the establishment of such tribunals, and we were entitled to them. However, there was strong opposition in the Senate to settling the claims in such a manner.

["Secretary Hughes was thus thrown back upon the alternative of negotiating a claims agreement with Germany. He corresponded frequently with Ambassador Houghton in working out his plan, which contemplated the use of a mixed commission, on which Germany would be represented, as a means of determining the amounts of the American claims. While he was in the midst of negotiations with Germany looking to an appropriate agreement to cover the matter, effort was made in Congress, during the summer of 1922, to enact a law treating the settlement of these claims as a purely domestic matter, through the medium of a commission that excluded German representation. This bill, introduced by Senator Underwood, after providing for the establishment of such a commission, provided that the former German property in the United States which had been seized during the War in accordance with the Trading with the Enemy Act, and was at that time being held temporarily by the Alien Property Custodian, should be used to satisfy claims that were not settled otherwise. (Senate Bill 3952, 67th Cong., 2d Sess.)

["This bill amounted in effect to confiscation by *ex parte* proceedings of the property held by the Alien Property Custodian. Secretary Hughes was anxious that we should not blot our record by such confiscation. He agreed, however, that we should hold the property until the question of claims had been agreed upon with Germany.

["When consulted concerning the Senate bill by Senator Nelson, chairman of the Senate Committee on the Judiciary, Secretary Hughes said, in part: 'To undertake to exclude a nation in a case like the present from any participation or voice in matters thus vitally affecting its interests and to deal with such matters by *ex parte* action would be, in my judgment, at variance with the principles and practice generally observed by nations in their relations with each other, and I should think it unfortunate if such a course were initiated by this government.' (Letter from Secretary Hughes to the Hon. Knute Nelson, July 29, 1922, in the Hughes Papers.)

["Secretary Hughes was apprehensive lest this bill might be passed by the Senate. Even if it did not pass, he would meet the opposition of those supporting the bill when he presented his completed claims agreement with Germany. He was thus confronted with a difficult problem. To solve it he devised the plan of proceeding under an old practice by which it was within the province of the Executive to adjust claims for its nationals. The Executive has the authority to make arrangements for the adjustments of such claims without the advice and consent of the Senate.

["The Secretary had his agreement along these lines worked out, with an American as umpire. He was ready to surprise the Senate, but he told the President that he didn't want to initiate a controversy with that body and asked the President to bring down Senator Borah for an interview. Secretary Hughes then unfolded to Senator Borah his abhorrence of confiscation and explained to him what he proposed to do to meet the problem of adjusting the claims against Germany. The Senator asked him for his authority on the principle of Executive action, and, after the Secretary had given it to him, said that he would not oppose such an agreement with Germany. Secretary Hughes then wired Ambassador Houghton to close the agreement.

["This was the origin of the claims agreement with Germany signed at Berlin on August 10th, 1922. United States Treaties, Volume 3, p. 2601 (Treaty Series, No. 665). It provided for a mixed claims commission comprising a representative of each country and also an umpire (whose judgment was to be decisive in case of disagreement between the two representatives), who were empowered to determine the amounts to be paid by Germany in satisfaction of her financial obligations under the treaty. Germany agreed contemporaneously, moreover, that the President of the United States might appoint the umpire, who might be an American citizen. This was probably the first time in history when two nations who had recently been at war with each other agreed to appoint a citizen of one of the two countries to decide a question of claims between them.

["Congress duly appropriated the funds necessary to defray such expenses as might be chargeable to the United States, and the adjudication of claims began. President Harding, with the approval of the German Government, appointed as umpire, upon the recommendation of Secretary Hughes, the Honorable William R. Day, Associate Justice of the Supreme Court of the United States, who had been Secretary of State in 1898. Failing health compelled Mr. Justice Day to retire shortly after his appointment. The President appointed as his successor the Honorable Edwin B. Parker of Texas. The commissioners of Germany and the United States, respectively, were Dr. Wilhelm Kiesselbach, and the Honorable Chandler P. Anderson, an international lawyer of distinction.

["Before Secretary Hughes left his office in March, 1925, the Mixed Claims Commission had completed a large part of the task assigned it. It had performed its functions as an arbitral tribunal expeditiously and impartially and had rendered awards in numerous classes of cases." [29]]

A Commercial Treaty was also negotiated with Germany. It was signed December 8, 1923. This Treaty contained provision for "unconditional most-favored-nation" treatment, the reason for which, as well as for "national treatment," are set forth in my letter to Senator Lodge, Chairman of

[29]U.S. Stat., Vol. 42, Pt. II, p. 2200; Beerits' Memorandum, ["Separate Peace with Germany"], pp. 22a–23e.

the Senate Foreign Relations Committee of March 13, 1924.[30] This is given in full in *Foreign Relations,* 1924, Vol. II, pp. 183–192.

The care with which this Treaty was prepared, so that it might serve as a model for commercial treaties with other countries, and my support of the proposed Treaty before the Senate Committee on Foreign Relations, are described by Beerits in his Memorandum, "The Commercial Treaty with Germany."

["To work on the drafting of this treaty an interdepartmental committee was formed, consisting of advisors from the State, Treasury, and Commerce Departments. The work of preparing the draft was worked on insistently and expertly, and in June, 1923, Secretary Hughes submitted to Germany the text of the draft on which the State Department pinned its faith. Germany was eager for a commercial treaty with the United States and was prepared to accept the proposal substantially as it stood. As a result of the negotiations between the two countries the treaty was signed on December 8th, 1923.

["The treaty dealt with three general matters: first, the conditions of life of nationals of either contracting party within the territories of the other; second, commerce and navigation; and third, consular representation. Articles covering the first of these were developed with great fullness, special effort being made to safeguard the rights of the resident alien throughout his various experiences in a foreign land. The articles on consular representation dealt minutely with the problems of the modern consul in respect to his rights and immunities, as well as his relationship to his countrymen and to the State in which he was sojourning. The problems of commerce and navigation required careful handling, for in certain matters they involved the inauguration of fresh policies, and in others the maintenance of long established ones. The use of the so-called most-favored-nation clause in relation to imports and exports was one of the former.

[". . . Secretary Hughes felt that the course of wisdom lay in assuring unconditional most-favored-nation treatment, in future treaties, to the commerce of any Power which might be willing to reciprocate. He presented the matter to President Harding, who acquiesced. He then presented the matter to Senator Lodge, Chairman of the Senate Committee on Foreign Relations, who likewise acquiesced. Consequently, in the draft of the commercial treaty submitted to Germany, Secretary Hughes proposed unconditional most-favored-nation treatment with respect to import and export duties and certain kindred matters.

["The treaty with Germany was signed in December, 1923, and Secretary Hughes was anxious that it be ratified by the Senate as promptly as possible. However it did not move in that body. Secretary Hughes would see points of objection raised to the treaty in the newspapers or in the Congressional Record, and he would write to Senator Lodge, giving answers to these objections, to be presented to the Senate

[30]U.S. Stat., Vol. 44, Pt. III, pp. 21, 32; *Foreign Relations,* 1923, Vol. II, pp. 22–45; 1924, Vol. III, pp. 183–192.

Committee. He had in this way submitted elaborate memoranda in explanation of the treaty, and the Senate had taken no action.

["The Secretary felt that so long as the Senate remained in doubt and withheld its action on the treaty, he could not well submit drafts of similar content to other nations; nor could he properly continue negotiations with other countries to which replicas of the Germany treaty had been submitted. He felt that the issue at hand was one of great concern to the United States, on the proper solution of which hung the fate of negotiations with maritime States generally.

["Senator Lodge died on November 9th, 1924. Senator Borah succeeded him as Chairman of the Committee on Foreign Relations. Secretary Hughes was satisfied that the treaty with Germany followed the only sound course to be pursued, and he felt that he ought to endeavor to convince the Senate Committee that such was the case. He took up the matter with Senator Borah, and, after talking the matter over, it was decided that the Secretary should go before the Senate Committee to explain the situation.

["(Secretary Hughes learned to his astonishment from Senator Borah that Senator Lodge had not presented to the Committee a single one of the Secretary's communications answering objections to the treaty. The Secretary had been sending these carefully prepared letters during an extended period of time, but they had been simply pigeon-holed by Senator Lodge.)

["On Sunday afternoon, February 1st, 1925, Secretary Hughes read to a group of subordinates gathered at his house an exhaustive memorandum which he had prepared on every phase of the matter. On the following day he argued his cause before the Committee on Foreign Relations." [31]]

THE MANDATES CONTROVERSY

This had arisen with respect to the Island of Yap, one of the islands included in the "C" Mandates covering the German Islands in the Pacific north of the Equator.[32]

31[Beerits' Memorandum, "The Commercial Treaty with Germany," pp. 2–3, and 6–8.]

32[Mandated territories were former colonies of the belligerents said in Article 22 of the Covenant of the League of Nations to be "inhabited by peoples not yet able to stand by themselves under the strenuous conditions of the modern world" and whose tutelage "should be entrusted to advanced nations." The Covenant provided for three kinds of Mandates: "A", referring to former units of the Turkish Empire almost ready for independence; "B", referring to territories of Central Africa which needed administrative supervision; and "C", referring to South-West Africa and certain Pacific Islands, which, "owing to their sparseness of their population, or their small size ... can be best administered under the laws of the Mandatory as integral portions of its territory ... "

[The discussion of the mandatory system started with the fifth of Woodrow Wilson's Fourteen Points: "A free, open-minded, and absolutely impartial adjustment of all colonial claims, based upon a strict observance of the principle that in determining all such questions of sovereignty the interests of the population concerned must have equal weight with the equitable claims of the Government whose title is to be determined." In its final form, the system represented a compromise between the proposition advanced by the advocates of annexation and the proposition put forward by those who wished to entrust

On May 7, 1919, the Council of Four had awarded the mandates for these Islands to Japan. Yap was an important cable center. President Wilson insisted that he had stipulated that Yap should be excepted from the mandate and that the question of its disposition should be reserved for future consideration. There had been correspondence on the subject before I took office. The Council of the League of Nations took the position that the allocation of all the mandated territories was a function of the Supreme Council and not of the Council of the League; that the League was concerned, not with the allocation but with the administration of those territories. And the President of the League concluded that "having been notified in the name of the Allied and Associated Powers that all the Islands North of the Equator had been allocated to Japan, the Council of the League merely fulfilled its responsibility of defining the terms of the Mandate." He added that if a misunderstanding existed as to the allocation of the Island of Yap, it would seem to be between the United States and the Principal Allied Powers rather than between the United States and the League.[33]

Great Britain had refused to concede the contention of our Government, stating "that all islands in the Pacific north of the Equator formerly in the possession of Germany, including the Island of Yap, were by decision of the Council of Four included in the mandate to be given to Japan"; that President Wilson was present when the decision was made; that no reservation appeared in the minutes; and that it did "not appear to be open to His Majesty's Government to regard the decision of May 7, 1919, as other than definitive."

Japan has made reply to the same effect. Our Government had reiterated its position, which was still contested. In its note of February 26, 1921, Japan, after referring to the contention of our Government with respect to the reservations as to Yap, stated:

> It follows that the question whether the Island of Yap is excluded from the mandatory territories assigned to Japan must be judged from the decision of May 7th by which the mandatory powers and their mandatory territories were for the first time and at the same time finally

---

the colonial territories to international administration. Wilson wanted the open door "or equal opportunity" written into the mandates. Leaving the open door out of the final draft created problems with which Hughes had to deal. See Gordon Levin, *Woodrow Wilson and World Politics* (New York, Oxford University Press, 1968), p. 245; Benjamin Gerig, *The Open Door and the Mandates System* (London, George Allen & Unwin, Ltd., 1930), pp. 85–104; Quincy Wright, *Mandates Under the League of Nations* (Chicago, The University of Chicago Press, 1930), pp. 33–62, 593–621 and 634–636.]

[33] [The Yap negotiations may be found in *Foreign Relations, 1921*, I, 87–95, and II, 263–284; Wright, *Mandates Under the League*, pp. 52–54.]

decided upon and it must be concluded that whatever utterances may have been made previous to that date were only preliminary conversations that took place before the decisions were reached and in themselves possess no such cogency as to qualify the meaning or limit the application of the decisions.

On taking office, I received a communication sent by President Wilson to the Department of State under date of March 3, 1921, in which he said:

> My first information of a contention that the so-called decision of May 7, 1919, by the Council of Four assigned to Japan a mandate for the Island of Yap, was conveyed to me by Mr. Norman Davis in October last.[34] I then informed him that I had never consented to the assignment of the Island of Yap to Japan.
>
> I had not previously given particular attention to the wording of the Council's minutes of May 7, 1919, which were only recently called to my attention. I had on several occasions prior to the date mentioned, made specific reservations regarding the Island of Yap and had taken the position that it should not be assigned under the mandate to any one power but should be internationalized for cable purposes. I assumed that this position would be duly considered in connection with the settlement of the cable question and that it therefore was no longer a matter for consideration in connection with the peace negotiations. I never abandoned or modified this position in respect to the Island of Yap, and I did not agree on May 7, 1919, or at any other time, that the Island of Yap should be included in the assignment of mandates to Japan.
>
> As a matter of fact, all agreements arrived at regarding the assignment of mandates were conditional upon a subsequent agreement being reached as to the specific terms of the mandates, and further, upon their acceptance by each of the Principal Allied and Associated Powers. The consent of the United States is essential both as to assignments of mandates and the terms and provisions of the mandates, after agreement as to their assignment or allocation.
>
> The consent of the United States, as you know, has never been given on either point, as to the Island of Yap.

I thought it important, not only as to Yap but as to all the mandated teritories, that we should stand on the proposition that the right to dispose of the overseas possessions of Germany was acquired only through the

[34] [Davis was Undersecretary of State at the time.]

victory of the Allied and Associated Powers; that the right thus accruing was shared by the United States; that there could be no valid or effective disposition of these possessions of Germany without the assent of the United States; that the Supreme Council had no authority to bind the United States and that the right accruing to the United States through the common victory could not be regarded as in any way ceded or surrendered to Japan, or to other nations, except by treaty, and that no such treaty had been made. It followed that the fact that the United States had not ratified the Treaty of Versailles could not detract from the rights which the United States had already acquired and that a treaty to which the United States was not a party could not affect those rights. In this view, it made no difference what the Supreme Council had decided and whether or not President Wilson's reservations had been reiterated when the Supreme Council undertook to allocate the German Islands, including Yap, to Japan.

This view I set forth in an identic note to the Principal Allied and Associated Powers on April 2, 1921.

In a later conversation (April 12, 1921) with the British Ambassador, it appeared that the British Government had agreed with Japan in 1916 to favor the awarding to Japan of the islands in the North Pacific. I asked if President Wilson was acquainted with this agreement and the Ambassador said that Mr. Balfour had given him a copy when he was here. I inquired if Mr. Balfour had called President Wilson's attention to it. The Ambassador replied that he did not know as to that but understood it was left with a number of papers. He added that President Wilson knew of it when he reached Paris.

Evidently Japan in view of the agreement with the British Government expected to get the islands and when the scheme of mandates was substituted for absolute cession she nevertheless contemplated doing what she pleased with the mandated territory. The mandates, however, prohibited fortifications, etc.

Beerits' Memorandum on "The Mandates Controversy" covers the subsequent negotiations pretty fully.

["In a conversation with the Japanese Ambassador, Baron Shidehara, on June 3rd, Secretary Hughes explained the stand taken by his Government on the mandates question. He stated that the principle was of general application to all the overseas possessions of Germany, and that there was no reason why the United States should be denied an equal participation; that this Government had no desire to advance the principle for the purpose of obtaining territory or of increasing its possessions, but merely for the purpose of protecting its interests so that wherever it was important, there should be no denial of equality of opportunity through any exclusive use by any of the other Powers of the possessions which formerly belonged to Germany. He said that he did not see upon what grounds it could be maintained, after we had entered the war and participated in obtaining victory, that those associated with us should attempt to deprive us of equal privileges in what were German possessions wherever we had interests to safeguard. The Secretary said that so far as the other islands north of the Equator were concerned, he was not advised that we had any interest with respect to which we desired to make representations, but that Yap was in a strategic position and that we should have the same rights and privileges there that were enjoyed by the other Powers.

["Baron Shidehara, after dwelling upon Japan's claim to exclusive jurisdiction over the islands, said that the claim had been made that they should be internationalized for cable purposes; that this might be arranged but that if the United States pressed for anything more, it would be extremely difficult. The Secretary said that if there was anything that the islands could be used for aside from cables, he saw no reason why the United States should not have its equal opportunity for such a use. He stated that the United States desired that whatever Power or Powers had administration of the islands, their authority should be subject to the equality of right, and administration should be maintained under suitable terms which would assure the maintenance of the privileges, not as those granted by a sovereign Power which was in possession of the islands, but as privileges in which all the Powers were entitled to share and subject to the exercise of which the island was administered.

["On June 18th Ambassador Shidehara presented Secretary Hughes with two memoranda — first, with respect to the general question of Yap; and second, with respect to the existing cables. The Secretary, in reading over the memoranda, objected to the fact that communication by radio had been excluded. The Ambassador said that it was of no practical consequence inasmuch as this Government had full opportunity for radio communication at the Island of Guam. The Secretary replied that however much or little the radio station at Yap might be used, he could not see why we should not have an equal opportunity and facility for the purpose; that the substantial thing was the communication itself, and that as the island appeared to be of importance only with respect to communication, he thought that it ought to be available to all nations alike for all purposes of communication whether by cable or otherwise.

["On August 19th Secretary Hughes presented Ambassador Shidehara with a memorandum regarding the Island of Yap. This included the provisions that the United States understood would be included in a formal agreement to settle the controversy over the island.

["In an interview on September 8th the Ambassador presented Secretary Hughes with a memorandum with respect to Yap. The latter then called attention to the fact that the "C" Mandates treated mandated territory for administration and legislation as an integral portion of the territory of the mandatory, and that this, unless qualified, would permit discrimination. He therefore suggested that the mandatories should guarantee to the United States most-favored-nation treatment. He also stated that the United States desired the Open Door policy to apply in these cases, so that there could be equality of industrial and commercial opportunity.

["In answer to the Ambassador's inquiry as to whether he thought that a treaty was necessary, the Secretary explained his view that as the United States was one of the parties to the cession by Germany it had become entitled to certain property and that this could not be disposed of validly under our constitutional system without a treaty or convention which would be negotiated by the President and ratified by the Senate. The Ambassador said that he recognized that the Mandate granted by the League of Nations was not binding upon the United States but that it was binding upon the other Powers, and therefore his Government desired that this matter should be settled by Convention directly between the United States and Japan as the other Powers had no right to question the Mandate already granted.

["The Secretary said that it had been the disposition of this Government in raising the question as to Yap and the other mandated territories not to seek any special privileges for itself, and it had presented its views in that aspect, but that the Ambassador was right in saying that the other Powers had given their consent and that the Secretary was disposed to think that there was no reason why this Government should undertake to deal with any situation but its own, and that he saw no objection to such a convention between the United States and Japan, as the Ambassador suggested.

["On September 15th Secretary Hughes presented Ambassador Shidehara with another memorandum relating to negotiations as to the Island of Yap and the other islands in the North Pacific formerly possessed by Germany, and various details of the memorandum were discussed. On September 22nd they again discussed details of the memorandum, pending receipt of instructions from his Government by the Ambassador.

["On October 17th Ambassador Shidehara left with Secretary Hughes a memorandum relating to Yap and the mandated islands north of the Equator. One outstanding point of difference between the two Governments related to the proposal of this Government that in the proposed American-Japanese Convention the existing treaties between Japan and the United States should apply to the islands which had been mandated to Japan. In the memorandum it was stated that this and the desired right of American citizens and vessels to have free access to all waters of the mandated territories, would practically lead to the recognition, in essential particulars, of the principle of equal opportunity for all nations; that Japan was willing to agree to this principle, provided the other mandatories of Class C should make a similar agreement. A long discussion of this point with the Ambassador followed . . .

["Quietly . . . the negotiations with Japan had been in progress since June. The terms of settlement were almost entirely agreed upon before the opening of the Conference on Limitations of Armament. In the atmosphere of good will pervading the Conference Secretary Hughes found his opportunity. He conferred with the Japanese delegates and won them over; he then conferred with the heads of the other Allied delegations and received their acquiescence. On December 12th he was able to announce to the press that the United States and Japan had reached an accord on Yap and the other mandated islands north of the Equator." [35]]

[35][Beerits, "The Mandates Controversy," pp. 6–13, bases his account on typescripts of Hughes's memoranda of conversations with the Japanese Ambassador, June 3, 18, August 19, September 8, 15, 22, and October 17, 1921, Hughes Papers. The public announcement to which he refers is in the *New York Times*, Dec. 13, 1921.]

Our Treaty with Japan, which was signed in February 1922, and later ratified and proclaimed, covered all the islands mandated to Japan, recited the provisions of the mandate prohibiting the establishment of military or naval bases or fortifications in the mandated territories and other provisions and gave to the United States all the benefits of Japan's engagements notwithstanding the fact that the United States was not a member of the League of Nations. The Treaty also provided for freedom of religion, for the protection of vested American property rights, for the application to the mandated islands of existing treaties between the United States and Japan, and for the receipt of a duplicate of the annual report on the administration of the Mandate which was to be made by Japan to the Council of the League of Nations. There followed special provisions with regard to the Island of Yap.[36]

When the Treaty was signed, interpretative notes were exchanged with respect to the right of our nationals and vessels to visit the mandated islands. The note signed by the Japanese Ambassador was as follows:[37]

Japanese Embassy
Washington, February 11, 1922

Sir:

In proceeding this day to the signature of the Convention between Japan and the United States with respect to the islands, under Japan's Mandate, situated in the Pacific Ocean and lying north of the Equator, I have the honor to assure you, under authorization of my Government, that the usual comity will be extended to nationals and vessels of the United States in visiting the harbors and waters of those islands.

Accept, Sir, the renewed assurances of my highest consideration.

K. Shidehara

Honorable Charles E. Hughes,
Secretary of State.

Despite the stipulations of the treaty, Japan proceeded to fortify the mandated islands. And this apparently was known to our Government as early as March 1933.[38] It appears that in 1936 our Government made "suggestions" that our ships be invited to visit ports in the mandated islands, pointing to the fact that we had granted the requests of Japan to allow its ships to visit Alaska harbors, even those which were "not open ordinarily

[36]U.S. Stat., Vol. 42, Pt. II, pp. 2149–2152. [The United States did not give its assent to the arrangements made for B mandates until July 1922; and for A mandates until 1925. Wright, *Mandates Under the League*, 58–62.]

[37][U.S. Stat., Vol. 42, Pt. II], pp. 2152, 2153.

[38]See Ambassador Grew's statement of March 27, 1933, in his *Ten Years in Japan* ([New York, Simon & Schuster,] 1944), pp. 84–85.

to foreign commerce." But these suggestions came to nothing and the State Department assumed that there was "no prospect" that the Japanese Government would take "favorable action." Our Government thought this "unfortunate" but apparently let the matter drop.[39] No attempt was made to bring pressure to enforce our important rights under the Treaty and Japan proceeded with the fortification of the islands, thus seriously jeopardizing the security of our Pacific possessions.

In the Report by Senator [David Ignatius] Walsh [of Massachusetts], Chairman of the Senate Committee on Naval Affairs, made on June 7, 1944, it is stated with respect to the efforts of the Committee to obtain information whether the Japanese Government had fortified the mandated islands:[40]

> The committee had several communications with the State Department which resulted in the committee being unable to obtain any definite information. The correspondence was kept confidential at the request of the State Department. The State Department, in reply to an inquiry made by the committee, stated: "With regard to the questions whether the terms of the treaty have been violated by Japan . . . the Government of the United States has at no time raised any question with the Japanese Government in regard to the obligations of Japan to the United States with respect to the Japanese mandated islands."
>
> In reply to another question by the committee requesting information as to whether the Japanese Government had denied nationals of the United States or naval vessels of the United States the privilege of visiting harbors and waters of the mandated islands, the Secretary of State in a letter dated April 5, 1939, stated: "In this connection I may state that the files of the Department show that the instances referred to were four in number and that in each instance only one naval vessel was concerned. In no instance was the request 'ignored,' the reply being the same in all four instances, namely, regret was expressed that the Japanese authorities were unable to give consent to the proposed visits."
>
> At the request of the State Department at the time, the information contained in the Department's letters to the committee were kept secret.

I suppose the inaction of the State Department was due to an unwillingness to come to a show-down with Japan and to the fear of strengthening

[39]*Foreign Relations of the United States — Japan, 1931–1941*, Vol. I, pp. 307–309 (Washington, U.S. Government Printing Office, 1943).

See article on "The Japanese Islands" by Huntington Gilchrist (one-time member of the International Secretariat of the League of Nations and Assistant Director of the Mandates Section), in *Foreign Affairs* [Vol. 22, No. 2] (July 1944), pp. 639–640.

[40]Sen. Doc. No. 202, 78th Cong., 2d Sess., p. 8.

the influence of her military clique. On the other hand, Japan was without any legal or moral right to fortify the islands and we did not lack ability or opportunity to put pressure upon her to fulfill her clear and definite obligations.

We also concluded treaties with other Powers as to mandated territories; with France as to the Cameroons and Togoland; with Belgium as to East Africa; and with Great Britain as to Palestine. While some of these treaties were ratified later, they were negotiated and signed before I left office.[41]

[The mandates controversy with Japan was aired at the Washington Arms Conference and the treaties with Japan to which Hughes refers were negotiated at the Conference. All of the tensions resulting from the failure of the United States to ratify the Treaty of Versailles were allowed to grow in anticipation of the Conference. It was hoped that these tensions would be relieved by a confrontation between the United States, Japan, and Great Britain.]

THE WASHINGTON CONFERENCE 1921–22

In order justly to appraise the work of the Conference, it is necessary to have regard (1) to the imperative public demand for limitations of armament; (2) to the standard adopted by the Conference in fixing naval ratios, that is, the then existing naval strength of the respective countries; and (3) to the effect of the naval treaty, negotiated on that basis, which not only safeguarded the relative position of the United States as it stood at that time, but with respect to the outlook for the future gave the United States a better relative position than it would otherwise have had in view of competitive programs.

As a result of her defeat, Germany had lost her naval vessels. While no agreement for the limitation of naval armament could be effected which did not embrace France and Italy, these powers, because of the losses sustained in the war, had not built up their navies and had not embarked on a definite building program.

[41]For these treaties see U.S. Stat., Vol. 43, Pt. II, pp. 1778, 1790, 1963; Vol. 44, Pt. III, pp. 2184, 2422, 2427, 2433. See also Beerits' Memorandum, ["Mandates Controversy"], Table of References, p. 6. [In the form of an Addendum, Hughes adds a lengthy quote from the Report of the Army Pearl Harbor Board, taken from the *New York Times*, August 30, 1945, p. 6, which strengthens his point "as to the failure to insist on our treaty rights with respect to the mandated islands." The material, taken from Section 3 of the Report, "United States Policy, 1922–1939," describes the provisions of the relevant treaties, already mentioned by Hughes, and laments that "the failure to have a showdown with Japan on her fortifications of the mandated islands" gave Japan an "enormous advantage" in the Pacific. The report is critical of United States policy which "appears to have been based upon a combination of fear of the Japanese and of an obsession not to give offense to the Japanese; a policy which . . . proved to be one of weakness rather than of strength. . ."]

At the Washington Conference, 1921

The great naval powers were the United States, Great Britain and Japan and these powers were engaged in a wasteful and injurious naval rivalry. Congress was reluctant to make the appropriations necessary to carry forward the immense naval building program which had been projected. Harold and Margaret Sprout of Princeton University, in their important work, *Toward a New Order of Sea Power*, have given a careful account of the public sentiment in this country.[42] This situation led to a demand in

[42][Harold and Margaret Sprout, *Toward a New Order of Sea Power*, (Princeton, Princeton University Press, 1940), pp. 102–114, say that the resistance to the Navy Department's ambitious plan began immediately after the armistice, and stressed the argument that there was no reason for the United States to build a navy second to none. The resistance to naval expansion evolved during the winter of 1920–1921 into a popular movement to check the competitive struggle for naval primacy. The change to an organized movement was precipitated by public discussion of the Navy Department building program, calling for laying down within three years a total of eighty-eight additional naval vessels, including four capital ships and thirty light cruisers. The building program, in turn, stimulated a demand in Great Britain to resume capital ship construction. Senator William E. Borah of Idaho assumed the leadership of the disarmament forces in Congress by virtue of the joint resolution he submitted on December 14, 1920, calling upon the President to open negotiations with Japan and Great Britain with the objective of cutting naval building by 50 percent in the succeeding five years. From this point on, the move-

Congress for negotiations with Great Britain and Japan for a limitation of armament.

There was general expectation that the new administration would arrange for the calling of a conference for [this purpose]. At the outset, I had suggested to President Harding that it would probably be advisable to call such a conference, and he seemed to be in entire accord with that idea as I had supposed he would be from his utterances before his inauguration. Indeed, he went so far as to say that a conference could be called whenever I thought the time was ripe for it. But the Navy was insistent and there was a strong desire on the part of certain leaders to go forward with the existing building program. The argument was that this would facilitate an agreement if a conference were held. It soon became apparent that President Harding had decided to throw his influence in support of that effort, at least until public sentiment to the contrary had further manifested itself.[43]

While I was under severe pressure in the work of the State Department, I kept in touch with the proceedings in Congress as closely as possible. The response to the drive of public opinion had demonstrated that there was no possibility that Congress would make the appropriations necessary to carry out even the existing building program, to say nothing of the additional building programs which the competition among the leading naval powers would require. President Harding was convinced of this. Senator Lodge, who had the reputation of being the "big navy" leader in the Senate, came to that conclusion and Senator [Oscar] Underwood [of Alabama], the minority leader, had the same view. In this connection, I may refer to their unequivocal statements at one of the first meetings of the American Delegation to the Conference (held in preparation for the Conference) as described by Professor Jessup in his biography of Elihu Root (Vol. II, p. 449):

---

ment rapidly gained momentum. More detailed versions of the same events are in John Chalmers Vinson, *The Parchment Peace: The United States Senate and the Washington Conference, 1921–1922* (Athens, Ga., The University of Georgia Press, 1955); Thomas H. Buckley, *The United States and the Washington Conference, 1921–1922* (Knoxville, University of Tennessee Press, 1970); and the forthcoming major work of Sadao Asada of Doshisha University in Kyoto.]

[43]Beerits' Memorandum, "The Washington Conference. Calling the Conference," pp. 2–4. See, also, article by Arthur Krock ["Our Fleet is Now Superior"] in the *New York Times*, October 24, 1943, Sec. IV, p. 3. [Hughes refers again to the Sprouts' book, *Toward a New Order of Sea Power*, pp. 118–121. Their account shows that Harding opposed all efforts to limit armaments until the existing naval building program was completed, probably in 1924. The administration's stand led the opponents of navalism to redouble their efforts. Vinson's study *Parchment Peace*, (pp. 90–96) shows that the Administration did a *volte face* in May and lent its support to the Borah Resolution which was passed as an amendment to the navy bill. The reason for the change seems to be that the Administration hoped to use a conference on naval armaments to negotiate the problems in the Far East it considered more important.]

At one of the first preliminary meetings of the American delegation, Root asked whether there was any likelihood that Congress would vote the necessary appropriations to continue the naval building program and the concomitant program for the fortification of the Philippines which was an essential element in American naval policy as it was then conceived. In the minds of the naval officers, the projected large navy was necessary to defend the Philippines and American "interests" in the Far East; this policy contemplated the creation in the Philippines of a naval base and fortifications equal to the huge British base at Singapore which was then under way. Senators Lodge and Underwood were emphatic in asserting that there was no possibility that Congress would appropriate the necessary funds. Some at least of the naval officers had come to the same conclusion and for that reason were the more ready to acquiesce in a plan which was widely interpreted as an unfortunate surrender by the United States of a dominant position. The history of the next decade and a half, when the United States did not even build up to the treaty limits, confirmed the soundness of the view which Root and his fellow delegates held in 1921.

It was perfectly clear that unless we could obtain an agreement for a limitation of naval armament, we were headed for a disastrous competition. I say "disastrous" because Great Britain had her plan for four "super-Hoods" and Japan had her program for eight "super-dreadnought battleships" and eight "giant battle cruisers." In addition to capital ships, "the Japanese Navy in 1921 included a long list of auxiliary combatant craft, built, building, and authorized . . . And there were clear intimations that all these totals might undergo further upward revision depending on the course of American naval construction." (Sprout, p. 94). If we went ahead with our building program, that would have to be followed by additional programs, demanding vast outlays in order to keep our place in the race, a wasteful and senseless rivalry. This was clearly brought out in an article (published sometime after the Conference) by Hector C. Bywater, the distinguished British naval expert.

["That Britain got by far the best of the bargain at the Washington parley, is, I know, an article of faith with many American naval officers. They are persuaded that their country was duped into renouncing the prize of sea supremacy which was almost within its grasp.

["Superficially, the evidence on this point may look convincing. The 13 ships scrapped would, when completed, have put the American battle fleet first in tonnage and gun power. There is, however, a tendency to overlook Japan's program, which consisted of 16 ships larger and even more formidable than the American vessels. This scheme was to have materialized by 1927–28, so that, to insure the maintenance of its temporary lead, the United States would have had to build many additional dreadnaughts, not to speak of the cruisers and other auxiliaries that make up a well-balanced fleet.

["And is it to be supposed that Britain would all this time have stood idle watching her fleet decline to second or third rank? Far from it. Already in 1921 she had begun to construct four post-Jutland ships which are said to have surpassed in fighting strength the largest American ships then in hand. Despite her financial burdens, it is unthinkable that she would have let the trident slip from her hands without making a strenuous effort to recover it.

["If the American people desired to gain and keep the primacy of the ocean, they would have had to go far beyond the program of August 1916. Appropriations for the navy must soon have reached a staggering total, for under the spur of foreign rivalry, ships would have grown steadily in number, size and cost, compelling the provision of new docks and harbor works, besides the building of numerous auxiliary vessels and a progressive increase in personnel. Does anyone seriously think the American nation would have stood for this riot of expenditure, not merely for one year or two, but indefinitely? If it would not, then all the talk about America having been tricked out of her naval supremacy at the Washington Conference is meaningless and vain."][44]

In short, if Congress, as was practically certain, was not going to provide the appropriations necessary even to complete the existing program and we had no agreement for limitation, we were destined to fall behind the other great naval powers and thus get the worst of the competition our projects had started.

While it became apparent that a conference would have to be called, events abroad precipitated our action. The Imperial Conference in London had been discussing the renewal of the Anglo-Japanese Alliance, and on July 7th Lloyd George stated in the House of Commons that the British Government had suggested to the United States that there should be a general conference which would deal with essential matters bearing upon Far Eastern questions. I had no word of such a proposal, and thinking it important that we should hold the initiative if a conference were called, I sent telegrams directing inquiries to be made of the British, Japanese, French and Italian Governments whether it would be agreeable to them to be invited to a conference, to be held in Washington, on limitation of armament. A few hours later, I received a telegram from Ambassador Harvey stating the suggestions that had been made by the British Government as to our calling a conference to consider Far Eastern questions. After communicating through Harvey with Lloyd George, who fully approved, I enlarged our proposal, so that the conference I had suggested would include discussion of all Far Eastern problems, and China would be

[44]The article was published in the Baltimore *Sun*. [The same material is in Hector C. Bywater, *Navies and Nations: A Review of Naval Developments Since the Great War* (London, Constable & Co., Ltd., 1927), pp. 103–177, and is reproduced here.]

asked to participate. I also prepared a public statement to be made by President Harding and to be released for publication simultaneously in Great Britain and the United States. Beerits details these proceedings. The telegrams are set forth in *Foreign Relations*.[45] Professor Griswold, in his book on *The Far Eastern Policy of the United States*, describes these preliminary steps and also the difficulties, later encountered, in connection with the British insistence on a preliminary conference, which I opposed (pp. 292–296).[46] My reasons are shown in the correspondence.[47] There were also questions with Japan and Great Britain as to the scope of the agenda. In the end, my proposals were substantially accepted.

But it was one thing to call a conference and to set out the agenda and quite another to make the conference a success. It was freely predicted that failure was almost inevitable.[48]

The question was manifestly one of obtaining an agreement which would fix relative naval strength. But on what yardstick of relative strength could the powers be brought to agreement? It was evident that each country would have its own conception of its needs; that general considerations of needs and aspirations could be brought forward by each power in justification of some hypothetical relation of naval strength and the result would be an endless discussion, getting us nowhere. Looking at the question from every angle, I found no hope of success unless the three great naval powers, United States, Great Britain and Japan, were willing to end their competition by a determination to *stop now*. It would be impossible to end competition in naval armament if the powers were to seek the advantages they hoped to gain in the competition itself. The only solution therefore was that the powers should take as the basis of limitation their actual existing naval strength at the time of the Conference. And as soon as the American delegation met, this basis was agreed upon. It at once appeared that Mr. Root had exactly the same view that I enter-

[45]Beerits, ["Calling the Conference"], pp. 6–9; *Foreign Relations*, 1921, Vol. I, pp. 18–25.

[46]See, also, Sprout, [*Toward a New Order of Sea Power*], pp. 131–134; and Griswold, [*Far Eastern Policy*], pp. 297–304.

[47]*Foreign Relations*, 1921, Vol. I, pp. 26–29, 32, 33, 36–38, 45–51. Beerits, ["Calling the Conference"], pp. 9–13.

[48]Beerits' Memorandum, "Treaty for the Limitation of Naval Armament," p. 1: ["Although the idea of holding an international conference on the limitation of armament was popular in this country, the people in general felt that no extensive material limitation could result from such a conference. Thus people experienced a paradoxical feeling; they felt that the conference itself was valuable, and at the same time they felt that the conference could accomplish little in the way of tangible results. This pessimistic view of the prospects of success for the Conference on Limitation of Armament, this apprehension of futility, was shared by peoples of other nations. Many thought it a chimera to believe that the nations of the world could come together and really agree on anything substantial. (Citing John McAuley Palmer, *Statesmanship or War* [New York, Doubleday, Page & Co., 1927], pp. 106–12)."]

tained[49] and Senators Lodge and Underwood, the other members of the American delegation, readily concurred. Accordingly, the basis of "existing strength" was put forward in the American proposal at the beginning of the Conference.[50]

There was general agreement among the naval experts that the American rule for determining existing naval strength was correct, that is, that it should be determined according to the tonnage of capital ships. The decision to adopt this yardstick did not mean that our ships under construction were to be ignored in the calculation. It was "the position of the American government that paper programs should not be counted, but only ships laid down or upon which money had been spent." It was also our position "that ships in course of construction should be counted to the extent to which construction had already progressed." That position was contested by Japan upon the ground "that a ship was not a ship unless it was completed and ready to fight." We insisted "that in case of an emergency a warship which was 90 percent completed was to that extent ready and that only the remaining 10 percent of construction was necessary; and, similarly, in the case of a ship 70 percent or 50 percent or other percent completed, the work done was so much of naval strength in hand." We said that the American Government, while ready to sacrifice its battleships and battle cruisers in course of construction, was not willing to ignore the percentage of naval strength represented by the amount already expended. We submitted to the naval experts of the other Governments our records with respect to the extent of the work which had been done on the unfinished ships. The negotiations resulted in an acceptance by both Great Britain and Japan of the ratio which we had proposed.[51]

I may emphasize another point. In the course of preparation for the Conference, I asked the Navy Department to give me a chart which would show what Great Britain and Japan should do in order to establish a fair equivalence, in case we scrapped our ships under construction. The Navy Department did so and to that advice as to equivalents the American Delegation steadily adhered.[52]

I have said that by taking existing naval strength as the standard, we not only safeguarded the relative position of the United States as it then

[49]Jessup, *[Root]*, Vol. II, p. 448.

[50]"Report of the American Delegation," pp. 19–20. A copy of this report is in the Hughes Papers. [It also is published as part of the Department of State publication, *Conference on the Limitation of Armament* (Washington, U.S. Government Printing Office, 1922).]

[51]*[Ibid.]*, pp. 20–21.

[52]Jessup, *[Root]*, Vol. II, p. 448.

stood, but obtained for the United States a better relative position with respect to future prospects, than it would have if our program of 1916 and the competitive programs of Great Britain and Japan were carried out.

This appears from the fact that if we had completed the program of 1916 and Great Britain and Japan had completed their programs, the ratios about the year 1928 would have been 100 to Great Britain's 106 and Japan's 87. Instead, by the Conference Treaty and on the basis of existing strength, the ratios were established at 100 to Great Britain's 100 and Japan's 60.

Senator Lodge referred to this fact in his speech in the Senate in the debate on the treaty. He said:[53]

> It might be of interest to him (the Senator from Missouri) as it will certainly be to the other Members of the Senate, to know exactly what the situation would have been as to the relative strength of the capital ships of the navies of the United States, Great Britain, and Japan had their contemplated building programs been completed. I have as an authority for the figures which I will now state no less a body than the General Board of the Navy. That board of officers has estimated that with our building program of 1916 and the building programs of the other two nations completed, namely about the year 1928, the relative tonnage of capital ships, excluding pre-dreadnaughts, would be as follows:

United States	100
Great Britain	106
Japan	87

> By the treaty we have fixed the relationship:

United States	100
Great Britain	100
Japan	60

Then, after discussing details, he added:

> Therefore in the effort to come to an equality in fighting strength with Great Britain and to a ratio of five to three with Japan it will be seen that the United States, while endeavoring in every way to preserve

[53]Cong. Rec., March 28, 1922, Vol. 62, Pt. V, 67 Cong., 2d Sess., p. 4683. [In his Notes, Hughes refers to the original print of the *Congressional Record* for March 28, 1922, p. 5105.] The Senate gave its consent to the Naval Treaty negotiated at the Washington Conference with but a single dissenting vote. The vote was 74 for the Treaty to one against it. Of the 21 Senators who were absent when the vote was taken, 20 Senators took pains to have it announced that if present they would vote for the Treaty. Cong. Rec., Vol. 62, Pt. V, 67th Cong., 2d Sess., March 29, 1922, pp. 4718–4719.

these fair ratios, has in no wise allowed her naval strength to be jeopardized.

Superficially more important, as Mr. Bywater pointed out, was our agreement to maintain the *status quo* as to fortifications and naval bases in the Philippines and Guam. I say "superficially more important" because in fact there was not the slightest ground for hoping that we would measurably increase our fortification of these possessions. When Japan asked for an agreement with respect to increase of fortifications and naval bases in the Pacific, I consulted Senators Lodge and Underwood as to the attitude of Congress. As the majority and minority leaders in the Senate, they were in the best position to form a sound judgment upon this point. They at once replied that "there should be no hesitation in making the agreement, since Congress would never consent to spend the vast sums required in adequately fortifying these islands." Mr. Root took the same view.[54]

Senator Lodge dealt with this question in his speech in the Senate, saying [on March 28, 1922]:

> To begin with, Wake Island is impossible to fortify. Next, Guam could not be made a great fleet base without a vast expenditure of money, because it is too small.
>
> Let me digress here to say that I have been a good deal amused at the agony of apprehension which some persons have expressed in regard to Guam. We took that island in the Spanish-American War; it was taken by the cruiser Charleston. We have had so little interest in the island that we have never passed a line of legislation in regard to it or to provide for its government or to make any provision about it at all. It has been left in the hands of the Navy, which captured it. The captain of the ship represents the captors and rules the island. That shows the amount of interest we have taken in Guam. We have never fortified it, and nobody would vote to spend money in fortifying it. All we provide in this treaty is that we will not fortify it so long as Japan does not fortify her islands.

And he made a similar statement as to the Philippines:

> Mr. McCormick: The critics of these treaties have never voted any great sums for the protection of the Philippine Islands.
>
> Mr. Lodge: Of course not. We shall never fortify them. It would cost hundreds of millions of dollars to fortify them and probably take half a

[54]Jessup, *[Root]*, Vol. II, p. 449. [Bywater discusses the problem of fortification in *Navies and Nations*, pp. 126–128 and 149–150.]

century to do it. We are not going to do it. Previously, however, we had no promise from anybody to respect the Philippine Islands, but now we have that promise from three great powers.

His statements found corroboration in subsequent events. Even after Japan's notice (December 1934) of its intention to terminate the naval limitation treaty in December 1936, and after Japan had begun its war on China and had openly associated itself with Germany, no plan was adopted to fortify Guam.

From the Report of the Chairman of the Senate Committee on Naval Affairs [Senator Walsh] (June 7, 1944),[55] it appears that, pursuant to an act of Congress, a Board headed by Admiral [Arthur J.] Hepburn [Commandant of the 12th Naval District] was appointed by the Secretary of the Navy to investigate and report on the need of additional air bases, etc. The Board recommended (1938) various projects (including those for the defense of the Philippines and Guam) at an estimated cost of $326,216,000. In January 1939, the Acting Secretary of the Navy forwarded to the Speaker of the House of Representatives a draft bill providing for some of the naval facilities recommended at a cost not to exceed $65,000,000. Of this amount, $5,000,000 was allotted to improvements at Guam, that is, for a breakwater, dredging and building seaplane ramps, etc.; in February 1939, the House, after debate, struck out this amount.

In the hearings on the bill before the Senate Committee, Admiral [William D.] Leahy [Chief of Naval Operations] explained that it was not intended to fortify Guam so as to make it an important and strongly defended naval base but merely to make certain harbor improvements. Admiral Leahy further stated that something in the neighborhood of $200,000,000 would be required to make a really safe base at Guam; that there was "no proposition before the Congress at the present time to establish any kind of a base at Guam."

I have emphasized these few points in relation to the Navy limitation treaty because they seemed to be overlooked in some recent comments.

The size and personnel of the American Delegation contributed greatly to the success of the Conference. Elihu Root was of outstanding ability, sagacious, experienced, and thoroughly informed. Senators Lodge and Underwood, leaders in the Senate, had an intimate knowledge of the mind of Congress, and their membership in the Delegation gave the best possible assurance of the Senate's sanction of the negotiated treaties. As there were only four of us, we had constant opportunity for informal contacts and these were had. While I had special duties as Chairman of the Conference and carried the burden of the discussion in the meetings of the Heads of the Delegations, I kept my associates in the American Dele-

[55] Sen. Doc. No. 202, 78th Cong., 2d. Sess., pp. 4–8.

gation fully advised of what took place in these meetings. They not only concurred in the initial proposal, which I made at the opening of the Conference, but all decisions throughout the Conference were taken with their complete agreement.

I shall not attempt to retraverse the ground covered fully in Beerits' Memoranda on "Calling the Conference," "The Four Power Treaty," the "Treaty for the Limitation of Naval Armament," "Article 19 of the Naval Treaty: Fortifications of the Pacific," and "Far Eastern Questions." Some of the papers Beerits examined and to which he refers in his tables of "References," appended to his memoranda respectively, may now be found in *Foreign Relations*.[56]

[In support of his argument that the Washington Arms Conference treaties had helped the United States and, with support from the Great Powers, would have continued to preserve the peace, Hughes points out that the London Naval Conference of 1930 applied the policy of limitation to auxiliary naval vessels and postponed the laying down of replacement tonnage. Hughes insisted that it was not the treaties that had failed, it was the United States — as much as any other power — which had failed to live up to the terms of the treaties. The United States had fallen down by not building enough ships. He continued:

["I should add that I expected, and so did the other members of the American Delegation to the Washington Conference, that our Government would maintain its fleet up to the limits permitted by the naval limitation treaty. Beerits quotes my statement in October 1922, in which I said: 'It is essential that we should maintain the relative naval strength of the United States. That, in my judgment, is the way to peace and security. It will be upon that basis that we would enter in future conferences or make agreements for limitation, and it would be folly to undermine our position.' [57]

["But this was not done and our Navy was permitted to fall far below the treaty limits." [58]]

[56]1921, Vols. I and II; 1922, Vol. I. See, also, Official Reports of the Proceedings of the Conference.

[In his several memoranda Beerits recounts the events leading up to the conference, describes the negotiations, and provides the outlines of the treaties which resulted. This same information is available in Vinson, *Parchment Peace*, pp. 97–218; Sprout, *Toward a New Order of Sea Power*, pp. 102 ff., and Griswold, *Far Eastern Policy*, pp. 269–332.]

[57][Beerits' Memorandum, "Naval Armament Limitation Treaty," Table of References, No. 32.]

[58][Sumner Welles, *The Time for Decision* (New York, Harper & Brothers, 1944), pp. 43–44. Hughes documents his assertions with lengthy quotes from the Senate Naval Affairs Committee Report of 1944, above, n. 55, and the Department of State publication, *Peace and War: United States Foreign Policy, 1931–1941* (Washington, U.S. Government Printing Office, 1943). Hughes points out references to the Washington Conference in the latter on pp. 9, 12, 244, 20, 21, 27, 28, 39, 40, 316, 44, 54, 55, 404. For good measure, he adds some quotations from Department of State, *Foreign Relations of the United States, Japan, 1931–1941* (Washington, U.S. Government Printing Office, 1943), pp. 244–251, 252–253, 282, 255, 257, 259–260, 261, 269–270, 274, 281–284 and refers the reader to pp. 294–306.]

JAPAN AND THE IMMIGRATION ACT

[Whatever the success of the Washington Conference in curtailing the competition in naval armaments, it did not relieve the tensions in the Far East. The Four-Power Treaty of December 13, 1921, ended the troublesome Anglo-Japanese Alliance. By its terms, the United States, England, France, and Japan agreed to respect their mutual rights "in relation to their insular possessions and insular dominions in the region of the Pacific Ocean." This was designed to end the mandates controversy. The Harding Administration had understood that without such a political settlement, effective disarmament was impossible. The public, however, focused its attention on the Five-Power Treaty on armaments and the Nine-Power Treaty of February 6, 1922, on China. The Senate was suspicious of the Four-Power Treaty. It looked too much like a secret alliance. In clarifying the Treaty, Hughes was forced to make a series of disclaimers to pacify the Senate. One of these left open the door to later trouble with Japan. It asserted that Congressional restrictions on immigration could not be brought before a four-power conference. These restrictions were repugnant to the Japanese and, in the following section, Hughes discusses the difficulties they created.]

In a message to our Government in September 1923, the Prime Minister of Japan (Yamamoto) said that the report of the "spontaneous and prompt measures, taken by the President, the Government and the people of the United States" to afford relief from the affects of the severe earthquake that had caused "a bewildering devastation" was creating "a profound impression in the grateful hearts of suffering Japan." This feeling of gratitude strengthened the measure of good will which had sprung from the belief that the "Versailles Treaty and the Washington Treaties," as the Prime Minister stated in the same message, had "laid the foundation of World Peace and will greatly promote human welfare." [59]

But this prospect of satisfactory relations with Japan was destroyed by the intemperate action of the Congress in the passage of the Immigration Act of 1924.

My efforts to prevent this action are recited by Beerits.[60] The memoran-

[59] *Foreign Relations*, 1923, Vol. II, pp. 472–473; see, also, pp. 473–503.

[60] Beerits' Memorandum, "Japan and the Immigration Act."

[According to Beerits, pp. 2–3, soon after the new immigration bill was introduced in Congress, Hughes told Representative Albert Johnson of Washington, who was Chairman of the House Committee on Immigration and Naturalization:

["The Japanese are a sensitive people, and unquestionably would regard such a legislative enactment as fixing a stigma upon them. I regret to be compelled to say that I believe such a legislative action would undo the work of the Washington Conference on Limitation of Armament, which so greatly improved our relations with Japan. The manifestation of American interest and generosity in providing relief to the sufferers from the recent earthquake disaster in Japan would not avail to diminish the resentment which would follow the enactment of such a measure, as this enactment would be regarded as an insult not to be palliated by any act of charity. It is useless to argue whether or not such a feeling would be justified; it is quite sufficient to say that it would exist. It has already been manifested in the discussions in Japan with respect to the pendency of this measure, and no amount of argument can avail to remove it."]

dum of my interview with Ambassador Hanihara on March 27, 1924, may now be found in *Foreign Relations*. Hanihara's note of April 10th with its unfortunate concluding paragraph in which he used the phrase "grave consequences," is also published.[61]

As Beerits says, I was placed in a difficult position. To refuse to receive the note would have led to obvious difficulties, to say nothing of the delay in giving to the Congress, which might act at any moment, the explicit summary set forth by Hanihara of the essential terms of the "Gentlemen's Agreement" (which were reaffirmed), the practice under it, and the willingness of Japan to cooperate with our Government in order effectively to prevent the entrance into the United States of such Japanese nationals as were not desired. Moreover, in view of the context there was no reason to expect that Hanihara's intent in the use of the words "grave consequences" would be so seriously misinterpreted.

Hanihara's explanation and his disavowal of any intention to convey a threat, a disavowal which I accepted, and the notes which were exchanged, are also in *Foreign Relations*.[62]

It appears that in a book recently published by Frederick Moore, who had been an adviser to the Foreign Office in Japan, it is stated that the paragraph containing the words "grave consequences" was inserted by the advice of the State Department which had approved the note when it was presented.[63] Miller Freeman of Seattle wrote me a letter to this effect under the date of August 23, 1944, as follows:

> My dear Justice Hughes:
>
> I note in the book by Frederick Moore in chapter six his statement:
>
> "It was at the State Department's suggestion that Hanihara (Japanese Ambassador) had strengthened his famous Note to our Government in which he gave warning of 'grave consequences' resulting in Japanese public opinion if the 'Gentlemen's Agreement' were terminated and no quota of immigrants were granted to Japan. Although the Department advised him to insert such a paragraph and approved it when the Note was presented, a group in Congress, led by Senator Henry Cabot Lodge, picked the two words quoted out of the Note's lengthy and generally friendly text, charged that they were a threat to the United States, and passed the bill in defiance of the wishes of Secretary Hughes and President Coolidge. When I told Secretary Hughes, some weeks after the passage of the bill, that Hanihara had been discredited among his own people and would have to resign, he told me that from the American

[61] *Foreign Relations, 1924*, pp. 337–338 and 369–373.

[62] *[Ibid.]*, pp. 379–383.

[63] [Frederick Moore, *With Japan's Leaders: An Intimate Record of Fourteen Years as Counsellor to the Japanese Government, Ending December 7, 1941* (New York, Charles Scribner's Sons, 1942). Hughes mistakenly indicates the book was published in 1944.]

point of view this was, of course, entirely unnecessary and he hoped the Ambassador would not be required to do so. I took this to Hanihara and he said while he appreciated it he had no alternative because of Japanese opinion. Mr. Hughes said to me also that the affair was the most regrettable of his experience in the State Department."

I will appreciate your informing me whether you were aware of or acquiesced in inserting the words, "grave consequences" in the Hanihara Note to the State Department. If not, who was responsible in the State Department?

Sincerely yours,
Miller Freeman.

Replying to Mr. Freeman, I stated emphatically that I had every reason to believe that the paragraph in question and the words "grave consequences" were Hanihara's own and that their insertion was not advised, suggested or approved by any member of the State Department. My reply, under date of August 31, 1941, written from my summer address at Skytop, Pa., is as follows:

My dear Mr. Freeman:

I have received your letter of August 23rd relating to the use of the phrase "grave consequences" in Ambassador Hanihara's Note. I have every reason to believe, and do believe, that the paragraph in question, and these words, were Hanihara's own and that their insertion was not advised, suggested, or approved, by any member of the State Department. I think that this would be corroborated by Mr. J. V. A. MacMurray who was then in charge of Far Eastern Affairs and in touch with Hanihara.

The volume of *Foreign Affairs* (1924), published by the State Department, is not accessible to me here, but I think it includes Hanihara's subsequent note, in which he explains his use of the phrase, and also my reply setting forth my attitude in the matter.

Sincerely yours,
Charles E. Hughes.

Mr. Freeman on receiving my letter wrote to Mr. MacMurray, to whom I had referred, and Mr. MacMurray, in a letter to Mr. Freeman dated October 14, 1944, fully corroborated what I had said. Mr. MacMurray sent me a copy of this letter, which I quote in full:

My dear Mr. Freeman:

I recently received at this address, where I am living since retiring from the Foreign Service, your undated letter enclosing an exchange of correspondence between yourself and former Secretary of State Hughes, in the course of which he referred you to me for corroboration of his belief that Ambassador Hanihara's use of the phrase "grave consequences", in his note on the subject of the so-called "Gentlemen's Agreement", was not advised, suggested or approved by any member of the State Department. Although your letter does not expressly ask for such corroboration, I wish, in order to avoid any possible misunderstanding, to give categorically, as the person who was most directly involved in the discussion of this matter with the Japanese Ambassador and his staff, my confirmation of Mr. Hughes' belief.

To reply to your specific inquiries:

The statement of Mr. Frederick Moore, which you quote from his book *With Japan's Leaders,* had not come to my attention before the receipt of your letter.

As regards your question whether I "challenge" that statement, I would prefer to reply, in terms less ambiguous and liable to misunderstanding, that I do not concur in Mr. Moore's statement implying that the Department had suggested that the Ambassador's note be "strengthened"; but I quite understand how even so informed and sincere an observer as Mr. Moore might in his position, so have construed the efforts of the Department's representatives to persuade the Ambassador and his Government to put an end to the secrecy which had theretofore shrouded the set of understandings constituting the "Gentlemen's Agreement" and bring into the open with entire frankness the substance of that agreement and the Japanese Government's view of the problems involved.

I regret that, not having had occasion to keep in touch with Far Eastern matters for a considerable period, I am not in a position to offer information as to the publication of records bearing on the subject of your inquiry.

Yours sincerely,
J. V. A. MacMurray.[64]

[The exchange of notes with Hanihara was submitted to Congress where it called forth some acrimonious statements. These statements and the Immigration Act itself exacerbated relations with Japan which Hughes had done so much to assuage.]

[64]The letters above set forth are in the Hughes Papers. [According to his daughter, Mrs. William T. Gossett, Hughes was very much exercised over his incident and considered it one of his greatest disappointments. (Interview with the editors, March 11, 1969.) Her testimony bears witness to the sincerity of Hughes's efforts on behalf of Japan and to the impotence of the Executive in the face of a determined Congress.]

Chapter XVI The Open Door and Other Issues

[The United States emerged from the war with a new sense of its importance as a World Power. The Congress and the electorate refused to accept the responsibilities of membership in the League of Nations; but there never was any suggestion that the United States would shun contact with other nations. The United States economy was the most powerful in the world. Before the war, Americans owed foreigners three billion dollars. By the end of the war, foreigners owed Americans — on government and private account — nine billion dollars. Europeans were convinced that American capital would be as important to their well being as it had been during the war. For their part, Americans believed that foreign customers for their goods and their capital were necessary for the continued good health of their economy. The Government accepted this belief and made the expansion of American markets abroad part of official policy. In addition to this general objective, the Government strove to attain three specific strategic objectives which affected American business interests. As a consequence of its experience during the war, the United States Government considered it imperative to control a supply of petroleum adequate to the needs of the United States Navy; to place under American control a communications network that would girdle the globe; and to insure that foreign capital could not suborn the sovereignty of any nation in which the United States had a vital interest. The achievement of these objectives often placed the Government in embarrassingly close relations with American business and, in so doing, exposed the Government to criticism of economic imperialism and accusations of being the willing tool of private interests.

[Many members of the Government, with Hughes among them, were disturbed by the ambiguity of the Government's relations with private interests overseas. One result of their deliberations was the Statement on Loans, March 3, 1922, in which the Department of State reiterated its desire to pass on all projects for foreign loans. At the same time, the Department insisted that passing on a loan in no way implied a favorable judgment on the financial aspects of the loan or a commitment of support for the bankers involved. To make clear his impartiality Hughes insisted over and over again that his Department was concerned only that American business be given an equal opportunity in the international competition for markets, loans, and concessions. Hughes and Secretary of Commerce Hoover opposed international monopolies. In the fight for American cable rights and petroleum concessions, the phrase employed over and over again to characterize American policy was "open door." It was used first in this context by Secretary of State Bainbridge Colby in his note to the British Government complaining of discrimination against American petroleum interests trying to participate in the exploitation of Mesopotamian oil fields. Hughes adopted the phrase, applied it also to the struggle for American-controlled cables, and finally, used it to explain the Government's interest in American economic expansion overseas.[1]]

OPEN DOOR POLICY

This policy was set forth more explicitly than theretofore, in relation to China, in the Nine-Power Treaty negotiated at the Washington Conference.[2]

The Second World War has emphasized "the absolutely vital-to-victory part" played by adequate supply of all petroleum products for our armed forces.[3] This proved dependence upon oil puts in a strong light my insistence twenty years ago on maintaining a fair and equal opportunity for our oil companies in developing the resources of territories held under mandate, an insistence which brought down upon me some ill-advised criticism at the time.

A particular question arose out of a claim to oil rights in Mesopotamia, under a concession alleged to have been granted by Turkey to the Turkish Petroleum Company in 1914.[4] The validity of this concession had been

[1][On economic policy after the war see Herbert Feis, *The Diplomacy of the Dollar: First Era, 1919–1932* (Baltimore, Johns Hopkins University Press, 1950); Joseph Brandes, *Herbert Hoover and Economic Diplomacy* (Pittsburgh, University of Pittsburgh Press, 1963); Carl J. Parrini, *Heir to Empire: United States Economic Diplomacy, 1916–1923* (Pittsburgh, University of Pittsburgh Press, 1969); and Joseph S. Tulchin, *The Aftermath of War: The Latin American Policy of the United States, 1918–1925* (New York, New York University Press, 1971). On the need for petroleum see Feis, *Diplomacy of the Dollar*; and John A. DeNovo, "The Movement for an Aggressive American Oil Policy Abroad, 1918–1920," *American Historical Review*, LXI (July 1956), 854–876, and *American Interests and Policies in the Middle East, 1900–1939* (Minneapolis, University of Minnesota Press, 1963). On the Statement on Loans, see Feis, *Diplomacy of the Dollar*; and Tulchin, *Aftermath of War*, pp. 182–243. For an example of the criticism of the State Department's seeming liaison with American business see Scott Nearing and Joseph Freeman, *Dollar Diplomacy* (New York, B. W. Heubsch and The Viking Press, 1925).]

[2]Treaty of February 6, 1922, concerning China; Art. III, 44 U.S. Stat., Pt. III, p. 2117.

[3]*American Year Book, 1943* (Washington, [D.C.], The Foreign Policy Association, 1944), p. 473.

[4]Beerits' Memorandum, "Relations with Turkey," pp. 18–19; Appendix thereto, Table of References, p. 6.

questioned by Secretary Colby who had asserted our demand for equality of treatment and opportunity. The British position had been stated in its note of March 1, 1921.[5]

I was convinced of the soundness of our position and I set forth succinctly the principles involved, in my instruction to our Ambassador in London on August 4, 1921. These views were embodied in a memorandum given to the British Government on August 24th. I restated our position as to the territories under mandate which by the Treaty of Versailles had been ceded to the Principal Allied and Associated Powers of which the United States was one. Then, with respect to the mandated territories other than those which were formerly possessions of Germany, I said that, while it was true that the United States did not declare war against Turkey, still the opportunity of the Allied Powers to secure the allocation of these territories was made posible only through the victory over Germany, and that we assumed in that view, and by reason of the principles recognized by the British Government, there would be no disposition to discriminate against the United States or to refuse to safeguard equality of opportunity. After a review of the various mandates, I stated that we were unable to conclude, upon the information we had, that any concession was validly granted to the Turkish Petroleum Company, and that if the claim of that company was still asserted it should be the subject of arbitration.

The grounds of my belief that this concession was invalid were set forth in the note which was addressed to the British Government under date of November 22, 1921, in accordance with my instruction of November 4th.

There followed negotiations between the private oil companies concerned, a detailed account of which may be found in memoranda prepared by Allen W. Dulles, Chief of the Division of Near Eastern Affairs, on file in the Department of State.[6]

Throughout this controversy, my insistence upon the open door policy was on behalf of all American companies which desired the opportunity to take part in the development of the oil resources in question and not on behalf of any particular company. And as a result of the negotiations,

[5]*Foreign Relations, 1920,* Vol. II, pp. 668–669; 1921, Vol. II, 80–84; [and, for the other documents to which Hughes refers see *Foreign Relations, 1921,* Vol. II, pp. 106–110, 279–280; 86–87; and 89–93; also, *Foreign Relations, 1924,* Vol. II, pp. 233–234].

[6]Beerits' Memorandum, ["Relations with Turkey"], Appendix, p. 8. [For a brief summary of the issues, see Feis, *Diplomacy of the Dollar,* pp. 48–60; Tulchin, *Aftermath of War,* pp. 128–134; and DeNovo, *American Interests and Policies in the Middle East,* pp. 167–184. The memoranda by Dulles concerning the negotiations over the concession of the Turkish Petroleum Company cover the period 1922 to 1926 and are filed under decimal file 890g.6363T84, part of the General Records of the Department of State (Record Group 59).]

participation was finally secured by an American group composed of all the American companies who wished to participate.[7]

My attitude toward American commercial enterprises abroad was stated in my letter to President Coolidge of November 8, 1923. After referring to the matter which was the occasion for the letter, I said:[8]

> This general question raises a point which I feel to be of sufficient importance to bring to your attention; namely, the proper attitude of this Government toward American commercial enterprise abroad. From time to time there has been some dissatisfaction expressed in business circles because this Department's attitude towards American business interests in the foreign field differs somewhat from the attitude in similar matters of the British, French and other European governments. The latter are not loath to interfere politically in support of the business interests of their nationals to a degree which is not followed by this Department. Our position is that we are always ready to give appropriate support to our nationals in seeking opportunities for business enterprise abroad, but we do not undertake to make the government a party to the business negotiations or use political pressure for the benefit of private interests in order to obtain particular concessions, or intervene in favor of one American interest as against another. We are persistent in our efforts to maintain the open door policy, or equality of commercial opportunity, but we do not attempt to assume obligations for the government, expressed or implied, which under our system we could not undertake to discharge.
>
> American companies which might prefer a policy of more direct interference on their behalf by the government are inclined, in my opinion, to overlook the fact that American prestige and reputation for fairness has been enhanced, and consequently business opportunities of our nationals have been increased, by the correct policy which this government has followed. I find that in many parts of the world, American business is welcomed largely because foreign countries realize that they can deal with American interests on a business basis without fearing political complications.
>
> It is hardly necessary to point out that the other course desired by some business men, intent on their own immediate interests, would not only be contrary to our traditions and foreign policy, but if persistently followed would involve us in political intrigues and in difficulties

[7] [Beerits' Memorandum, "Relations with Turkey"], p. 19, Appendix, pp. 7–8; *Foreign Relations*, 1924, Vol. II, pp. 233–234.

[8] *Foreign Relations, 1923,* Vol. II, pp. 717–718.

which other governments with different exigencies and aims find it impossible to escape and from which we have happily been free.

THE DAWES PLAN

[The United States was involved intimately with the economic recovery of Europe. Here, Government and private interests had to work together. Europe needed American goods and American capital; but her ability to pay for those goods and repay the loans was, for the Allies, dependent upon how much money they would receive from Germany in the form of reparations and in what manner they would have to repay the United States Government for loans extended to them during the war. The reparations imbroglio went back to the Pre-Armistice Agreement in which the Allies demanded that Germany make compensation "for all damages done to the civilian population of the Allies and their property . . ." This was written into the peace treaty in the famous "war guilt" clause, Article 231, which held Germany responsible "for causing all the loss and damage to which the Allied and associated Governments and their nationals have been subjected as a consequence of the war imposed upon them by the aggression of Germany and her allies." The exact amount of the reparations was to be determined by a Reparation Commission provided for in the treaty. The figure of $33 billion was set in 1921. Germany made two payments and then defaulted in 1922. Before a settlement could be reached, France and Belgium occupied the Ruhr.

[The European governments suggested that reparations be combined with the war debts to the United States, or that the latter be cancelled altogether as a first step toward a solution of the political and economic tangle in Europe. Both the Wilson and Harding administrations steadfastly refused to consider reparations together with debts owed to the United States, taking the position that the debts were purely an economic problem. Hughes's efforts led to the creation of the Dawes Commission which provided for a rational schedule of payments geared to Germany's ability to pay. This, however, did not settle the reparations problem. Despite American claims to the contrary, reparations and debts were intertwined. American capital flowed into the German economy, helping Germany meet her reparations payments. As those payments were met, the Allies met their payments on American loans.]

A telegram to Ambassador Herrick, on October 9, 1922, refers to the suggestions I had made to the Ambassador during his visit to Washington in September 1922. These were to the effect that he should take up with M. Poincaré the proposal that a committee of independent financial experts should be constituted to ascertain what Germany could pay in the way of reparations and to work out and recommend to the Governments concerned a financial plan for such payments. The Ambassador did so. I took the matter up with Ambassador Jusserand in Washington. The text of my speech at New Haven, on December 29, 1922, before the American

Historical Association, also appears in *Foreign Relations*.[9] Notwithstanding the favor with which the proposal was received, Poincaré was unwilling to agree to the proposed plan and the occupation of the Ruhr followed.

[The following account of the New Haven speech was written by the Solicitor in the Department of State, Charles Cheney Hyde. Hyde cleared the text with Hughes before publishing it and, therefore, it may be considered a semi-official version of the events.

["On the morning of the 27th of December 1922 Secretary Hughes awoke very early with an idea as to an appropriate mode of making clear his position. It so happened that he had prepared an address to be delivered at New Haven on the evening of December 29, before the American Historical Association, on some aspects of the foreign policy of the United States. The address was then completed. It occurred to its author that he might well insert the terms of the proposal which he had made. He immediately arose and began to write a statement of his plan. He finished the task in about an hour. Before breakfast he telephoned the White House to inquire whether President Harding could see him on his way to the Department. About nine o'clock he called upon the President and read to him the written statement. The President warmly approved. The Secretary went to the Department and had the insertion incorporated in the text of his address and in the so-called press releases for publication on the morning of December 30. Copies were sent to the embassies at Washington of every Allied power.

["It was under such circumstances that the Secretary of State made public his constructive suggestions, which proved ultimately to be as influential as any that he had offered to countries other than his own.

["In his address he stated that the economic conditions in Europe were of the greatest concern to the United States, which could not escape the injurious consequences of failure to settle problems for which those conditions were responsible. He said that these problems were essentially European, in the sense that they could not be solved without the consent of European governments. The crux of the European situation lay, he declared, in the settlement of reparations. Until a definite and acceptable basis for the discharge of reparation claims had been fixed, he asserted that there would be no adjustment of other needs. He asked how the United States might help in the matter. He stated that it was not seeking "general reparations," although it did ask for reimbursement of the cost of the American Army of Occupation. He declared that the capacity of Germany

[9] 1922, Vol. II, pp. 199–202. Beerits' Memorandum, "The Dawes Plan," pp. 9–13. [It is also reprinted in Hughes, *The Pathway of Peace*, pp. 32–58.] The course of the negotiations now appears in *Foreign Relations, 1922*, Vol. II, pp. 165–198; 1923, Vol. II, pp. 46–110. [For further information on reparations see Bernard M. Baruch, *The Making of the Reparation and Economic Sections of the Treaty* (New York, Harper & Brothers, 1920); and Harold G. Moulton and Leo Pasvolsky, *World War Debt Settlements* (New York, The Macmillan Company, 1926). Background on United States conflicts with the former allies is in Daniel M. Smith, *Aftermath of War: Bainbridge Colby and Wilsonian Diplomacy, 1920–21* (Philadelphia, American Philosophical Society, 1970), pp. 32–74.]

to pay was not at all affected by the indebtedness of any of the Allied powers to the United States, and that that indebtedness did not diminish Germany's capacity, and that its removal would not affect her capacity.

["Concerning the attitude of the United States towards the question of reparations, standing itself as a distinct question, he said that his country had no desire to see Germany relieved of her responsibility for the war, or of her just obligations to make reparation for the injuries due to her aggression, and that there was not the slightest desire that France should lose any part of her just claims. On the other hand, he declared that the United States did not wish to see a prostrate Germany, and that there could be no economic recuperation in Europe unless Germany herself recuperated, and that there would be no permanent peace unless economic satisfactions were enjoyed. "There must be hope," he said, "and industry must have promise of reward if there is to be prosperity. We should view with disfavor measures which instead of producing reparations would threaten disaster." He declared that the first condition of a satisfactory settlement was that "the question should be taken out of politics." He expressed the hope that statesmen would effect a settlement of the issue, as the alternative of forcible measures to obtain reparations was not an attractive one. If, however, statesmen could not so agree, and such an alternative was faced, he asked what could be done. He proposed himself the following response:

[" 'Why should they not invite men of the highest authority in finance in their respective countries—men of such prestige, experience and honor that their agreement upon the amount to be paid, and upon a financial plan for working out the payments, would be accepted throughout the world as the most authoritative expression obtainable? Governments need not bind themselves in advance to accept the recommendation, but they can at least make possible such an inquiry with their approval and free the men who may represent their country in such a commission from any responsibility to Foreign Offices and from men of such standing and in such circumstances of freedom as will insure a reply prompted only by knowledge and conscience. I have no doubt that distinguished Americans would be willing to serve in such a commission. If Governments saw fit to reject the recommendation upon which such a body agreed, they would be free to do so, but they would have the advantage of impartial advice and of an enlightened public opinion. People would be informed, the question would be rescued from assertion and counter-assertion, and the problem put upon its way to solution.

[" 'I do not believe that any general conference would answer the purpose better, much less that any political conference would accomplish a result which Premiers find it impossible to reach. But I do believe that a small group, given proper freedom of action, would be able soon to devise a proper plan. It would be time enough to consider forcible measures after such an opportunity had been exhausted. Such a body would not only be expert but friendly. It would not be bound by special official obligations; it would have no animus and no duty but to find and state the truth. In a situation which requires an absence of technicality and immunity away from interference, I hope that the way may soon be found for a frank discussion and determination of what is essentially an economic problem.' "[10]]

The endorsement of my proposal by Mr. Lloyd George in connection with his visit to the United States in the summer of 1923 and its immediate effect are described by Mr. Bertram D. Hulen, correspondent of the *New York Times*, in his book entitled *Inside the Department of State*, pp. 125–129. After further negotiations in which I resisted efforts to limit the scope of the committee's investigation and insisted upon its opportunity to make an adequate inquiry, the Dawes committee was constituted.

Throughout this entire undertaking I had to work within the limitation that the Government could not be represented in any body, agency or commission, acting under the Treaty of Versailles, without the consent of Congress. This was also the explanation of my statement in the Aide-Memoire of October 15, 1923, that our Government could not appoint a member of the Reparation Commission unless Congress consented. This restriction was due to the reservation made by the Senate in ratifying the Treaty of Berlin to the effect "that the United States shall not be represented or participate in any body, agency or commission, nor shall any person represent the United States as a member of any body, agency or commission in which the United States is authorized to participate by this Treaty, unless and until an Act of Congress of the United States shall provide for such representation or participation."[11]

If I had sought to obtain the consent of Congress to the appointment of a committee officially representing our Government, I should have been involved in a controversy which would have defeated the entire plan.[12] By the method I adopted a committee was established to make an economic inquiry and recommendations—without authority to represent our Government but with distinguished American members—and thus it became possible for us to throw our influence to the carrying out of the plan the committee proposed. Beerits refers to my efforts to that end in connection with my visit to Europe in the Summer of 1924 as President of the American Bar Association. My visit to London happened to be at the time when the Conference was being held to deal with the Dawes Committee's report. My interviews there were followed by interviews in Paris with Poincaré and with the representatives of the German Government in Berlin.

[10][C. C. Hyde, "Charles Evans Hughes," in S. F. Bemis, ed., *The American Secretaries of State and Their Diplomacy* (New York, Alfred A. Knopf, 1929), X, 376–379.]

[11]Treaty of Berlin, August 25, 1921, *Foreign Relations, 1921*, Vol. II, p. 33; 1923, Vol. II, p. 72.

[12]See speech at The Pilgrims' Dinner in London on July 21, 1924, reprinted in *The Pathway of Peace*, pp. 108ff.

In connection with the distribution of the amounts to be paid by Germany under the Dawes Plan, questions arose as to the right of the United States to participate in these payments to the extent of obtaining reimbursement for the costs of our Army of Occupation and to meet the types of claims which were the subject of adjudication by the Mixed Claims Commission under the agreement with Germany of August 10, 1922. Our Army of Occupation had been maintained under the distinct agreement that the claim for army costs was to be paid on a parity with similar claims by the Allied Powers and ahead of reparations.[13] With regard to the right of participation in the payments made by Germany, in order to meet the claims established by the Mixed Claims Commission, we felt that the Allied Powers could not justly take for their own purposes of reparation the entire amount that Germany had capacity to pay and ignore the rights of the United States.[14]

Having asserted and maintained our rights, we were willing to make, and did make, a liberal concession in fixing the amount of our participation.[15]

THE SOVIET UNION

As Beerits states in his Memorandum, while the repudiation of the debt owing to the United States for the loan made to the Kerensky Government and the confiscation of the property of our nationals, were important considerations, the chief reason for withholding recognition from the Soviet regime lay in the subversive efforts which it had sponsored in this country. Of these, the State Department had abundant evidence.[16] Senator

[13] *Foreign Relations, 1922,* Vol. II, pp. 262, 264; *Foreign Relations, 1924,* Vol. II, p. 9.

[14] See the text of reply, December 9, 1924, to British Note, which reviews this matter. *Foreign Relations, 1924,* Vol. II, pp. 102–107 (especially pp. 103, 106); 127–132. Beerits' Memorandum, ["The Dawes Plan"], pp. 29–30.

[15] *Foreign Relations, 1924,* Vol. II, pp. 133–134.

[16] Beerits' Memorandum, "Relations with Soviet Russia," pp. 9–10: ["The Department of State possessed evidence establishing the unity of the various Bolshevik organizations known as the Communist party, the Soviet Government, and the Third Communist Internationale, all controlled by a small group of individuals constituting the political bureau of the Russian Communist party. The evidence also established a solid connection between the Moscow group and its representative in the United States in the form of the American Communist Party, and its legal counterpart, the Workers' party.

Secretary Hughes, possessing incontrovertible evidence that the revolutionary organizations in the United States were directed from Moscow and were to some extent subsidized by Moscow, was unwilling to deal with the diplomatic representations of a regime committed to such a program. He had no desire to burden his Government with the task of safeguarding itself against communist activities fomenting discontent and disorder throughout the country, and inspired under the roof of a Russian embassy in Washington."] *Hearings in relation to Recognition of Russia,* 1924, before a sub-committee of the Committee on Foreign Relations, United States Senate, 68th Cong. 1st Sess.

Root in his speech at the dinner, which was given to me after I had resigned as Secretary of State, strongly emphasized this point.[17] The policy of non-recognition, initiated by the Wilson administration and followed during the administration of Harding and Coolidge, was continued under Hoover. As late as December 1930, Secretary Stimson was reported as saying that "the United States would not recognize the Soviet government until the latter had acknowledged its debts, guaranteed proper compensation for American property confiscated in Russia, and ceased to agitate for the overthrow of American institutions by revolution."[18]

When recognition was finally accorded in 1933, it was upon the explicit pledge that the Soviet Government would refrain from interfering in any manner in the internal affairs of the United States, its territories or possessions, and would restrain all persons in government service and all organizations in receipt of any financial assistance from it, from any act overt or covert liable in any way whatsoever to injure the tranquility, prosperity, order, or security of the whole or any part of the United States.[19]

My relation with the first Soviet Ambassador to Washington, Alexander Troyanovsky, were most agreeable. It was the custom for Ambassadors and Ministers, after they had presented their credentials and had been received at the State Department, to call upon the Chief Justice, and so I made the Ambassador's acquaintance soon after his arrival. I was his guest several times at the Soviet Embassy.[20] On one of these occasions, at the end of May 1938, he sat with me after the dinner and talked at considerable length of Hitler's threatening proceedings. The Ambassador said rather emphatically that he believed Hitler, as soon as he was ready, would attack France.

The agreement between the Soviet Union and Hitler in 1939 and the attack on Poland keenly disappointed many of the friends of Russia in this country, but when Hitler invaded the Soviet Union in June 1941, Winston Churchill's announcement that "any man or State who fights against Nazism will have our aid," found strong support in the United States. Military supplies were made available to Russia and were increased as rapidly as production and transportation would permit.

The dissolution of the Comintern was welcome evidence that the Soviet Union was disposed to abandon its sponsorship of Communistic

[17]Beerits' Memorandum ["Relations with Soviet Russia"], pp. 12–13. A copy of this speech is in the Hughes Papers. See, also, Jessup, *[Root]*, Vol. II, p. 370 [and Hyde, "Hughes" in Bemis, ed., *American Secretaries of State*, X, 280–288].

[18][Quoted in Vera Micheles Dean, ed.], *The American Year Book for 1933* (Washington, The Foreign Policy Association, 1934), p. 66.

[19]*[Ibid.]*, p. 67.

[20]The Soviet Ambassador gave three large dinners at which Mrs. Hughes and I were the guests of honor. These were on May 18, 1935, February 20, 1937 and May 28, 1938.

activities in this country and leave the Communists here to fare for themselves. The revival of intense patriotic ardor in Russia, the unity, tenacity and prodigious sacrifices of the Russian people, the extraordinary efficiency displayed in the production of matériel, and the military skill with which the hordes of Hitler's Germany were met and beaten back, aroused our unstinted admiration. Stalin's masterful leadership and Russia's victories established an unprecedented prestige for the Soviet Union among the European peoples, of which Stalin has not been disinclined to take full advantage in his diplomatic enterprises. With Germany doomed to complete defeat, with the countries of Continental Europe ravaged and their peoples impoverished, with Great Britain facing the most serious economic difficulties, the Soviet Union is destined to emerge from the War the greatest Power in Europe, and the hopes of peace and progress largely depend upon her cooperation in all future programs. That cooperation Stalin seems willing to give in relation to plans to prevent aggression, as indicated by the Moscow Declaration of the Foreign Secretaries in 1943 and Stalin's recently expressed support of the Dumbarton Oaks proprosals. This attitude, however, is evidently not deemed by Stalin to be inconsistent with an apparent determination to hold for the Soviet Union the Baltic provinces and a large slice of pre-war Poland, and to be assured of friendly governments in contiguous countries. Nor is it likely that he will view with displeasure the growth of communistic influence in European countries, although he may carefully abstain from any overt action to stimulate it. All the aims of Stalin's diplomacy are not yet fully revealed.[21]

LATIN AMERICA

At the close of the Wilson Administration, our relations with the countries of Latin America were far from satisfactory. In 1916, I had reviewed and severely criticised the course which had been taken in connection with Mexican affairs. It had provoked resentment. "Decrying interference, we interfered most exasperatingly."[22] In 1921, the wounds thus inflicted had not yet healed. And we were still faced with the fundamental problem of safe-guarding American rights. In the Caribbean area, a most serious situation had developed. Our troops were in Santo Domingo, in Haiti, and in Nicaragua. Panama and Costa Rica were about to engage in war.

A stabilizing policy was demanded, and what Professor Bemis has called "the liquidation of imperialism." As he says, it was my policy "to liqui-

[21]This was written in November 1944.

[22]Address in accepting the Republican nomination for President. Copy in the Hughes Papers.

date the interventions of the United States in the Caribbean and Central America as promptly as political stability should seem to be established and the safety of foreign nationals reasonably assured."[23]

In my public utterances, I sought to set forth the true American policy and to dissipate the notions that we had any desire to interfere in the internal concerns of the Latin American states. Professor Bemis quotes what I said in Brazil, when I attended the celebration of the centenary of the Brazilian independence.[24] In harmony with these declarations I set forth our policy in relation to Mexico.[25]

It was manifest that a restatement of the true import of the Monroe Doctrine was called for. And this I undertook to give in two addresses, one at the annual meeting of the American Bar Association in Minneapolis in August 1923, and the other at the meeting held in Philadelphia, under the auspices of the Academy of Political Science, in November of that year, to celebrate the centenary of the Doctrine.[26]

But utterances of this sort, though backed by official position, were not enough. There were concrete conditions to be dealt with.

Mexico. In September 1920, General [Alvaro] Obregón was elected President of Mexico and the time seemed to be ripe for arrangements to secure a satisfactory settlement of our claims for the injuries which our nationals had sustained in their persons and property.[27] The recognition of the government of General [Venustiano] Carranza by the Wilson Administration had been based upon his explicit assurances that there would be no confiscation of American properties. However, there were subsequent confiscatory measures. In the poltical campaign of 1920 in the United States, both

[23]Samuel F. Bemis, *The Latin American Policy of the United States,* [New York, Harcourt, Brace & Co., 1943], Chap. XII, "The Republican Restoration and the Liquidation of Imperialism," pp. 203, 389. See, also, Sumner Welles, *The Time for Decision,* [New York, Harper and Brothers, 1944], p. 187. [Smith, *Aftermath of War,* pp. 102–154, defends Wilson; and Tulchin, *Aftermath of War,* chapters 2 and 3, stresses the impact of World War I on policy and continuities between the Wilson and Harding administrations.]

[24]September 1922. Bemis, *[Latin American Policy],* p. 203. See Beerits' Memorandum, "The Brazilian Trip of 1922." [This memorandum is largely an account of the ocean voyage and good will festivities in Brazil.]

[25]See my review of "Foreign Relations" (1924), p. 55. Printed pamphlet in the Hughes Papers.

[26]These addresses are reprinted in *The Pathway of Peace,* pp. 113ff, and pp. 142ff.

[27]See Beerits' Memorandum, "Relations with Mexico." [A more detailed discussion of this and the other Latin American situations mentioned by Hughes, laying great emphasis on the continuity of policy between the Wilson and Harding administrations is Tulchin, *Aftermath of War.* For a discussion that focuses exclusively on Hughes see George Navarrete, "The Latin American Policy of Charles Evans Hughes, 1921–1925" (Ph.D. dissertation, University of California, Berkeley, 1965); and Nathaniel Stephen Kane, "Charles Evans Hughes and Mexican-American Relations, 1921–1924" (Ph.D. dissertation, University of Colorado, 1970).]

parties had pledged themselves not to recognize the Mexican government without an undertaking for the adjudication, that is, by appropriate arbitration, of American claims. This could not be achieved during the remaining period of the Wilson Administration and so the government of Obregón had not been recognized when I took office.

I thought it advisable, if possible, to establish our relations and the protection of American interests by a formal treaty, which should be coincident with recognition.[28] This proposal led to a considerable correspondence. Not being able to carry out this plan, and being most desirous to come to an understanding with the Mexican authorities in any way that seemed feasible and consistent with American rights, I was glad to agree to the appointment of a Commission composed of the representatives of both countries who should seek a satisfactory solution of the pending questions. In my letter of instructions to our Commissioners (May 8, 1823) I reviewed the prior negotiations, and set forth the objects to be attained.[29] The American Commissioners submitted a report of the understanding reached with the Mexican Commissioners concerning subsoil and agrarian matters, which was approved by the President of the United States and the President of Mexico, and thereupon the Obregón government was recognized and formal diplomatic relations were resumed. Two Claims Conventions were agreed upon, a general one, and an additional, or special one for claims relating to losses through revolutionary acts.

The assurances thus given and the arrangements for judicial settlement of claims thus arrived at went as far as it was possible at the time to establish a basis for peaceful and mutually beneficial relations with our sister republic. We were optimistic enough to "look forward to a new era of friendship and cooperation."[30]

The Caribbean Area—Central America. At the beginning of March 1921, Costa Rica and Panama were on the verge of war. Beerits' Memorandum, "Latin-American Boundary Disputes," states the circumstances [pp. 1–3].

[28]Bemis, *[Latin American Policy]*, pp. 215–216. This idea of coupling the recognition of a new government with an appropriate engagement on its part in relation to American interests was not novel. See *Hamilton Fish: The Inner History of the Grant Administration*, by Allan Nevins, [New York, Dodd, Mead & Co., 1937], Appendix I, p. 913. [The Wilson Administration had tried the same policy. See *Foreign Relations, 1920*, Vol. III, pp. 189–196.]

[29]Letters to Commissioners Charles Beecher Warren and John Barton Payne, *Foreign Relations, 1923*, Vol. II, pp. 536–548. [The subsequent negotiations and resulting Claims Convention are *ibid.*, pp. 550–567.]

[30]See my Princeton lectures on *Our Relations to the Nations of the Western Hemisphere* (Princeton, 1928), pp. 42–46. Professor Bemis describes the course of subsequent events—down to 1943, *[Latin American Policy]*, pp. 216–218; 345–350.

[As Hughes "entered office there was a serious outbreak between Panama and Costa Rica over a tract of land known as the Coto district, the boundary of which had long been the subject of dispute. The dispute had been submitted for arbitration to President Loubet of France in 1900. He had made an award, but question arose as to precisely what his award meant. By a convention between Panama and Costa Rica of March 17th, 1910, the matter was submitted for further arbitration to Chief Justice White of the United States Supreme Court for his decision as to what President Loubet had meant by his award. Chief Justice White's decision was presented on September 12th, 1914.

["Just as the Harding Administration was about to be inaugurated in March, 1921, dissatisfaction over the terms of the award, which had long been smouldering, broke out into open hostilities between the two countries that were parties to the dispute. On February 24th Panamans (sic) attacked the Costa Rica Consulate on news of the invasion of their country. The following day the Panamans armed to oust the alleged invaders of the Coto district. President Porras, of Panama, signed a proclamation declaring war, but withheld it. A special session of the National Assembly was called, while forces were being rushed to the border. On the 28th the Costa Rican force occupying Coto was captured. The United States sent warnings to both Governments; and the League of Nations started an inquiry. On March 1st the special session of the Panaman Assembly took up defense measures. Costa Rica sent troops to the frontier. American troops saved President Porras from a war-hungry mob. The following day fighting was renewed in the Coto district. The Panamans captured a vessel and 100 men. On March 4 an American gunboat was on its way to Panama.

["On March 5th Secretary Hughes entered office."]

This was a crisis in a long-standing boundary dispute: It had been referred to Chief Justice White as arbitrator and, in 1914, he had finally determined the true boundary. But Panama refused to accept the award.

It was evident that the outbreak of hostilities might have far-reaching consequences and that, in particular, the integrity of judicial settlements was involved.

I at once took the position that the award of Chief Justice White, which both countries had agreed to accept, must be regarded as conclusive and that arrangements should be made to carry it out in an orderly manner. My reasons were fully set forth in my note of March 15, 1921. I directed attention to the fact that by Article 1 of the Hay-Bunau Varilla Treaty the United States had guaranteed the independence of the Republic of Panama; that in order to fulfill its obligations, it was necessary for the United States to advise itself as to the extent of Panama's sovereignty and hence of its territorial limits; that it appeared that the boundary line on the Pacific side had been determined by an arbitral award of the President of France in 1900, and that the controversy which remained as to the Atlantic side had been submitted to the Chief Justice of the United States for final determination; that the award of the Chief Justice, in 1914, was "definite and unmistakable," and that there was no basis for the contention that the arbitrator had exceeded his powers.

Hostilities were checked and, after a few months and several exchanges of views with Panama, the dispute was ended and Costa Rica was confirmed in the peaceful possession of the territory to which she was entitled.[31]

The attitude of our Government in sustaining the position of Costa Rica under the arbitral award, as against Panama to whom we sustained an exceptionally close relation, was a demonstration to Central America, and to the other countries of Latin America as well, of our impartiality and our desire to see all controversies settled amicably and judicial determinations upheld.

Honduras—Nicaragua—Salvador. The Governments of Honduras and Nicaragua accused each other of assisting revolutionists in the invasion of their respective countries. Salvador also became involved. The outbreak of a general Central American war was feared. Our Government invited the Presidents of the three countries to a confernce on the U.S.S. *Tacoma* in August 1922. This was held and an agreement was reached.[32]

Central American Conference, 1922–23. The conference on the *Tacoma* had brought about better relations for the time being, but I felt that something more definite was needed to make permanent what had been gained and to accomplish other needed reforms. Accordingly I recommended to President Harding the calling of a conference of the Central American Powers.[33] The President approved, our invitations were accepted, and the Conference met in Washington in December 1922, and adjourned in February 1923. The delegates of our Government were myself and Sumner Welles.

There was a very friendly atmosphere and the results were highly encouraging. A General Treaty of Peace and Amity was signed, together with a large number of Conventions. Beerits gives a summary and Professor Bemis provides a commentary.[34]

[31] [These notes are in] *Foreign Relations, 1921,* Vol. I, pp. 182–228. [For the efforts of the previous administration, see *Foreign Relations, 1921,* Vol. I, pp. 175–189.]

[32] *Foreign Relations, 1922,* Vol. I, pp. 417–426.

[33] *[Ibid.],* p. 428.

[34] Beerits' Memorandum, "Latin American Conferences," pp. 1–9; Bemis, *[Latin American Policy],* pp. 205–209. The proceedings of the Central American Conference, together with the text of the agreement concluded, are set forth in the official Report, *Conference on Central American Affairs* (Washington, Government Printing Office, 1923). See also my pamphlet, "Foreign Relations" (1924), pp. 60–1, in the Hughes Papers.

[The conference, wrote Beerits, resulted in "a general treaty of peace and amity and a series of eleven conventions, among them being conventions for the establishment of a Central American Tribunal, for the limitation of armaments, for a permanent Central American commission for extradition, for the preparation of projects of electoral legislation, for the unification of protective laws for workmen and laborers, for the establishment of stations for agricultural experiments and animal industries, and for the reciprocal exchange of Central American students.

["To a remarkable degree these treaties conserved the best interests of the Central American Republics as well as those which Secretary Hughes had declared to be peculiar to his own country. The United States was a party to the convention for the establishment of international commissions of inquiry. The convention providing for the establishment of an International Central American Tribunal was of special interest to the United States, not only because of the scope of the differences to be adjusted by judicial process, but also by reason of the fact that five of the thirty jurists who were to constitute a permanent panel were to be chosen from a list of fifteen jurists to be submitted by the United States, which was not a party to the convention.

["The treaty of peace and amity contained those provisions of a similar treaty of 1907 which had been found to be of practical value and additional provisions which the conference believed would promote the objects in view. The most important provision was one by which the parties agreed, in order to uphold constitutional government and maintain free institutions, not to recognize any Central American government which might come into power through a *coup d'etat* or a revolution against a recognized government, so long as the freely elected representatives of the people had not constitutionally reorganized the country."

[In his commentary, Bemis says: "The Washington Conference of 1922–1923 on Central American Affairs produced, under Secretary Hughes' chairmanship, thirteen treaties between the five republics of Central America for the general purpose of conserving peace and solidarity among themselves, for disarmament, for free trade (except Costa Rica), for the study and inauguration of elaborate programs of education, labor legislation, social welfare, finances, transportation, common jurisprudence, and reciprocal rights of citizenship.

["Outstanding were the conventions that established a Central American Tribunal and international commissions of inquiry into disputes between the states . . .

["The hub of these Washington treaties of 1923, about which all the others were constructed, was the treaty of peace and amity. It pledged the five republics mutually to the Tobar Doctrine, repeated in more specific detail than in 1907: not to assist or recognize revolutions or coups d'etat of the Huerta type of Mexican history. They agreed not to intervene in their neighbors' affairs in case of civil wars. The signatories consecrated themselves to the constitutional principle—so salutary at least in tropical countries—of non-reelection to the office of president or vice president. Further, each party agreed 'not to intervene, under any circumstances, directly or indirectly, in the internal political affairs of any other Central American republic.' This last-mentioned article was a model for a similar provision in the later famous Pan American Treaty on the Rights and Duties of States, signed at Montevideo in December, 1933, and for the special non-intervention protocol of 1936.

["Although the United States was not a contracting party to twelve of the thirteen treaties, every one of them contained in the preamble this direct testimony of its tutelage and its moral responsibility (similar to the preamble of 1907, except for the absence of Mexico in 1923): 'By virtue of the invitation sent to the Government of the United States of America by the Governments of the five Central American republics, there were present at the deliberations of the Conference, as delegates of the Government of the United States of America, the Honorable Charles E. Hughes, Secretary of State of the United States of America, and the Honorable Sumner Welles, Envoy Extraordinary and Minister Plenipotentiary'."]

While I acted as Chairman of the Conference, I had the invaluable assistance of Sumner Welles. When I took office I found him in charge of the Latin American division of the State Department and I continued him as its Chief. I came into close contact with him in dealing with the Panama-Costa Rica affair and I recognized at once his exceptional ability, his poise and force of character. The Central American Conference showed that special aptitude for the conduct of delicate negotiations with our Latin American friends, which he so brilliantly displayed in the later conferences when he was associated with Secretary [Cordell] Hull.

The effectiveness of joint action along the lines provided for by the conference treaties was demonstrated even before their ratification. Because of the failure of an election for President of Honduras, in October 1923, there was no constitutional government when the President's term expired in February 1924. There was resort to revolution. There were several revolutionary armies in the field within a few weeks. Conditions throughout the country, and particularly within the capital, were appalling, and there appeared to be little prospect for the early establishment of orderly government. In these circumstances President Coolidge, on my recommendation, sent Sumner Welles as his personal representative to offer the good offices of our Government in an effort to restore peace. A preliminary agreement was reached by which all factions agreed upon the selection of a Provisional President to hold office until the Constitution could be revised and a constitutional government elected. This preliminary agreement was accepted and made definite at a conference in which all Central American Governments, as well as that of the United States, were represented. Order was restored.

In view of the conference treaties, and the prospect of peaceful conditions, our Government gave notice to Nicaragua, in November 1923, of our intention to withdraw what remained of our forces there (the legation guard). This was to follow a free election in 1924 that was to be held under a new electoral law in the preparation of which Harold W. Dodds (now President of Princeton) had given expert assistance as electoral advisor.[35]

Santo Domingo. Whatever may have been the excuse for the military intervention of our Government in Santo Domingo, in 1916, I was convinced that we should evacuate our troops as soon as possible. Sumner Welles has called the intervention "unjustifiable" and considers that the interventions in the Dominican Republic and in Haiti, "carried out in the years prior to 1917, when Wilson was gravely preoccupied with the problems arising from the first World War, at once alienated the sympathies of the other American nations and fatally undermined their confidence in the sincerity of Wilson himself.[36]

Study of the situation convinced me that the time was opportune for arrangements for our withdrawal, and it was not long after I became Secretary of State that I was able to take steps to that end. Under my instructions a proclamation was issued on June 14, 1921, setting forth a detailed plan. But difficulties arose, through a misunderstanding of our purpose, and after consultations with Dominican leaders a further plan was developed. In March 1922, on my request, Sumner Welles was appointed Commissioner, with the rank of Minister, to represent President Harding in the negotiation of an appropriate agreement for our withdrawal. Mr. Welles performed his duties most ably, and through his untiring efforts all obstacles were finally surmounted. Pursuant to an orderly election a new government was installed in 1924. Our forces were entirely removed, and, as Mr. Welles has said, "a new era of liberty and independence had commenced." We thus gave a demonstration of the sincerity of our intentions.[37]

Haiti. It was my desire to withdraw also from Haiti, but as this did not appear to be feasible at the time, I sought in every way possible to ameliorate conditions and pave the way for the termination of our control.[38]

[35][Harold Willis Dodds (1889–   ) taught at various institutions before going to Princeton in 1927 as Professor of Politics. He became President of the University in 1933. In addition to his teaching, he was Secretary of the National Municipal League from 1920–1928. His expertise led to his appointment as Electoral Adviser to the Government of Nicaragua 1922–1924, Technical Adviser to the president of the Tacna–Arica Plebiscitary Commission, 1925–26, Chief Adviser to the president of the National Board of Elections of Nicaragua, 1928, and Arbiter in the Cuban Election Dispute, 1935.]

[36]See my address on the Monroe Doctrine in *The Pathway of Peace*, pp. 129–130; and Welles, *The Time for Decision*, p. 186.

[37]Mr. Welles has given a detailed account of all these proceedings in his book entitled *Naboth's Vineyard* (New York, Payson and Clark, Ltd., 1928), pp. 838–859. See, also, Beerits' Memorandum, "Latin American Intervention and the Monroe Doctrine," pp. 1–12.

[38]Beerits, ["Latin American Intervention"], pp. 12–17; *The Pathway of Peace*, pp. 131–134.

Cuba. The corrupt administration in Cuba under President [Alfredo] Zayas, and the importance of promoting administrative reforms, gave us no little difficulty.

Under the Platt Amendment we had a peculiar relation to Cuba, but it is especially noteworthy that all our efforts were to aid the people of Cuba to establish sound administration and our interventions were "reluctant and temporary." [39] As I said in my Princeton lectures:[40]

> We did intervene originally without treaty and in the interest of humanity to free Cuba from Spanish domination. We need make no apology for that either to Europe or to Latin America. We abated a nuisance at our door and gave Cuba her opportunity for a new and vigorous national life. In so doing, we expressly reserved, to avoid the recurrence of intolerable conditions, "the right to intervene for the preservation of Cuban independence, the maintenance of a government adequate for the protection of life, property and individual liberty, and for discharging the obligations with respect to Cuba imposed by the Treaty of Paris on the United States" which were assumed by the Government of Cuba. Without reviewing the circumstances of our action under this treaty, or our endeavors to promote the interests of the Cuban people, *it is plain that the significant thing in our interventions was not that we went in but that we came out.* We demonstrated our interest in Cuban freedom at the beginning and we have kept on demonstrating it since. We wish for Cuba the prosperity and stability of an independent State and instead of looking for opportunities to take advantage of the treaty right, the dominant sentiment of our people is just the reverse, and we should be happy to have no thought of the exercise of the right because of the absence of any exigency in which it could with any propriety be invoked. [Emphasis added by Hughes.]

I shall not attempt to review the various proceedings in connection with the Special Mission in Cuba of General [Enoch] Crowder (later Ambassador) which are set forth in *Foreign Relations.*[41] One helpful action which was greatly appreciated in Cuba was the ratification of the Treaty of 1904 relating to the Isle of Pines. Our Senate had delayed ratification for many years because of serious opposition, due to the idea that the interests of American citizens in the island would be imperiled if our Government definitely renounced all claim of title. The final ratification, in March 1925, was had after I left office, but I think that I may properly say that it was due in no small degree to my efforts to secure it. I had

[39] *[Ibid.]*, pp. 128–129; Bemis, *[Latin American Policy]*, pp. 140–141, and 278.
[40] *Our Relations to the Nations of the Western Hemisphere*, p. 76.
[41] *Foreign Relations, 1921, 1922, 1923, 1924*, title "Cuba."

taken the matter up with Senators and had communicated my views in support of the Treaty. In my letter to Senator [Joseph Taylor] Robinson [of Arkansas] of January 2, 1925, I said that

> The present undetermined status of the Isle of Pines constitutes one of the few remaining questions capable of prejudicing the intimate relations between the United States and Cuba, and it is my earnest hope that the Senate in its present session will give its consent to the ratification of the Treaty.[42]

Boundary Disputes. While declarations of principles and pronouncements of good intentions are desirable, the surest way to promote peace and friendly relations between countries is to remove grievances. In Latin America, boundary disputes have been festering sores. I have given a great deal of thought and effort to healing them so far as possible.

I have already referred to the disputes between *Panama and Costa Rica.*

The ratification in 1921 of the Treaty of 1914 between Colombia and the United States paved the way for the settlement of the boundary question between *Colombia and Panama.*[43]

In accordance with the request of the three Governments, I had given my good offices for the settlement of the boundary controversy between *Brazil, Colombia and Peru.* The settlement was arrived at on my last day in office.[44]

Chile-Peru. Tacna-Arica. The most troublesome and acrid boundary dispute was between Chile and Peru. It had lasted for about forty years. It was described as "the long-standing controversy over the unfulfilled provisions of the Treaty of Ancon." This was a treaty of peace and the unfulfilled provisions were in Article 3 relating to the disposition of the provinces of *Tacna* and *Arica.*

I shall not attempt to review my efforts to settle this dispute; the long and difficult negotiations leading to the arbitration by President Coolidge; the terms of the submission and the Award; and the difficulties which were encountered in the endeavor to carry out the Award. It is sufficient

[42] *Foreign Relations, 1925,* Vol. II, p. 2. See, also, Memorandum, which was prepared under my direction, as to the status of the Isle of Pines, enclosed with my letter to Senator Robinson, *[Ibid.],* pp. 7–11.

Our Senate ratified the Treaty on March 13, 1925, with a reservation to which Cuba assented on March 18, 1925. *[Ibid.],* pp. 11, 14.

[43] *Foreign Relations, 1921,* Vol. I, pp. 638–645; Beerits' Memorandum, "Latin American Boundary Disputes," p. 7.

[44] *Foreign Relations, 1925,* Vol. I, pp. 461–463. For the earlier negotiations, see *[ibid.],* pp. 436–460. Beerits, ["Latin American Boundary Disputes"], pp. 8–9.

to refer to the documents found in *Foreign Relations*, to the summary of Beerits, and to the general statement I made in my Princeton lectures.[45] The nub of the matter was that at the close of the war between Chile and Peru, and when the Treaty of Ancon was made, Chile was in possession and control of the disputed territory. The Treaty provided that at the end of ten years there should be a plebiscite to decide whether these provinces should "remain definitely under the dominion and sovereignty of Chile," or should continue "to constitute a part of Peru." The plebiscite was not held as provided, and in the ensuing years there were acrimonious disputes on various grounds. By the submission to arbitration the parties agreed that the Arbitrator should determine whether a plebiscite should or should not be held. The Arbitrator ruled that it should be held and, in accordance with the submission on that point, prescribed the conditions.

Throughout the entire period of the controversy Chile had remained in possession of the provinces in question and had exercised the powers of sovereignty. She was not willing to surrender this control, and she made it so secure that in the absence of an agreement she could be dislodged only by force of arms. In the light of that fundamental fact, it was impossible to arrange for arbitration save on the condition that if a plebiscite were not directed, and pending an agreement as to the disposition of the territory, the administrative organization of the provinces should not be disturbed.

Despite every effort of the Plebiscitary Commission, for which the Award provided, it turned out to be impossible to hold a fair plebiscite in accordance with the prescribed conditions. And it was manifestly not feasible for our Government to intervene by sending an army to the scene of the dispute. Thus there remained only the resources of diplomacy.

While the breakdown in the proceedings for a plebiscite was most regrettable, still the Award was by no means futile. Previously, and for a generation, there had been no possibility of an amicable settlement. This was chiefly because of a disagreement as to the legal rights of the parties under the Treaty of Ancon. With these questions determined by the Arbitrator the way was at last open to a diplomatic adjustment and, although there was considerable delay, this was finally attained.

Guatemala—Honduras. My connection with boundary disputes was not to end with my term of office as Secretary of State. Later, in 1930, when I was Chief Justice, Guatemala and Honduras agreed to submit their claims to a Special Boundary Tribunal, of which I was to be President. Although

[45] *Foreign Relations, 1922*, Vol. I, pp. 447 et seq; 1925, Vol. I, pp. 305 *et seq;* Beerits, ["Latin American Boundary Disputes"], pp. 10–21; and *Our Relations to the Nations of the Western Hemisphere*, pp. 87–91.

this imposed a burden which in view of the work of the Court it would be extremely difficult to bear, I felt that I should accept the appointment. The Award, establishing the boundary, was made in 1933 and was accepted by both parties.[46]

Pan-American Conferences. It was my privilege to be associated with three of these Conferences: Santiago, Chile (1923); Havana (1928); Washington (1928–29). Beerits has given a general description of all three, and I shall make only a brief comment.[47]

The Fifth Pan-American Conference was held at Santiago while I was Secretary of State. The American Delegation was headed by Henry P. Fletcher, who had been Under Secretary of State, and among its members were Senators Frank B. Kellogg and Atlee Pomerene, and George E. Vincent. Important agreements were made. There was provision for a number of special conferences on subjects bearing upon commerce and culture.[48] Further, a treaty was signed "to avoid or prevent conflicts between American States" commonly called "Gondra Conciliatory Convention."[49]

While out of office, I was appointed Chairman of the American Delegation to the Sixth Pan-American Conference held at Havana in 1928. Those who understood the situation looked forward to this meeting with no little anxiety. Haiti was still under our control; and while our troops had been removed from Nicaragua in 1925, as I had provided, there had been another revolutionary outbreak and our armed forces had returned. Just before the Conference met additional Marines had been landed. Our action had been widely criticized.[50] Our relations with Mexico had deteriorated, and while they were being improved by the skillful efforts of Dwight Morrow, there was lingering resentment at the attitude which our Government had taken.[51] Argentina was restive under the restraint our Government had imposed, for sanitary reasons, on the importation of beef, and Argentina's opposition to this restriction was not without interest to other Latin-American countries.

[46]Beerits, ["Latin American Boundary Disputes"], pp. 22–27.

[47]Beerits' Memorandum, "Latin American Conferences," pp. 10–53. [These conferences are described in Bemis, *[Latin American Policy]*, pp. 242–55; and J. Lloyd Mecham, *The United States and Inter-American Security, 1889–1960* (Austin, University of Texas Press, 1961), pp. 94–111.]

[48]I referred to this provision in my address on the Monroe Doctrine in *The Pathway of Peace*, pp. 137–138.

[49]*Foreign Relations, 1923*, Vol. I, pp. 309 *et seq*. See, also, my radio address on "Latin American Relations" (January 1925), in *The Pathway of Peace*, pp. 165–166.

[50]*American Year Book*, 1928, ed. Albert Bushnell Hart (New York, American Year Book Corp., 1929), pp. 17, 164.

[51]Sumner Welles, *Naboth's Vineyard*, p. 189.

I fully realized that the Conference would present serious difficulties and I accepted the appointment with misgivings. I had associates of high distinction, including Henry P. Fletcher, Senator Oscar W. Underwood, Dwight Morrow, James Brown Scott and Ray Lyman Wilbur.[52] We were advised that the Conference had "not been called to sit in judgment of the conduct of any nation or to attempt to redress alleged wrongs." And we were instructed to strive to keep off the agenda all controversial subjects not already there, and to resist the doctrine of absolute non-intervention. The State Department gave us a review of the topics on the agenda and a "Special Political Memorandum." [53] The latter stated:

> The past year has seen the development of a vigorous anti-American propaganda throughout Latin America based on charges of "imperialism" and characterized by violent criticism of the relations existing between the United States and Mexico and the American policy in Nicaragua. For the most part the Latin American Governments have refrained from participating in this propaganda, which has been carried on by private individuals and private organizations created expressly for that purpose, and in the press. Nevertheless, it is possible that an effort may be made by some delegates to the Sixth Pan American Conference to bring up controversial matters which the United States would not consider appropriate for a gathering of this nature, and it is not improbable that in the course of their remarks certain delegates may attack the policy of the United States Government towards Latin America with special references to its relations with Mexico, Nicaragua, Panama and Haiti. Every effort should be made to have the topics discussed at the Conference confined to those on the prearranged agenda, or such additional topics *as do not involve any discussion or criticisms of the foreign policy of this or any other country* . . .
>
> The United States cannot enter into any discussion at Havana of

[52][Dwight Whitney Morrow (1873–1931) was a senior partner in J. P. Morgan & Co. and a friend of President Calvin Coolidge. As Ambassador to Mexico, 1927–1930, he restored harmonious U.S. relations with that republic. See Harold Nicolson, *Dwight Morrow* (New York, Harcourt, Brace & Company, 1935).

[James Brown Scott (1866–1943), one of the outstanding authorities on international law of his day, was Solicitor of the Department of State, 1906–1910; trustee of the Carnegie Endowment for International Peace; technical adviser at the Hague Peace Conference, 1907, the Paris Peace Conference, 1919, Washington Arms Conference, 1921–1922, and many others. He was Editor-in-Chief of the *American Journal of International Law* from 1907 to 1924. During the course of his long career he was appointed to more than a dozen peace commissions and arbitration boards all over the world.

[Ray Lyman Wilbur (1875–1949) was Secretary of the Interior under Hoover and a member of the California State War Problems Board during World War II.]

[53]*Foreign Relations*, 1928, Vol. I, p. 535, and pp. 536–573; and Bemis, *[Latin American Policy]*, p. 251.

matters of purely domestic concern, such as its immigration and tariff acts, or of its foreign policy or relations with individual countries, since these are considered to be subjects which can properly be discussed only between the nations concerned and not in an open forum of nations not directly affected. [Emphasis added by Hughes.]

While carefully following these instructions, I gave strong support to the Declaration of Rights and Duties of States which had been prepared by the American Institute of International Law in 1916 and which I had endorsed when in office in 1923.

The work of the Conference is reviewed in the Report of the American Delegation.[54] Beerits has given a general account of the proceedings, including a somewhat detailed description of the dramatic incident in the closing session of the Conference, with references to the generous appraisal by the American press of my part in it (pp. 13–34):[55]

["In 1927 an International Commission of Jurists had met in Rio de Janeiro to determine the items on public international law to be submitted for consideration at the Sixth Pan American Conference. One of the proposals of the commission had been that no American country had the right to intervene in the affairs of any other American country. Hughes did not want to oppose the proposal, but its intent precluded U.S. intervention even to protect American life and property in Latin America. After discussion in a subcommittee of which Hughes was chairman, Dr. Honorio Pueyrredón, Chief of the Argentine delegation, suggested reluctantly that the proposal be dropped because of irreconcilable difference, and it was agreed finally to reconsider the matter at the next Pan American Conference, which was to be held in five years. Pueyrredon stalked out of the Conference in disgust. On the last day of the plenary session of the Conference when the proposal of the Committee on Public International Law came up that the subject of intervention be considered at the next Pan American Conference, Dr. Laurentina Olascoaga of Argentina leapt to his feet and argued in favor of non-intervention."

["At once," wrote Beerits, "the atmosphere of the Great Hall changed as though a current of electricity had run through it, and the air became charged with tense excitement. Delegate after delegate arose to affirm the ideas of the Argentine delegate. Then Guerrero [of El Salvador], who had promised to drop the matter, arose and said [that] if the Conference were unanimous, as it appeared to him it was, he saw no reason why it should not go on record on the subject of intervention. (Without making a formal motion he proposed the following:) 'The Sixth Conference of the American Republics, taking into consideration that each one of the Delegates

[54]Washington, Government Printing Office, 1928. See, also, the *American Year Book*, 1928, pp. 17, 28, 58, 59; Bemis, *[Latin American Policy]*, pp. 251–253.

[55]See, also, *American Year Book*, 1928, pp. 16–17. [For an Argentine interpretation of these events see Alberto A. Conil Paz, *La Argentina y los Estados Unidos en La Sexta Conferencia Panamericana (La Habana, 1928)*, (Buenos Aires, Editorial Huemul, 1965).]

has expressed his firm decision that the principle of non-intervention and the absolute juridical equality of States should be roundly and categorically stated, resolves: No State has the right to intervene in the internal affairs of another.' At this the Cubans in the gallery broke into thundering applause.

["At this point the Great Hall was invaded by the dignitaries of the University, gorgeously gowned, and for an hour learned doctors of law, science and philosophy delivered long speeches. But while the doctors were speaking the delegates were whispering. Fernandez of Brazil and Olaya of Colombia came to Mr. Hughes and protested that this action by Guerrero was a breach of honor, and that it was impossible that it be tolerated. Mr. Hughes replied that he could not be put in the position of stopping discussion on the matter. He sent word to Dr. Antonio Sanchez de Bustamante (Judge of the Permanent Court of International Justice), who was chairman of the Conference, on no account to adjourn the session until the matter was settled.

["The interruption in the proceedings of the Conference served only to increase the fierce flame of excitement. After the dignitaries had concluded their addresses, the delegates launched forth into a fierce debate on the non-intervention proposal. It was as tense and exciting a meeting as Mr. Hughes ever witnessed. Maúrtua of Peru arose and attacked Guerrero. One of the Nicaraguan delegates defended the United States. Fiery speech followed upon fiery speech, and the air was becoming more and more tense. Dr. Bustamante at one point found it necessary to call the meeting to order so as to prevent a heated personal exchange between Jesús M. Yepes of Colombia and Guerrero from reaching a state where nothing but pistols for two would have been acceptable to wounded Latin-American honor.

["While all this discussion was taking place, the position of Mr. Hughes was a very delicate one. If the votes were there to defeat the non-intervention resolution, it was better that he did not appear to prevent its passage. If, on the other hand, the votes were not there to prevent its passage, it was essential that he speak in an attempt to defeat it. It was an exceedingly tense experience for him and he never felt more strongly his responsibility for America.

["The Great Hall was ringing with violent applause and excited cries each time one of the delegates spoke in favor of the non-intervention proposal. Mr. Hughes finally decided that the time had come when he must speak.

["Immediately the room became hushed with eager expectancy. Mr. Hughes started speaking with firm and measured tones. He gave the history of the decision to postpone discussion of the question of intervention, in view of the fact that unanimity on the question could not be then attained. Then he took up with great candor the question of intervention, and explained very frankly the policy of his country with respect to this matter. In conclusion he stated:

[" 'I am too proud of my country to stand before you as in any way suggesting a defense of aggression or of assault upon the sovereignty or independence of any State. I stand before you to tell you we unite with you in the aspiration for complete sovereignty and the realization of complete independence.

[" 'I stand here with you ready to cooperate in every way in establishing the ideals of justice by institutions in every land which will promote fairness of dealing between man and man and nation and nation.

["'I cannot sacrifice the rights of my country but I will join with you in declaring the law. I will try to help you in coming to a just conclusion as to the law; but it must be the law of justice infused with the spirit which has given us from the days of Grotius this wonderful development of the law of nations, by which we find ourselves bound.'

["Mr. Hughes never had greater success in his life. When he finished speaking, the galleries rang with applause. A marked change had taken place in the tempo of the audience while he spoke. As the New York *Times* put it, 'as Mr. Hughes sat down there was a sudden tension over the whole chamber. It seemed as if everyone realized that the resolution for an immediate decision on the question of intervention was beaten. Mr. Hughes had beaten it, by the sheer force of his personality, his eloquence and deep sincerity.'

["The result was that the Conference voted to postpone consideration of the question of intervention until the meeting of the Seventh Pan American Conference, to be held five years later. Thus the stormy session adjourned, and the delegates finally appeared for their dinner at 10:30 that night.

["Mr. Hughes by his masterly speech had prevented the Conference from ending on a harsh note of discord, and thus had saved Pan Americanism from suffering a serious setback. This was the first Conference at which every one of the twenty-one members of the Pan American Union was represented. It resulted in many tangible achievements, but perhaps its greatest achievement was an increase in Pan American understanding and good will."]

Professor Bemis makes this comment (p. 264):

> Not until Havana in 1928 did the twenty Latin American republics, by that time safe after the First World War from any danger of non-American intervention, really attempt to debate live questions with the "Colossus of the North". Even though Mr. Hughes successfully fought off the Argentine effort to inject intervention formally into the program in order to lead an attack on it, the atmosphere at Havana crackled with that potential issue. Had it been released, it might have broken up the Conference and perhaps have wrecked the whole Pan American movement then and there. This risk the Argentine delegation had been ready, even eager, to take — and we recall that the head of the delegation bolted the Conference when his effort failed. It is well for the solidarity of the New World that the issue was postponed to more propitious days, to which Mr. Hughes himself looked forward sincerely; the time when the interventions of the United States would have been more largely liquidated.

Pursuant to a resolution adopted by the Havana Conference, a special conference to deal with the question of obligatory arbitration was convened in Washington in December 1928. Beerits gives the text of the resolution (pp. 35–36). I was associated with Secretary Kellogg as a delegate to the Conference, and as the Secretary was extremely busy with his departmental duties, I had the laboring oar.

The Conference was held in a friendly atmosphere and resulted in two treaties.[56] One was for "Inter-American Conciliation" carrying forward with improvements the Santiago Convention of 1923, and another was for "Inter-American Arbitration." [57]

I reviewed the work of the Conference in my lectures at Yale in 1929.[58]

As I approached the end of four years of service [in 1925], I desired to be relieved of the responsibilities of office and again to enjoy the privileges and immunities of private life. I was tired and needed a long rest, which I did not feel at liberty to take while continuing in office. For several years before I became Secretary, I had had exceptionally hard work with little opportunity for relaxation. There was none whatever in 1917 and 1918; and 1919 and 1920 were difficult years with constant and heavy demands. As Secretary, I had had only short periods of respite; none in 1921; a couple of weeks in Bermuda after the Washington Conference, and the trip to Brazil at the end of the Summer (1922), a visit crowded with official engagements.[59] In 1923 I had a couple of weeks at Hot Springs in September and, in 1924, the trip to London, Paris, Brussels and Berlin, which packed into a brief period a round of exacting labors.[60] Then I tried to meet all the social requirements which seemed to be inseparable from the office of Secretary of State, and this had imposed a very heavy burden on my wife who was eager for relief. I must say, however, that I fully appreciated the advantages of those social contacts with members of the diplomatic corps, and I seldom went to a dinner party without gaining some information which helped me in my work. And many highly prized friendships resulted from these meetings.

Of course, if there had been any critical situation which I felt demanded my continuance in the Department, I should have remained in office in accordance with President Coolidge's wishes, but there was no such situation at that time; my policies were well understood and I had made my contribution in carrying them out. There appeared to be no sufficient reason why I should not resign and return, as I desired, while still vigorous, to professional practice. So, in January 1925, I tendered my resigna-

[56]Beerits, ["Latin American Conferences"], pp. 36–53; *Proceedings* (Washington, Government Printing Office, 1929).

[57]*Foreign Relations, 1929,* Vol. II, pp. 653–663.

[58]Printed by the Yale University Press under the title *Pan American Peace Plans.* See, also, Bemis, *[Latin American Policy]*, pp. 253–255.

[59]Beerits' Memorandum, "The Brazilian Trip of 1922."

[60]Beerits' Memorandum, "The European Trip of 1924."

tion to take effect on March 4, 1925. My letter to President Coolidge of January 5th, and his reply of January 10th, are quoted [below].[61]

["Washington, Jan. 5, 1925.

["My dear Mr. President:

["The period of service which was in contemplation when I took office is now drawing to a close and, in accordance with the intention I have heretofore expressed, I beg leave to tender my resignation as Secretary of State to take effect on March 4, 1925. It will then be twenty years since I undertook public work in New York, and during that time, with the exception of a little more than two years after the armistice, I have been engaged almost continuously in the discharge of public duties. I feel that I must now ask to be relieved of official responsibility and to be permitted to return to private life. As foreign affairs are perennial, I know of no more appropriate time to do this than at the end of the present Administration.

["Permit me again to express my deep appreciation of the confidence you have reposed in me and of the privilege of serving under your leadership. I shall have an abiding memory of your unfailing kindness.

["Assuring you of my earnest support of your Administration and of my hope that, although out of office, I may still be able to be of service, I am, my dear Mr. President, with highest esteem,

Faithfully yours,
(Sgd.) Charles E. Hughes"

[President Coolidge's response was as follows:

"The White House,
Washington,
Jan. 10, 1925.

["My dear Mr. Secretary:

["Your favor of recent date, advising me that you have irrevocably decided to adopt your long-cherished intention of retiring on the 4th of March I have received with much regret.

["I can well appreciate that you are personally entitled after twenty years of public service, to seek some of the satisfactions of private life. But I cannot refrain from expressing my feeling of personal loss at the prospect of your retirement, and also the loss that must inevitably ensue when one of your ability and experience goes out of an office which he is so well qualified to fill.

["I realize, however, that this is in the nature of things, and so wish to put my emphasis upon the appreciation that I feel for your loyalty at all times to me, your many expressions by word and deed of a friendship upon which I could not set too high a value, and the exalted character and disinterested nature of the important public service that has come so constantly under my observation. I trust that you may have a well-merited repose and that satisfaction which alone can come from a consciousness that the duties of this life have been well performed.

["With kindest regards, I am

"Very cordially yours,
"(Sgd.) Calvin Coolidge."]

[61][The letters are in the Hughes Papers and quoted in] Beerits' Memorandum, "Activities During the Years 1925–1930," pp. 1–2.

The announcement of my intention to retire elicited very generous comments.[62] One of the most notable was in the London *Times*, sent by its Washington correspondent.[63]

[The article said, in part,

["As always happens when a member of the Cabinet retires, the suggestion that he goes as the result of a break with the President is made here and there, but in this case it can, with complete confidence, be set aside. Mr. Hughes has merited, and has enjoyed, the fullest confidence of both the late President Harding and President Coolidge. He has had charge of foreign affairs during a period when, important as have been the problems demanding solution, they nevertheless have had to take second place in the mind of the President . . . Add to this that neither Mr. Harding nor Mr. Coolidge had, or have, much knowledge of movements outside the borders of the United States, or the inclination to make a study of them, and the degree to which the conduct of foreign policy has been in the hands of Mr. Hughes can be judged. He will be counted, and justly, as one of the greatest of the distinguished line of Secretaries of State . . .

["When he entered the Department of State on March 4, 1921, the affairs of the world, and particularly the questions affecting America's concern with them, were in a dismaying state of muddle. Today he can see some degree of order emerging from this confusion, and he need not hesitate to take to himself a large share of credit for this improvement. The Arms Conference at Washington in 1921 and 1922, highly as it must rank, is but one of the means whereby he has helped in the reconstruction of international relationships. At the close of 1922 he made the speech at New Haven out of which came the arrangement under which Europe is seeking to adjust the question of German reparations, and whose results will be probably even more far-reaching than those of the Arms Conference. His was the plan of adherence to the World Court which was submitted to the Senate under President Harding. He has brought Mexico and the United States into amicable relationship again; he has done more than any before him found possible to correct the long-standing animosity between Chile and Peru, and in innumerable ways he has been instrumental in improving the relations between his country and Latin America and the Orient. His grasp of foreign affairs is unequaled in this country (U.S.), and his power of work is no less remarkable. His departure will be a loss not only to America, but to the rest of the world."

[On the next day, January 13, 1925, the London *Times* ran an editorial in praise of Hughes's foreign policy:[64]

["The retirement of Mr. Hughes has come as a surprise, and it is an event of more than personal significance. For nearly four anxious years Mr. Hughes has been responsible under two successive Presidents for the conduct of the foreign policy of the United States. The features of that policy which are now most familiar to the world are those with which he is particularly identified. They bear the clear impress of his intellect, of his courage, and of his shrewd sense of very complex

[62] Beerits' Memorandum, "1925–1930," pp. 5–15.
[63] London *Times*, January 12, 1925, p. 12.
[64] London *Times*, January 13, 1925, p. 13.

realities. His going means a good deal, not because it signifies or is likely to lead to any sudden change in the direction of American foreign policy, but because this policy is one thing with him and may be rather a different thing without him. Mr. Hughes, at any rate, was intelligible. The workings of his able mind had become familiar. It was possible to depend upon his interpretation of that great force which is America. He knew his America and he knew the world. He also understood, as perhaps no one else did during a very difficult period, the nature of the relations between a changing America and a world that was changing still more swiftly. He knew, moreover — and this is his chief title to fame — how to interpret these unstable and uncertain relations in a policy that was at once coherent and convincing to people at home and people abroad. He maintained the balance. He was neither retrograde nor Utopian. He knew exactly how far he could go at any given moment. Acutely sensitive to the confused impulses of the great nation which he represented, and at the same time acutely aware of the crying needs and the inveterate rivalries of the great world outside, he succeeded in conveying to the world, in speech and in action and in the manner of his restraint, something like the exact attitude of America to the chief world problems. His retirement means the removal of a very definite and familiar personal influence. It is perhaps too early to suggest that it may signify a quickening of the speed of transition in American politics. The reason given for Mr. Hughes's resignation — namely, that he wishes to devote his attention to his own private affairs — is probably quite adequate. There is no occasion to analyse in the present instance possible changes of atmosphere in Washington. It is sufficient for the present to observe that Mr. Hughes has exercised the functions of the great office he has laid down — and has exercised them with remarkable effect — during a period of swift transition in the life of the American nation. He was above all an interpreter of subtly changing moods.

["Mr. Hughes became Secretary of State, or Minister of Foreign Affairs, early in 1921, at the very moment when the United States was stoutly and emphatically affirming a strong revulsion of feeling from all those universal and absolute ideals that were identified with the name of President Wilson. It was a moment for taking stock . . . The first and natural impulse after President Wilson had set all the goals so far away in space and time was to hasten back to the familiar and the known, to return to America, and to recover in this changing world a very clear and certain sense of national identity. It was this condition of the American mind that Mr. Hughes had to interpret to the world, and he has done it extraordinarily well. It is significant that he, together with President Harding, began by diverting attention from Europe, which had grown utterly unintelligible, to the Pacific, where the United States had one urgent and intelligible problem and where the cooperation of European Powers was both possible and necessary. The experiment of the Washington Conference, in which Mr. Hughes played a leading part, was entirely successful in its immediate purpose, and it was most useful in accustoming the American people to a new form of association with European Powers in a region that particularly and obviously concerned the United States. To divert attention from the troubles of Europe to the changes of the Pacific, and to bring the representatives of Europe to Washington to consider these dangers, was the best way, at that particular moment, of instilling into the American people a sober and practical view of the new realities of world politics. After the Washington Conference the troubles of Europe did, however, remain the chief and most urgent concern of the world. Mr. Hughes, who realized this, showed great skill and caution in his method of approach. He avoided such burning issues as the League of Nations. With his strong practical mind he excluded Soviet Russia from the sphere of American relations. He approached the reparations problem gradually, merely dropping in his New Haven speech at the end of 1922 that fruitful hint which led at the end of 1923 to the institution of the Committees of Experts and in 1924, with active but circumspect American cooperation, to the adoption of the Dawes Report. Mr. Hughes has been the skillful exponent of the foreign policy of a great nation that is immersed in the trying problems of a period of transition.

["His retirement emphasizes the impression of gradual change in America; but in this country, at any rate, the fact that Mr. Kellogg has been chosen as his successor will be regarded as reassuring. During his short term as American Ambassador in London Mr. Kellogg has not merely won popularity. He has conveyed the impression that he is the 'kind' of American whose wide and genuine sympathies may be a most important factor in the coming phase of American international policy. Moreover, he has had profound and direct experience of the results of the general policy so subtly and carefully initiated by Mr. Hughes. He played a very prominent and active part in last year's London Conference, which brought about an agreement on the application of the Dawes scheme. At present he is directing his attention to those European and American financial problems which form the subject-matter of the important discussions at the Paris Conference. He has seen Europe during a very critical period. He knows personally the chief European statesman. He is especially familiar with the problems and intimate hopes of the people of this country. He will bring home a vivid and personal impression of those new conditions in Europe to which the American people is now directing a calmer and less anxious attention. His presence in Washington and his knowledge of affairs at home and abroad should be a great support to President Coolidge."]

But the friendly expression which touched me most deeply was at the luncheon given by the staff of the State Department at which Under Secretary Grew presided.[65]

[Grew said, "There are certain moments in life when one's inmost thoughts and feelings surge to the surface and cannot be denied expression — moments when conventional phrases would be wholly inadequate, wholly misplaced. Today, if only today, we are privileged to express the thoughts and feelings that are held by every man and woman at this table, every man and woman in the Department and in the field. We are at the parting of the ways with our chief, who, through four strenuous years, has held in unstinted measure our admiration and respect, our devoted loyalty, and, what is more, our deep personal affection . . . Every one of us

[65] *New York Times*, March 4, 1925, p. 18.

today must be taking stock of the influence the Secretary has exerted upon our lives; influence that will be turned to account according to our several capacities. If any greater monument to his work can be erected than the specific achievements of the last four years, it may be found in the inspiring and enduring influence he has exerted upon those around him. Because of it we shall always be better servants of the Government, better men.

["During the last four years the Department of State has attained a cohesion, an enthusiasm and an esprit de corps which has never before been equalled; a department where every man and woman works for the joy of working, and knows that his work is being directed into the right channels to constructive ends."]

During my four years in the Department I had kept careful memoranda of my interviews with Ministers and Ambassadors. These I had regarded as personal notes. But Secretary Kellogg asked me to leave them with him for a time and I did so. After they had remained in the Department for a long period, I was asked to leave them permanently as a part of the Department's official files, and I readily consented. The Department gave me a complete copy of these memoranda, which is with my papers on deposit in the Library of Congress.

Chapter XVII Practice Again *1925–1930*

I felt that I should take a long rest before resuming practice, and on March 7, 1925, with my wife and our daughter Elizabeth, I sailed for Bermuda. We remained there until June, save for my return for a few days at the end of April to deliver addresses before the American Society of International Law (of which I had been elected President), the Chamber of Commerce in New York, and the New York City Bar Association. The Summer, except for a few engagements, was spent at Lake George. And in September, after attending the annual meeting of the American Bar Association at Detroit, I took up active work at the bar. I received a warm welcome.[1]

I rejoined my old firm, Hughes, Rounds, Schurman & Dwight, and thus I had the privilege of once more enjoying an intimate professional relation with my son.

My practice was large, varied and lucrative. I shall not attempt to enumerate, much less to describe, the interesting, important and difficult cases in which I appeared.[2] As in the years before I became Secretary of State, I maintained a position of complete independence at the bar, taking cases which I thought should be argued, regardless of popular feeling, and refusing those in which for one reason or another I did not care to appear. I should add that after my son became Solicitor General of the United States (about May 1929), I refused to take cases against the Government.

When I retired from the State Department, I was quite sure that though out of office I should have abundant opportunities for public service. And so it turned out. I welcomed these opportunities and did not permit my practice to engross all my time.

[1]Beerits' Memorandum, "Activities During the Years 1925–1930," pp. 17–22. Report of the address of Senator Root at the dinner on November 10, 1925, and my reply, are in the Hughes Papers. [See, also, *New York Times*, November 11, 1925, pp. 1 and 6.]

[2]Beerits' Memorandum mentions only those to which he found references in the newspapers. [Beerits' references are taken from the files of the *New York Times*.]

Beerits' Memorandum recites many of these activities. I may mention in particular the following:

(1) Service as Chairman of the Committee on the Reorganization of the Government of New York State (1925–1926).

(2) Service as Special Master for the Supreme Court in the two references in the *Great Lakes Cases* dealing with the diversion by the Chicago Sanitary District of water from Lake Michigan involving extensive hearings and elaborate reports (1926–1929).[3]

(3) Attendance, as Chairman of the American delegation, at the Sixth Pan American Conference in Havana, Cuba (January–February 1928).[4]

(4) Attendance at the Pan American Conference at Washington on Conciliation and Arbitration (December 1928–January 1929).[5]

(5) Service as Judge of the Permanent Court of International Justice at The Hague. I was elected by the Council and Assembly of the League of Nations in September 1928 and sat in the Court during its session from May 1929 to September 1929.[6]

Also during this period, I gave my lectures at Columbia University on the Supreme Court of the United States (January–February 1927);[7] at Princeton on Our Relations with the Nations of the Western Hemisphere (May 1928);[8] and at Yale on Pan American Peace Plans (March 1929).[9]

In addition, I gave my support to various public enterprises and made

[3]Wisconsin v. Illinois, 278 U.S. 367 [1929]; 281 U.S. 179 [1930]. I may refer, in relation to my compensation for this service, to the letter of April 17, 1930, addressed to Mr. Justice Holmes (who had written the last opinion) by Newton D. Baker, chief counsel for the Great Lakes States. This letter was evidently written in reply to an inquiry by Mr. Justice Holmes. It gave a generous appraisal of my work as Special Master and stated that all of the Attorneys General of the complaining States recommended that my compensation be fixed at $60,000, plus expenses. It also stated that counsel for the Chicago Sanitary District were unwilling to join in that recommendation because they thought the amount was "grossly inadequate," their view being that $100,000 should be the minimum and that $125,000 would be "in their judgment more appropriate." Of course I was unwilling to accept and the Court could not properly grant any such sums and my compensation was fixed by the Court at $30,000 (plus my expenses of $2,775.90), which I gladly accepted.

Mr. Baker's letter, which was given to me by Justice Holmes, will be found in the Hughes Papers.

[4]See above, chapter 16.

[5]See above, chapter 16.

[6]Beerits' Memorandum, ["1925–1930"], pp. 32–37; 40, 41. On January 16, 1930, I delivered an address before the New York City Bar Association on the organization and methods of the Permanent Court. The text of this address is with my papers in the Library of Congress. Beerits' Memorandum, ["1925–1930"], p. 41, Appendix thereto No. 185.

[7][Charles Evans Hughes, *The Supreme Court of the United States* (New York, Columbia University Press, 1928).]

[8][Charles Evans Hughes, *Our Relations to the Nations of the Western Hemisphere* (Princeton, Princeton University Press, 1928).]

[9][Charles Evans Hughes, *Pan American Peace Plans* (New Haven, Yale University Press, 1929).]

Judge Hughes and his colleagues at the Permanent Court of International Justice, 1929

many speeches as chronicled by Beerits.[10] I also took an active part in the Hoover presidential campaign in the Fall of 1928.

This intense activity was made possible only by a severe regimen. By getting up very early in the morning (5 o'clock and sometimes earlier), by working at home in the morning hours so as to escape the demands at my office, I managed to find time for writing my lectures, preparing briefs for arguments, etc. As the demands upon my time, whenever available, were continuous and exacting, I sought relaxation and kept generally in good health by trips to Europe each year. These trips were made the more delightful by the fact that we journeyed through various parts of western Europe by motor and thus found opportunities for more intimate acquaintance with the countryside and the cities and villages which we visited than would otherwise have been possible.

At one time, however, in the Spring of 1927, I almost suffered a break-

[10]Beerits' Memorandum, ["1925–1930"]. [Beerits also discusses the activities to which Hughes refers below.]

Hughes with Will Rogers

down. This was due to the extra work in writing the Columbia lectures and in conducting the hearings on the first reference in the *Great Lakes Cases.* I argued my cases with difficulty and one day, walking to my hotel from the Supreme Court I suddenly felt as though a curtain had fallen over my left eye. I went at once to an oculist and found that this was caused by the breaking of a small blood vessel. Fortunately no serious harm was done, but I was strongly advised to slow up my pace. I followed this advice so far as possible and soon regained my usual vigor. In addition to our summer trips abroad, I took two winter vacations at Bermuda (February 23—March 12, 1929; December 23, 1929—January 11, 1930).

Chapter XVIII Chief Justice *1930–1941*

Soon after the death of Chief Justice White (May 19, 1921), Henry P. Fletcher, Under Secretary of State, came into my room with the air of one having an important communication, and asked me whether I should like to be Chief Justice. I immediately said, "No." There was no discussion. While Fletcher was close to President Harding, I did not take the suggestion seriously — (1) because I wished to continue as Secretary of State. I had put my hand to the plow and did not intend to turn back. And (2) because I believed from what I had heard that the President was committed to the appointment of Mr. Taft. I had the notion that Fletcher's inquiry might have been inspired by some of the irreconcilables in the Senate who feared they would wake up some fine morning and find the country in the League of Nations; they would be well satisfied if I were taken out of the diplomatic sphere.

In the early part of 1925, while I was still Secretary of State, but after I had announced my intention to leave the Department on March 4th, President Coolidge asked me if I wished to be Chief Justice, and I at once said, "No." Again, I gave the matter no serious thought as Chief Justice Taft was going strong and I had no reason to doubt that he would outlive the time when by any chance I could be deemed available.

After the election of 1928, Mr. Hoover asked me to be Secretary of State. I refused. He then sent his friend Henry M. Robinson (who had been one of the American Representatives in the formulation of the Dawes Plan) to urge me to accept, but I was firm in declining. This was because I had recently been elected by the League of Nations as a Judge of the Permanent Court of International Justice, to succeed John Bassett Moore[1] who had resigned. I was keenly interested in the Permanent Court and wished it to have the support of our Government. I feared the effect both here and in

[1][John Bassett Moore (1860–1947) was professor of international law at Columbia University, member of the Hague Tribunal (1912–1928), and judge on the Permanent Court of International Justice (1921–1928).]

other countries of my resignation, following that of Judge Moore, so soon after my election and before I had even attended a session of the Court. I wished at least to serve out the term of Judge Moore which would expire in 1930 — when a new election would be in order. Another reason, although a subordinate one, for my refusal of Mr. Hoover's offer, was that I did not wish my wife to be subjected to the heavy social demands which we had found were entailed by the position of Secretary of State.

Sometime later — but long before the Inauguration — in an interview with Mr. Hoover at his home in Washington, he remarked casually, "I don't suppose you would care to go to England." I understood that he referred to the Ambassadorship and I said, "No," adding "There is certainly one man who does not wish any office, and that is myself." This remark was doubtless prompted by the many demands that were being made upon the President-elect.

From the time of my resignation as Associate Justice in 1916, I had no desire to return to the Bench. I should certainly have refused an offer of an Associate Justiceship, and I did not for a moment contemplate being chosen as Chief Justice. I was greatly surprised when this was proposed near the end of January 1930. At President Hoover's request, I came to Washington on the night of Thursday, January 30th, and saw the President at the White House early the next morning. It appeared that Chief Justice Taft was failing rapidly; there was no hope of his recovery, and the fear was entertained that unless he resigned at once he might lapse into a mental condition which would make it impossible for him to resign and in which he might continue for an indefinite period. The President wished to be ready for the contingency of the Chief Justice's resignation and proposed my appointment. I demurred, referring to my age (I should be 68 in the following April), and my desire not to assume further and heavy responsibilities. After some discussion in which the President strongly urged me to accept, I finally told him that I would, making the qualification that I did not wish my nomination to evoke any contest over confirmation. I made this qualification because I had taken an important part in the Republican campaign of 1928 and had also been very active in my law practice. The President did not seem to think there would be opposition and urged that my acceptance would be very satisfactory to the country.

Chief Justice Taft resigned the next day (February 1st) and on the following Monday (February 3rd) the President sent my nomination to the Senate. The Senate confirmed it on February 13th.

In one of a series of biographical sketches by Henry F. Pringle, published in *The New Yorker* (July 13, 1935), Mr. Pringle said in relation to my nomination as Chief Justice:

> Mr. Hoover, according to the best information, desired to promote Associate Justice Stone, his close friend. He confided this to the late Under Secretary of State Cotton, who said that it was out of the question to pass over Mr. Hughes. But Hughes, he added, would not accept. He was earning enormous fees in private practice. Besides, Charles E. Hughes, Jr., would have to resign as Solicitor-General if his father became Chief Justice. "Offer it to Mr. Hughes," suggested Cotton. "He'll decline and then you can pick Justice Stone." — It was offered to Hughes and he promptly accepted.

I was sure that this statement was inaccurate, as it was entirely inconsistent with what President Hoover had said to me. But I did not wish to take the matter up with him or attempt to pry into what he might regard as his personal affair.

Sometime later, in the book by Pearson and Allen, *Nine Old Men*,[2] this supposed incident was somewhat elaborated. I understand that it was also stated that Mr. Hoover had made the offer to me by telephone. I have not read the book, but from extracts I have seen I judge that it has many misstatements.

In February 1937, Mr. Hoover's attention was called to this book and the story to which I have referred. On February 19, 1937, he wrote me as follows:

> My attention has been called to the serializing of a scurrilous book on the Supreme Court in one of the newspapers here, in which a purported conversation of mine with Joe Cotton at the time of your appointment is related.
>
> I scarcely need to say that no such conversation ever took place, and your own recollections will confirm mine that I never had any telephone conversations with you at all on the subject. I only write this so that you might file it away in your memoirs, although I think it is hardly necessary.
>
> I am not capable of expressing my indignation at that book and its authors. One of those men was discharged from the *Baltimore Sun* and the other from the *Christian Science Monitor* for deliberate lying. The discharge, however, did not seem to effect any moral regeneration.

I made the following reply the next day:

> I am very glad to receive your letter of the 19th. I assume you refer to the book entitled *The Nine Old Men*. I have not read it, but of course

[2][Drew Pearson and Robert S. Allen, *The Nine Old Men* (New York, Doubleday, Doran & Co., 1937), pp. 74–75.]

> I have heard a good deal about it. The story of a conversation between you and Cotton, at the time of my appointment, first appears, I think, in July, 1935, in an article by Henry F. Pringle in *The New Yorker.* Pringle is a serious writer and was friendly. What he said about your conversation with Cotton greatly disturbed me, as it was utterly inconsistent with your offer to me and with all I knew of the circumstances of my appointment. I thought of writing you about the matter, but let it pass. Your letter disposing of this story is most welcome and I shall treasure it as a valuable item for those who in the future wish to write with accuracy.
>
> I wonder if you would let me quote to Mr. Pringle the first two paragraphs of your letter. I understand that he is writing Mr. Taft's biography and he has important articles from time to time in magazines and reviews. He may be tempted to repeat this story and I should like to see it suppressed.

Mr. Hoover then wrote me again, under date of February 25, 1937, giving fully his recollection of the matter. He said:

> I was not aware when I wrote you on the 19th that this telephone story had other antecedents than those two particular imaginative minds. I had not heard of Mr. Pringle's story. You can, of course, use my letter of the 19th as you state.
>
> The whole story falls to the ground from the fact that no telephone conversation as to your appointment as Chief Justice ever took place. That you and I can both confirm. If our joint word is no good, one would think it improbable that Presidents use the telephone in such vital matters, especially in extraordinarily confidential circumstances that surrounded this incident.
>
> You may be interested in that background. I have had it locked up in the Presidential files and I have checked my memory from the White House Secretary concerned.
>
> Chief Justice Taft became indisposed early in January, 1930, and went to North Carolina for a rest. Late in the month I received word from a member of the family that unless the Chief Justice soon showed improvement, he would be compelled to resign in order to have complete rest and that this contingency was almost certain. I at once discussed the question of his possible successor with the Attorney General. To my great satisfaction, Mr. Mitchell urged your appointment. The question required no consultation with others. It was the obvious appointment.
>
> I discussed it with but one other gentleman and that was not Mr. Cotton. Mr. Cotton was Under Secretary of State and had nothing to do with judicial appointments.

I then sent word to you asking you to come to the White House. You did so on January 31. I proposed that you undertake the work. I wanted to be ready for the contingency of Mr. Taft's resignation so that I could announce it instantly and thus prevent all the political pulling and hauling that takes place over an open vacancy.

My recollection of that interview you can also confirm. We discussed the subject at great length. I urged many reasons for your taking it. You felt you should be allowed to finish your life in peace. You felt it might interfere with the career of Charles, Jr. I stated that we were anxious to keep him in the Government in some other equally important post. I urged the confidence your acceptance would bring to the whole country and that it would meet great response in the people. You promised to let me know in a day or so.

I was convinced your sense of public service would compel you to accept, and I reported to the Attorney General that he could consider it settled if Mr. Taft felt he must retire. A day or so later you sent word to me, either through Charles, Jr. or the Attorney General that you would accept.

I received Mr. Taft's resignation on February 3, and I announced your appointment the same day.

Life would certainly be better and sweeter if there were more decencies in it.

I answered this letter on March 8, 1937, as follows:

Mr. Richey has handed me your letter of February 25th and I am greatly pleased to have your statement about the circumstances of my appointment as Chief Justice.

I have a vivid memory of our interview at the White House in which you made the offer. My recollection agrees with yours in every respect, except I think that I gave my acceptance at the time of our interview subject only to the qualification that I did not wish my nomination to evoke a contest over confirmation. However, that is an unimportant detail. You were entirely at liberty to report to the Attorney General, as you did, that he could consider the matter settled if Chief Justice Taft felt that he must retire. I do not recall sending you a confirmatory message. I may add that I heard at the time that Chief Justice Taft was failing so fast that members of his family felt that he must resign at once or he might not be able even to resign. He did resign forthwith.

I am glad to have your emphatic repudiation of the absurd story which it seems has gained considerable currency. I suppose a good deal of such unfounded gossip passes into history![3]

[3]Mr. Hoover's original letters and copies of my answers are [in the Hughes Papers].

My nomination called forth generous comment in the press.[4] But despite President Hoover's confidence that there would be no important opposition in the Senate to my appointment — a confidence which I understood was confirmed by his inquiries of Senate leaders — I was most bitterly and unjustly attacked. This was on two grounds: (1) that I was reactionary in my views, having represented in my practice before the courts important corporate interests; and (2) some thought (I understand this was the attitude of Senator Glass) that in my opinions as Associate Justice as to the extent of the power of Congress over interstate commerce I had unduly interfered with the authority of the States.

While my integrity was not assailed, the attack caused me great distress. Its baselessness, as to the first ground, I thought was sufficiently shown by my work in the Insurance Investigation, by my record as Governor of New York, and by my opinions as Associate Justice. As to the second ground, it seemed to be forgotten that the Federal power which I had sustained in my opinion in the Shreveport Case,[5] to protect interstate commerce against unjust discriminations by interstate carriers through intrastate rates, had been definitely asserted by Congress itself in the Transportation Act, 1920,[6] and the ruling in the *Shreveport Case* had been reaffirmed by the Supreme Court.[7]

Not less regrettable was the exhibition of prejudice arising from a misconception of the character and effect of the activities of a lawyer in active practice. Professor Zechariah Chafee, in his work on *Free Speech in the United States*,[8] has dealt with this mistaken and essentially illiberal attitude. He observes:

> After all, the right of every man to the service of a lawyer is as much a part of our Bill of Rights and American traditions as the right of free speech. The great service of the American Civil Liberties Union consists in upholding both traditions in the face of malignant attacks. If the Union had not existed or been less efficient, hundreds of men would have gone defenseless, with only a slim chance of obtaining liberty of speech or a fair trial. We liberals cannot have it both ways. If we blame a prominent lawyer like Mr. Hughes for some of his clients, we are merely chiming in with those who constantly call the American Civil

[4]Beerits' Memorandum, "Activities During the Years 1925–1930," No. 30 on his list, pp. 48, 49; Appendix thereto, No. 198, referring to clippings [in the Hughes Papers].

[5][Houston & Texas Ry. v. United States] 234 U.S. 342 (1914). [See chap. 11, n. 44.]

[6][See Act of February 28, 1920, Ch. 91, §416(4), 41 Stat. 484, *as amended* 49 U.S.C. §13(4) (1964).]

[7]Illinois Central R. R. Co. v. Public Util. Comm'n: 245 U.S. 493, 506 [1918]; Wisconsin R.R. Comm'n v. Chicago B. & Q. R.R., 257 U.S. 563, 579 [1922].

[8][Zechariah Chafee, *Free Speech in the United States*] (Cambridge, Harvard University Press, 1941), pp. 358–62.

Liberties Union communistic because it has represented Communists along with the great many other defendants. Senator Newberry and the St. Paul Reorganization Committee are as much entitled to an able presentation of their causes as Gitlow and the I.W.W.'s. Surely liberals and radicals, above everybody else, ought to realize the dangers of spreading the doctrine that no decent lawyer should take the case of a man accused of conduct which is considered to be especially antisocial. The doctrine of guilt by association is abhorrent enough in the criminal and deportations fields without being extended into the relation between lawyer and client.

Any lawyer who is eminent enough to be named to the Supreme Court of the United States has too able and complex a mind to admit of such an easy explanation. Probably the best place to look, if you want to guess his future attitude toward important cases, is not in his file of clients or in his safe-deposit box but at the books in his private library at home.

Then, after a further discussion of the general question, he deals with my particular case as follows:

However this may be, a deeper consideration of Mr. Hughes's record would have lessened the apprehensions of men like Senator Norris. Many acts of his political career were not those of a reactionary. During the life-insurance investigations of 1906, he was considered such a dangerous radical that the leading trustees of his own university were outraged at his being invited to give a Commencement address to the alumni and stayed away from the meeting to avoid hearing him speak.[9] As Governor of New York he put the state into the forefront of progressive legislation. The best evidence of his qualifications for Chief Justice was the hundred and fifty opinions he had written as Associate Justice between 1910 and 1916 — the years when the national current had turned strongly toward social democracy and was bearing the Court along with it. Many of these opinions combined an intimate knowledge of economic problems with a forward outlook. Moreover, his subsequent representation of large business interests in court was no sure indication of his position on the bench. An office lawyer may have some difficulty in ceasing to think like the heads of wealthy corporations with whom he has spent years in close collaboration, but Mr. Hughes took merely a few weeks preparing a case, presented it in court, and then turned to the affairs of a wholly different client like the United

[9] I did not know of this. Brown University gave me the degree of LL.D. in June 1906, and then, and in later years, I always received a warm welcome there.

Mine Workers. Furthermore, this period of advocacy came long after his opinions had matured. It was unlikely that the liberalism of his earlier years was completely submerged by the arguments made after he resumed practice at sixty-two. Mr. Hughes was primarily a lawyer, and as such he felt it his duty to represent loyally the client for whom he happened to be working. While in the Republican administration he was its strongest advocate, at the bar he spoke for those who had retained him. On the bench his client is the people of the United States, and there has never been any danger that he would be inclined to represent any other.

On freedom of speech, his attitude was unmistakable. We last saw him in this book upholding the cause of the Socialist Assemblymen in New York. In an address to the graduates of Harvard Law School in June, 1920, he took a strong stand in favor of maintaining the Bill of Rights and denounced deportation outrages about which his fellow-statesmen were preserving a discreet silence. And even the unkind characterization of him by a political opponent as "One of the best minds of the eighteenth century" was praise when applied to issues of liberty. The standards of individual freedom were set high by the century of Voltaire, Jefferson, and Madison.

It was not long, I think, before it came apparent that my opponents in the Senate had been wrong in their judgment. At all events, in later years, some of the Senators who had voted against confirmation took occasion in the course of their remarks on the floor of the Senate to commend my work as Chief Justice. Several others privately expressed regret that they had opposed my appointment. I recall one interesting incident. Senator Swanson of Virginia, meeting me one day in the corridor of the Capitol not long after my appointment, voiced his congratulations, and referring to the support of my nomination by himself and other leading Democrats, he said: "I told them when the Wilson Administration was in trouble during the War because of the situation in relation to aircraft production, to whom did our President turn to get an honest and impartial investigation? It was to Mr. Hughes, and one to whom President Wilson gave that confidence we can afford to trust." [10] This struck me as an extraordinary by-product of my hard task in the Aircraft Inquiry.

[10]Beerits' Memorandum, ["1925–1930"], p. 55, gives a slightly different version. The above text gives Senator Swanson's words as nearly as I recall them. [According to Beerits, Senator Swanson said: "When our President Wilson was in the greatest straits during the War and we were attacked for irregularities in the aircraft industry, we wanted someone to make an honest, fair, and impartial investigation, someone who wouldn't capitalize the findings for political purposes. He chose Mr. Hughes, who vindicated his choice by conducting the aircraft inquiry in just that manner. It is up to us to support

Immediately on confirmation I wound up my business affairs in New York so that I was able to take my place on the Bench on February 24th, 1930. All the Justices gave me a cordial welcome.

Only three of my former associates on the Court were still in service — Justices Holmes, Van Devanter and McReynolds. Of course, I knew the others as I had frequently appeared before them as counsel and had met them from time to time. Justice Stone,[11] able, scholarly and experienced, I had known in New York, and during my last year as Secretary of State I had sat with him in the Cabinet, when he was Attorney General.

Justice Brandeis, who came to the Court just as I was leaving in 1916, was an old friend. I recall our first meeting; it was during my clerkship in the old office. Mr. Carter, always eager to boost young lawyers of ability, came to the door of the clerks' room with a keen-eyed slender young man in his wake, whom he introduced as "Louis Brandeis, the coming leader of the Boston bar." Later, and during the years before I was elected Governor, Brandeis' firm (Brandeis, Dunbar & Nutter) was the correspondent of my firms in New York and we handled for each other various legal matters.[12]

Justice Roberts,[13] a strong judge of most engaging personality, who had won high distinction at the bar by his ability, forcefulness and forensic skill, and who had been commended to the general public by his successful representation of the Government in the oil cases,[14] was appointed in May 1930 to succeed Justice Sanford.[15] My companionship with Justice Roberts was most agreeable throughout the entire period of my service as Chief Justice.

Justice Holmes resigned on January 12, 1932. He had given me a warm greeting when I returned to the Bench, and our old-time comradeship was

---

Mr. Hughes now." Claude Augustus Swanson (1862–1939) was a Congressman for twelve years and Governor of Virginia before he was appointed to the Senate to fill an unexpired term. He was elected four times in his own right, 1911–1933, and resigned to become Secretary of the Navy under President Franklin D. Roosevelt.]

[11][Harlan Fiske Stone (1872–1946) was professor of law (1902–1905) and dean of the law school (1910–1923) at Columbia University, U.S. Attorney General (1924–1925), and Supreme Court Justice (1925–1941). In 1941, he succeeded Hughes as Chief Justice and served in that office until his death in 1946.]

[12]In connection with his 75th birthday, I wrote a tribute to Justice Brandeis for the *Columbia Law Review*, XXXI (1931), pp. 1071–72.

[13][Owen Josephus Roberts (1875–1955) served on the Supreme Court from 1930 to 1945.]

[14]When counsel for the Government in the oil cases were selected, President Coolidge asked my opinion and I was glad heartily to endorse the selection of Owen J. Roberts, although I then knew him only by reputation.

[15][Edward Terry Sanford (1865–1930) served on the Supreme Court from 1923 to 1930.] Justice Sanford and Chief Justice Taft died on the same day (March 8, 1930.) See my tributes to them in the memorial exercises before the Court on June 1, 1931. 285 U.S. XXVIII–XXXVI, LIII–LVII.

Hughes and Holmes a short time before Holmes retired in 1932

at once resumed. I was amazed at the degree of vigor which he maintained in his 90th year.[16] He was still full of zest and intense in his devotion to his task. I observed that he kept his notes of arguments with the same care as in previous years, and his opinions showed no abatement of his power.[17] In the term beginning in October 1931, however, it appeared that he was slipping. While he was still able to write clearly, it became evident in the conferences of the Justices that he could no longer do his full share in the mastery of the work of the Court. In January 1932, a majority of the Justices asked me to request him to resign. I consulted Justice Brandeis who agreed that the time had come for Justice Holmes to retire and that I was the one who should take the matter up with him. The other Justices were of the same view. This was for me a highly disagreeable duty, but Justice Holmes received my suggestion, which was made as tactfully as possible, without the slightest indication of his resentment or opposition. At his request I got out from his bookshelves the applicable statute and he wrote out his resignation with his usual felicity of expression.[18]

Justice Holmes was succeeded by Justice Cardozo, whom I had known from his boyhood[19] and had frequently met at the bar of New York during my practice. There was thus brought to the Court one of the outstanding jurists of his time, a rare spirit with whom it was a privilege and constant

[16]See my radio address on the 90th birthday of Justice Holmes, [Hughes Papers].

[17]See, e.g., Wisconsin v. Illinois 281 U.S. 179 [1930]; New Jersey v. New York, 283 U.S. 336 [1931].

[18]His resignation appears in 284 U.S. VII [1932].

[19]See [chapter 5], "Early Experiences at the Bar."

delight to be associated.[20] From the time of his appointment (1932) until the retirement of Justice Van Devanter in 1937, there was no break in the membership of the Court.

When I became Chief Justice, I was well aware of the cleavage in the Court. Justices Van Devanter, McReynolds, Sutherland[21] and Butler,[22] all able men of high character, generally acted together. They had similar views as to the construction of constitutional provisions, and were classed by many as a conservative *bloc.* In my address before the Judicial Conference of the Fourth Circuit, in June 1932, I referred to the popular method of classifying judges and judicial opinions as "liberal" or "conservative," saying:[23]

> A young student wrote me the other day to ask whether I regarded myself as a "liberal" or "conservative." I answered that these labels do not interest me. I know of no accepted criterion. Some think opinions are conservative which others would regard as essentially liberal, and some opinions classed as liberal might be regarded from another point of view as decidedly illiberal. Such characterizations are not infrequently used to foster prejudices and they serve as a very poor substitute for intelligent criticism. A judge who does his work in an objective spirit, as a judge should, will address himself conscientiously to each case, and will not trouble himself about labels.

Justice Van Devanter, during the period of my service as Associate Justice, was certainly not an ultraconservative.[24] And Justice Sutherland had written broadly of the police power of the State, overruling contentions under the due process clause in sustaining the validity of a zoning ordinance in the case of *Village of Euclid v. Ambler [Realty] Co.*[25] It will be noted that in that case Justice Sutherland separated from Justices Van Devanter, McReynolds and Butler, who dissented.[26] Justice McReynolds and Justice Butler, men of exceptional vigor and of resolute determination to maintain their conceptions of the constitutional protection of property rights, were disposed to agree with each other, and they — especially

[20]Justice Cardozo died on July 9, 1938. See my announcement of his death, 305 U.S. V [1938] and my tribute to him in the memorial exercises before the Court, *[ibid.]* at XXII.

[21][George Sutherland (1862–1942) was a member of the House of Representatives (1901–1903) and the Senate (1905–1917). He was appointed to the Supreme Court in 1922 and served until 1938.]

[22][Pierce Butler (1866–1939) served on the Supreme Court from 1923 to 1939.]

[23]A printed copy of this address is in [the Hughes Papers].

[24]See [chapter 11], "The Supreme Court, 1910–1916."

[25]272 U.S. 365 [1926].

[26]See my tribute to Justices Van Devanter and Sutherland, on their retirement, in my remarks before the American Law Institute, *Proceedings,* XV (1958), pp. 32–34.

Justice Butler[27] — had a strong influence on Justices Van Devanter and Sutherland. The disposition of these Justices to work together was strengthened by their common disagreement with certain views held by Justice Brandeis, and his elaborate and forceful expositions intensified opposition.

Justice Brandeis was a resourceful colleague. As Justice Holmes became more and more conscious of the limitations of age he was inclined to depend upon the judgment of his close friend. Chief Justice Taft thought that Justice Brandeis had "two votes instead of one."[28] Justice Stone frequently agreed with Justice Brandeis, but was careful to maintain his independence and had often expressed his views in a separate opinion. Later, Justice Stone and Justice Cardozo were generally in accord in their judicial work. But not always. In *Panama Refining Company v. Ryan*,[29] holding that a section of the National Industrial Recovery Act constituted an unconstitutional attempt to delegate legislative power, Justice Stone concurred in my opinion and Justice Cardozo was the sole dissenter. In *Perry v. United States*,[30] dealing with the gold clause in Government bonds, Justice Cardozo thought, as he told me, that I was "100 percent right" and agreed on the point of unconstitutionality, while Justice Stone, concurring in the view that the plaintiff had not shown damage, thought it unnecessary to consider the constitutional question. In both cases Justice Brandeis agreed with my opinions.

As I remarked in the address (above quoted) at the Fourth Circuit Conference, I paid no attention to labels and was careful not to identify myself with any group in the Court. Very rarely, and then only casually, did I discuss cases with any Justice in advance of the conferences of all the Justices. I conceived it to be my duty as Chief Justice to make an independent study of each case and to present to the conference accurately and comprehensively, but succinctly, the questions presented and then to state my own views, seeking thus to afford a basis for the discussion of essential points.

It is frequently and mistakenly said that in these conferences the Chief Justice gives his verbal opinion last.[31] On the contrary, it is the tradition and regular practice for the Chief Justice to lead the discussion of each case by stating his opinion first and then to call for the views of the other Justices in the order of seniority. The mistaken notion is due to a con-

[27]See my tribute to Justice Butler in the memorial exercises before the Court in May 1940. 310 U.S. XV (1940).

[28]Pringle, [*The Life and Times of William Howard Taft*, 2 vols. (New York, Farrar & Rinehard, Inc., 1939)], II, 969.

[29]293 U.S. 388 (1935).

[30]294 U.S. 330 (1935).

[31]Pringle, *[Taft]*, II, 961.

fusion of the order of discussion with the order of voting. When the discussion has reached the point where the Justices are ready to vote, the Chief Justice calls the roll in the inverse order of seniority and thus casts the last vote.[32]

My heaviest work was thus in preparing for conference, not only to present adequately the argued cases but also the host of applications to be heard, that is, petitions for certiorari. My most delicate task was in the assigning of opinions.[33] I endeavored to do this with due regard to the feelings of the senior Justices and to give to each Justice the same proportion of important cases while at the same time equalizing so far as possible the burden of work. Of course, in making assignments I often had in mind the special fitness of a Justice for writing in the particular case. In all parts of my work I carefully avoided any showing of partiality. My relations with all the Justices — both with the seniors and those who came to the Court in the later years — were most happy, and whatever disagreements there were from time to time did not affect our friendship.

Justice Van Devanter retired in June 1937, and Justice Sutherland in January 1938.[34] I have reason to believe that they would have retired earlier, had it not been for the failure of Congress to make good its promise to continue to pay in full the salaries of Justices who resigned.

By the Act of April 10, 1869,[35] Congress provided: "That any judge of any court of the United States, who, having held his commission as such at least ten years, shall, after having attained the age of seventy years, resign his office, shall thereafter, during the residue of his natural life, receive the same salary which was by law payable to him at the time of his resignation."

This provision was regarded as a highly important safeguard of the independence of the federal judges. It assured one who withdrew from the opportunities of professional practice, and gave presumably his best years to judicial service, security for his old age. It was never doubted that Congress would faithfully perform its pledge. Justice Holmes referred to this provision in his letter of resignation.[36] But, after his resignation, Congress reduced his compensation. This was notice to all the Justices that they could no longer rely upon the congressional promise and their attention was drawn to the provision of the Constitution which only prohibited the diminution of their compensation "during their Continuance

[32]See my lectures, *The Supreme Court of the United States* (New York, Columbia University Press, 1928), pp. 58–60, [which I gave] before I became Chief Justice.

[33]*Ibid.*

[34]302 U.S. III [1937]; 303 U.S. IV [1938].

[35][R.S. §714 (1878), *repealed and now found at* 28 U.S.C., §371 (1964), *amending* 28 U.S.C. §375 (1940).]

[36]284 U.S. VII [1932].

in Office." [37] The Justices of the Supreme Court did not then have the privilege of retirement, as distinguished from resignation, which was accorded to the judges of the lower federal courts.[38] The result was that Justices of the Supreme Court who otherwise would have retired remained on the Bench.

This situation was remedied by the Act of 1937 which gave to the Justices of the Supreme Court "the same rights and privileges with regard to retiring, instead of resigning," which had been granted to the other federal judges, with the provision that a Justice of the Supreme Court "so retired may nevertheless be called upon by the Chief Justice and be by him authorized to perform such judicial duties, in any judicial circuit, including those of a circuit justice in such circuit, as such retired justice may be willing to undertake." [39]

It was under the provision of this Act that Justices Van Devanter and Sutherland retired.[40] Justice Van Devanter waited until the close of the current Term, and Justice Sutherland, who did not wish to create a second vacancy until the first had been filled, did not retire until the next Term (October Term, 1937) was well under way; but both had determined to retire when the privilege was accorded by the Act of 1937.

During the next two years there were three more vacancies. Justice Cardozo died in July 1938; Justice Brandeis retired in February 1939; and Justice Butler died in November 1939.[41]

On February 5, 1937, President Roosevelt startled the country by proposing the passage of a bill "To reorganize the judicial branch of the Government." [42] This provided for the appointment of an additional judge to a federal court whenever any judge of that court had attained the age of 70 years, had held his commission for at least 10 years, and within six months thereafter had neither resigned nor retired. Appointments were not to be made to the Supreme Court if they would result in more than fifteen members, and two-thirds of its members were to constitute a quorum.

[37]U.S. Const. Art. III, §1.
[38][28 U.S.C. §375 (1940), *as amended*, 28 U.S.C. §371(b) (1964).]
[39]Act of March 1, 1937, c. 21, 50 Stat. 24.
[40]302 U.S. III [1937]; 303 U.S. IV [1938].
[41]305 U.S. III [1938]; 306 U.S. III [1939]; 308 U.S. III [1939].
When (in 1941) I felt that I must no longer attempt to carry the heavy burden of the Chief Justiceship, I had a strong inclination, as I had considerable means, to "resign" and not take advantage of the retirement allowance. But on full consideration I came to the conclusion, as did Justice Brandeis whose fortune was far greater than mine, that this would make an undesirable precedent. Congress had passed the Retirement Act without qualification, and it was in the interest of the Court that the policy of the statute should be maintained.
[42]S. 1392, 75th Cong., 1st Sess. [(1937); the text of the bill is found at 81 Cong. Rec. 881 (1937)].

This proposal — viewed in the light of its chief purpose with respect to the Supreme Court — was justly regarded as an assault upon the independence of the Court and evoked strong opposition, regardless of party, in Congress and throughout the nation. The Justices of the Supreme Court took no part in the discussion of the measure, save as I dealt with the state of the business of the Court in the letter about to be mentioned.

The President in his message, evidently relying on the statements of Attorney General Cummings,[43] had stressed the need for additional judges to expedite the work of the federal courts.[44] Of course, so far as the lower federal courts were concerned, the Judicial Conference of Senior Circuit Judges met regularly in accordance with the applicable statute, considered most carefully with their special knowledge the needs of all the federal districts and circuits, and annually recommended provision for additional judges whenever this was found to be desirable. So far as the Supreme Court was concerned, there was no ground for asserting that the Court was behind in its work. On the contrary, during all the years I was Chief Justice, all cases and applications which were ready to be heard had been disposed of by the Court at each Term when it rose for the annual summer vacation.

It was true that the average age of the Justices of the Supreme Court was high. But the plain remedy, as I have already indicated, was to provide for retirement instead of resignation, thus according to the Justices of the Supreme Court a privilege similar to that granted to the judges of the lower federal courts. When that privilege was granted by the Act of March 1, 1937, retirements followed. However, despite the advanced age of several Justices, the work of the Court had been performed with thoroughness and promptness.

I made this clear in the following circumstances. Hearings on the proposed bill were had before the Judiciary Committee of the Senate.[45] As the opponents of the bill were about to present their case, Senators Wheeler, King, and Austin called upon me — I think it was on Thursday, March 18th, 1937 — and asked me to appear before the Committee.[46] I was entirely willing to do so for the purpose of giving the facts as to the work of the Court. Even in appearing for such a purpose, however, I thought it inadvisable, in view of the delicacy of the situation, that I should appear

[43][Homer Stille Cummings (1870–1956) was U.S. Attorney General from 1933 to 1939.]

[44][Message of the President to the Congress is found at 81 Cong. Rec. 877 (1937); statement of Attorney General Cummings *(ibid.)* at 879.]

[45][*Hearings on S. 1392 to Reorganize the Federal Judiciary Before the Senate Comm. on the Judiciary*, 75th Cong., 1st Sess. (1937).]

[46][Burton K. Wheeler of Montana (1882–).
[William H. King of Utah (1863–1949).
[Warren Austin of Vermont (1877–1962).]

alone. It seemed to me that at least one other member of the Court should accompany me — preferably Justice Brandeis — because of his standing as a Democrat and his reputation as a liberal judge.

I so informed the Committee. But when I consulted Justice Brandeis I found that he was strongly opposed to my appearing — or to any Justice appearing — before the Committee. I stated the desire of the Committee to have the facts as to the state of the work of the Court and suggested that I might, in response to a request, write a letter for that purpose. With that suggestion Justice Brandeis fully agreed. I found that Justice Van Devanter took the same view.

Accordingly, I telephoned to Senator King and to Senator Wheeler on the morning of Friday, March 19, 1937, that I had found that there was a very strong feeling that the Court should not come into the controversy in any way, and that it was better that I should not appear; but that if the Committee desired particular information on any matters relating to the actual work of the Court, I should be glad to answer in writing giving the facts.[47]

Later — on Saturday, as I recall it — Senator Wheeler, who I understood had seen Justice Brandeis in the interval, called on me and asked me to write such a letter. He said that the Committee desired this letter so that it could be used on Monday morning at the opening of the hearing on behalf of the opponents of the bill. This gave me very limited time but I proceeded at once to assemble the necessary data, and on Sunday, March 21st, the letter was completed. I at once took it to Justice Brandeis and to Justice Van Devanter, and each went over it carefully and approved it. I then sent it to Senator Wheeler so that he could present it at the hearing on the following morning. I had no time to consult the other Justices.[48]

[47]Memoranda of these telephone conversations [are in the Hughes Papers].

[48]Later, at the very first opportunity when the Justices were all together, I described the above circumstances and my inability to consult all the Justices, and said that I hoped that they all approved my action. Several Justices at once spoke up, saying that they did, and the others seemed to me to acquiesce. No Justice, either then or later, expressed to me a contrary view, nor throughout the period when the bill was before the Senate did I hear that any of the Justices were in any way dissatisfied with my action.

I was greatly surprised when over a year later, in an article [by Marquis Childs, "The Supreme Court Today,"] in *Harpers Magazine* (May 1938), pp. 587, 588, it was stated that certain Justices had not approved my course and that a "quarrel might well have been engendered" if it had not been avoided "by the forbearance of those who felt the Chief Justice's action had been unwarranted." [In the margin of his copy of *Harpers*, Hughes wrote: "Matter brought up in conference — & no objection to letter voiced. On the contrary, there appeared to be emphatic approval."] The article also contained some criticisms of Justice Black which in *Newsweek* (May 23, 1938) were attributed to Justice Stone. (See clippings, placed with the article in *Harpers* [in Hughes Papers], but I understand that Justice Stone later denied that he was the source of the aspersions in the article.) [Stone was, however, the source of Childs's article. See Alpheus Thomas Mason, *Harlan Fiske Stone: Pillar of the Law* (New York, Viking Press, 1956), pp. 451–455, 472–475.]

In this letter I said:[49]

> 1. The Supreme Court is fully abreast of its work. When we rose on March 15 (for the present recess) we had heard argument in cases in which certiorari had been granted only 4 weeks before — February 15. . . There is no congestion of cases upon our calendar.
>
> This gratifying condition has obtained for several years. We have been able for several terms to adjourn after disposing of all cases which are ready to be heard.

I then proceeded to describe the dockets of the Court and to give a comparative statement of the disposition of cases for the preceding six terms. This was followed by a reference to the Act of 1925, governing our appellate jurisdiction, and to our practice in dealing with petitions for certiorari. With respect to an increase in the number of Justices, I said:

> An increase in the number of Justices of the Supreme Court, apart from any question of policy, which I do not discuss, would not promote the efficiency of the Court. It is believed that it would impair that efficiency so long as the Court acts as a unit. There would be more judges to hear, more judges to confer, more judges to discuss, more judges to be convinced and to decide. The present number of justices is thought to be large enough so far as the prompt, adequate, and efficient conduct of the work of the Court is concerned. As I have said, I do not speak of any other considerations in view of the appropriate attitude of the Court in relation to questions of policy.

This letter appears to have had a devastating effect by destroying the specious contention as to the need of additional justices to expedite the work of the Court.[50] It had the effect of focusing attention on the real purpose of the bill.

And after the *Harpers'* article was published in 1938, its statement, to which I have referred, did not elicit the slightest confirmation. Certainly if there was any feeling in the Court adverse to my action in writing my letter of March 21, 1937, it was most carefully concealed.

[49]A copy of this letter appears as Appendix C (page 38) in the printed copy of the Adverse Report (June 7, 1937) of the Judiciary Committee of the Senate upon the bill. [S. Rep. No. 711, 75th Cong., 1st Sess. 38 (1937).] There are certain typographical errors in the print (page 39) which I have noted in my copy. In the same Folder are two typewritten copies as well as my original notes for the letter. [These documents are in the Hughes Papers.]

[50]Mr. Justice Jackson, in an address quoted in the *American Bar Association Journal* for August 1943 (p. 424), said that the letter "did more than any one thing to turn the tide of the Court struggle."

As the Judiciary Committee of the Senate said in its Report (June 7, 1937): "No amount of sophistry can cover up this fact. The effect of this bill is not to provide for an increase in the number of Justices composing the Supreme Court. The effect is to provide a forced retirement or, failing this, to take from the Justices affected a free exercise of their independent judgment." [51]

And after quoting from the President's address to the Nation of March 9, 1937, the Committee added: "Here is the frank acknowledgment that neither speed nor 'new blood' in the judiciary is the object of this legislation, but a change in the decisions of the Court — a subordination of the views of the judges to the views of the executive and legislative, a change to be brought about by forcing certain judges off the bench or increasing their number." [52]

The controvery had the good effect of revealing the strength of public sentiment in support of the independence of the Court. That independence is not a vague, collective attribute; it means the actual independence of the Justices. They are supposed to have shown at the bar or on the bench the learning, integrity and stability which will assure the expert, independent, and conscientious discharge of the supreme duty of maintaining the provisions of the organic law against either executive or legislative departures.

To demonstrate the lack of any sound basis for the President's assault, the Judiciary Committee reviewed the decisions of the Court, referring in particular to the cases dealing with statutes enacted after the Administration came into power in the year 1933. The Committee found that there were only eleven of these statutes which in whole or part had been invalid. Five of these decisions were by a unanimous Court and in two others eight Justices concurred.[53]

Whatever grounds for criticism of these decisions the partisans or particular theories may find, certainly when Justices Brandeis, Stone, Cardozo and Roberts, or three of them, to say nothing of myself, concurred in the decisions, it is idle to charge that they were attributable to an illiberal bias.

In two of the five unanimous decisions, Justice Brandeis wrote the opinion: *Lynch v. United States*,[54] holding void the attempt of the Economy Act of 1933 to take away certain contractual rights secured by policies of renewable term insurance issued under the War Risk Insurance Act; and *Louisville Bank v. Radford*,[55] holding invalid the Farm Mortgage

[51][S. Rep. No. 711, 75th Cong., 1st Sess. 9 (1937).]
[52][*Ibid.* at 10.]
[53][*Ibid.* at 46.] Pages 9 and 10 of printed copy in [the Hughes Papers].
[54]292 U.S. 571 [1934].
[55]295 U.S. 555 [1935].

Act (Frazier-Lempke Act) of 1934. In another of the five cases, *Hopkins [Federal Savings & Loan] Association v. Cleary,*[56] holding invalid Section 5 of the Federal Home Owner's Loan Act of 1933, Justice Cardozo wrote the opinion. In *Booth v. United States,*[57] holding unconstitutional the reduction of the compensation of a retired federal judge the opinion was delivered by Justice Roberts. In *Schechter Poultry Corporation v. United States,*[58] holding invalid the code provisions of the National Industrial Recovery Act of 1933, I wrote the opinion for the Court and Justice Cardozo wrote a separate concurring opinion in which Justice Stone joined.[59]

The two decisions which had the support of eight Justices were *Panama Refining Company v. Ryan,*[60] invalidating Section 9 (c) of the National Industrial Recovery Act because of an unconstitutional attempt to delegate legislative power, and *Perry v. United States,*[61] holding invalid the Gold Clause Resolution of 1933 as applicable to the gold clause in government obligations. I wrote the opinion for the Court in both cases. In that of the *Panama Refining Company,* Justice Cardozo was the sole dissenter,[62] while in the *Perry* case Justice Cardozo agreed with my opinion, but Justice Stone, concurring in the result upon the ground that the plaintiff had shown no damage, thought it unnecessary to pass upon the constitutional question.[63] In the other Gold Clause cases,[64] the Court sustained the validity of the Gold Clause Resolution as applied to private contracts.[65]

The remaining four statutes, of the eleven to which the Judiciary Committee refers, were the Railroad Retirement Pension Act;[66] the Agricultural

[56]296 U.S. 315 [1935].

[57]291 U.S. 339 [1934].

[58]295 U.S. 495 [1935].

[59][295 U.S. at 551 (Cardozo & Stone, J.J., concurring).] Justice Brandeis in returning my opinion in the Schechter case, wrote: "Yes. This is clear and strong — and marches to the inevitable doom."

[60]293 U.S. 388 [1935].

[61]294 U.S. 330 [1935].

[62][293 U.S. 388, 433 (1935) (Cardozo, J., dissenting).]

[63][294 U.S. 330, 358 (1935) (Stone, J., concurring).]

[64]Norman v. Baltimore & O. R.R., 294 U.S. 240 [1935]; Nortz v. United States, 294 U.S. 317 [1935].

[65]In the case of the *Panama Refining Company,* Justice Brandeis put the following endorsement upon my opinion: "Yes Sir. Complete and even the layman can understand." Commenting upon my three opinions in the Gold Clause cases *(Norman, Nortz,* and *Perry),* Justice Brandeis wrote: "The three opinions are clear and forceful. You have said all that should be said in support of our view." And Justice Cardozo, commenting separately, said as to the opinion in the Norman case: "I agree. I think this amounts to a demonstration"; and in the Perry case, Justice Cardozo wrote: "I agree, and I think it has been finely worked out."

The general dissent of four Justices in these Gold Clause cases necessarily upheld the ruling in the Perry case so far as it there held the statute invalid.

[66]Railroad Retirement Bd. v. Alton R.R., 295 U.S. 330 [1935], in which I dissented, p. 374.

Adjustment Act of 1933,[67] the Guffey Coal Act of 1935,[68] and the Municipal Bankruptcy Act of 1934.[69]

As the Committee observes, "The Municipal Bankruptcy Act, the Farm Mortgage Act, and the Railroad Pension Act, were not what have been commonly denominated administration measures." The Committee added, "When he attached his signature to the Railroad Pension Act, the President was quoted as having expressed his personal doubt as to the constitutionality of the measure."[70] The Committee also noted that the Farm Mortgage Act was later rewritten by Congress and in its new form was sustained by the Court.[71] The same may be said with respect to the Municipal Bankruptcy Act which, when reenacted with the former ground of objection removed, was sustained.[72]

In the case of the Agricultural Adjustment Act of 1933, there was a division in the Court upon the question of whether the statutory provisions were in effect coercive, in relation to agricultural production within the States. The majority of the Court were of opinion that the provisions were coercive, and that, in any view, they constituted an attempt to control and reduce production of agricultural commodities, a control of local activities which was sought to be exerted irrespective of any relation to interstate commerce. The minority, while vigorously opposing the decision, did not appear to question the invalidity of the scheme if it could be deemed coercive, saying: "The power to tax and spend is not without constitutional restraints. One restriction is that the purpose must be truly national. Another is that it may not be used to coerce action left to state control." [73] In that relation the minority opinion referred, as if to point a contrast, to the Bankhead Act of 1934 with respect to cotton production.[74]

While the Justices were thus divided upon the question as to the coercive effect of the statute, there was no division with respect to the correct interpretation of the constitutional clause giving the power "to lay and collect taxes."[75] And the most significant and important ruling in the *Butler* case was the adoption of the view of Hamilton and Story, in pref-

[67] United States v. Butler, 297 U.S. 1 [1936].

[68] Carter v. Carter Coal Co., 298 U.S. 238 [1936].

[69] Ashton v. Cameron Water Dist., 298 U.S. 513 [1936].

[70] S. Rep. No. 711, *supra*, note 49, at 18.

[71] Wright v. Vinton Branch Bank, 300 U.S. 440 [1937].

[72] United States v. Bekins, 304 U.S. 27 [1938].

[73] [United States v. Butler], 297 U.S. at 78 [(1936) (Stone, J., with Brandeis & Cardozo, JJ. dissenting)].

[74] *Ibid.*, p. 82. Compare p. 71.

[75] [U.S. Const. Art I, §8, Cl. 1.]

erence to that of Madison, as to the scope of the taxing power.[76] That this interpretation was settled by the *Butler* case was expressly recognized in the opinion of the Court upholding the Social Security Act.[77]

When Congress, acting under the commerce clause, dealt with interstate commerce in agricultural commodities in the Tobacco Inspection Act of 1935 and the Agricultural Adjustment Act of 1938, its action was sustained.[78]

In the case of *Carter v. Carter Coal Company*,[79] dealing with the Guffey Coal Act of 1935, there were three opinions. The majority, by Justice Sutherland, held that the provisions of the Act looking to the control of wages, hours and working conditions of miners engaged in the production of coal were beyond the power of Congress as an attempt to control local production, before the coal became an article of commerce. The price-fixing provisions were deemed not to be separable and their constitutionality were not considered. Justices Brandeis and Stone concurred in a dissenting opinion by Justice Cardozo.[80] He sustained the price-fixing provisions as applied to interstate commerce and to intrastate sales "where interstate prices are directly or intimately affected." He said that these provisions were separable from the labor provisions and expressed no opinion as the validity of the latter.

I wrote a separate opinion[81] to the effect that mining, which precedes commerce, is not in itself commerce, that the power to regulate commerce, while not a power to regulate industry within the State, did embrace the power to protect interstate commerce "from injury whatever may be the source of the dangers which threaten it, and to adopt any appropriate means to that end"; that Congress had adequate authority to maintain the orderly conduct of interstate commerce and to provide for the peaceful settlement of disputes which threaten it; that the labor provisions of the Act were invalid upon three counts: (1) they attempted a broad delegation

[76]I had taken this view in an opinion which I gave, while at the bar, with respect to the validity of that Federal Farm Loan Act of 1916 and of the Federal Farm Loan bonds to be issued under the Act. [Chapter 13], "1917–1921."

[Madison argued that the federal government's power to tax and spend for the public welfare, under Art. I, §8, was limited to Congress' enumerated powers also in Art. I, §8. The Court, in *Butler*, expressly rejects Madison's interpretation and adopts the Hamiltonian position, by ruling that "the power of Congress to authorize expenditure of public moneys for public purposes is not limited by the direct grants of legislative power found in the Constitution" (297 U.S. at 66). In other words, Congress' taxing power under Art. I, §8 is in addition to the enumerated powers and is limited only by the requirement that federal taxes be levied and spent for the general welfare of the country.

[Validity of the Farm Loan Act was sustained in Smith v. Kansas City Title Co., 255 U.S. 180 (1921).]

[77]Helvering v. Davis, 301 U.S. 619, 640 [1937].

[78]Currin v. Wallace, 306 U.S. 1 [1939], Mulford v. Smith, 307 U.S. 38 [1939].

[79]298 U.S. 238 [1936].

[80]*[Ibid.]* at 324.

[81]*[Ibid.]* at 317.

of legislative power without standards or limitations, (2) they permitted a group of producers and employees, according to their own views of expediency, to make rules as to hours and wages for other producers and employees who were not parties to the agreement, and (3) they went beyond any proper measure of protection of interstate commerce and attempted a broad regulation of industry within the State. I then supported the power to regulate the prices of coal sold in interstate commerce and to prohibit unfair methods of competition, and also expressed the view that the provisions in relation to interstate commerce transactions were separable from the labor provisions of the Act and should be sustained.

After the decision in the *Carter* case, the Bituminous Coal Act of 1937 was enacted. That Act eliminated the labor provisions of the earlier Act which had been held invalid and made other substantial and structural changes. The new Act was upheld by the Court in *Sunshine Coal Company v. Adkins.*[82] After pointing to the changes above noted, the Court, by Justice Douglas, observed (pp. 396, 397): "There is nothing in the *Carter* case which stands in the way. The majority of the Court in that case did not pass on the price-fixing features of the earlier Act. The Chief Justice and Mr. Justice Cardozo in separate minority opinions expressed the view that the price-fixing features of the earlier Act were constitutional. We rest on their conclusions for sustaining the present Act." [83]

The Judiciary Committee of the Senate also listed the Acts, enacted since March 4, 1933, which had been held constitutional in whole or part.[84]

It has been insinuated, and some have made, I understand, a direct charge, that the Court during the pendency of the President's bill, and for the purpose of defeating it, changed front. The reference has been to two cases, that of *West Coast Hotel Company v. Parrish,*[85] sustaining the Minimum Wage Act of the State of Washington, and *National Labor Relations Board v. Jones & Laughlin Steel Corporation,*[86] upholding the National Labor Relations Act.

These cases, both because of their intrinsic importance and because of their setting aroused public interest in an unusual degree. But the notion that either of these cases, or any others, were influenced in the slightest degree by the President's attitude, or his proposal to reorganize the Court, is utterly baseless.

While what I am about to say would ordinarily be held in confidence, I

[82]310 U.S. 381 [1940].
[83][*Ibid.*] at 396.
[84]S. Rep. No. 711, *supra*, note 49, at 47.
[85]300 U.S. 379 [1937].
[86]301 U.S. 1 [1937].

feel that I am justified in revealing it in defense of the Court's integrity. The case of the *West Coast Hotel Company* was argued, and was brought before the conference of the Justices for decision, before the President's attack upon the Court had been made or anyone had any notion that it was coming. It then appeared that four Justices, that is, myself, and Justices Brandeis, Roberts and Cardozo, were in favor of sustaining the statute and overruling the case of *Adkins v. Children's Hospital.*[87] At that time, Justice Stone was absent on account of illness, but his view that a minimum wage statute, such as that under consideration, was within the state's power was well known and had been definitely expressed in his dissenting opinion in the case of *Morehead v. New York ex rel. Tipaldo.*[88] As four of the Justices were in favor of sustaining the Washington statute, it was manifest that there would be a majority of five Justices as soon as Justice Stone was able to attend conference. Accordingly we decided to hold the case. Justice Stone returned about February 1, 1937, and agreed to the affirmance of the Washington judgment. The opinions, majority and minority, were prepared in due course and were announced on March 29th. The President's proposal had not the slightest effect on our decision.

As to my personal position, I may say that my views with respect to the limitations of "liberty of contract" had been stated, when I was an Associate Justice, in writing the opinion for the Court in *Chicago, Burlington & Quincy R.R. Co. v. McGuire.*[89] And when the Oregon Minimum Wage Act was before the Court in 1916, just before I left the Bench, I had expressed in conference my view in support of that statute. At that time reargument was ordered and later, after I had resigned, the case was reargued and the judgment of the state court was affirmed by an equally divided court [in] *Stettler v. O'Hara.*[90] I was not a member of the Court when the *Adkins* case was decided in 1923.

I wrote the opinions for the Court in the *Jones & Laughlin* case,[91] and other cases sustaining the National Labor Relations Act. These opinions were in no sense a departure from the views I had long held and expressed. As Justice Stone said in his article in the *American Bar Association Journal* upon my retirement as Chief Justice, they upheld "under the Commerce Clause the constitutional validity of the National Labor Relations Act upon principles which twenty-four years before" I had stated with clarity and precision in the *Minnesota Rate Cases.*"[92] And Justice

[87] 261 U.S. 525 [1923].
[88] 298 U.S. 587, 631 [1936].
[89] 219 U.S. 549 [1911].
[90] 243 U.S. 629 [1917].
[91] 301 U.S. 1 [1937].
[92] *American Bar Association Journal*, XXVII, (1941), p. 408.

Jackson[93] (then Attorney General) in his article in the same issue referred to my opinion in 1911 in the *McGuire* case as laying "the foundation" which later enabled me "to sustain state regulation of minimum wages, and thereby overrule the much-criticized decision which had meanwhile been rendered" in the *Adkins* case.[94] Attorney General Biddle, referring to my opinions sustaining the National Labor Relations Act, observed that "this was not new ground for the author of the *Minnesota Rate Cases.*"[95]

Nor can it be supposed that the President's proposal had any effect upon the views of Justices Brandeis, Stone and Cardozo in relation to the National Labor Relations Act. And as to Justice Roberts, I feel that I am able to say with definiteness that his view in favor of these decisions of the Court would have been the same if the President's bill had never been proposed. The Court acted with complete independence.[96]

In considering the President's proposal, I have thought it advisable to refer to the few cases I have mentioned in that connection, but it is not my purpose to review the opinions of the Court during my Chief Justiceship. I have set forth in my opinions the reasons I deemed controlling and I leave these to be appraised by others.[97]

My personal relations with President Roosevelt have always been agreeable. In his occasional letters and whenever I have seen him, he has shown the utmost cordiality and friendliness. I may mention one interesting incident. When King George and Queen Elizabeth visited Washington in June 1939, I was unable to attend the state dinner. The President, learning this, personally called Mrs. Hughes on the telephone and, expressing his regret, said in his usual gay manner that he wished her to come and that he was going to seat her next to the King. And this he did.

After I had administered to him the oath of office for the third time, I told him that I had an impish desire to break the solemnity of that occasion by remarking: "Franklin, don't you think this is getting to be a trifle monotonous!"[98]

The Jurisdictional Act of February 13, 1925, makes it possible for the Supreme Court to devote itself to those cases which demand consideration

93[Robert Houghwout Jackson (1892–1954) was U.S. Solicitor General (1938–1939), U.S. Attorney General (1940–1941) and Supreme Court Justice (1941–1954).]

94*Ibid.*, p. 410.

95*Columbia Law Review*, XLI (1941), pp. 1157, 1158.

96[Justice Roberts left a memoir on the *West Coast Hotel* case. See Felix Frankfurter, "Mr. Justice Roberts," *University of Pennsylvania Review*, CIV (1955), 313–316.]

97[See F. D. G. Ribble, "The Constitutional Doctrines of Chief Justice Hughes," *Columbia Law Review*, XLI (1941), 1190–1215; Samuel Hendel, *Charles Evans Hughes and the Supreme Court* (New York, Russell & Russell, 1951), chapters 9–21.]

98This was a conversation in his Library at the White House after a Judicial Dinner.

because of the public importance of the questions involved.[99] But while the Supreme Court was thus able to keep abreast of its work, and it controlled its own procedure, there was serious need of improvement in the procedure of the lower Federal Courts and the Supreme Court gave this matter considerable attention.

One of the most pressing needs was the expediting of appeals in criminal cases. On the recommendation of Attorney General Mitchell, Congress passed the Act of February 24, 1933,[100] giving the Supreme Court authority to prescribe rules with respect to proceedings in criminal cases in the Federal Courts, after verdict; this was amended by the Act of March 8, 1934,[101] so as to make the Act applicable to proceedings after finding of guilt by a trial court where a jury is waived. The Department of Justice, under the supervision of Solicitor General Thacher, made a careful study of federal practice and procedure, and there was correspondence with the Federal Judges and with representatives of the bar. The ensuing recommendations were submitted to the Supreme Court, and I also laid the matter before the Senior Circuit Judges.[102] The Court promulgated its rules as to criminal appeals on May 7, 1934.[103]

Procedural reform in civil cases in the Federal Courts was another subject demanding attention. For many years the American Bar Association had sought to have Congress provide for uniformity in federal procedure in actions at law by the passage of an Act conferring upon the Supreme Court authority in such cases similar to that which the Court exercised with respect to equity practice. The proposal had been strongly opposed by lawyers who wished to retain in actions at law the practice with which they had become familiar in the state courts. And many lawyers and judges in some States felt that their particular practice was so free from procedural difficulties that it should be left alone. This was especially the case in New England.

Finally, Congress, having broken the ice in dealing with criminal appeals, passed the Act of June 19, 1934,[104] authorizing the Supreme Court to prescribe general rules to govern procedure in civil actions at law, and

[99]The method of the Court in the operation of the Jurisdictional Act was described in my remarks before the American Law Institute in May 1937. *American Law Institute Proceedings*, XIV [1937], pp. 35, 36. See, also, my letter to Senator Wheeler of March 21, 1937; [S. Rep. No. 711.] *supra*, [note 42], pp. 38, 39.

[100][47 Stat. 904 (1933), *as amended* 18 U.S.C. §3772 (1964).]

[101][48 Stat. 399 (1934), *as amended* 18 U.S.C. §3772 (1964).]

[102]See my remarks before the American Law Institute in May 1934. *Proceedings*, XI [1934], pp. 316–318. [Thomas Day Thacher (1881–1950). He was a U.S. District Judge (1925–1930), U.S. Solicitor General (1930–1933), and later a New York Court of Appeals judge (1943–1948).]

[103]292 U.S. 659 (1934).

[104][48 Stat. 1064 (1934), *as amended*, 28 U.S.C. §2072 (Supp. V, 1970).]

at the same time the Court was also authorized, at its option, to set up a uniform system of procedure for both actions at law and suits in equity. In the latter event, the rules were not to become effective until after the close of a regular session of Congress at the beginning of which the rules had been reported to Congress by the Attorney General. After careful consideration, the Court decided not to prepare rules limited to common law cases but to provide a unified system so far as that might be done without the violation of any substantive right. The desirability of such a system had been emphasized by Chief Justice Taft, and in my remarks before the American Law Institute at its meeting in May 1935, I discussed the pros and cons in connection with the announcement of the Court's action.[105]

It was manifestly necessary that the Supreme Court should have the most expert assistance in devising the new rules, and for this purpose the Court appointed an Advisory Committee. Among its members were professors of law who had specialized in the study of procedure and experienced practitioners from all parts of the country. This highly competent committee worked diligently at its task. Its preliminary draft of rules was distributed for the criticism of judges and lawyers throughout the country and the rules were debated in local conferences. After considering various criticisms and suggestions, the committee prepared a final draft. This was examined by the Supreme Court and, with certain changes, the proposed rules were adopted. They were forwarded to the Attorney General in December 1937,[106] were presented by him to Congress at the beginning of the regular session in January 1938,[107] and after the close of that session were promulgated.[108]

These new Federal Rules of Civil Procedure have worked well.[109] This happy result was followed by another notable advance in promoting procedural reform in criminal cases. I have already referred to the rules related to proceedings after verdict, or after finding of guilt in case tried without a jury. By the Act of June 29, 1940, the Supreme Court was authorized to prescribe rules in all criminal proceedings prior to verdict or finding. The Court promptly followed the same method which had been so successful in the drafting of the civil rules, by appointing an Advisory Committee composed of professors of law who had specialized in the study of criminal procedure and of eminent lawyers from different parts of the country.[110] This committee has been assiduous in its work and

[105]American Law Institute, *Proceedings*, XII [1935], pp. 56–60.
[106]308 U.S. 649 [1937].
[107]*[Ibid.]* at 647.
[108]*[Ibid.]* at 645. See American Law Institute *Proceedings*, XIII [1935–36], pp. 61, 63; XIV [1936–1937], pp. 32, 37; XV [1937–38], pp. 32, 34.
[109]*Ibid.*, XVII [1939–1940], pp. 28, 29.
[110]American Law Institute, *Proceedings*, XVIII, [1940–41], pp. 24, 25.

it is expected that in due course a satisfactory body of rules will be promulgated.

More was needed than the formulation and adoption of rules. To secure promptness and efficiency in administering federal justice, it was desirable to have machinery for constant and adequate supervision of the work of the courts. Under the Act of September 14, 1922,[111] the Senior Circuit Judges held a conference each year in Washington just before the opening of the October Term. The Chief Justice of the Supreme Court, under the statute, called the conference and acted as its presiding officer. The Attorney General attended the opening session and submitted his report of the condition of the dockets and his recommendations. The Senior Circuit Judges were required to submit reports (furnished to them respectively by the District Judges) of the state of business in the District Courts with recommendations as to the need of additional judicial assistance.[112]

I was deeply interested in the work of this conference which gave a general view of conditions in the various districts, the number and kind of litigated cases, and the extent of delays in their disposition. It seemed to me that here was the nucleus of a supervisory organization.

This statutory conference was supplemented by voluntary conferences of the Judges in several of the circuits. These conferences gave an admirable opportunity for bringing the District and Circuit Judges together, with members of the bar, to consider local conditions and means of improvement.

It became apparent, however, that there should be a more thoroughgoing organization. Complaints of delays, and occasionally of maladministration, would come to members of Congress, and there was danger that some sort of an organization would be set up putting the courts under direct executive or legislative supervision. This was thought to portend what might be a menace to judicial independence. Judges also had their complaints of difficulties in having adequate attention paid to their needs by the administrative agency of the Department of Justice, and the Department desired to be relieved of its duties with respect to budgetary requirements, supplies, etc.

Attorney General Cummings had procured the introduction of a bill in Congress for the creation of an administrative office of the United States courts in order to give to the courts the management of their own affairs and to secure an improved supervision of their work. And the Attorney General sought the approval of this bill by the Conference of the Senior

[111] [Ch. 306, §2, 42 Stat. 837 (1922).]

[112] Reports of the proceedings of these annual conferences, issued by the Chief Justice, were included in the Annual Reports of the Attorney General.

Circuit Judges at its meeting in September 1938. I had given the matter close consideration and made my recommendations. The Conference appointed a committee under the chairmanship of Chief Justice Groner of the Court of Appeals of the District of Columbia to perfect the pending measure. Through the efforts of this committee, especially those of Chief Justice [D. Lawrence] Groner [1873–1957] and Judges John J. Parker [1885–1958] and Kimbrough Stone [1875–1958], in collaboration with the Attorney General and with sympathetic consideration of the Judiciary Committees of the House and Senate, the Act of August 7, 1939,[113] for the administration of the United States Courts was passed.

I discussed this Act in my remarks before the American Law Institute in May 1940.[114] I noted that the Administrative office, created by the Act, has two distinct functions: One, to deal with the business affairs of the federal courts, previously handled by the Department of Justice, which embraces budgets, audits, personnel, and the procurement of facilities and supplies; and the other the appropriate supervision of the work of the courts. There were thus two main divisions of the office (1) The Division of Business Administration and (2) The Division of Procedural Studies and Statistics. It was expected that thus there would be real progress in the development of an adequate system of judicial statistics. I also noted that one of the best features of the plan is that it provides for a natural and helpful evolution of the Conference of Senior Circuit Judges. The Conference has the power and duty to supervise and direct the Director of the Administrative Office and thus has the immediate responsibility of looking after the work of the federal courts, other than the Supreme Court. Another provision of the Act gives opportunity for speedy correction of local defects in administration and for consultation as to local problems. All the Circuit Judges in a circuit are constituted as a Judicial Council for that circuit and to that Council the Senior Circuit Judge submits the reports that he has received and his recommendations. The District Judges are to carry out promptly the directions of the Council as to the administration of business in their respective courts. While there is to be no interference with judicial prerogatives and proper judicial independence, the Circuit Judges are thus empowered to maintain a constant supervision of the administration of justice in their circuits. Then provision was made for the holding annually in each circuit a Conference of all the Judges of the Circuit, both District Judges and Circuit Judges, with participation by representatives of the bar, if that is desired. This constitutes a forum dealing with local difficulties in administration, and

[113][53 Stat. 1223 (1939), *as amended*, 28 U.S.C. §601 (1964).]
[114]American Law Institute, *Proceedings*, XVII [1939–1940], pp. 30, 31.

through these judicial conferences in the circuits it is expected that matters will be developed for the consideration of the Conference of Senior Circuit Judges.

Under the Act, the Director of the Administrative Office and the Assistant Director were appointed by the Supreme Court of the United States. The Court was most fortunate in obtaining the services of Henry P. Chandler [1880–] as Director and Elmore Whitehurst as Assistant Director, aided by Will Shafroth [1894–] as Chief of the Division of Procedural Studies and Statistics. The Administrative Office was thus thoroughly organized and has amply fulfilled the promise of the Act.[115]

In addition to the work of the Court, I met a large number of incidental demands. In August 1930, I attended the meeting of the American Bar Association in Chicago when we welcomed the members of the British Bar who returned the visit of the American lawyers to Great Britain (1924). And in September 1930, I gave a historical address at the 100th anniversary of the Founding of the Rhode Island Chapter of Phi Beta Kappa at Brown University. In September 1931, I spoke at the unveiling of the bust of Chief Justice Taney at Frederick, Maryland, and at a similar ceremony in honor of Madison at Richmond, Virginia.

In June of 1932, 1933 and 1934, I attended the Conference of the Judges of the Fourth Circuit at Asheville, North Carolina. In October 1932, I spoke at the laying of the cornerstone of the new Supreme Court Building.

It was also in the years 1931–1932 that I was engaged in the difficult task of determining the boundary between Guatemala and Honduras under the Arbitration Treaty of 1930. By this Treaty a Special Boundary Tribunal was constituted, consisting of myself as President, Luis Castro Urena of Costa Rica, and Emilio Bello-Codesido of Chile, Arbitrators. The Award was made in January 1933. It was unanimous and was accepted by both States.

During the period above mentioned, I also yielded to a number of requests for speeches, but in later years I accepted few invitations. I made an exception of the large gathering of judges and lawyers at the annual meetings of the American Law Institute, held at Washington in May, when I gave a brief address at the opening session.

I spoke at the college commencements in June 1937, on the graduation of my grandsons, Charles E. Hughes, 3d (at Brown), and Henry Stuart Hughes (at Amherst). On March 4, 1939, I had the privilege of speaking at the Joint Session of the Houses of Congress in Celebration of the 150th Anniversary of the Commencement of the First Congress.[116]

[115] *Ibid.*, XVIII [1940–1941], p. 25.

[116] [84 Cong. Rec. 2249 (1939).] Copies of various speeches are in [the Hughes Papers].

The Chief Justice addressing Congress on March 4, 1939

Hughes and his family on his eightieth birthday

Hughes and his daughter, Mrs. William T. Gossett, at the Wianno Club, Cape Cod, shortly before his death in 1948

I made good use of the summer vacations in order to obtain a change of scene and physical and intellectual refreshment. We made three trips to Europe. In 1930, we landed at Cherbourg, motored through Normandy and then, after proceeding up the Rhine, spent a few days at Lausanne. From there we journeyed to Paris and sailed for home in time to attend the meeting of the American Bar Association in Chicago in the middle of August. In 1931, we took the Mediterranean route, stopping at Sicily, where we spent about a week, and thence we went by airplane to Ostia, and after a short stay in Rome we motored to Florence, Siena, Bologna, the Italian Lakes, and St. Moritz. We made a long stay in the Engadine, and from there we went directly to London, which we made our headquarters for many delightful motor trips. We returned early in September.

Our next and last trip to Europe was in 1938. We again took the Mediterranean route, landing at Naples, whence we motored by easy stages to

Rome, Florence, Venice, The Dolomites, and then to St. Moritz, Lucerne, Lausanne and Paris. We returned to New York on August 22d.

In the other years, we traveled quite extensively in northern United States and Canada. In 1932, we motored to Montreal and on to Quebec and Murray Bay, returning through Maine and New Hampshire. In 1933, we visited the North Shore (Magnolia, Mass.), the White Mountains and the Adirondacks. In 1934, we went again to the White Mountains and from there to the Seigniory Club (between Montreal and Ottawa). We then motored south to Skytop, Pa., which became one of our best liked resorts. In 1935, after again visiting the White Mountains, we took the trip by steamer through the Great Lakes from Buffalo to Duluth. Thence we journeyed to Minneapolis and went on to the Yellowstone Park. From there we motored to Glacier Park and to Banff and Lake Louise, returning by train to Montreal. In 1936, we enjoyed a visit to St. Andrews, New Brunswick, going and returning by motor. In 1937, we found our way to Jasper Park, Alberta, and in that charming spot we spent a large part of the summer in the years 1939 to 1942, inclusive.

There was a large amount of work to be done during each summer in preparation for the October Term of the Court. This was in examining the host of applications for certioraris, the jurisdictional statements upon appeals, and the applications to be heard *in forma pauperis*. The law clerks of the Justices did the preliminary work in examining records and briefs and preparing copious memoranda. I had highly competent law clerks. Reynolds Robertson, Francis R. Kirkham, Richard W. Hogue, Jr., and Edwin McElwain served in succession with great ability. But, while availing myself of their memoranda, I made it a practice to check them by my own examination of the records and briefs and I made my own notes, which were as succinct as possible. I presented each case with my views to the conferences of the Court which were held in the opening week of the Term, when we passed upon the various applications.

For this preparation, the records and briefs in all cases were sent to me by mail during the Summer, wherever I made a long stay, as in the White Mountains and in Canada, the sending of the mail bags to Jasper Park, Canada, and their return being facilitated by arrangement between the United States and Canadian postal authorities.

When we made our trips to Europe, I returned to New York in time to catch up with my work by continuous application until the Term opened. (In 1931, while at St. Moritz, I prepared in large part my speeches on Taney and Madison for which I had taken notes and material.)

In 1939 and 1940, I hit upon the expedient of employing at Skytop, in the latter part of August and in September, a court stenographer from Scranton to help me finish the Summer's task.

While I was Secretary of State, I maintained a residence in Washington at 1529 18th Street, Northwest, which I held under lease. I retained, however, my legal residence in New York. But when I became Chief Justice, I decided to establish my permanent home and legal residence in Washington and in the Spring of 1930 I purchased the house at 2223 R Street, Northwest. That has been our residence since September 1930.

I had excellent health during my service as Chief Justice until March 1939. Then I suddenly found myself becoming very weak. When on March 4th I spoke at the Joint Session held in celebration of the 150th Anniversary of the first session of Congress, I was not sure that I could reach the rostrum. But I summoned all my reserves and made my speech with what appeared to be my usual vigor. This day (Saturday) also was our conference day and I had a long afternoon of hard work. In the evening, Mrs. Hughes and I gave one of our large dinners. On the following Monday, I called my physician and discovered that I had a bleeding duodenal ulcer and had sustained a serious loss of blood. This compelled me to give up work for a few weeks, but my trouble yielded to rest and diet, and by the middle of April I was able to resume under full steam. At the close of the Term (in the beginning of June) I thought that I was threatened with a recurrence. This turned out to be a false alarm, but the necessary explorations laid me up for a few days.

With these exceptions (in the Spring of 1939) I did not miss a session of the Court, or a court conference, or indeed a single hour of the work of the Court from the time I took my seat in February 1930 until June 1941.

While I was still in good health, I then realized that the work was too heavy for me at my age, as it was increasingly difficult to maintain the necessary number of hours of sustained effort. I had criticized judges for trying to hang on after they were unable to bring full vigor to their task.[117] As I felt that I could not keep the pace that I had set for myself as Chief Justice, I decided that the time had come to follow my own advice.

My retirement was announced on the last day of the Term, to take effect on July 1, 1941.[118]

Soon after, the President asked me to take lunch with him at the Executive offices and discussed with me the appointment of my successor. I strongly recommended Mr. Justice Stone.

In bringing these notes to a close, I should not fail to add that throughout the eleven years of my Chief Justiceship and since my retirement I have had the faithful and efficient service of my secretary, Wendell W. Mischler, who had served Chief Justice Taft in a like capacity.

[117]See my lectures on the Supreme Court [*The Supreme Court of the United States* (New York, Columbia University Press, 1928), pp. 74–77].

[118][313 U.S. III (1941).]

Appendix I Ancestry

David Charles Hughes was the youngest of six children. He had three brothers, Samuel, Jabez and John Richard, and two sisters, Jane and Eliza. Samuel died in his young manhood. My father had great respect for the intellectual ability of his brother Jabez who I understand was a man of wide reading and independence of character. I saw him when I was in South Wales in 1873 and I remember him as a kindly man, full of humor.[1] In that summer we also visited the home of John Richard Hughes in Anglesey, North Wales. He was an eminent preacher of the Calvinistic Methodist denomination and I have a vivid memory of his eloquence. It deeply affected me althought I was but a boy and could not understand a word he said. He had what the Welsh call "hwyl" or what a recent writer has described as "that mysterious power of the Celtic temperament which makes the orator say what he hardly knows he is saying, and excites his listeners without their knowing why they are excited." [2] I also found my Uncle John to be a delightful companion. I visited him again on my trip to Wales in 1885 and spent two days with him. He was most interested in everything concerning the United States and was very well informed with respect to our government and "way of life." He died in 1893 in his sixty-fifth year.[3] His son, Howell Harris Hughes, has had a distinguished career as a preacher and for some years has been Principal of the Theological

[1]After the death of my Uncle Jabez, a few years later, his widow and their daughter, Mary Ann Hughes, with the latter's husband, T. P. Thomas, came to the United States about 1880 and made their home in Texas. I am informed that Mrs. Jabez Hughes died soon after their arrival and that her daughter died in 1919. T. P. Thomas died in 1936 and was survived by three daughters and a son. In recent years I have had some correspondence with one of the daughters, Mrs. J. F. Scarff, of Waco, Texas, and with the son, R. A. Thomas, of Benbrook, Texas.

[2]André Maurois, referring to Lloyd George in *The Edwardian Era* [translated by Hamish Miles (New York, D. Appleton Century Company, 1933)], p. 261.

[3]I have a memorial card showing the date of his death and a photograph; also an interesting letter from him to my father, dated September 12th, 1873, in which he refers to our visit in that summer and the birth of his son, Howell Harris Hughes.

College of the Presbyterian Church of Wales in Aberystwyth. Another son is J. R. Lloyd Hughes, a journalist, connected with the Yorkshire *Post.* I understand that he has written popular stories of Anglesey life. A daughter of John Richard Hughes is Mrs. Eames, the wife of W. Eames, who was editor, until his retirement, of the *Manchester Guardian Commercial.* Mrs. Eames is the author of a Welsh "Cookery Book." [4]

My father's sister Jane was a resolute woman with a dominating personality and had considerable business ability. She took great umbrage at my father's determination to come to this country. She married Edward Jones, a colliery agent at Abertillery, Monmouthshire, who was a man of importance in that community. He had a general store and after his death, which took place before my visit to Wales in 1873, my Aunt Jane continued the business and was the local postmistress. Her eldest son Richard came to the United States about 1870 and soon after met a tragic death through an accident at a mine in southern Illinois.[5] Another son, Samuel, whom I met on my visit to South Wales in 1873, and again in 1885, was a man of parts. He remained, I believe, at Abertillery, became a local magistrate, and rose to distinction in that part of the country. Augustus Jones, another son of my Aunt Jane, died about 1886 at the age of twenty-four or twenty-five. My Aunt Jane's daughter Lizzie married a preacher, Mr. Rhys.[6]

My father's other sister, Eliza, married Mr. Thomas Roberts who kept an inn at Brynmawr. She died in 1867. She had two children, Thomas Roberts who resided in Manchester, England, and, I understand, died many years ago, and Annie Roberts who married a Mr. Rogers. The latter had a large family and lived in South Wales. I visited them in 1885, at Aberbeeg, and found a delightful group of exceptionally fine boys and girls.[7]

[My mother's] maternal line went back to Jacob Burhans who came to this country from The Netherlands and settled at Wiltwyck (Kingston, New York) about 1660. In that year he appears as a soldier in the Nether-

[4]My authority for the above as to J. R. L. Hughes and Mrs. W. Eames is a clipping which I find among my papers. A son of Howell Harris Hughes, named Arthur Emlyn Harris Hughes, came to Canada in 1936 and wrote me. I made inquiry of his father and received a letter in reply under date of July 14, 1936.

I frequently receive letters from persons bearing the name of Hughes claiming relationship. Their claims have always appeared to be unfounded. I have no knowledge of any relative by the name of Hughes in the United States.

[5]I believe that he was employed as a superintendent or inspector at the time.

[6]See letter from Mrs. Lizzie Rhys, dated November 18, 1906, [Hughes Papers].

In 1924, when I was in London with the members of the American Bar Association, my cousin Lizzie with her daughter, the latter's husband and their daughter, came to London and I had the pleasure of calling upon them. Their home was in Cardiff.

[7]See letter from my cousin, Lizzie Jones, to Mrs. D. C. Hughes, dated Dec. 24, 1867. I assume that the Aunt there mentioned was my Aunt Eliza. See, also, letter from Mrs. Annie Rogers to D. C. Hughes and Mrs. Hughes, dated March 21, 1907, [Hughes Papers].

landish service on the *Esopus* in the company of "his Noble Honor the Director-General." His name is third on the list of church members at Wiltwyck when the First Dutch Reformed Church was organized. It appears that he was appointed "Collector by the Hon. Lord Petrus Stuyvesant on the 21st of November, 1661," and that in 1666 he was elected and confirmed as Schepen (Justice-Magistrate) of the court at Wiltwyck. His son, Jan Burhans, arrived in America in 1663 on the ship *Bonte Koe* (Spotted Cow). Jan Burhans with two others obtained a patent at Brabant (Esopus). In 1673 he was appointed Magistrate for the town of Swaenburgh and in 1693 he became Magistrate of the Town Court at Kingston. He married Helena Traphagen.[8]

Mr. Justice Willis Van Devanter of the Supreme Court (whose wife, Hannah Dorman [Dollie] Burhans, was a descendant of Jacob Burhans),[9] by his researches in Holland in 1935 discovered additional data. He found that Jacob Burhans was a son of Barent Burhans and his first wife Elizabeth, who were married in Deventer, Holland, on November 11, 1593. The church entry recites that both had come from Wesel, Germany, a place near the Dutch frontier.[10] They had three children, born in Deventer, one of whom was the Jacob Burhans who came to America and was living in Wiltwyck (Kingston, New York) in 1660. Barent was a weaver and had two houses on Polstraat in Deventer, one called "The Cotton Tree" and the other "The Blue Sheep" — and was for several years an Elder in the Reformed Dutch Church in Deventer. His first wife, Elizabeth, died in 1603. Barent Burhans died in 1622. His son Jacob was then a minor, although approaching maturity. Guardians were appointed for him and in 1625 he received his share of the proceeds of his father's estate. It also appears that Jacob Burhans had two sons, one called Barent and the other Jan. Barent arrived in New Amsterdam in 1663 with his brother Jan. Nothing more is known of him. In the records at Deventer the family name is variously spelled Burhans, Boerhans and Buerhans, but the records make it plain that these are mere variations in the spelling of the same name. Mr. Justice Van Devanter also states that "the house in which Barent Burhans lived in Deventer was just across the street from the house in which an ancestor of mine lived at the time." [11] It is not unlikely that over 300 years ago my ancestor and Justice Van Devanter's were

[8][Samuel] Burhans *Genealogy [:Descendants from the First Ancestors in America — Jacob Burhans, 1660, and His Son Jan Burhans, 1663, to 1893.* (New York, printed for private distribution, 1894).]

[9]*Ibid.*, p. 195, No. 3537.

[10]Wesel is also near Alt Schermbeck, Germany, to which the compiler of the Burhans *Genealogy* refers. He adds that it "is quite certain that the ancestors of the American Burhans family were of Holland extraction." *Ibid.*, Preface, p. iv.

[11]See Mr. Justice Van Devanter's letter to me under date of November 2, 1935, with memorandum entitled "Supplement to Burhans *Genealogy*," [Hughes Papers].

chatting over their schnapps and testifying to the virtues of the remarkable new plant being imported from Virginia, quite unable to imagine the part their remote descendants would be called upon to play in the marvelous New World.

My mother was in the eighth generation from Jacob Burhans, being descended from David Burhans, the ninth son of Jan Burhans.[12] The line was Dutch, save for an infusion of German in the fifth generation, when Deborah Ostrander, the granddaughter of David Burhans, married Leonard Krows. The latter was born in Kingston, the son of John Krows of Germany and Mareitje Beem, widow of Jacob Terpenning. Both John Krows and his son Leonard fought in the Revolutionary War as soldiers of the First Regiment of Ulster County.[13] It appears that Leonard Krows enlisted when he was only sixteen years old. He was wounded in battle and received a pension.[14] The eldest daughter of Leonard Krows (Mariah) married Tjerck Vilie Terpenning,[15] whose father, Henricus (Henry) Terpenning fought in the Revolution and received a commission from General Washington.[16] Tjerck Vilie Terpening and Mariah Krows (Terpenning) were the parents of Margaret Ann Terpenning, my maternal grandmother, who was born in 1810 and died in 1882. She married William Connelly, Jr., on July 11, 1829.[17]

William Connelly, Jr., who was born in Shandaken, Ulster County, New York, in 1807 and died in 1884, was the son of William Connelly and Lydia Merihew (Connelly), the latter being of English descent.[18] The elder William Connelly was born in 1769 and died in 1835. He was a physician of repute,[19] making his home in Saugerties, about 12 miles from Kingston. He was the son of Michael Connelly. I know nothing of the forbears of the latter. The tradition in the family is that they came from the province of Ulster in Northern Ireland to Ulster County, New York. I do not know the date or place of birth of Michael. He died in 1806.[20] "Michael Con-

[12]Burhans *Genealogy*, p. 609, No. 11703; p. 601, No. 11542.

[13][Berthold Fernow], *New York in the Revolution* (Albany, [Weed, Parsons & Company], 1904), pp. 189, 260, 403.

[14]See clipping in Folder, "Family Items," [Hughes Papers].

[15]Burhans *Genealogy*, p. 602, No. 11557.

[16][Fernow], *New York in the Revolution*, p. 137, and "Supplement," pp. 206, 211.

[17]Burhans *Genealogy*, p. 604, No. 11598.

[18]See Family Record in the Bible of my great grandfather, William Connelly.

[19]In a printed obituary notice found in the old Bible, it is stated that he was a Baptist Minister as well as a physician. I have no information confirming this.

[20]There are two references to Michael Connelly in the Family Record in the Bible of my great grandfather, William Connelly. One states that William was the son of Michael; the other that Michael died May 10, 1806. In a loose paper in my mother's handwriting, placed with the Family Record, is a statement that Michael Connelly was the father of Dr. Wm. Connelly. It gives the date of Michael's death and the names of his eight children.

nelly" appears as one of the freeholders and inhabitants of Kingston who signed the "Agreement to Maintain Constitutional Rights," dated July 1, 1775.[21] This may be the Michael Connelly (or possibly *his* father) who was the father of William Connelly, Senior. According to the family tradition, it was this Michael Connelly, the father of William, who was an officer in the Revolutionary Army and served as an aide to General George Clinton. General Clinton was himself an Ulster County man and Michael Connelly enjoyed his confidence. The name appears in the Clinton Papers as Connolly, Connelly, Conolly and Connely.[22] This is not surprising as the various spellings of the old Irish family name have often been noted, e.g., Connelly, Connolly, Connally, Conneally, etc.

Michael was entrusted with various important duties.[23] He was devoted to "his General," for whom he vigorously recruited in Ulster County against no little opposition. His experiences are picturesquely narrated in his letters to General Clinton.[24] On July 11, 1777, General Clinton recommended him to General Washington for a commission in a designated regiment of the Continental Army saying: "The Bearer Mr. Connolly is the Person I formerly mentioned to your Excellency as a supernumerary Officer, I having given a Warrant to him as a 1st Lieutenant after the 4 Companies officered by me were compleat. He has taken great Pains to recruit Men, tho' his Success has not been great, owing to the Resolve of this State in favor of the 5 Regiments to be raised in it. There are two

[21][Marius] Schoonmaker, *History of Kingston* [New York, Burr Printing House] (1888), pp. 517–518.

[22]*Public Papers of George Clinton as First Governor of New York.* [Albany,] Published by the State, 1899.

See, also, [Fernow], *New York in the Revolution*, pp. 29, 55; "Supplement," p. 76. Note that the name is spelled "Connolly" in the text, but in the index to the "Supplement," p. 294, it is spelled "Connelly."

[23]Michael Connolly is mentioned as having been engaged in enlisting men on the frontier. *Clinton Papers*, Vol. I, p. 566. On February 23, 1777, General Clinton entrusted him with a message to the President of the Convention of the State of New York. *Ibid.*, pp. 616–617. He proposed to raise a company and seize pipes of wine belonging to Royalists. *Ibid.*, p. 635. On March 17, 1777, General Clinton authorizes him to purchase certain rum, which had been seized, if the claimant proved title. *Ibid.*, p. 669.

[24]He had his own way of spelling, but there was no question of his patriotic ardor. Describing, in his letter of May 24, 1777, the treatment he had received from the "Counssel" which objected to his proceedings, he says: "I told them I Judged I was in the line of my Dutey but wo'd Say or Do no more Untill I Acquaint'd General Clinton; Mr. Contine Answered with a Rinkel'd Cockt'd Knos, that he wo'd have General Clinton & me to know that the Military was Not to Rule Civil . . . a Day or 2 Ago I Inlist'd a man in the Steatehouse About 10 O'Clock, Amoungest the thick of the Counssel; the[y] Look'd Very grim at me, but I am Resolv'd to part with No Man that will Inlist for money. I wo'd been over to Dutches County Amoungest the frightn'd Torries was it not to See the Event here . . . Capt'n Bovier & Mrs. Pawling seems Very Desirous I sho'd Joine their Regiment if the[re] was a Vacancey; I told them I Co'd say Nothing to that for General Clinton had the Dissposal of me — but if the pepol Call'd me out, Capt'n Oh how well it Wo'd please your Most Obeedant Serv't, Mich'l Connolly. To Genrl. Geo. Clinton." *Ibid.*, pp. 839, 840.

Vacancies in Col. Du Bois's Regiment of first Lieutenants, & I find it would be more agreeable to him to be provided for in that, than any other Corps, & I doubt not, should your Excellency gratify him in having him appointed in that Regim't, he will make an Active & very useful Officer." [25] Later he performed numerous services of importance.[26]

In this connection, I may refer to an amusing incident in 1908 when Mr. Taft was Secretary of War and I was Governor of New York. We were both guests of the Friendly Sons of St. Patrick at a dinner in New York City on St. Patrick's Day. It was well understood that Mr. Taft was President Roosevelt's candidate for the presidential nomination by the Republican Party. Mr. Taft delivered a flowery and eloquent speech extolling Ireland and the Irish. In a humorous reference to the exuberance of his rhetoric, he remarked that he had kissed the Blarney Stone. When it came my turn to speak, I said that I had no doubt that Secretary of War had given a veracious account of his experiences in Ireland but that I should like to have a picture of him kissing the Blarney Stone. Mr. Taft was then very large and the Sons of St. Patrick, well knowing the location of the Stone, were greatly amused. (The next day, one of the newspapers had a cartoon showing the Secretary being hoisted by a derrick to reach the Stone.) After that, I trotted out my great great grandfather, Michael Connelly, and put in my own claim to Irish good will. I was admitted to full fellowship with that genial company.

My grandfather, William Connelly, Junior, did not follow in the footsteps of his father as a medical practitioner, but made his start as a contractor and builder. In that work he was obliged to establish temporary bases of operations at places distant from Kingston, and it was in such an enterprise that he took his young wife to the beautiful hills — still unspoiled — of Delaware County, where, as I have said, my mother was

[25] *Ibid.*, Vol. II, pp. 102, 103, and Vol. V, p. 705.

[26] In November 1777, he carried a letter from General Clinton to Col. Webb and carried money from Webb to Clinton. *Ibid.*, Vol. II, pp. 505, 512. In November 1778, Col. Malcom reports that "Lt. Connelly" (note the spelling — "Connelly") brought in "a fine Reinforcement of Torys, from Peeks Kill." *Ibid.*, Vol. IV, p. 301. In February 1780, he joins a number of officers in addressing a request to General Washington for leave to retire from service on account of the failure of the Legislature to make adequate provision for them, and Clinton transmits the request to Washington inviting his consideration of the matter. *Ibid.*, Vol. V, p. 477–481. In July 1780, General George Clinton writes to General James Clinton stating that it is necessary to have a recruiting officer from the latter's brigade and suggesting "Mr. Connolly for this service as well on account of his activity & industry as his genl. acquaintance with the Officers & Men stationed on the frontiers of Orange & Ulster." *Ibid.*, Vol. V, p. 908. See, also, *ibid.*, Vol. VI, p. 492. In August 1780, Governor Clinton supersedes Captain Black by "Lieut. Mich'l Connely" in providing for the collection and distribution of clothing for New York troops. *Ibid.*, Vol. VI, pp. 74, 130. See, also, Vol. VI, pp. 234–236. In December 1780, he appears as Paymaster to the Fifth New York Regiment. *Ibid.*, Vol. VI, p. 476. He was also Paymaster to the Second New York Regiment. *Ibid.*, Vol. VI, p. 918.

born. Later, I believe that my grandfather had a general store in Eddyville, and when his son Henry took that over, he turned to farming. In his last years he had a fruit farm at Port Ewen (near Rondout) overlooking the Hudson River. There in my boyhood I spent many happy summer days.

I have received a letter from my cousin, Reverend Howell Harris Hughes, under date of January 8, 1947, giving additional information about my Hughes forebears. He enclosed a script entitled "The Hughes Family," which he had received some years ago from a friend who had access to the diaries and manuscripts at Trevecca, in South Wales, where the evangelist Howell Harris established his community.

It appears from this script that my grandfather Nathan Hughes was the eldest child of Hugh Hughes, who had hailed from Carnarvonshire, North Wales, and had joined the "Family" at Trevecca sometime before 1769. There, in 1773, he married Jane Owen, the daughter of John and Elizabeth Owen, who had come from Carnarvonshire to Trevecca in 1754.

Hugh and Jane Hughes had three children, the eldest of whom was my grandfather Nathan Hughes, baptized February 9, 1780. Nathan was apprenticed to the printing trade at Trevecca. It is said that "He was naturally gifted and had literary tastes." It appears that he prepared and printed in Wales a short biography of Howell Harris. Sometime before 1828 he married and moved to Tredegar in Monmouthshire where he engaged in business and also was a schoolmaster. Thence he moved to Aberbeeg, then Abercarn, and finally to Caerphilly, all in Monmouthshire, where he was buried September 22, 1845, age 65.

The script gives an interesting account of Howell Harris and the establishment at Trevecca, as follows:

> In the year 1735 Howell Harris, of Trevecka near Talgarth, a small township in Breconshire, Wales, was "converted," and in 1738 John Wesley went through a similar experience in a service at Aldersgate, London. These two events mark the beginning of the religious awakening known as the Methodist Revival, a movement which began simultaneously tho' quite separately in England and Wales, and in both cases within the Established Church, but eventually led to the formation of two separate Communions, the Wesleyan Methodist Church in England and the Calvinistic Methodist Church (also known as the Presbyterian Church of Wales) in Wales.
>
> The two movements had several features in common. They were similar in their methods: itinerant evangelical preaching followed up by forming the converts into "societies" for the fostering of their spiritual life. At the head of each movement there was a man of commanding personality and great organizing abilities, John Wesley and Howell

Harris. In each there was a man gifted far above the ordinary as a preacher of the Gospel, and worthy to be ranked among the greatest preachers of the ages: George Whitefield in England and Daniel Rowland in Wales. To each also there was given a man who was inspired to express in immortal hymns the spiritual experiences and aspirations of the saints and thus add to the fervour and power of the revival: Charles Wesley in England and William Williams, Pentycelyn, in Wales. The leaders of the two movements came early into contact with one another, but eventually the two Methodist bodies drifted apart on doctrinal issues, the Welsh body leaning to Calvinism and the English, under Wesley, to Arminianism. Whitefield, however, was a Calvinist and still more so the Countess of Huntington, who had joined the Methodists, appointed Whitefield as her chaplain, and built several chapels in various parts of the country and maintained ministers there at her own expense.

In 1750, on doctrinal and other grounds, a serious rift occurred between Harris and the other leaders of the Welsh Methodists, resulting in a separation which lasted until 1763. Harris at once began to gather his "people" together, re-arranging them into Bands under new Exhorters and with new periodical Councils to direct the work. The "Rowlandists" did the same. In 1751 Harris's health broke down, and for many months he was confined to his house at Trevecka. By the middle of 1752 he realized that he could no longer hope to maintain a following in the country in opposition to the "Rowlandists", but during his enforced seclusion he conceived another plan by which he might yet minister to those who desired to place themselves under his spiritual care. As early as 1736 he had been greatly impressed by an account of the Pietistic Institutions of Professor Franke, the Moravian of Halle, Germany, and in his diary dated that year he writes: "Reading of Professor Franke, I was disposed to God's glory, and thought of how poor people could hear me. Then it came to me as a solution to sell all I have . . . and build an Alms House and School House and employ as many as I could have of followers." That idea seems never to have left him, but it was during his illness after the separation that he found both the occasion and the leisure to give it serious thought and a definite form. The old homestead at Trevecka was pulled down, and the foundations of a new building laid in April, 1752, wherein Howell Harris carried on until his death (1773) with strange success a marvellous experiment of "a farm and labour colony, a reformatory and a monastery all in one." After his death the trades there were one by one abandoned, the "Family" steadily dwindled, but printing continued until 1805, when the press was removed to Talgarth. As many as 60 trades were followed by different members of the community, including farming, wool spinning and weaving, shoemaking, tailoring, cheese making, wooden spoon and ladle making, carpentry, brewing, curriers, printing and bookbinding. John Wesley writes in his Journal in August, 1763, after a visit to Trevecka: "About six score people are now in the Family; all diligently employed, all fearing God and working righteousness." At least one-half this number were married couples with children (whom, probably, Wesley does not include in his figure), the rest being single men and women and a few paupers and, occasionally, one or more sent there for reformatory discipline. From all the counties of Wales there came at least one family to join the Community. The recruiting agent from the very start was Evan Moses (a tailor from Aberdare and itinerant preacher) who visited wakes and fairs in North and South Wales, especially where Howell Harris had been most successful in securing converts, to invite the most zealous to come under his constant care at Trevecka. Joining the "Family" involved casting all personal possessions into the common purse, submitting to strict discipline including three religious services a day, the first at five o'clock in the morning, very much after the style of the Moravians.

In 1764 the Countess of Huntington visited Trevecka and was greatly impressed by all she saw there. She discussed with Howell Harris the idea of instituting at Trevecka a School for the training of Preachers, and four years later (1768) the workmen of the Family rebuilt the premises of Trevecka Isaf (Lower) as a residential College. The two institutions were in close touch with one another; Howell Harris addressed the students on one or two days every week, and the young preachers in turn conducted the devotional services at the communal settlement. In 1791 her ladyship's College was removed to Cheshunt, Hertfordshire, and ultimately to Cambridge. Early in the following century, owing to the break-up of the old Family, the House and College at Trevecka were sold by the last survivors to the Breconshire Presbytery, who, in turn, in 1842, offered them to the South Wales Association (Synod), who desired to establish a Theological College. From 1842 to 1862 it was used as a residential College, under the Principalship of Rev. David Charles, son of the famous Rev. Thomas Charles of Bala, who (David) had already joined with the Rev. (later Dr.) Lewis Edwards a few years earlier in starting a School for Preachers at Bala, out of which arose the Theological College there. In 1906 the College was removed to Aberystwyth, the premises at Trevecka being used as a Preparatory College for ministerial students. In 1922 the two Colleges were amalgamated, the Aberystwyth building being retained as a residential College, where the students follow a course of two or three years in Theology, proceeding thereafter to Bala for a further one year course in "Practical Theology".

In my letter to my cousin, under date of April 7, 1947, acknowledging receipt of the script, I noted certain inaccuracies in the script, as follows:

> Thus it is said that our grandfather, Nathan Hughes, "had three sons and one daughter." My information is that he had four sons and two daughters. I distinctly remember my father speaking of an elder brother Samuel, who died when a young man before my father came to the United States in 1885. My father often spoke of him with great admiration. Then there was your father, John Richard Hughes, and another brother, Jabez Hughes. I met the latter when I was in Wales as a boy in 1873. After his death, his wife and daughter (who married a Mr. Thomas) came to this country and settled in Texas. The two daughters were Jane, who married Edward Jones of Abertillery, and Eliza, who married a Mr. [Roberts] of Bryn Mawr. Eliza died before my visit to Wales in 1873, but I met his daughter Annie, her husband, Mr. Rogers, and their children, on my visit in 1885.
>
> The script refers to my father, David Charles Hughes, as "a preacher with the Baptists" and as coming to this country in 1857. He came here in 1855, as I have said, and at that time he was a licensed preacher of the Wesleyan Methodist connexion. He joined the Baptists in New York a few years after his arrival.

I also referred to the statement in the script that the manuscript of Nathan Hughes's biography of Howell Harris, together with a woodcut preserving the only portrait of the latter known to exist, were supposed to be in my possession. I said that this was a mistake, as I have neither the manuscript nor the portrait.

My cousin in his letter to me of January 8, 1947, gives information with respect to his own family. He states that his brother, J. R. Lloyd Hughes, was editor, during the years of the War, of *Y Cymro*, a leading Welsh weekly. He is now seventy and has retired from the editor's chair but is still in close contact with the paper. My cousin's sister (to whom I referred in my notes as Mrs. Eames), and her husband moved to Cardiff during the War where he had a post in connection with the Ministry of Information, with special reference to the Welsh press. He was the first Editor of the *Manchester Guardian Commercial*, and my cousin says that he "did some very hard work to make it the success it has become."

Appendix II Speeches—Methods

Since I came under the public eye in 1905, I have made an inordinate number of speeches. In extenuation, I may say that I have refused at least ninety-five percent of requests. While on the Bench as Associate Justice and Chief Justice, I had a comparative immunity although even then the requests for speeches were numerous. During my service as Governor of New York and Secretary of State, and while at the bar, they were extremely burdensome, entailing interviews and correspondence at a time when I was in the midst of urgent official or professional demands. Not infrequently one invitation would be reenforced by many letters from prominent persons to whom as a matter of courtesy I had to make personal replies.

When I was Governor, I made many speeches in the interest of the policies of my administration, taking my case to the people of the State, and other speeches on occasions when my appearance seemed to be a quasi-public obligation. Rarely had I a chance to write out a speech and I adopted the plan of having stenographers (at my personal expense) take my speech in relays so that the reporters would have it complete within a few minutes after delivery. I found this necessary in order to avoid the publication of inaccurate or purely sensational scraps based on the hurried notes of a reporter. I often "bunched my hits," appearing sometimes at two or even three dinners in New York City in a single evening.

My speeches during the campaigns for Governor in New York in 1906 and 1908 (except the initial speeches on accepting the nomination, which were written) were extemporaneous and were reported stenographically. In 1908, Mr. Taft asked me to open the campaign for him in Ohio and this I did at Youngstown about the beginning of September. I wrote out that speech and gave copies to the press for release on delivery. In view of its effect,[1] Mr. Taft and his managers insisted that I should campaign

[1]As to its effect, see Beerits' Memorandum, "First Term as Governor," pp. 67 *et seq.* and references; also Mark Sullivan, *Our Times* [*:The United States, 1906–1925.* 6 Vols. (New York, Charles Scribner's Sons, 1926–1935)], Vol. 4, p. 306, Note.

for him in the Middle West. I demurred, insisting that I had a hard campaign for reelection in New York but I finally yielded. I insisted, however, that I should be limited to two indoor speeches a day, one in the afternoon and another in the evening. This was because I did not wish to lose my voice by outdoor speaking. While the understanding was clear, there was no resisting the local demands when we were on tour and I spoke constantly outdoors at all sorts of stations making as many as twenty speeches a day. One incident of that campaign has always stood out in my memory as an illustration of the friendliness and generosity of the American people which even the bitter contests of political campaigns cannot wholly obscure. One evening, shortly before my train arrived at Hastings, Nebraska, there was a severe storm which tore down the tent in which I was to speak. The only hall in the town at that time was taken and already filled by the Democrats who were awaiting the arrival of their speaker. We concluded that we could not have a meeting, but a committee of the Democrats came to the train and invited me to speak at their hall. Their orator's train was an hour or so late. They made the condition that I should appear on the platform alone, without any Republican associates, as their invitation was a courtesy extended to me as Governor of New York, but I was at liberty to speak as I pleased. A straggling lot of Republicans followed me to the hall and crowded in as best they could. To the amazement of the Democratic audience I appeared on the platform, introduced myself, thanked the Democratic committee for its courtesy and said that they would not have any respect for me if I did not make the speech I had intended to make at Hastings. I then launched out as usual. The audience gave me a rousing welcome and the hall rang with their applause as I extolled the American spirit of fair play and concluded with a number of questions for the Democratic orator to answer on his arrival, which was shortly after I left.

In the campaign of 1916, aside from my prepared speech at Carnegie Hall on accepting the nomination, I spoke extemporaneously, the speeches being taken down by stenographers. With many speeches a day,[2] I had no time to write them. Of course, I thought the points out in advance and once in a while I jotted down a few headings on a scrap of paper. This seemed to help my memory, although it remained in my pocket and was not used while I was speaking.

Later, when at the bar, while I made a number of extemporaneous speeches, I prepared with as much care as was possible in the limited time at my disposal various addresses on important occasions. When Secretary of State, I made addresses bearing on departmental policies and action.[3]

The increasing use of the radio changed methods, notably in political

[2]See copies of itineraries in [the Hughes Papers].

[3]See published collection entitled *The Pathway of Peace.*

campaigns. The radio has greatly reduced the number of speeches that are necessary and thus the almost intolerable burden of campaigning in the manner of earlier days. But the radio demands precision, a decent restraint and a more careful speech-structure. The repetitious utterances of the campaign orator, his excessive emotional outbursts, his strenuous efforts to reach his climaxes, may be condoned by his immediate audience largely composed of his fellow partisans — who shout their approval and sympathize with his struggles — but go ill with the larger and more important audience of radio listeners. In order to assure the precision and care in construction which will appeal to the radio audience, it is advisable to write out the speech in advance. But at the same time, the demands of the thousands who attend the campaign rally must be met. The speaker does not like to have the audience walk out on him. And the audience does not like a speech that is read, unless perchance the speaker can read so easily and with such elocutionary effect that his use of manuscript is but little noticed. There is also the demand of the press for copies in advance. In the nineteen-twenties, in view of the radio, I made a practice of writing or dictating my speeches but rarely used manuscript in delivery, save on those formal occasions when reading would be expected and it would seem almost an affectation to deliver a set speech otherwise.

Fortunately, I did not find it difficult to memorize a speech — even a long one. I have been blessed, to a fair degree, with visual or what is sometimes called a photographic memory. That is, having composed a speech, I find that reading it a few times — always from the same typewritten copy — fixes the type in my mind's eye so that in speaking I am almost reading the pages. When I wished to interpolate, introducing something that was suggested or required by the occasion, or paused to answer a question, I put a mental finger at the place on the page, and after interpolation or interruption I could easily resume where I had left off. Reporters sitting before me with copies of my speech have flattered me sometimes by saying that I had reproduced the written speech with verbal exactness. But that is an exaggeration. To follow the written speech so that the reporters were satisfied that I was not delivering a speech different from the one given out, answered the purpose. I did not try to be verbally exact, although what I had carefully written or dictated naturally was remembered in the same form. My speeches at Westminster Hall and at the Pilgrim's Dinner in London in 1924, on the occasion of the visit of the American Bar, were delivered in this way without notes, as I understood that it was not customary in England to use notes. But my speeches on the visit of the bar to Paris were read, as I recall it, as I thought that speaking without manuscript might be regarded by the French as too informal for the occasion.

I should add that all my written speeches (and these have been very numerous although relatively few — as compared with the number delivered extemporaneously) have been prepared under extreme pressure, as it has always been my lot to have more to do, either officially or professionally, than I could do comfortably or without the urgent drive of engagements. Often I have risen at 5 o'clock, or even earlier, in the morning, in order to write before going to the office to meet the demands of the day. Aside from the Historical Address at Brown University (1914) and my lectures on the Supreme Court at Columbia (which because of so many references and details had to be worked over for some time) I do not recall an instance in which I prepared an address with the pleasing consciousness that I could work at leisure and completely satisfy my ambition. Time was always of the essence, and one demand had to be got out of the way to make room for another on its heels.

Appendix III Memorandum

THE FOURTEENTH AMENDMENT AND FREEDOM OF SPEECH AND OF THE PRESS

A striking development in the jurisprudence of the Supreme Court of the United States is in relation to the application of the due process clause of the Fourteenth Amendment to state action restricting freedom of speech and of the press.

As late as 1922, the Supreme Court declared that "the right of free speech" was not within the protection of the Fourteenth Amendment.

In the case of *Prudential Insurance Company v. Cheek,* 259 U.S. 530 [1922], the question was as to the validity of the Service Letter Law of Missouri requiring corporations to furnish to any employee when discharged a letter stating the cause of his leaving. The Court held that this requirement was within the regulatory power of the State over foreign and domestic corporations. The Court stated (p. 538) that "the Constitution of the United States imposes upon the States no obligation to confer upon those within their jurisdiction either the right of free speech or the right of silence." Again the Court said (p. 543): "But, as we have stated, neither the Fourteenth Amendment nor any other provision of the Constitution of the United States imposes upon the States any restrictions about 'freedom of speech' or the 'liberty of silence'; nor, we may add, does it confer any right of privacy upon either persons or corporations."

It is interesting to note that Justice Holmes and Justice Brandeis concurred in the opinion of the Court in this case. Chief Justice [Taft], Justice Van Devanter and Justice McReynolds noted that their dissent but did not write.

There had been earlier references to the subject. In *Patterson v. Colorado,* 205 U.S. 454 (1907), Justice Holmes, in writing the opinion for the Court, said (p. 462):

We leave undecided the question whether there is to be found in the

> Fourteenth Amendment a prohibition similar to that in the First. But even if we were to assume that freedom of speech and freedom of the press were protected from abridgements on the part not only of the United States but also of the states, still we should be far from the conclusion that the plaintiff in error would have us reach.

In *Schaefer v. United States,* 251 U.S. 466 (1920), dealing with the Federal Espionage Act, the Court (p. 474) observed "That freedom of speech and of the press are elements of liberty all will acclaim." Still, two years later, in the *Prudential* case, the Court made the flat statement, quoted above, that freedom of speech was not protected by the Fourteenth Amendment.

In *Gilbert v. Minnesota,* 254 U.S. 325 (1920), it was argued that the statute of Minnesota making it a misdemeanor to advocate that a citizen of the State should not assist the United States in carrying on war, was violative of the right of free speech. The Court, without "deciding or considering the freedom asserted as guaranteed or secured either by the Constitution of the United States or by the constitution of the State," and examining the contention that the right of free speech was a "natural and inherent right" (p. 332), concluded that if so the right was not absolute but was subject to restriction, and that the Minnesota statute was valid. Justice Holmes concurred in the result. Justice Brandeis, dissenting (p. 343), considered the statute to be invalid "because it interferes with federal functions and with the right of a citizen of the United States to discuss them" and he saw "no occasion to consider whether it violates also the Fourteenth Amendment." But he had difficulty in believing that the liberty guaranteed by the Constitution did not include liberty to teach the doctrine of pacifism and he said that he could not believe that "the liberty guaranteed by the Fourteenth Amendment includes only liberty to acquire and to enjoy property." Yet, later, Justice Brandeis joined in the opinion in the *Prudential* case.

Then, three years after the *Prudential* decision, in *Gitlow v. People of New York,* 268 U.S. 652 (1925), the Court had the question whether the New York statute against "criminal anarchy" violated the due process clause of the Fourteenth Amendment. For the purposes of the decision, the Court assumed (p. 666) that the Fourteenth Amendment did protect freedom of speech and of the press and regarded the question as still open despite the statement in the *Prudential* case. The Court said:

> For present purposes we may and do assume that freedom of speech and of the press — which are protected by the First Amendment from abridgement by Congress — are among the fundamental personal rights

> and "liberties" protected by the due process clause of the Fourteenth Amendment from impairment by the States. We do not regard the incidental statement in *Prudential Ins. Co. v. Cheek,* 259 U.S. 530, 543, that the Fourteenth Amendment imposes no restrictions on the States concerning freedom of speech, as determinative of this question.

The New York statute was sustained. Justice Holmes wrote a dissenting opinion, in which Justice Brandeis concurred, holding that the judgment should be reversed. He said: "The general principle of free speech, it seems to me, must be taken to be included in the Fourteenth Amendment, in view of the scope that has been given to the word 'liberty' as there used, although perhaps it may be accepted with a somewhat larger latitude of interpretation than is allowed to Congress by the sweeping language that governs or ought to govern the laws of the United States."

What was assumed by the majority in the *Gitlow* case was evidently regarded as the law in *Whitney v. California,* 274 U.S. 357 (1927), and the validity of the "Criminal Syndicalism Act" of California was sustained over the contention that it violated the due process clause of the Fourteenth Amendment (p. 371). Justice Brandeis, concurring, said: "Despite arguments to the contrary which had seemed to me persuasive, it is settled that the due process clause of the Fourteenth Amendment applies to matters of substantive law as well as to matters of procedure. Thus all fundamental rights comprised within the term 'liberty' are protected by the Federal Constitution from invasion by the States. The right of free speech, the right to teach and the right of assembly are, of course, fundamental rights" (p. 373). Justice Holmes concurred in Justice Brandeis' opinion. Then in the next case, *Fiske v. Kansas,* 275 U.S. 380 (1927), the Court unanimously reversed the conviction of the plaintiff in error under the "Criminal Syndicalism Act" of Kansas, holding that the Act as applied in that instance was "repugnant to the due process clause of the Fourteenth Amendment."

It fell to my lot as Chief Justice, in 1930, to write the opinions for the Court in *Stromberg v. California,* 283 U.S. 359 [1931], and in *Near v. Minnesota,* 283 U.S. 697 [1931], holding that freedom of speech and of the press was embraced in the concept of liberty protected against state action by the Fourteenth Amendment.

Near v. Minnesota dealt with freedom of the press as curtailed by a Minnesota statute directed at "alleged defamatory newspapers." The Court held that the statute was not aimed at the redress of individual or private wrongs but at the continued publication by newspapers and periodicals of charges against public officers of corruption, malfeasance in office or serious neglect of duty, and that the statute operated not only to suppress the offending newspaper or periodical but to put the publisher under a federal censorship. (See Chafee, *Free Speech in the United States*, 1941, pp. 375, 381.)

The final decision as to the application of the Fourteenth Amendment has had two important general results, apart from their immediate application. As Justice Brandeis pointed out in his concurring opinion in *Whitney v. California*, it is recognized as settled that the due process clause of the Fourteenth Amendment applies to matters of substantive law as well as to matters of procedure. The contention that it was limited to matters of procedure was widely held by those who endeavored to restrict the application of the due process clause when it was considered in relation to property rights. The conclusion that the clause covered matters of substantive law has always seemed to me to be in accord with the original intention when the Fifth Amendment was adopted. As I have pointed out in my Columbia lectures on the Supreme Court (p. 187), Madison, who probably drafted the Fifth Amendment, said that under it the judicial tribunals would be "an impenetrable bulwark against every assumption of power in the Legislative or Executive."[1]

Another result has been that the right to "liberty," in relation to freedom of speech and of the press, has received a broader interpretation under the Fourteenth Amendment than has been given to the right of property, although the due process clause makes no such distinction. The suggestion of Justice Holmes in the *Gitlow* case that the States "might be allowed a somewhat larger latitude of interpretation" than is allowed to Congress by the sweeping language of the First Amendment, has not been followed. On the contrary, the scope of freedom of speech and of the press under the Fourteenth Amendment has been regarded as quite as broad as that which obtains under the First Amendment.

In writing for the Court in *St. Joseph Stock Yards Co. v. United States*, 298 U.S. 38, 52 (1936), I opposed the view that findings of fact of legislative agencies "may be made conclusive where constitutional rights of liberty and property are involved, although the evidence clearly establishes that the findings are wrong and constitutional rights have been evaded." I stated that no distinction may properly be made in this respect under the due process clause between constitutional rights pertaining to liberty and those pertaining to property. Justice Brandeis in his concurring opinion observed that "a citizen who claims that his liberty is being infringed is entitled, upon habeas corpus, to the opportunity of a judicial determination of the facts," but he thought (p. 77) that a distinction should be made when dealing with property.

[1][See Charles Evans Hughes, *The Supreme Court of the United States* (New York, Columbia University Press, 1928), pp. 160, 187.]

In writing the opinion for the Court, I had this to say upon the point:

> It is said that we can retain judicial authority to examine the weight of evidence when the question concerns the right of personal liberty But if this be so, it is not because we are privileged to perform our judicial duty in that case and for reasons of convenience to disregard it in others. The principle applies when rights either of person or of property are protected by constitutional restrictions. Under our system there is no warrant for the view that the judicial power of a competent court can be circumscribed by any legislative arrangement designed to give effect to administrative action going beyond the limits of constitutional authority.
>
> But this judicial duty to exercise an independent judgment does not require or justify disregard of the weight which may properly attach to findings upon hearing and evidence. On the contrary, the judicial duty is performed in the light of the proceeding already had . . .

The Court concluded that appellant had failed to prove confiscation and the decree of the District Court was affirmed.

Stone and Cardozo also agreed with Brandeis.

Appendix IV Hughes as Governor

BY ROBERT H. FULLER
SECRETARY TO GOVERNOR HUGHES, 1907–1910

When Charles E. Hughes was Governor of the State of New York it was sometimes said of him that "Nobody ever slapped him on the back and called him Charlie." This statement was praise when made by his friends and reproach when made by his opponents. In any case, it was true.

It would be difficult to imagine any one slapping Napoleon on the back, or Cromwell, or Washington, or Lincoln, or, in fact, any of the men who gave the best that was in them to the service of their fellows. There is a seriousness of purpose which clothes such men in a dignity that is proof against the "hail fellow well met" familiarities of the street corner.

While he was Governor, and in every field of his public service, Mr. Hughes has given his best. No duty was ever too small to receive the closest attention and no obligation was ever too great to cause him to shrink from its performance. Absorption in the performance of these duties, small and great, has so occupied his time that he has had little leisure to devote to the cultivation of personal relationships upon an extended scale. This does not mean that Mr. Hughes is averse to meeting men and exchanging views with them. Few men have a wider range of sympathies than he, and few have a broader understanding of the aims and aspirations of Americans. Mr. Hughes was a poor boy and he knows what it is to overcome modest circumstances by hard work; he has occupied positions of power and trust which invite the flattery of the men who are usually looked upon as the demi-gods of American industrial and commercial life. To him, they are all alike, each according to his talents. That a man is poor does not constitute a demerit to the Governor's mind and that he happens to be rich does not add a tittle to his claim for consideration.

Perhaps the dominating characteristic of Mr. Hughes in public life, aside from his wonderful capacity for prolonged and sustained application to any task that may be before him, is his self-reliance. When he has a problem to solve he likes to take counsel from all who are familiar with the facts and competent to make suggestions, but in the end he must settle the problem for himself. His mind is not content until it has reached the solution which satisfies it. His faculty of weighing facts and arguments and of reducing conflicting considerations to a conclusion seems sometimes to onlookers to be almost automatic. When he once takes up a problem it is always present in his mind until it has been solved. He may, meanwhile, be doing other things, perhaps talking with people who do not suspect that in the background of his mind the problem is always under consideration. The process of reduction seems to eliminate not only all immaterial considerations, but even his own wishes or preferences. The only important thing is that the solution shall be satisfying.

With this judicial faculty of mind, Mr. Hughes has a rare power of concentration. This, too, seems to be a natural gift rather than one that has been acquired by cultivation. His memory is unusually retentive, a faculty which has been of great use to him in his public career.

Mr. Hughes's administration of public office has always followed in the strictest sense the dictum of President Cleveland, that it is a public trust. In no instance, however trifling, has he ever used the powers of office for his own advantage or for the advantage of his friends or relatives. This scrupulousness with regard to public office helped in a measure to gain him a reputation for austerity which his absorption in the various problems presented to him, tended to create. This reputation, it may be said in passing, was deepened by his attacks upon intrenched privilege and upon defiance of law which were incidents of his administration as Governor and which "good fellows," who are unable to see any harm in helping themselves and their friends at the public expense, looked upon as too severe. During the Governor's attack upon race-track gambling, which was being practiced in the State in defiance of the plain mandate of the constitution against it, an ingenius phrase-maker christened the Governor, "Charles the Baptist," a title reminiscent of the preachings of John the Baptist in the wilderness. In truth, the ancient prophet could hardly have been more forceful or sincere than was Governor Hughes in uprooting what he believed to be an evil more dangerous to the commonwealth in its defiance of fundamental law, than the current crop of orchids which resulted from it would indicate.

Mr. Hughes is a fervent believer in the American form of government and in the great destiny of the American nation. He believes that the institutions, upon which the rule of the people in this country is founded, ought to be permitted to work freely; that every public official should faithfully discharge all the duties laid upon him by law and that he should not interfere or encroach upon the duties laid upon other public officials. He believes that constitutions are intended to be obeyed and that was the chief reason why he attacked race-track gambling in the State of New York.

The criticism is sometimes made of him that he did not get the Legislature to do things that he wanted to have done. It has been and still is the custom for State executives practically to bribe and bully legislators into carrying out their wishes. Nothing is more common than for a Governor to send for members of the legislature and promise them appointments or the approval of bills in return for their votes upon measures in which the Governor happens to be interested. Nothing is more common, when needed votes cannot be obtained in this way, than for the Governor to refuse his signature to measures that he ought to sign, because they were introduced by recalcitrant legislators and, if signed, would help them in their home districts; or to bring about the dismissal from office of the political friends and supporters of legislators who will not take dictation. It is almost the customary practice for executives who are aspirants for other offices, to reward their friends and punish their enemies by the use of official power or public office. Governor Hughes never did any of these things. His abstention from them was so unusual when he was in Albany that the Old Guard of that day regarded it as a reflection upon them. The legislative leader, with votes at his command, who tried the back door of the Executive Chamber and found it locked, went away with a sense of injury. The politician who came to the Governor with legislative votes to be bargained for and who was compelled to state his case in full view of the public, became convinced that Mr. Hughes ought not to occupy public office. As a matter of fact, the Governor was merely insisting that the republican method of government in the State of New York should have free play. While some of the politicians and some of the legislative leaders thought that he was foolish to attempt such a thing, he usually had his way in the end, and the people not only of his own State, but of the country at large came to feel that they could rely upon him to represent them and no other interest.

The "appeal to the people" was Governor Hughes's substitute for bribery, bulldozing and intrigue as it had been practiced up to his time. When he found himself opposed in the Legislature, he did not immediately conclude that it was his duty to compel obedience. He reasoned that the members of the Legislature represented certain constituencies defined by law; that it was their duty to carry out the will of these constituencies; that if they failed to do so the constituencies would retire them to private life and choose other representatives. Therefore the Governor, as he felt that he had a right to do under a representative form of government, went directly to the constituencies with his proposals and his reasons for supporting them. The presentation of these reasons was usually sufficient to kindle a backfire which either brought the legislators into line or else terminated their careers. Although it may seem incredible, this "appeal to the people" was denounced in the Legislature as an unwarranted and indefensible attempt to coerce a co-ordinate branch of the government.

Governor Hughes's views upon running for office are as "peculiar" as his views with regard to holding office. He has never been a candidate for a political nomination although he has been nominated for Mayor of the City of New York, twice for Governor of the State of New York and for President of the United States. His feeling is that, ordinarily at least, the American citizen ought not to endeavor to sway the judgment of his fellow-citizens with regard to the choice of an official to represent them, but that if he is selected to run for office he should do his utmost to win that office. This is the reason why the Governor absolutely refused before he was nominated for President to encourage in the slightest degree the movement in his favor, and why he has since announced that he is now "100 per cent a candidate."

The underlying idea of all of Governor Hughes's public service has always been that every public official should confine himself strictly to the law which defines his powers and his duties. Only by such restriction can defects in the law be made apparent so that they can be corrected.

Index

Bei Fragen zur Produktsicherheit wenden Sie sich bitte an:
If you have any questions regarding product safety,
please contact:

Walter de Gruyter GmbH
Genthiner Straße 13
10785 Berlin
productsafety@degruyterbrill.com